William Lindsay White, 1900–1973

In the Shadow of His Father

William Lindsay White, 1900–1973

In the Shadow of His Father

by E. Jay Jernigan

UNIVERSITY OF OKLAHOMA PRESS : NORMAN AND LONDON

This book is published with the generous assistance of Edith Gaylord Harper.

PN4874
.W525
J47
1997

Also by E. Jay Jernigan

Henry Demarest Lloyd (Boston, 1976)
William Allen White (Boston, 1983)

Library of Congress Cataloging-in-Publication Data

Jernigan, E. Jay, 1935–
    William Lindsay White, 1900–1973 : in the shadow of his
father / by E. Jay Jernigan.
        p.   cm.
    Includes bibliographical references and index.
    ISBN 0-8061-2902-6 (alk. paper)
    1. White, William Lindsay, 1900–1973. 2. Journalists—
United States—20th century—Biography. 3. Editors—United
States—20th century—Biography.   I. Title.
PN4874.W525J47   1997
070' .92—dc20
[B]   96-32782
                                                            CIP

Text design by Debora Hackworth.

1 2 3 4 5 6 7 8 9 10

For Louise, Nathan, and David

Contents

Illustrations

Acknowledgments

I should from the outset acknowledge that I am originally from Emporia, Kansas. Though I attended high school in Osage City, a small town thirty-five miles to the northeast, I spent my childhood and college undergraduate years in Emporia, growing up casually aware of the local legends about William Allen White and reactions to his eccentric son and heir. I left Emporia in 1957 to take up teaching and, after several jobs and two graduate degrees, ended up in 1965 a member of the English faculty at Eastern Michigan University, where I have taught ever since. Over the years, though, I have returned periodically to Emporia and its vicinity to visit family and friends and to catch up on local gossip, objectified somewhat by my residence a thousand miles away and in a different ambiance. So I am at heart a Kansan, which may be why I have written a biography of William Allen White (published by Twayne in 1983) and now this biography of William Lindsay (W. L.) White.

I owe my largest research debt to Barbara W. Walker, the daughter
of W. L. White, who gave me open access to the many family
manuscripts still held by her and her husband, David Walker, and
permission to quote from those materials. She cooperated fully
and selflessly with my study, suggesting further sources while
carefully allowing me to develop my own focus and come to my
own conclusions. For that I am most grateful.

My largest personal debt I owe to my wife, Louise, who is herself
a busy full professor in the School of Education at Eastern
Michigan University. She consistently encouraged my work on
this project, helping me solve the arcane mysteries of computer
word processing, listening patiently to my many tales of research
and writing woes, and often offering useful solutions, while at
the same time being a homemaker and mother to our two sons.

Many others have contributed significantly to my writing of
this book and because of that I am somewhat at a loss whom
to mention next. For example, my longtime friend Mary Matheny,
director of the Lyon County Historical Museum, buoyed me with
her unfailing enthusiasm for this project and proved a sage
commentator on local history. Another dear friend, Municipal
Judge Robert L. Morton, helped me sort out local politics when
written sources or my family's collective memory failed me. Judy
Price, secretary to Kathrine White and to Barbara Walker,
cheerfully helped me locate materials within the unindexed *Gazette*
archives.

Mary Bogan, special collections librarian at Emporia State
University, assisted me with numerous research leads. One of those
leads, a fellow former Emporian and W. L. White's best boyhood
friend, Cecil ("Teet") Carle, gave me permission to use his
unpublished reminiscences and corresponded with me about his
friendship with W. L. White. A former *Gazette* reporter and a
Kansas editor of notable stature, Whitley Austin, provided me
with unique views of both W. L. and Kathrine White. Another
Gazette reporter, who became vice-chancellor for academic affairs
at the University of Kansas, Del Brinkman, wrote in support of
my successful request for a sabbatical from Eastern Michigan
University, then later commented helpfully on the initial
manuscript. Robert Bader, Kansas historian and former dean of

arts and sciences at the University of Missouri at St. Louis, also supported my sabbatical application and gave me helpful research advice. Sheryl Williams, curator of the Kansas Collection in the Spencer Research Library at the University of Kansas, gave me unfettered access to its uncatalogued White collection and helped with photocopying relevant materials. And photographer Jerry Pippig of El Dorado, Kansas, opened his studio to reproduce photos for me on short notice during a Christmas vacation.

Among Emporians whom I have interviewed I wish particularly to mention Gail Rindom, Mrs. Ted McDaniel, Professor Samuel Dicks, Kenneth Scott, Ray Call, Philip Winter, and Robert Foncannon, Sr. Others outside of Kansas who knew of W. L. and who proved especially helpful as correspondents or interview sources were Lambert Davis, Professor Jean Folkerts, James (J. V.) Spadea, Sally Baroness Ostman van der Leye (formerly Mrs. Edward Keith), Mrs. Russell Barnes, Joseph M. Lindsay, Mrs. Kathy ("Chuck") Southard, Irene Corbally Kuhn, Kathy Pasquale, Mrs. Martin Herrick, Hobart Lewis, and William F. Buckley, Jr.

Friends within the American Journalism Historians Association proved generous with constructive criticism and encouragement, especially Professor James Startt of Valparaiso University. Edison McIntyre, as a graduate student at the University of North Carolina, graciously shared with me his interview of the Harcourt, Brace editor Lambert Davis and court records of lawsuits over the movie version of W. L.'s *They Were Expendable*. My nephew Kelly Jernigan dug out information that I could not find from the University of Kansas institutional archives. My colleague James Angle read the manuscript twice for stylistic errors, my colleague Curt Stadtfeld gave me good counsel about errors in my discussion of W. L.'s *Report on the Russians*, and my colleague Frank McHugh briefed me about undergraduate customs at Harvard. My son Nathan read the next-to-final manuscript version closely to suggest numerous cuts for better narrative flow. But regardless of all the help and suggestions I have had, I must acknowledge the final selection, the interpretation, the phrasing, and whatever faux pas have resulted therefrom are stubbornly my own. My University of Oklahoma Press editors—Kimberly Wiar, Sarah Iselin, and freelancer Barbara Siegemund-Broka—have provided much-appreciated advice and encouragement.

Finally, I wish to thank my sister and brother-in-law, Evalee and Ernie Williams, for their hospitality during my numerous research trips to Emporia, and my brother and sister-in-law, Dean and Pat Jernigan, of Overland Park, Kansas, for their hospitality while I worked with manuscript materials at the University of Kansas.

E. JAY JERNIGAN

Ypsilanti, Michigan

William Lindsay White, 1900–1973

In the Shadow of His Father

Prologue

In the Shadow

Popular journalist William Lindsay White (1900–73), born in Emporia, Kansas, son of William Allen White, the most famous small-town newspaper editor of the first half of this century, established his own byline separate from his father's at the beginning of World War II. His widely syndicated newspaper column "Take a Look," his CBS radio broadcasts from the Russo-Finnish front, and his magazine reports about Great Britain under attack attracted widespread national attention from 1939 through 1941. Then *They Were Expendable*, his story of the PT boat squadron that brought Gen. Douglas MacArthur out of Bataan, became a Book-of-the-Month Club best-seller in 1942. Metro-Goldwyn-Mayer made it and his 1941 book, *Journey for Margaret*, into highly acclaimed wartime propaganda films. And the book version of his story *Queens Die Proudly*, retailing the adventures of a Philippine-based B-17 crew after the Japanese bombed Clark Field, gained best-seller status in 1943. Unfortunately, early in 1945 his critical *Report on the Russians* turned into an international cause célèbre that alienated many Progressives in that period of anxious hopes, between the Yalta and Potsdam conferences, and created lingering doubts about his honesty as a reporter.

Employed after the war as a New York–based roving editor for the *Reader's Digest,* "Young Bill" also made significant contributions to regional journalism as the publisher-editor of the family-owned *Emporia Gazette* from 1944 to 1973. Yet during the warmest part of the cold war he maintained his primary focus back east, where he had come to know scores of prominent Americans and became himself prominent, serving on the governing boards of such organizations as Freedom House, Radio Liberty, the American Civil Liberties Union, and Harvard University.

In his lifetime Bill White published thirteen books, over ninety magazine pieces, and several thousand signed newspaper commentaries. But his name was and is overshadowed by his father's. Indeed, Young Bill found growing up the only son of William Allen White a heavy burden. Sometimes, of course, that relationship proved a boon; as part of his father's busy life, he met presidents and prime ministers, novelists and syndicated columnists, book publishers and Broadway actresses. Yet as the son of the self-appointed teetotalist Conscience of the Midwest, he was his state's quintessential "preacher's kid." As he once observed, his father "was the best-known citizen of our state, far more in the limelight than any Governor or Senator, with the result it was impossible for me to lead a relaxed and normal life in my boyhood."[1] The glare of that publicity cast his father's shadow over him well after the older player had strutted his hour on the stage.

This is the story of how Young Bill White stepped out from behind that shadow and into the same professional limelight, only to find that shade still hovering in the wings. For in some respects, to the end of his life Bill was considered a chip off the old block; he too was an endemic Kansas humorist and small-town editor-booster. And like his father he too earned much of his national reputation writing for popular magazines. But, unlike his father, for many years he made New York City, not Emporia, his home. Yet he maintained legal residence in Emporia. That small town both nourished and repelled him, an ambivalence that contributed to unresolved conflicts in personal loyalties, that pitted the homely provincialism of Kansas against the sophisticated ambiance of the East Coast and juxtaposed his familial allegiance to the *Emporia Gazette* against his professional commitment to the *Reader's Digest*.

Unknown to most, that patrimony and ambivalence created a neurosis that affected Bill off and on for much of his adult life. Undiagnosed at first, his emotional disorder was subsequently misdiagnosed and treated as schizophrenia, though his real problem was manic-depression, a family trait. Outside the family few knew about his erratic emotional health or how much he struggled during the hard times of the 1930s to earn a place in New York City and establish a name separate from his father's. Few in his hometown knew of his later frustrations working as a roving editor for the *Reader's Digest* while at the same time overseeing the *Gazette*. And few realized how much his ties to Emporia truly meant to him, and to the town.

World War I initiated Bill's break from Kansas and his resulting ambivalence. While an army private in the University of Kansas Student Army Training Corps in 1918, Bill persuaded his father to get him released early to accompany him to the Paris Peace Conference. Fascinated by Paris and by European mores, Bill found the University of Kansas boring after his return and a year later transferred to Harvard, graduating with the class of 1924. He hoped to take a Rhodes Scholarship, but his parents insisted he work for a while on the family newspaper, then take over as its managing editor. Except for two five-month trips to Europe and occasional forays to New York City, he stayed in Emporia with the *Gazette* for ten years, writing many editorials attributed to his father and managing the paper during his absences.

At that time an operations point on the Santa Fe Railroad 125 miles southwest of Kansas City, Emporia was a cattle town of about fourteen thousand people, the seat of Lyon County. Near the center of a 150-mile oval of native tall-grass prairie known as the Bluestem Flint Hills, the town and its way of life could best be described as quiet. So could Young Bill. At a slender 5 feet 10 inches, with a round face, receding hairline, oddly rambling gait, and hesitant drawl, he appeared unprepossessing at first glance. His public manner as the town's junior editor, though occasionally tainted with an East Coast affectation, was inevitably polite, even diffident. But that masked a hyperbolic sense of humor, betrayed by wide-open brown eyes under heavy uplifted brows, an uneven but ready smile, and a laconic wit. Unlike his temperance-committed father, Bill drank immoderately at times, with great discretion, of course, while living in "dry" Kansas, and smoked Chesterfield cigarettes incessantly. In private, when an idea or subject appealed to him, he could become unusually animated. To those few who knew him well, he was far from quiet.

But compared to his father, Bill certainly seemed quiet. An ebullient roly-poly extrovert, Will A. White was an accomplished publicist, expert at garnering national attention from his editor's desk in Emporia, at a daily with a circulation less than six thousand. From there he had become a state and national leader of the liberal wing of the Republican party, the confidant of presidents, and the humorously sage voice of the midwestern middle class. He had been a prominent member of Samuel S. McClure's famous band of muckrakers; his political commentary was often syndicated and his editorials were widely copied. The winner of two Pulitzer Prizes, he wrote copy for twenty-five books in his lifetime and hundreds of magazine pieces, reviews, and speeches. He was also the chief booster and claim-to-fame of Emporia, Kansas. For his son that was a tough act to follow.[2]

In 1931 in New York City Bill married Kathrine Klinkenberg, a strong-minded, attractive, blue-eyed blonde. A fellow Kansan who escaped to the East Coast, she had worked nearly five years for *Time* magazine. In Emporia the young couple moved into a duplex across the street from the family home. Kathrine soon found living so close to her intrusive in-laws in small-town Kansas unbearable, with her discontent whetting Bill's. Both felt even more dissatisfied after a depression-bred school bond scandal rocked the state, perpetrated by the Whites' closest hometown friends, Warren Finney and son Ronald, well-known local bankers.

Early in 1934 Bill and Kathrine left for New York and then Boston, where she ostensibly sought medical treatment for gynecological problems. Away from the confines of Emporia and the *Gazette*, Bill started to write a novel, with Kathrine's help, about the Finney bond scandal, while at the same time sending home editorial copy to justify his *Gazette* paycheck. By the summer of 1935 both father and son realized that he and Kathrine could not return happily to Emporia. Instead he took a job in Washington, D.C., with the scholastic newsletter the *National Observer*, then moved into an editor's slot at the *Washington Post*, where he lasted only a short time. After months of joblessness, mutual unhappiness, and indecision, he and Kathrine moved in the fall of 1936 to New York City's Greenwich Village, where, with financial help from his parents, Bill continued to work on his novel.

In "The Sage of Emporia," a speech Bill delivered at the University of Kansas to commemorate his father's centennial, he remembered that

> some rough years followed. I had no literary reputation of my own, yet editors, particularly unsure or inexperienced ones, were eager to hire me on the theory that they were buying a slice of the Sage of Emporia at a substantial cash discount. When I tried to tell them I was an entirely different person with other talents and another viewpoint, they wouldn't listen. When I proved to be right, they felt I had swindled or betrayed them. The period was I think more painful for my father than it was for me, for no man wants his son to fail, and when the son of the Sage of Emporia is floundering around, this can hardly be kept a secret within the trade.

But in 1939 Bill established a newspaper column through the *Des Moines Register–Tribune* Syndicate, which more than fifty newspapers carried at its peak. And his Christmas Eve commentary from the Finnish Mannerheim line won the National Headliners Club citation for best European broadcast of the year, the the radio equivalent of a Pulitzer Prize. So Bill recalled that his father

> was now enormously proud of me, even telephoning me in Helsinki from Emporia. In the years that followed, he would watch my books rising on the best-seller lists, and buy them by the arm-load, paying the full retail price, to send out to his friends. He was very happy. I also liked it because intensely

well-meaning people had quit asking me if I thought I was a
chip off the old block.[3]

But that was a selective, honorary memory only. In truth Will
White ruined his son's budding radio career by ambivalently
motivated, deceptive advice to Bill's syndicate, advice that also
contributed to the demise of his newspaper column. And much
of the public never stopped viewing Bill by the reflected light of
his father.

In the fall of 1940 Bill sailed to an embattled Britain aboard
a Land-Lease destroyer as a stringer for the *Reader's Digest* and
a different newspaper syndicate. He did that purposefully with
no direct help or advice from his father. His subsequent London
material so interested DeWitt Wallace, publisher of the *Digest*, that
he signed Bill on late in 1941 as one of its first roving editors.
Bill kept that post the rest of his life because it gave him an identity
and an income separate from his father and the *Gazette*.

Though his father died in 1944, leaving Bill in control of the
family newspaper, for a decade his primary interest was his *Reader's
Digest* assignments. So he continued to reside chiefly in New York
City, running the *Gazette* as an absentee publisher-editor and
writing such books as *Land of Milk and Honey* (1949), the story
of a Russian defector, and *Back Down the Ridge* (1953), a narrative
about Korean War medical units. But after 1954 he began living
in Emporia for longer periods to monitor the newspaper more
closely, as he completely revamped its back shop and worked with
the staff on more graphically interesting layouts. Under his closer
supervision the *Gazette* eventually won seven national awards,
including the prestigious Ayer Cup in 1960 as the best newspaper
in the United States in typography and format.

Many of the townspeople, however, did not welcome his
increased local attention. Over the years they had come to regard
his occasional editorials about hometown civics as patronizing
interference from a New York transplant, a self-made exotic who
sported a monocle and sometimes a Harvard accent, one who
no longer understood the town and its needs. That perception
aggravated the ambivalence with which Bill and many Emporians
regarded each other. Yet, according to Whitley Austin, an old

friend and fellow Kansas publisher, Bill enjoyed his more active role as a small-town editor, "puttering with the *Gazette*'s typography and writing long pieces in an attempt to eclipse the reputation of his late father."[4] But to many of the hometown folk he never surpassed his father. To them he was still Young Bill to the day of his death, in Emporia, in 1973.

Ed Shupe, a former reporter for the *Gazette*, observed after Bill's death that

> WL's biggest trouble was that he was living in the shadow of his father, but he was probably at least as capable, if not more so, in a different way, than his father was. But he had a heck of a reputation to live down, and I think he worried about it more than anybody else; . . . it made him do things that would try to center more attention on himself. In other words, he'd do more radical things, even in his personal dress and his habits, just because he wanted to be known as W. L. White and not Young Bill. I think that this was really a cross that he carried around with him all his adult life.[5]

In large part this book is about that burden. It is the life story of a son who pursued the same profession as his more famous father, carrying virtually the same name. He did so at first with unassuming anonymity. But after making himself a literary craftsman equal to, and in some ways better than, his father, he attained a popular national byline on his own, through much persistence and some luck. Later, he too made the *Emporia Gazette* a nationally prominent small-town newspaper, for its makeup if not its commentary. So this is a story of acquiescence and rebellion, of influence and serendipity, of failure and undeniable success, of escape and return. It is an archetypal story of the covert conflict between a famous father and a dutiful son, as that father both helped and hindered the son's career. As background for this story we must start with the father, in the year his son was born.

Chapter One

A Small-Town Kansas Childhood, with a Harvard Finish, 1900–1924

In June of 1900 William Allen White, the thirty-two-year-old editor of the *Emporia Gazette*, a small-town Kansas daily, canceled plans to cover the Republican convention in Philadelphia, Pennsylvania, for Samuel McClure's national newspaper syndicate. Instead he stayed home with his sick wife, Sallie, during her final month of pregnancy. He was worried because they had earlier lost a baby after a similarly troubled pregnancy. Sallie again had a difficult labor but on June 17 bore a healthy ten-pound son, whom they named William Lindsay, the second name being her maiden name. In a jaunty mood Will wrote John Phillips, associate editor of *McClure's Magazine*: "There is a little baby boy 24 hours old in the White household. His name is Bill. If any one calls him Willie, or William or Will, Boxers [Chinese revolutionaries] will organize and wipe that person off the face of the earth. Little Bill was a dilatory youth, and . . . has been hanging around reluctant to leave the gates until I do not know what kind of dislocation he has got us in."[1] Soon the full realization of his wife's ordeal dampened his parental enthusiasm. A week later he wrote Maud Johnston, a mutual friend whose husband was managing editor of the *Kansas City* [Missouri] *Star*, that Sallie "has gone down into the valley of the Great Shadow and has come up and is getting well and strong. Of the boy—I can't get interested in him for a long time. Till I know that all possible danger to Sallie is over."[2]

His son's late arrival and his wife's slow recovery forced him to delay other travel plans, to New York City, where he planned to join Auguste Jaccaci, art editor for *McClure's*, and to sail on July 10 for Paris on a trip to be sponsored by the magazine. That would be his first trip to Europe, and Sallie urged him to take it. Reassured by her that all was well, he left for New York on June 28 but returned hastily to Emporia within a week because Sallie, weakened by pregnancy and childbirth, had become gravely ill with a fever, so he informed John Phillips, associate editor of *McClure's*. White also reluctantly wrote Jaccaci, "You do not know how it pains me and how disappointed I am, not to be with you now, but the call to come home was imperative, and I had to give it up. . . . My wife has been very low with Malarial fever; but is now recovering. . . . I hope that I have not disarranged your plans."[3] Little Bill certainly disarranged his.

Otherwise, the birth of a son did not slow the frenetic pace he had set five years earlier when he bought with three thousand borrowed dollars the smaller of the two dailies in Emporia. At first he struggled just to make expenses and establish a local name. But in the summer of 1896 he catapulted onto the national stage with an angry editorial denouncing the ascendant Populists statewide, which Sen. Mark Hanna of Ohio, chairman of the Republican National Committee, distributed widely in support of William McKinley's presidential campaign. Soon nearly every sizable Republican newspaper in the country reprinted it. Will capitalized on the publicity by publishing that fall his first book of short stories, which introduced him to the New York City magazine market. Four years after that editorial, he had paid off his original note, put an equal amount of money into new press machinery, and built a new *Gazette* building, mostly with earnings from freelance magazine articles.

Late in the fall of 1900 he started a novel while working at his newspaper by day and writing magazine copy by night. Then, just a year after his son's birth, he pledged a series of biographical sketches to *McClure's* and another series of short stories to *Scribner's Magazine* for a loan to buy the impressive, ten-room house he was renting at 927 Exchange Street. In addition to all his writing he was busy too as a stage manager in Kansas politics. Being home in July 1900 because of Sallie's illness, he rode the Republican campaign train through Kansas with vice-presidential candidate Theodore Roosevelt, for whom he handled local introductions.

Then just after the election he and Sallie, now recovered, traveled to New York City for nearly a month. While back East, Sallie left the baby with Mary Ann White, Will's mother. Grandma White was a short, stout, dour Irishwoman, emotional but completely humorless, who was to become increasingly morose as she grew older. When Young Bill was in his thirties, his parents worried that he had inherited her moodiness. Just as likely, he had inherited her sentimentality, a leavening quality subsumed in the best of his mature writings. Whatever the inheritance, Grandma White had a decided influence on his childhood. She had lived with the young couple since their marriage, then in 1903 they built a house for her next door, at 923 Exchange, though she continued until her death in 1924 to take her evening meals with them.

Billy literally cut his teeth in the *Gazette* newsroom, where Sallie placed him in a large mesh basket next to her desk. For her and Will that newspaper had become part of their marriage. She wrote local and society items and, when he was out-of-town on political or magazine errands, took over as managing editor.[4] And she always worked with him on his fiction and his feature articles, curbing his impulsiveness and honing his style. Fortunately for that hard-working partnership, Billy was a good baby and grew into an outwardly docile, shy but affectionate child, with a slyly irreverent, quirky sense of humor.

In addition to Grandma White another implacable influence on Young Bill was the neighborhood around 927 Exchange. Known locally as the Red Rocks, the house was a turreted Victorian structure built in 1885 of Colorado red sandstone. But it was located in Precinct Two of the less fashionable, northeast Fourth Ward, near Stringtown, the "colored" section. Despite being the son of the town's famous editor, Billy grew up in that neighborhood learning the social realities of small-town life. His playmates were blue-collar and lower-middle-class children; he attended integrated public schools with neighborhood blacks; and he carried a newspaper route for four years along three blocks of the nearby southeast Second Ward, a largely working-class section where the Roman Catholic church stood. So he knew his side of town well, and it knew him.

When he was born, Emporia was a county-seat country market town with a population of 8,724. Kansas State Normal School (renamed Kansas State Teachers College in 1923), the small Presbyterian College of Emporia, and a downtown business college were located there. In that age of steam the town was to become in the next two decades a division headquarters for the Santa Fe Railroad, with two locomotive roundhouses and a large switching yard. It also marked the junction of the east-west Santa Fe and the north-south Missouri, Kansas, and Texas Railway Company (the MKT, or "Katy"). Located in east-central Kansas between the rich bottomlands of the Cottonwood and the Neosho rivers, Emporia stood amid the rolling Bluestem Flint Hill prairies as a self-conscious commercial and cultural oasis. Farming and cattle ranching sustained its economy, and Kansas provincialism determined its mores. Genteel life focused on the two academic colleges. Its many Protestant churches, led by the Methodists, frowned on such frivolities as dancing and card playing or Sunday entertainment, other than religious services. The town council had enforced a Prohibition ordinance since 1874, until the state in 1938 allowed taverns that served beer with a lowered 3.2 percent alcohol content. In 1948 the state allowed county-option packaged liquor stores. The sale of ready-made cigarettes and even cigarette papers was illegal statewide from 1907 until 1927. Nonsmoking, teetotaling, church-going editor Will A. White could live comfortably with that self-righteously intrusive provincialism, partly because he often escaped from it. Young Bill, however, ostensibly conformed to it yet quietly flaunted it, paradoxically attracted to and repelled by it all his life.

When Sallie and Will returned from New York City in December 1900, he increased his pace by adding to his *McClure's* and *Scribner's* commitments an occasional article and short story for the *Saturday Evening Post*. His workload increased further; before long he had added *Collier's* to his list. In the spring of 1901, for example, he went east to interview former presidents Benjamin Harrison and Grover Cleveland for interpretive biographical sketches in *McClure's*. Then in July he covered the opening of Indian lands in Oklahoma for the *Saturday Evening Post*, while at the same time working on a series of short stories. Early in August he met with Vice President Roosevelt in Colorado Springs, Colorado, to help set up a 1904 presidential campaign. Then in the last week of August he again went east, this time to interview Pres. William McKinley in Ohio and Sen. Thomas C. Platt in New York City for more *McClure's* sketches, and to confer further with Teddy Roosevelt. While Will was in New York City, McKinley was assassinated and Roosevelt became president. Young William Allen White of Emporia, Kansas, was one of his most ardent supporters and closest political confidants.

In that dual role he published his sketch of Senator Platt, an intraparty foe of Roosevelt's, in the December issue of *McClure's*. It was a whimsically vitriolic attack picturing Platt as a corrupt political intriguer, an "earthworm" undermining popular government at both state and national levels. The senator was furious and threatened an expensive libel suit. Will put up a brave, even flippant front but soon realized that the expenses of a competent legal defense could cost him the *Gazette*. After much bluster Platt did not file, but that threat, added to the previous years of near-manic bustle, took its toll on White. In the middle of January 1902, while writing another political sketch for *McClure's*, he collapsed into total nervous prostration.

Accompanied by Sallie, he went to Los Angeles, California, to consult Dr. Merrit Hitt, a "nerve specialist," then on his advice rented a cottage on sparsely settled Catalina Island for a complete rest. Eighteen-month-old Billy was left at home in the care of Grandma White, who was joined by Sallie's mother, Francis (Fannie) Lindsay. The two grandmothers were good friends, though temperamentally different, with Mrs. Lindsay reportedly as cheerfully easygoing as Mrs. White was dour.[5] Will rationalized in his autobiography, "One grandmother will spoil a baby. Two working together will bring him up in the way he should go, for each will suspect the other of spoiling him and will check it."[6] When he and Sallie returned to Emporia in June, Will still did not feel fully recovered, but by that fall he was again working at his former hectic pace.

Years later Young Bill would write Cecil ("Teet") Carle, his closest boyhood friend, recalling regretfully how in their childhood "your father [a laconic house painter] talked to you and paid more attention to you than my father did to me."[7] For Will's frenetic pattern of work, with strenuous social entertaining and occasional breaks for travel or rest, established the parental lifestyle with which Billy White grew up. Not surprisingly, several more times Will or Sallie broke down so completely that they had to take months off to recuperate. For Sallie too suffered from bouts with ill health or depression throughout her life.[8] She was the daughter of a former Confederate cavalry captain from Kentucky, one of Morgan's Raiders, who had settled in Kansas City, Kansas, where he earned a modest salary as yard superintendent for the Fowler Packing Company. When Will married her, she was a twenty-three-year-old elementary school teacher, intelligent, pretty, and, in contrast to his exuberance, quietly level-headed. He came to rely on her judgment implicitly.[9]

Though Will grew up an only child, Sallie had seven younger brothers and sisters who survived infancy, to whom she felt the eldest child's responsibility. Mutual family loyalties were a fact of married life for her and Will. For example, after the second week of their honeymoon at a resort hotel in New Mexico, they met his mother in Santa Fe, then the three of them went to Manitou Springs, Colorado, where his maternal aunt, Kate, ran a small hotel.[10] There they were joined by Sallie's thirteen-year-old brother, Milt Lindsay. Like Grandma White one or more of the Lindsay clan was usually at 927 Exchange while Billy was a child. Thus Bill came to know his uncles and aunts well.

In 1904 Sallie was pregnant and again having a difficult time. On June 18 she bore a daughter whom they named Mary Katherine after Grandma Mary Ann White. According to Everett

Rich, one of Will White's biographers, during this pregnancy Sallie's doctor gave her "a stimulant to strengthen her heart" that affected the baby's health.[11] Whatever the cause, for the first several years of Mary's life she was a colicky child who required much care and nursing, with both grandmothers helping out. Because of Sallie's and the baby's frail health, the family escaped the punishing heat of Kansas summers for the next several years by spending those months in a cottage at Manitou Springs, Colorado, on the slopes of Pikes Peak and near Grandma White's sister, Kate. During those months, so Will records in his autobiography: "I shuttled between Colorado Springs and Emporia many times. Bill sometimes lived with me and his grandmother White; sometimes he was with his mother and [sister] Mary. There never was a better little boy or a more satisfactory baby than he. He tried so hard to make it easy for us. He was so gentle and considerate that his mother and I were afraid that God might be shy of angels somewhere and send for him. But he was a robust youngster and full of joy and mischief and insatiable curiosity, and most affectionate."[12]

In contrast young Mary grew up no angel. After her initial sickliness she became a nervously vibrant tomboy, rambunctious and rebellious, fearless around horses, a frequent trial to her parents. Unlike Bill she was not a warm, considerate child but expressed her spirits by flagrant teasing and flamboyant reckless-ness. That led to many childhood arguments, of course, but they grew up very close, with Bill the somewhat pompous big brother and Mary the bedeviling gamin of a little sister.

When Bill was six, his parents sent him to Century, the public elementary school serving the Fourth Ward. Built in 1900, hence its name, it stood only three blocks from home. For some reason it contained but six classrooms, so Fourth Ward children had to attend seventh and eighth grades at Union Street School, only a six-block walk for Bill. Emporia did not build a junior high until 1925. Most of the black children in town also attended Century after their own neighborhood school partially collapsed before Bill was in first grade. So Bill quickly experienced the not-so-subtle social barriers for "coloreds" even in "free" Kansas. He learned that his first-grade teacher, Miss May Hancock, would not allow white boys to sit with black girls and discovered in the second grade that his mother would not invite black schoolmates to his birthday party. Perhaps that fostered the open sympathy for blacks apparent in his later life and writings.[13] As a child Bill was left-handed, but at Century, in accord with current pedagogy, he was forced to switch to his right, which may have caused several personal quirks: though he became ambidextrous, throughout his life he easily became confused about directions and when under pressure was prone to spoonerisms. But in general he excelled in grade school and had a typical small-town midwestern boyhood. He had a fox terrier named Teddy, after the president, and played with a gang of neighborhood boys, several of whom were to remain lifelong friends. Chief among them was Teet Carle, who lived half a block north.

In March 1909, soon after returning from Teddy Roosevelt's last presidential reception and William Howard Taft's inauguration, Will and Sallie took the children and Grandma White on a long-planned six-month tour of Europe, their first. The timing was right for the entire family. Billy was just shy of nine years old and Mary of five; Grandma White was an intrepid seventy-nine. Will had finally finished his novel A Certain Rich Man, a loyal and capable staff ran the Gazette, and the Progressive wing of the Republican party seemed to hold Kansas and the nation firmly in its hands. They sailed slowly from New York City to Naples on a small White Star liner, then did a full version of the grand tour, staying in pensions or modest tourist hotels and taking in the galleries, shops, and sights of Europe.

In his autobiography Will remembered that trip as "a milepost. In the new environment of Europe, I saw myself in perspective."[14] Billy, however, viewed that journey with a child's eyes, unready to focus on mileposts, recording but a blur of impressions. It did force him, though, after their homecoming to see himself too in a new perspective, one that stayed with him the rest of his life. For while the Whites were in Europe, A Certain Rich Man had become, unknown to Will, a national best-seller. That plus his widely copied travel letters to the Gazette, written in the humor and style of Mark Twain's Innocents Abroad, had stirred his staff and fellow townspeople to expansive pride in their editor. When the Whites' train pulled into Emporia that September, the town's brass band saluted them, a welcoming committee escorted them to nearby Humbolt Park where townsfolk presented skits from the novel, then two flower-bedecked open hacks paraded them home past the *Gazette* building and down Commercial Street. On his deathbed Bill recalled his realization as a boy of nine during that parade that "we did occupy a kind of God-like position in this little town." But his first concern on getting home was to escape the ceremonies, strip off "his shoes and socks and go find the boys."[15]

From then on, though, he would never again be just one of the boys—he was the son of William Allen White, a famous author and highly respected editor. And he learned that the town judged him by a different standard. That became clear to him in the sixth grade when as a practical joke during recess he tried to plant a "dirty" note in Teet Carle's pocket inviting Augusta Bang, the prim daughter of Louis Bang, leading merchant and school board member, to a nearby barn for a tryst in the hayloft. He planned to tease Teet later, after he discovered it. By accident the note fell on to the playground and was turned in to Miss Frances Riggs, the principal, who called Teet up before Mr. Bang and Lloyd Lowther, school superintendent. Threatened with reform school and physically shaken, Teet blurted out that Billy White had probably written the note in fun. Believing that a lie, they sent for him and to their consternation he confessed. Reassessing the situation, they agreed it was but a boyish prank and gave him a letter to carry home to his mother about his being "naughty." Perhaps wiser than they, she made him go to the Bang house, knock on the door, and apologize to Augusta in "anguished humiliation."[16] Being the son of the town's famous editor had both advantages and handicaps. But his innate irreverence and sense of humor were not dampened by that realization; they were just quietly sublimated.

Will, a boisterous extrovert unaware of his son's burden, saw only his outward reticence at that time and commented in a letter to Gene Howe, son of Ed Howe, a fellow Kansas novelist and the nationally known editor of the *Atchison Globe*, "I am glad to know you are working on the *Globe*. I shall be mighty proud when my boy, Bill, gets that far along. I don't think Bill will be worth very much. He is a good boy and that is the trouble. He is too good a boy and does not make me any trouble and I'm afraid he won't make anybody else any trouble and never get very far."[17] Years later, after Bill's controversial *Report on the Russians* first appeared in the *Reader's Digest*, Soviet premier Joseph Stalin undoubtedly wished that prophecy had come true. And Will, by the time of his death, had seen two of his son's books make the national best-seller list.[18]

In the summer of 1911 Will and Sallie rented a cottage in Moraine Park, Colorado, just within Rocky Mountain National Reserve, from Prof. Frank Hodder of the University of Kansas. Will had been mulling over a second novel and wanted some time to write free from *Gazette* chores, magazine editors and the intraparty struggle then raging between Progressive and standpat Republicans. The next summer he bought the Hodder property and the family returned to Colorado. That cabin became the summer base for at least some of the family the rest of Will's life. For Bill and Mary it became the vacation home of their youth and introduced them to rustic outdoor living among a neighborly summer colony of mostly University of Kansas faculty and their families, whom Will knew because from 1905 to 1912 he was one of the university's regents. On the slopes of a mountain, overlooking a valley, and with a spectacular view of Longs Peak to the south, Moraine Park in those days had no telephone and got its news chiefly from the flamboyantly yellow Rocky Mountain *Post*, and its mail and staples at the Sam Service general store in the nearby village of Estes Park. As a youth, Bill was captivated by that Rocky Mountain retreat with its quiet, rugged way of life diversified by a kaleidoscope of visiting friends and family.

During the 1912 political tornado that swept the Progressives away from the Republicans and into the temporary shelter of their own Bull Moose party, Will braved the storm of national convention and election politics with his usual gusto. As a syndicated reporter, an unofficial publicist for and press advisor to Teddy Roosevelt, and a Kansas political boss, he could barely catch his breath in the midst of the whirlwind. But with the election of Democrat Woodrow Wilson that November came the inevitable aftermath, and Will found himself becalmed in Emporia, his second novel nearly forgotten, his political base in jeopardy. But this time it was Sallie who suffered a nervous collapse. She fell ill in September and by the middle of December Will decided to take her to California for a rest.[19] They rented a beach house in La Jolla for five months. Will also took along the children, Grandma White, and their "hired girl," Martha. Catherine Boynton, Will's cousin and Grandma White's niece, lived in Los Angeles where, after her husband died, she had trained and then practiced as an osteopathic physician, so even there the Whites were not far from family.[20] In La Jolla Sallie rested and walked the shoreline while Will puttered away on his novel. Bill finished the seventh grade and Mary the third at the local two-story red schoolhouse. After class he and Mary searched the tidal pools and jousted with breaking waves as their parents or Grandma White looked on. On weekends they toured San Diego and its environs. For Billy La Jolla was a pleasant interlude.[21]

In June 1913 the family returned to Emporia for several weeks; then Will decided Sallie was still not fully rested and took the family to Colorado for July and August. In September Bill enrolled again at Union, where he entered the eighth grade, but just after school started he fell seriously ill with typhoid, which kept him home several weeks. During the second half of that school year, with the approval of his teacher, he edited a little handwritten newspaper called the *Union Bugle*, which caught the interest of his classmates because it contained, in addition to news items, a serial Wild West story he wrote entitled "The Sombrero."[22] This school year he also took on his paper route and joined the Arrow Patrol of the Boy Scouts, based at the Congregational church, which his family attended.

But Bill was never much interested in merit badges and Boy Scout heartiness. Bookish and unobtrusive, he had no real interest in sports, though he was robust enough. Instead, in high school he found his outlet in the school newspaper, the yearbook, and the drama club. But he could not be called a sissy either. At least parts of the five summers after 1913 he spent hiking or fishing in Moraine Park. Other times he spent at his uncle Charles Lindsay's farm northwest of town, near the small village of

Americus. There he helped do chores and worked in the fields, sometimes with his grandfather, Joe Lindsay, who had retired from the cattle yards of Kansas City and with his wife moved in with his son when Bill was in high school. In answer to a *Gazette* subscriber's charge much later that Bill knew nothing about farming and thus as editor should not comment about it, he replied:

> I often spent long periods of the summer vacation out [at my uncle's farm]. After the milk had been put through my aunt's separator I have taken the skimmed milk out to the pigs and chickens. . . . I know how to ride and service a corn planter. I was not big enough to be allowed to drive the reaper, but I followed along behind it picking up the wheat bundles and stacking them into shocks.[23]

Likewise, he learned to box and shoot from his uncle Bob, who was only eight years older. In a letter to his aunt and cousins on learning of his uncle's death, he wrote:

> [Bob] was very good to me. I had never had a brother, while your grandfather Lindsay's family was a big one—teaming with boys. The older boys bossed the younger ones around, but they also trained them, and always defended them, if anyone outside the family got into an argument with them. And Bob took me on in this capacity—a younger boy that he both trained and defended. . . . For instance he taught me how to shoot, and in time I inherited his rifle (he had graduated to a shotgun). It was a wonderful .22, which held 16 shots in its magazine, as good as any they make today.[24]

In fact, Bill's visits as a young boy to the Lindsays home in a working-class neighborhood of Kansas City, Kansas, perched on a bluff overlooking the Kansas and Missouri rivers, enlarged his view of life in many ways. As he remembered it, in the upstairs bedrooms there was no heat at all, so "you learned to dress in nothing flat, and to make a run downstairs to where the stove and gas burner were. As for plumbing, my memory is that they had a two-hole privy out back of the house and just beside the barn, which raised the finest, healthiest crop of blue-bottle flies that I have ever seen." That family of eight living children included five boys, each an avid sportsman who hunted and fished along the two rivers. The three girls also hunted, not for game, but for "Paw's" bottle. As Bill recalled, "'Paw' was supposed to be an alcoholic. At the time I accepted the statement as true. Now I wonder if 'Paw' was not on the side of normal, and that maybe his wife and daughters were violent prohibitionists."[25] Grandfather Lindsay's perceived alcoholism undoubtedly accounted for his daughter Sallie's insistence that Will A. White take the pledge before she married him and for their later concern about their son's drinking habits. At any rate, his close ties to his mother's family broadened his perspective and his sympathy, an asset to his later career as a writer.

When Bill entered classes at Emporia's new high school building in the fall of 1914, he was still Billy White, at least the 1915 yearbook, the Re-Echo, listed him so as one of the two freshman reporters on the school newspaper, the Echo. Billy learned that year to churn out copy, not only at school but also at the Gazette, for his father had hired him and Teet that fall to collect personals. Bill's beat was north of Sixth Avenue, which included the high school. Every afternoon after school they scoured the town for two-, three-, or four-line items of local interest, each containing one or more personal names, then met at the Gazette newsroom and typed up their results for next day's edition. Will paid them fifty cents per pasted-up column; if they hustled they could earn about two dollars a week. For two high school freshmen that was good money and, what was more important, excellent training, with the Gazette staff unstinting in editorial advice.

Now that Billy stood at the edge of adulthood, an intelligent, quietly inquisitive adolescent, his involvement in his father's world increased. During the election years of 1914 and 1916 Will fought heroically alongside his fellow Progressives to prevent the complete rout of the Bull Moose party. They failed. But during the final battle, in the summer of 1916, Bill joined his father at the national conventions in Chicago, Illinois, and St. Louis, Missouri. There he experienced the excitement of political combat and watched his father function as a national columnist for the Adams Syndicate. Undoubtedly that gave him a better idea of his father's stature as a journalist and behind-the-scenes politician.

Bill continued as an occasional part-time reporter for the *Gazette* and at the same time carried his paper route. He worked on the *Echo* some his sophomore year, this time as Bill, not Billy, but not his junior year, when that paper nearly ceased publication amid student accusations of administrative censorship. It was reorganized his senior year with Teet and him elected coeditors over a staff of twenty-five, including his sister, who was a "sub-freshman." For that paper Bill wrote a humorous personals column entitled "Horse Laffs." He also worked on the 1918 yearbook and played one of the leads in the senior class play.

But his sense of humor got him in trouble several times his senior year. For example, Roy Cook, the high school principal, had scheduled a student-hated inspirational assembly every Friday morning at ten o'clock. For one Friday in March he announced a special program by the evangelical Fletcher Thomas, an official from the Young Men's Christian Association (YMCA) state headquarters in Topeka, Kansas. Unimpressed, a group of six senior boys, including Bill, decided to make Mr. Thomas's speech memorable. They pooled their cash, bought ten cheap alarm clocks, set them to ring at two-minute intervals, then hid them on the stage and in the lighting fixtures of the auditorium. The alarms went off on schedule, starting just after ten o'clock Friday morning. They thought their scheme detection-proof, but the druggist who sold the clocks remembered who bought them and was a brother-in-law of a school board member. So Bill and friends endured a brief suspension and an official reprimand. As the elder White once said, to stay out of trouble any small-town journalist must know the local "kineology."

But for that senior class World War I overshadowed both studies and pranks. The United States had declared war against Germany on April 6, 1917, after several years of escalating tension. An unprecedented paroxysm of patriotism swept the nation. Bill joined the hastily organized Emporia Junior Militia in the fall of 1917 and registered for induction just after high school graduation when he turned eighteen. As the country mobilized clumsily for continuing trench warfare, which in the summer of 1918 seemed a several-year prospect, he was sure he would be called up and was uncertain about the coming year. Tentatively, he planned to enroll at the University of Kansas.

The war was especially immediate for him his senior year in high school because his father had sailed for France in August 1917 as a colonel in the Red Cross to observe its involvement with American troops there. Along with his good friend Henry Allen, publisher of the *Wichita Eagle*, Will spent two months in Europe, sometimes at the battlefronts, then returned home in November to publicize Red Cross war efforts. While in Europe, he sent back a number of letters about the war that Sallie published in the *Gazette*. After his return he combined them at her urging with his syndicated articles for the Red Cross to form the thinly fictitious, sometimes humorous book-length narrative *The Martial Adventures of Henry and Me*,[26] which sold well. Bill, of course, was impressed by his father's role as a small-town newspaper editor turned war correspondent, especially since at age seventeen he could himself be inducted into the army within a year.

With his father gone he now felt proprietary about the family business. In a letter to his father soon after he sailed, Bill expressed that interest clearly but awkwardly. For in it is sometimes the voice of an adolescent son speaking to a revered father, with speaker and auditor at clearly different levels, and sometimes the voice of one newspaperman talking to another on the same level. That confusion of voice, of attitude, characterized and troubled their future relationship for years. Bill wrote from Kansas City, Missouri, where he had undergone minor sinus surgery:

> I don't know what in the deuce will become of my [paper] route, but I think I can get home day-after-tomorrow . . . and have ten days to collect and put it in shape before school opens. . . . I still have a scheme in mind to get up a "High School Notes" column when school starts. I think I could do about a column every other day. The paper sure has been looking rotten since you left. The [Kansas City] Star had something to the effect that the editorial page had been filled up with boiler plate. . . . As for the society column, it just ain't, that's all there is to

say. . . . But cheer up, maybe it isn't going to the dogs as fast
as I think it is. Don't forget to bring me home some kind of
a souvenir for my room, like a trench helmet or a soldier's coat
or hat.[27]

After Bill's graduation from high school the Whites invited Teet
Carle to join them for a summer in Colorado, because both boys
faced possible military duty that fall. While they hiked the
mountain trails of Rocky Mountain National Park, idealistically
preparing for the rigors of army life, the federal government decided
to form a Student Army Training Corps (SATC) at some five
hundred colleges and universities. When the boys returned home,
Teet joined the unit at the College of Emporia and Bill enrolled
in the unit at the University of Kansas in Lawrence. As a member
of the SATC he was officially in the United States Army; he was
to receive uniforms, equipment, barracks housing, board, university fees, thirty dollars a month, and military training. But when
he reported for duty on September 16, he found the university
in chaos. Barracks were unfinished, food services were unready,
and a military-oriented curriculum based on the quarter instead
of the traditional semester system was not yet implemented.

For several weeks Bill stayed at his father's old fraternity, Phi Delta
Theta, which he pledged amid the initial disorder of the term. But
by the first week of October, military structure emerged, and he
found himself in Company B, assigned to a barracks and a cot.
At the end of the second week of October, though, an outbreak
of the Spanish flu closed the university and put SATC discipline
to a severe test. The university remained closed for a month while
the SATC commander tried to drill his recruits and the flu marched
unchecked through the new pine barracks. Bill was one of its many
victims and for a day or two thought he was going to die.[28] But
that flu left Lawrence as quickly as it appeared, and with the signing
of the armistice on November 11, the university reopened. Academically, the quarter was a disaster. To the great relief of faculty and
students the university disbanded its SATC unit and mustered out
most of its members before Christmas.

But Bill did not share that relief. Just after the false armistice
report of November 7 he wrote his father asking his help to transfer

to an officer training camp: "Well, it seems you were wrong about the war lasting till next year. . . . I wish there was some way for me to be transferred to a draft camp and get into officers camp some way. . . . Don't you suppose it could possibly be managed? . . . I have an awful hankering to get over in France, even if it is all over, and I am put to filling up trenches, for I have a hunch that there will be some fighting before Europe is politically reconstructed."[29] Will too hankered to be in France, not to fill in trenches, but to report on the prospects for peace. When his bid to join President Wilson's entourage to Paris failed, he turned to the Red Cross and to his newspaper syndicate. Both quickly accredited him to cover the Paris Peace Conference. Young Bill then begged his father to take him along. Sallie strongly seconded his plea. So Will contacted Capt. B. F. Scher, university comman- dant, to expedite Bill's release from the SATC, and by December 12 they were at White's New York base, the National Arts Club.

In the midst of meeting with editors and Red Cross officials and repacking to board the small, crowded, permanently listing French liner, oddly named the SS *Chicago*, Will discovered he could not get his son a passport without his having some sort of official standing among the dignitaries flocking to Paris. So he quickly arranged for the Red Cross to appoint Bill his aide and grant him the brevet rank of second lieutenant, a heady promotion for an eighteen-year-old SATC private. As a Red Cross staff officer, Bill got his passport. Will was characteristically amused by his son's all-too-human reaction to that unexpected commission, for he wrote Sallie: "Bill is tremendously funny about his clothes. He bought him an officer's chin strap, and I made him take it off. It just bordered the line of pretense, and while a Red Cross second loot is a loot, after all he is only a play-loot! I made Bill pack his leather putties in the trunk and the trunk is in the hold. But he has his officer's coat and rain coat which is as far as I'll let him go."[30] Will himself bought two new colonel's uniforms.

For Young Bill White, Paris in 1919 was tremendously exhila- rating, especially in the company of his father. Most of Will's New York City magazine cronies were there, and Young Bill soon became acquainted with them—with Samuel S. McClure, Ida Tarbell, Lincoln Steffens, Auguste Jaccacci, Walter Lippmann, and

Ray Stannard Baker, who was in charge of press relations for the American Commission to Negotiate Peace. President Wilson's personal aide, Col. Edward House, was a good friend of Will's, as were many other American observers, officials, and journalists, such as Thomas Lamont of the Morgan banking interests, Herbert Hoover and Vernon Kellogg of the American Food Administration, the novelist Dorothy Canfield Fisher, Arthur Krock of the *New York Times*, Herbert Swope of the *New York World*, David Lawrence of the *New York Evening Post*, and Oswald Villard of the *Nation*. Young Bill met them all. During the conference President Wilson appointed Will, together with diplomat George D. Herron, to meet at Prinkipo, a Turkish island off the Dardenelles, with representatives of the Soviet Union, France, Britain, and sundry Baltic states to discuss establishing diplomatic relations with the Soviets. After prolonged negotiations in Paris, the French blocked that meeting. But one result was that Bill, who functioned as his father's interpreter with two years of high school French plus Parisian tutoring, received from those negotiations a crash course in pragmatic international politics, European style.

Actually, his education started on the SS *Chicago*. The Whites shared their cabin and table with the British journalist Norman Angell, later Sir Norman, an international affairs expert and winner of a Nobel Peace Prize in 1933.[31] Will, as usual, was miserably seasick and took to his bunk for the duration. So Bill found himself at table with Angell and fellow Emporians Willis and Mary Kerr, librarians from the normal school charged with setting up a reference collection for Americans at the conference. Table conversation focused on the status of Europe and its prospects for peace, challenging topics for a one-term freshman at the University of Kansas. After landing at Bordeaux on December 31 and enduring a week in Paris at the frigid Hotel Normandy, a small out-of-the-way hotel where they had been billeted by the Red Cross, the Whites followed Norman Angell to the well-heated Hotel Vouillemont, located near the American Embassy on the Place de la Concorde. It was a fortunate choice because many others of the foreign press corps located there. Guided by his father, a food enthusiast, Bill became well acquainted with French cuisine and moderately priced Parisian restaurants, in addition to gaining fluency in the language.

While the elder White attended press conferences and wrote magazine commentary and cable dispatches, the younger roamed Paris, exploring its many facets.[32] In the evenings he accompanied his father to dinners, concerts, and the theater. And he went with him on two extended junkets—one starting in late January to Strasbourg to interview French officers in Alsace-Lorraine, then on to Koblenz in Germany to observe the American Army of Occupation; the other in early March through the battlefields northeast of Paris to Cambrai near the Belgian border. Both he described in two long letters to his mother, who published them in the *Gazette*, along with several others he wrote about Paris.

In the tour letters he tells with obvious satisfaction how in his Red Cross uniform he was treated as an American officer, even being called on to arrest an army deserter. And he describes with some sensitivity the physical and social costs of the war, as he observed the aftermath. Yet he was still a boy, in spite of the uniform. For example, he tells about hunting for souvenir field helmets in the trenches at Tergnier, ostensibly for his sister. There he came upon a former Russian soldier, recently a German prisoner, who was scrubbing pots in an old shell hole for a nearby French camp. The Russian saw his officer's uniform, jumped to stiff attention and held a salute while Bill tried to speak to him unsuccessfully in English, French, and some tags of German. He then comments compassionately: "They are tragic figures, these Russians. They died blindly and like sheep for the Allied cause, and now are wandering, homeless and forgotten, through the land of their former Allies, doing the menial work, no better off than they were under their enemies, with 4,000 miles separating them from their native villages, and with no prospect of ever returning, for the government that sent them forth has gone from this world, and no one is responsible for their welfare or return." In the next sentences, though, he returns to his souvenir hunt and reports: "These trenches, through which I had been walking, . . . were dotted with German and French helmets, and such stuff, which I had no way of getting to Paris, where I could mail them to the boys in Emporia, and at the Phi Delt house, or I certainly would have done so."[33] Bill was only eighteen years old; among his Parisian souvenirs was a collection of risqué magazines which he quietly mailed to Teet Carle to hold until he got home.

By May the elder White had had enough of the conference, with its misleading salon press briefings, backroom politics, and secret treaties. Instead of heading directly home, though, he accepted an invitation from Norman Angell to visit England for several weeks to get firsthand impressions for commentary about British reactions to the peace treaty. In London he met with leaders of the Labour party, strengthened ties with his British publisher, Sir Frederick Macmillan, and renewed friendships with such writers as H. G. Wells and Sir John Buchan, at that time director of information for Lloyd George's government. Son Bill quickly adapted to British formality at their stodgy hotel, the Artillery Mansions, near St. James Park. When not attending his father, he roamed London as he had Paris, a happy tourist. Early in June the Whites left for Ireland. Will wanted to determine for himself the strength of the Sinn Fein movement because he knew the Irish back home were adamantly opposed to the League of Nations, convinced it would strengthen British imperialism. He, in contrast, believed that in the league lay Wilson's only chance to attain a workable peace. After two weeks in Ireland, where Will finished articles for several London magazines warning of potent Irish-American opposition to the league, the Whites sailed for New York City, returning to Emporia in the last week of July. They had been gone for seven months.

Will, dismayed by Republican opposition to both the treaty and the league, threw himself immediately into the fight for ratification. That August he stumped Wisconsin for one week for the League to Enforce Peace and quickly wrote two *Saturday Evening Post* articles of support. Meanwhile, Bill settled back into small-town life, catching up with high school friends, visiting Lindsay relatives, and preparing to reenroll at the University of Kansas. Classes did not begin until September 15, but Bill returned to Lawrence early to help with fraternity rush week. He moved into the Phi Delt house and at first enjoyed the trivia of fraternity life. In several letters home that fall he detailed his busy social calendar, partially to rationalize his constant and, to him at least, perplexing lack of ready cash; for example: "All the rest of the Phi Delt chapter is departing in a body for Lincoln, Nebr., except for me. I am going to stay here for two reasons, i.e., I haven't the nec. $25.00, and I have a date with the Alice Carney whom father knows about."[34] Not surprisingly, after six months in Europe, often in the company of prominent American journalists and other near notables, Bill grew dissatisfied with Greek life at the university and found no compensating challenge elsewhere on campus. In an introspective mood late in life he remembered joining the Phi Delts only out of filial loyalty, remarking, "I don't think [my father] gave a damn what I did, but I got the idea I'd be disloyal to him if I pledged anything else."[35]

To most acquaintances Young Bill seemed reserved or distant or at best reluctantly sociable. But his friends, throughout his life, remarked on his unfailing personal courtesy and warm sense of humor. In contrast, casual associates often mistook an essentially modest demeanor as patronizing aloofness or barely concealed disdain.[36] That apparently anomalous attitude contributed to some of his discomfort at the university. For he sensed that fellow students saw him as the "stuck-up" son of William Allen White; he believed they resented that and tested him to see if he could "take it." In a letter during World War II to a former member of Company B in his old SATC unit, he recalled being put on KP (kitchen police) more than others and suggested that "one of the sergeants upstairs was 'testing my character.' Probably the most annoying thing about the first half of my life was the fact that every new acquaintance had to test my character. You see, it was presumed that since I was William Allen White's son, perhaps I was haughty and putting on airs, and everybody wanted to find out whether this was true. The quickest way of testing my character was to pester or insult me in some way and see how I would react."[37] Once in explaining to the grandson of Herbert Hoover the "severe burden" of his father's position as the son of a former president, he compared it to his own: "[My father] was a passionate advocate of Prohibition in the period when most of my generation were in revolt against it. When I started off to my first year at the University of Kansas, he called me in one day and said 'Bill, as a favor to me I hope you won't do even that small amount of occasional drinking that is normal for a college boy. I ask this because there is considerable likelihood that it might be seized on and blown up into a considerable story."[38] That was a difficult request of a future Phi Delt. But he honored it, at least in Kansas, until he was older.

Actually, his discontent with the University of Kansas had been whetted by Ronald Finney, son of his parents' best Emporia friends, Warren and Mabel Finney. A year ahead of Bill in school, Ronald had gone first to Washburn College in Topeka, where he also pledged Phi Delta Theta, then in the fall of 1919 to Cornell University in Ithaca, New York. Both families owned cabins in Moraine Park; the boys grew up together and were close friends. Ronald was quick to point out to Bill during Christmas vacation that year the advantages of an Ivy League education. Sometime during the second semester Bill decided to leave Kansas for Harvard University, if he could get his parents to agree. In the *Autobiography* his father reported the family decision:

> One day, in the spring before we went to Estes Park, Bill came to us and said: "I don't want to go back to K.U. . . . I want to be where folks talk things over; I mean politics and things like that. And it seems to me Harvard is the place I need."
>
> So long as he had that much wisdom, we trusted his judgment as we always have trusted it in matters relating to his own affairs and his own destiny. So the Harvard decision had been made before we came to the park. He took his year and a half's grades from the Kansas University and easily made a freshman entrance.[39]

Bill entered Harvard in September 1920 with approximately seven hundred others in the class of 1924. But his father's claim of unwavering trust then and later was to be sorely tried and sometimes proven equivocal.

First and foremost Harvard offered Bill the opportunity to escape his father's shadow. Ironically, during Bill's four years there his father became even more famous nationally, with a yearlong editorial page for *Judge* (a popular comic weekly), followed by a column of commentary in the *New York Sunday Tribune* for another year and by his winning a Pulitzer Prize in 1923 for a

Gazette editorial about free speech. Yet fellow classmates saw Bill as an indistinguishable son of but another notable father or prominent family; moreover, he was a midwestern product of public schools, an outsider who had to earn his Harvard friendships and recognition. In 1920 for Young Bill White of Emporia, Kansas, such lack of attention brought welcome release.

For example, free from Kansas scrutiny he immediately stepped out of his father's Republican traces and bolted to socialism. He recalled that mugwumpery later in a reminiscent letter to former classmates: "In my Freshman and Sophomore years I was maybe not quite a college Red, but a vigorous shade of pink. The first thing I was invited to join was the Student Liberal Club, which I would now call a Lonely Heart Society with Marxist leanings[;] . . . we often had bull sessions lasting far into the night, concerning what was wrong with the world, and how it should be changed— maybe even by violent overthrow. They were fun. I learned much from the clash of ideas."[40] In that first flush of youthful questioning he also joined the Harvard Christian Association, which he viewed as a nonsectarian combination against nascent Fundamentalism. Elected secretary his sophomore year, he went as one of three Harvard delegates to a weekend symposium on campus Christianity at Dartmouth College, explaining to his parents in an unusually sober letter that in fighting Methodist and Baptist antievolutionary theology "we are today only defending ourselves from an attempt, very nearly successful, to throttle education."[41] Another of those Harvard delegates was fellow Liberal Club member Corliss Lamont, brilliant son of Thomas Lamont, the powerful House of Morgan banker and a friend of Will White's. Corliss would become a well-known humanist and civil libertarian, but also a stalwart apologist for Soviet socialism who late in 1944 contributed to a virulent Communist attack against Bill's book *Report on the Russians*. In such company, a year after Atty. Gen. A. Mitchell Palmer's infamous "Red hunt" and three years before the Scopes trial, Bill enjoyed questioning conservative verities outside the parochial bounds of Kansas.

Yet sustained, studious seriousness was not his forte; instead he excelled in somewhat whimsical journalism. He tried out for the Harvard *Crimson*, the campus daily, and made the cut from twenty-five freshmen to five, but then had to resign to try to rescue his grades, which characteristically he had let slide in his rush to sample life in and around Cambridge, Massachusetts. For he was interested too in the theater and during his freshman year wrote weekly drama reviews for several months for the *Boston Transcript*, one of the regular dailies.[42] Prodded by letters from his father, he also read widely but erratically that first year in current American literature—John Dos Passos, F. Scott Fitzgerald, and H. L. Mencken, for example. Then on the advice of his father, he applied for admission to Professor Charles Copeland's renowned rhetoric course, English 12. To his delight "Copey" accepted him as a student his sophomore year. Intrigued and challenged by that histrionic taskmaster, he stayed in his course for two years, though he earned only a C– and remembered himself as a "very docile student." Later he told Copeland's biographer that "of the myriads who hold classes and write books purporting to teach writing, he was the only one who taught me anything."[43]

As an upperclassman Bill continued successfully to follow his extracurricular journalistic interests, often at the peril of his grades. He gravitated naturally toward the Harvard *Lampoon*, the campus comic magazine, and worked hard his sophomore year for election to its editorial board. He won a place on its masthead on May 31, 1922, along with the other newly elected. Being on the board of the *Lampoon* was as much a social as a journalistic honor, with its dinners memorable for practical jokes and food fights. To the detriment of his dinner jacket, he remained on the *Lampoon* through his senior year. Though not at first elected to the Institute of 1770, a club of upperclassmen who usually selected as initiates only the most socially eligible 20 percent of the sophomore class, he did make membership in the Hasty Pudding Club his junior year and then the institute, its sponsor. In fact, he coauthored two of its opéra bouffe productions. The first was *Who's Who*, produced in 1924, "an unqualified failure," according to the club's historian. The other was *1776*, so successfully produced in 1926, after he graduated, that its cast performed it to "wide acclaim" in seven cities during spring break.[44] And in his junior year he joined the Signet Society, a prestigious club for Harvard's less fashionable intelligentsia, according to historian Samuel Eliot Morison.[45]

Academically, though, Bill was usually in trouble. At the University of Kansas he had earned A's and B's; at Harvard he was a low C student overall, and in his sophomore year came close to academic dismissal. Officially, he did graduate with the class of 1924, but the College withheld his degree until he completed exam deficiencies. Yet the midwesterner W. L. White had become a socially acceptable, even popular classmate. In 1950, after he had become known as an author, his class nominated him for the prestigious Harvard Board of Overseers and the alumni elected him to a six-year term.

That summary of activities highlights the generally positive nature of his Harvard experience, but by no means was his decision to go there entirely beneficial. A more anecdotal account reveals the development of troublesome conflicting loyalties, interests, and emotions that remained unresolved to the end of his life. His years in Cambridge set up a social and cultural ambivalence that eventually fixed him uncomfortably between two worlds, those of Kansas and the East Coast, which diffused rather than sharpened his sense of identity. They created in him a discontent with small-town Kansas, yet those hometown roots nourished much of his later writing. For that reason we need to take a closer look at his Harvard experience.

His first year in Cambridge he shared a room in Matthews Hall, a freshman dormitory on Harvard Yard, with Albert J. Byington, Jr., later a prominent lawyer in Brazil. The social tradition of the time was that sophomores and juniors would try to move into one of several college dormitories on a section of Mount Auburn Street nicknamed the Gold Coast. Bill managed his second year to get a room there in Randolph Hall with Arthur ("Art") Houghton Tully, a poorer member of the Corning Glass Houghton family, who later became a wealthy stockbroker. Art Tully became Bill's best college friend; they shared the same sense of humor and worked together on the Lampoon. For their fourth year Bill and Tully obtained a room in one of the senior dormitories back on the Yard, again the socially accepted thing to do in the 1920s. Remembering Art after his death, Bill wrote:

We liked and disliked—or were amused by—the other inmates
of the Class of '24, and always for the same reasons. . . .
Together we ventured out across the Charles River to explore
Boston. There were the "Pop" concerts of its Symphony
Orchestra. . . . There was the Athens Cafe on Tremont Street
where we found out about Greek Olives, Shish Kebab, Yogurt,
Baklava, and Turkish Coffee. . . . There was, down in Scollay
Square (a wicked place), Posillippos, where you would start off
with Spaghetti or Ravioli, and then move through Veal
Scallopini to Zabaglioni (a kind of eggnog flavored with sweet
Marsala wine). . . . There was, a few doors from Posillippos,
a strip-tease show of ancient lineage, with an honored name
going back almost as far as that of Harvard College.[46]

Bill also made the occasional trip to New York City, where his
father belonged to several clubs and had many literary and
journalistic friends. Bill had family there too, his mother's sister
Mrs. Jessie Kane and his father's second cousin Mrs. Gwen Behr.
Spring break his freshman year he "had the most gorgeous week"
of his life in New York, so he wrote in a seven-page letter to his
parents thanking them for arranging the visit. He stayed at the
National Arts Club and was taken in hand by three former *Gazette*
employees, Brock and Murdock Pemberton and Elbert Severance,
who with occasional help from others of Will's coterie would serve
as New York godfathers to Young Bill for several decades. A close
family friend also in town that March was the novelist and
playwright Edna Ferber, whom Will and Sallie regarded as an
adopted daughter.

The two Pembertons were nephews of Brent Murdock, former
Kansas political boss and editor of the *El Dorado* [Kansas]
Republican, where Will had gotten his start. Will gave *Gazette* jobs
to both boys, then through his good friend Franklin P. Adams
(F. P. A.), the newspaper humorist, helped them get started in New
York City. Brock became a famous theater director-producer and
in March 1921 had two hits on Broadway, *Enter Madame* and *Miss
Lulu Bett*, which won a Pulitzer Prize that year. Murdock, his
younger brother, was in 1921 a busy New York journalist who
later became the first art critic for the *New Yorker*. He started the

tradition of lunch at the Algonquin Hotel, which evolved into its famous literary Round Table, whose members included such notables as George S. Kaufman, Dorothy Parker, Sherwood Anderson, Harold Ross, Robert Benchley, and Alexander Woollcott.[47] Elbert ("Sev") Severance in 1921 was one of the better-known Broadway press agents working for the Chanin Theaters, with the mammoth Hippodrome as his account.

Excerpts from Bill's letter to his parents reveal the extraordinary connections he enjoyed as his father's son, even back East:

> I came to New York to see shows with a serious purpose and a note book. I abandoned the note book after the first few shows, but I am sure I retained the serious purpose. Monday morning I dropped in at the Hippodrome, when Murdock invited me to lunch at the Algonquin, and Sev. invited me out to dinner the following night, and to a show afterward. I accepted both. The lunch was the hit of the day. [Robert] Benchley, [Heywood] Broun and [Alexander] Woollcott were all there, and I was so impressed I didn't open my mouth. . . .
>
> Tuesday morning up, and to see Frank[lin P.] Adams, who was in a good humor, and I told him I thought Benchley was the best critic in New York, thereby getting our names in the Conning Tower next day. . . . Lunched at the Algonquin, where I met Woollcott again, and he invited me to see the 47 Work Shop (Professor Baker's class) give its first public performance. I went with him and felt very grand sitting in one of the New York Times seats. . . . At the Algonquin dinner Tuesday, I met . . . a close friend of John Drinkwater [the British poet and dramatist], and when I told him I was interested in shows, he offered me tickets for "The Bad Man" (Holbrook Blin) and "Mary Stuart" (Clare Eames), which I accepted, so I asked Edna [Ferber] to "Mary Stuart." She in turn invited me to a dinner she was giving at the Crillon to meet Alex Woollcott and Mr. and Mrs. Louis Untermeyer. . . .
>
> Gwen [Behr, the cousin] was as father said she would be, very intelligent and very interesting, and she knows among other people the Gilmores who are very good actresses around New York. Ruth Gilmore is now playing the leading part in "Rollo's

Wild Oat," and Margalot Gilmore the ingénue part in the
"Famous Mrs. Fair" which I recommended to Ronald [Finney]
as the best show in Boston when he and Elizabeth were here.
She asked me if I wanted to meet Ruth Gilmore and I said *of
course* so she called up and announced my coming for that
afternoon after the matinee. . . . After the show I took Ruth
Gilmore to the Algonquin for tea.[48]

Bill saw eighteen plays, mostly on comps, met a number of literary
lights, and, best of all from his youthful perspective, took the
leading lady of a hit Broadway comedy to tea. Not a bad week
for a Harvard freshman, especially one from Emporia, Kansas.

Subsequent trips to New York City were just as packed. In fact,
he wrote his parents about a similar trip his sophomore year during
which he dropped in on F.P.A., who "was fine to me, let me stick
around his office in the 'World,' kidded around and cracked 'nifties'
with me, . . . introduced me to Dorothy Parker . . . and when
I told him I was going to 'Bulldog Drummond' he got me a girl,
Miss Margaret Cade who is working on 'The Sun,'" and whose
father owned the Algonquin Hotel, where they had a late supper
after the show.[49]

At Harvard he could not cut his Kansas roots entirely. Just after
his first New York fling, Gov. Henry Allen, his father's partner
in Kansas politics, spoke before Harvard's Liberal Club about his
state's new Industrial Court for compulsory labor arbitration. Bill
headed a student committee to greet him at his hotel on behalf
of the club then stayed behind to help him into his tux and to
chat a while, a conversation Governor Allen reported to Sallie
when he got back to Topeka: "I had a fine, though brief, visit
with Bill in Boston . . . [and] a mighty satisfactory talk with him
on his opinion of the Students' Liberal Club. He showed fine sense.
I hope he will not get to be in any sense a parlor socialist and
I don't believe he will."[50]

Two weeks after Governor Allen's appearance in Boston Bill
found himself hastily arranging train connections home. Tuesday
evening, May 10, his sister's horse shied and gave her a tumble.
At first she seemed essentially unhurt but in shock, then overnight
her condition grew critical, and Sallie telegraphed Bill and Will,

who was on a business tour back East, calling them home. When Bill's train stopped in Kansas City Saturday morning, May 14, he picked up a newspaper and read with disbelief the Associated Press dispatch announcing Mary's death at age sixteen from a cerebral hemorrhage.

That death profoundly affected him and his parents. His mother never fully recovered. For years afterward she suffered periodic bouts of depression, with Mary never far from her thoughts. At the time of the accident the Whites were living temporarily several houses south of 927 Exchange, which they were rebuilding after an extensive fire the year before. Sallie insisted on finishing the restoration of Mary's room as planned and keeping all her effects until her own death in 1950. Reacting in a nearly opposite fashion, Will abandoned his partially written biography of Teddy Roosevelt and a series of humorous *Saturday Evening Post* short stories about family life. Both projects evoked too many memories of his daughter. In fact, he never again wrote fiction. Still, as an anodyne, he took refuge in work, soliciting an even heavier load of outside writing assignments for the next several years. Bill too was very close to Mary. The final lines of his last letter just to her, dated April 2, indicate the teasing, affectionate rapport they had:

> I want to put on some shows this summer, and if you are any good at it, there is no reason why you shouldn't be in them. I wrote it all in a letter to Teetle [Carle], and it will pay you to walk down to his house, and tell him I told you you could read it, after he crosses out any "damns" or "hells" I may have inadvertently put in. But any cultured young fellow who can use a word like inadvertently right, as I did, just right off the bat without thinking, shouldn't let damn and hell worry him. Especially if he is able to crack a clever joke about it, as per above.[51]

The elder Whites had planned to send Mary to college back East, to Wellesley, near Harvard. To prepare for that they were thinking of enrolling her in a girls' preparatory school during her senior year of high school. Apparently, she was willing but wanted to go to a coeducational school in California. For she too found her position in Emporia difficult at times. As she confessed to

Teet: "I got it double. I'm not just William Allen White's little
girl. I'm also Bill White's kid sister. Folks won't forget that."[52] As
a protective but somewhat patronizing older brother, Bill was
bothered by her social rebelliousness and ostensible insouciance,
especially from his new Ivy League perspective. In a letter of May
7 he wrote his mother in exasperation,

> I am glad Mary is doing well on the Annual, and I hope in
> the name of heaven she is going to boarding school next year.
> You don't get much sympathy with the family from your scheme
> of sending her to California. She needs to go someplace where
> she can get social poise more than anything else, for she does
> not know anything more about it than a hog does about
> Sunday. . . . I suppose the work on the Annual looks good to
> her, but it won't get her nearly as far in Wellesley as will the
> ability to handle herself socially and not be a gawk, which is
> what she is now.[53]

A week later his younger sister was dead.

Together, his parents expressed their grief in a touching obituary
editorial written the day after her funeral. But Bill had no such
immediate release, though his grief was deep. Teet Carle remembered staying with him the night he got home and waking to hear
him "sobbing gently. I heard his hushed, but anguished words:
'Poor little girl. Poor little girl.'"[54] He then held Bill until he sobbed
himself to sleep, the only time in their long friendship he ever
lost his emotional reserve, according to Teet. Two days after the
funeral Bill had to return to Harvard because final exams were
to begin on June 2, and he was far behind in course work. In
his letters later and in his other writings he seldom referred to
Mary's death. He did write to his parents a year after her accident,
"Since I have left Emporia, where the thing is around me, the
fact of Mary's death easily slips from my mind. I find myself
thinking naturally of her opinions on different things, of plans
for the future which naturally include her. Then it comes back
with a dull wrench."[55] But usually he kept his deeper emotions
to himself.

When he returned home for summer vacations, though, he did
not keep to himself his impatience with what he perceived as

small-town provincialism. Emporia youth who went on to college customarily attended one of the two local schools or, if their parents could afford it, went to the University of Kansas or the state agricultural college. But few could afford or even desired to go out of state, especially to an Ivy League school. Many regarded that as being "uppity," even unpatriotic. Bill sensed this and reacted with teasing defensiveness, affecting Boston vowels and genteel mannerisms, such as carrying a fashionable walking cane one summer. His father tried to laugh him out of most such responses but tolerated those he could not. He did admit, though, in a letter to Bill afterward, that "the cane gave me a slow, low, persistent pain."[56] Bill's teasing alienated townsfolk more often than it amused them, because his humor was not just defensive; too often it was smug. Unfortunately, his youthful impatience with small-town ways developed later into a paternalism that soured relations with many in the town.

The summer after Mary's death the Whites did not take their usual August vacation in Moraine Park; instead the elder Whites motored for a week through the Ozarks with their best friends, the Finneys. The extra month in town gave Bill his chance to follow his plan to bring culture to Emporia. In concert with Teet Carle he persuaded Frank L. Gilson, head of dramatics at the normal school, to use local talent to direct and produce two one-act plays, Lord Edward Dunsany's philosophical thriller *A Night at an Inn* and G. B. Shaw's farce *How He Lied to Her Husband.* He enlisted Frank Beach, the normal's music director, to review for the *Gazette* a special preview performance of the Dunsany play before one hundred invited guests. In a paragraph added to that sympathetic review, Bill's father wrote, "A note from the low-brow editor of the Gazette may as well be appended to tell the truth, . . . [that] Emporia, even in its selected quintessence such as was brewed in the audience last night is too much inclined to giggle at the climaxes, and the need for thought on a hot night makes Dunsany seem an acquired taste."[57]

Unchastened, Bill plugged the production shamelessly in the *Gazette,* writing in a front-page advance story that "the Gazette intends to whoop it up for the show . . . because it is the kind of show the town ought to like. . . . It should be a blunt answer

to metropolitans who yawp about the soulless clods who rule the
country town. Gopher Prairie will not only pay to see Bernard
Shaw and Lord Dunsany, but can produce them itself."[58] And
he challenged townspeople in several inside-page four-column
advertisements to put up "four bits for a ticket" to prove they
had a "cultivated sense of humor."[59] The show played publicly
on August 31, but most townsfolk were not amused by Bill's
comparing Emporia to Gopher Prairie, Sinclair Lewis's fictional
evocation of a smug midwestern small town, and humorlessly held
onto their fifty cents. The *Gazette* reviewer commented
diplomatically, "The midsummer audience was not large but was
interested."[60] Eventually, Bill would learn he could not cultivate
his hometown with a harrow.

His last two summers home were less culturally ambitious, in
part because Teet Carle, his collaborator, left town the summer
of 1922 not to return for seven years, and then but for a brief
visit. Teet followed his girlfriend's family to Los Angeles, where
he enrolled at the University of Southern California, married the
girl, and eventually became chief publicist for Paramount Studios,
a job he later compared to that of a camphor ball in a urinal.[61]
In contrast, the Whites assumed Bill would return to Emporia
after college, work on the *Gazette*, then become its next editor
at some indefinite future time. But Young Bill was not so certain.
In New York between terms early in 1922 Edna Ferber asked him
what he intended to do after graduation. He wrote his father,

> I said there were a number of things I wanted to do. . . .
> "How old are you, Bill?" she asked. I told her.
> "Twenty-one isn't so young as it used to be," she said.
> "Youngsters these days even under that are showing great
> promise."
> That's why . . . I've got to get to work this summer, and I
> have a nebulous idea that I would prefer some place in the East,
> that I have got to get away from Emporia. Being the "Boss's
> Son" is very poor training, although it is partly compensated
> by the fact that you are the boss and an excellent trainer. But
> I've begun to think I ought to get out on my own soon if I ever
> do anything.[62]

Perhaps it was that letter that motivated Sallie to suggest he go to Europe that summer with a tour organized by the YMCA Collegiate Student Council. The organization promised to limit the cost to five hundred dollars. But he objected to the cloistered nature of a YMCA tour, claiming that in the previous year participants were asked to cover their eyes in the presence of nude statues. Instead, he countered that he could tour Europe on his own cheaper and more profitably. His mother did not agree. Before he could muster his arguments, the YMCA deadline passed, and she withdrew the offer.

But the possibility of Bill's not returning home for the summer caused Will to realize how much he missed his son and to think about his future role at the *Gazette*. Thus in April 1922 he wrote his son about his plans for them and the paper: "I wish you were here to help. . . . We ought to push the circulation to six or seven thousand, which would, of course, increase the profits. . . . The paper ought to make thirty-five or forty thousand a year under those conditions, and give you time for leisure in writing in a few years, when you get ready. I would like to get out of it as soon as I reasonably can, and devote all my time to writing."[63] With that in mind he promised Bill the courthouse beat that summer so that "you can get used to the folks," he wrote, "and the folks can get used to you."[64] So Bill came home to cover the Lyon County courthouse during June and July.

When home he also served as the family chauffeur because his father never learned to drive, though he first bought a car in 1915. In August, as usual, Bill drove his parents to Moraine Park for a month. Those leisurely auto trips to Colorado introduced Bill to his father's statewide political network, useful connections for a young editor-to-be. Recalling those drives years later, he remarked that when his father "crossed Kansas it was a kind of pageant. At every county seat he would hunt up his local chairman" or drop by the newspaper office.[65] Stopping every fifty miles or so during the shimmering heat of August to shake hands with versions of George Babbitt must have deeply pained that Harvard undergraduate, especially when he could have been in Europe instead. In fact, seventeen years later, in his syndicated column "Take a Look," in commenting on the lack of summer jobs for

young people during the depression years, Bill remembered that
earlier, in the 1920s, "all the boys had [a job] except a few rich
kids who had to drive their families' cars on vacation tours, and
most of them wished they had one."[66]

The summer of 1923 he was again back on the courthouse beat.
But he also worked up some editorial copy, to be set in galley and
used while the Whites were on break that August in Santa Fe,
New Mexico. One of those editorials was about nondescript Vice
President Calvin Coolidge and how unfortunate it would be
should he inherit the presidency if Warren Harding succumbed
to a reported bronchial illness, an outcome that seemed unlikely.
In that editorial Bill wrote, "This runty, aloof little man who quacks
through his nose when he speaks has become vice-president
through his unique gift for platitudes, which are at the same time
childishly clear and utterly untrustworthy. He has attained high
office by saying nothing when he talks."[67] Unfortunately, that
commentary ran the night before Harding died. All *Gazette*
editorials appeared unsigned then, thus many readers ascribed that
analysis to Editor W. A. White, to his embarrassment. Not until
1938, in his second, much more scholarly biography of Coolidge,
did Will himself publicly arrive at the same opinion.

Back in Cambridge his junior and senior years, Bill sorely tried
his father's patience with an excessively casual attitude toward
money and studies. Some of Will's letters to his son read like Lord
Chesterfield's to his—urbane observations and advice about
literature, writing, current political affairs, deportment, and whom
to get to know. But some demonstrate a humorously indulgent
exasperation never betrayed by the eighteenth-century gentleman.
For instance, in the fall of 1922 Bill and his former roommate
Albert Byington thought they needed a car. Bill wrote his parents
arguing the whys and hows; both were opposed. His father replied,
"I suppose Mother has written you what we think about the car.
There is this helpful suggestion which I have. Why don't you buy
a wheelbarrow and a cream separator and try and Burbank a
Ford?"[68] Instead of concocting such a hybrid, the two bought a
used Model T for three hundred and fifty dollars. After a few
months Bill became the sole owner, leading to a litany of
maintenance and storage woes in his letters home. Will put up

with that recital for over a year until he exploded: "For heaven's sake sell that old junk heap of a car!"[69]

Much of Bill's Harvard education was social. For example, he learned the proper conduct and the proper dress for formal occasions, accomplishments little valued in small-town Kansas. By his senior year he was known on the Yard as a natty dresser, with an often overdue account at Brooks Brothers. In his junior year hundred-dollar raccoon coats were in, but he knew that to coax his father into letting him buy one he would have to make him a promise: "I promise never to show up in it in Emporia, and I also promise to sell it a year from this coming spring, and to put the money into the Harvard Y.M.C.A. or foot warmers for the ladies aid in Emporia."[70] He got his coat. But for a while Will firmly turned down a request for a tux: "You don't need a full dress suit. . . . You ought to be able to borrow one without any trouble if they are common around Cambridge; if they are unusual and rare, you don't need one."[71]

In the fall semester of that junior year, when Bill was still in danger of academic dismissal, both parents repeatedly wrote him asking about his studies. He finally replied in the middle of November: "If you must know about my grades, and *will* tease so, here it is. To remain in Harvard College, I require two 'Cs.' To rejoin my class I require three 'Cs.' Well, I have four grades which are either C or above. One of these I know to be an honor grade, B. . . . So you see, it will take two derricks, a steam shovel, a writ of habeas corpus and a stick of striped candy to get me out of Harvard College."[72] But his father did not buy into that optimism, especially after receiving a letter from the college soon afterward regarding his son's excessive absences: "The Dean writes me you haven't been able to square yourself about those seven cuts. A boy with an average of B could get away with them but a boy with an average of D last year and C– this year ought no more to think of cutting than of spitting in the Professor's ear just to show he's on terms with him. When will you learn you can't do some things that other boys do unless you do other things they do?"[73] That was a lesson Bill took many years to learn, if he ever did.

In the fall of 1923, his senior year, Bill was not at all sure he wanted to return to Emporia immediately after graduation. True, he was prepared to write for a living; his work in Copey's classes and on the *Crimson* and the *Lampoon* testify to that. Clearly, his father expected him to take over the *Gazette*. But Bill enjoyed college life and had thought of a way of continuing on: apply for a Rhodes Scholarship to Oxford. Enthusiastically, he wired his parents about trying for that three-year award. With his father's influence and his Harvard degree he knew he had a solid chance for nomination by the Kansas committee, headed by Dr. Frank Strong, chancellor of the University of Kansas. Both his parents, though, were adamantly opposed, even to his accepting a one-year fellowship. His father replied to his initial telegrams firmly and specifically:

> Of course it is all right for you to want to go but I think you ought to realize rather definitely that if you take the Rhodes Scholarship and leave America and particularly the middle-west for two or three years, or even for a year, you incapacitate yourself just that much more for your job. You ought to decide rather definitely that if you accept the Rhodes Scholarship, you will give up all thought of coming back to run the Gazette. . . .
> I can imagine that you would be very happy in some eastern school teaching history or literature and the Gazette when we are done with it would be sold for enough to supplement your professorial salary seven or eight thousand a year easily enough. . . . But to make from seven to fifteen thousand a year on the Gazette, you will have to learn the business end of it well. That means two or three years grubbing in that department. If you shrink from it, then go ahead in the academic path and luck to you. But if you go to England next year, kiss the Gazette good-bye."[74]

Bill continued to plead with his parents, but they steadfastly refused to endorse his application. Without their support he knew Oxford was out. Reluctantly, then, he accepted his father's advice that he "would do better to come back to Emporia—work a couple of years and then take six months for travel, either around the world or in Europe."[75]

But first he had to graduate. An appendicitis attack in February, accompanied by surgical complications, put him behind in his studies, as did his social life and extracurricular commitments. To his fellows his pose was that of a Jazz-Age bon vivant and "gentleman scholar." The strain of maintaining that pose, while falling behind again in his studies, together with his continued ambivalence about returning to Emporia, brought on an attack of "nervous exhaustion," a syndrome that haunted him the rest of his life. As a result he did not complete his major exams in history and literature and, though he went through graduation ceremonies with his class, did not at that time receive his degree.

For his father that was especially disappointing because he had long regretted having dropped out of the University of Kansas in his final semester. He and Sallie did attend their son's commencement, which Will sourly described in a letter to his brother-in-law Milt Lindsay as a "hollow mockery." But his main concern in that letter was Bill's nervousness and evident exhaustion. Milt, a bachelor, had himself been a burden on the Whites for several years, having become a semi-invalid from an indeterminate, recurrent fever eventually diagnosed as tuberculosis. Other Lindsays helped care for him, but Sallie carried most of the load. That winter, for example, she had taken him to Santa Fe for the desert air. Will proposed that Bill join Uncle Milt in Santa Fe after commencement, rest up, then drive him to the family compound in Moraine Park: "By that time, very likely, Jessie or Mary [Sallie's sisters] will be out there and can take care of you. I would suggest that you let Bill get a good rest before he starts. He is tremendously tired . . . [and] needs to be held in check because he is very nervous and liable to overdo himself all the time, until he gets his nerves down and gets to sleeping."[76] After driving his uncle to Colorado, Bill returned to Emporia and to the *Gazette* payroll, destined, it seemed, to play second fiddle until his father retired, whenever that would be.[77]

Chapter Two

The Heir Apparent, 1924–1934

For the next ten years Bill worked on the *Gazette*, with his title and ostensible duties changing from reporter to circulation manager to associate editor to business manager. As the heir apparent, however, such titles did not define his true position. Until he married, in 1931, he lived at home and shared with his parents the everyday events of the town and the family newspaper. Whenever his father was out of town, which was increasingly more often, Bill functioned as managing editor, a role his mother had previously filled when not accompanying her husband.

But in fact the demands of that role were limited because Walter Hughes, the business manager until his death in 1932 from a heart attack at age fifty-eight, ran the production end of the paper no matter which White was in charge. Hughes had been printer's devil when Will bought the paper in 1895 and by 1907 was listed on the masthead as manager, next to W. A. White, editor and owner. For years Will had referred most business and back-shop matters to him and expected Bill to do the same, as acknowledged in the *Gazette*'s front-page obituary for Hughes: "During later years Mr. Hughes has taken over all of the business affairs of The Gazette and its owners. He has managed all business in connection with the office, taking care of the bank accounts, supervising every department and in the absence of Mr. and Mrs. White, Mr. Hughes was the final boss. His word always prevailed."[1]

From his birth Bill had known Walter Hughes as the family's stern financial advisor and had grown up at the *Gazette* under his authority. Clearly, until his sudden death, Hughes was second in command. That, and Bill's habitual pose of humorous diffidence, caused the staff to regard him more as a fellow than a boss. To them he was Bill or Young Bill; his father was always Mr. White.

Yet Bill, whatever his title, made many of the newsroom and staffing decisions and wrote many of the editorials from late 1924 until he left in 1934 for the East Coast. When he joined the paper in 1924, his father was fifty-six years old and eager to turn the editorial duties over to his son. Will wanted more time to read, to write longer pieces, and to play his emergent national role as Sage of Emporia. He had just completed a book-length biography of Woodrow Wilson and in the spring of 1925 delivered a series of lectures on American democracy at the University of North Carolina, which he then edited for book publication. The same year he wrote for *Collier's* a series of biographical sketches of Calvin Coolidge, which he also edited for book publication. Then in 1926 he became one of the original five judges for Harry Scherman's Book-of-the-Month Club. Until Will's death eighteen years later, he either met monthly with the other judges in New York City or telegraphed them his opinions about the assigned readings, which ran from three to ten books a month, in either manuscript or proof. The task increasingly absorbed his and Sallie's leisure time as the club—the first book club in the United States—flourished, becoming a major influence on middle-class tastes and publishers' sales.

Young Bill wrote many of the *Gazette*'s editorials during that decade, most of which were unsigned and ascribed to his father, leading to the occasional contretemps, like that over Bill's 1923 Coolidge piece deploring the vice president's mediocrity. For at this time as a stylist Bill was nearly indistinguishable from his father, yet brasher and more liberal politically. In an editorial of

May 1, 1928, for example, Bill praised Herbert Hoover's well-built bandwagon as it rolled toward a presidential nomination at the Republican convention that June. His father helped construct that vehicle. But Bill concluded his commentary by comparing Hoover negatively to the other leading candidates by criticizing his lack of focus and leadership, remarking, "In the Republican shambles, he is vaguely reminiscent of a plump and timorous capon, fluttering anxiously on the outskirts of a free-for-all cock-fight."[2] In the subsequent campaign many bemusedly attributed that comparison to the elder White, who, though embarrassed, never publicly denied authorship, in keeping with his policy of unsigned *Gazette* commentary, which spoke for the paper and for him.[3]

Writing many editorials wrongly credited to his father over that decade, and subservient to his authority, Bill grew quietly to resent the secondary role he seemingly had chosen. How much he resented it came out many years later when for the first time he publicly sketched his own view of his father in a 1968 address at the University of Kansas commemorating his father's centennial. In it he recalled that

> a few years after I left Emporia [my father] mailed me a book gotten up by some scholar who had come to Emporia to make a compilation of Gazette editorials. With the book was a note, saying that he rather thought that some of the editorials in it had been written by me. Reading through it, I found that, in the period when I had been actively on the editorial page, about two thirds of those editorials picked by this scholar as the Gazette's best actually had been written by me. Nobody was at fault here. If there was blame it was on *me*, for not having left Emporia sooner.[4]

After 1930 Bill did insist on initialing his longer, more analytical commentary about financial conditions, especially when he knew it did not represent his father's views. And one of the first policy changes he instituted when he took over the *Gazette* in 1944 was to affix authors' initials to all editorials.

Soon after returning to Emporia in 1924 Bill found himself not at a reporter's desk but behind the wheel of a 1919 Dodge touring car chauffeuring his father across Kansas in a quixotic independent campaign for governor. In the August Republican primary his father's Progressive allies had lost the gubernatorial nomination to a standpat conservative, Ben Paulen. That bothered Will. But what bothered him more was Paulen's refusal to denounce support from the Ku Klux Klan. That secret society, with its appeal to unthinking "Americanism" and its easily identifiable religious and racial scapegoats, had after World War I become a national, state, and local political force. The Democratic gubernatorial candidate, incumbent Jonathan Davis, also refused to denounce Klan support. Will had satirized the reactionary and secretive qualities of the Klan in editorials since 1921, but Emporia elected a Klan-backed candidate as mayor in 1923, and *Gazette* reporters were then denied access to local police reports.

At first Will tried to persuade either Henry Allen, his old friend and former governor, or former Senator Joseph Bristow to run as an independent against Paulen, but both Bull Moosers refused to bolt the party again. After a September 9 meeting of disgruntled Republican Progressives failed to find a candidate to oppose Paulen, Will started a petition drive to get himself on the ballot as an independent, in spite of his vow when he bought the *Gazette* never to run for political office. He soon received the necessary signatures and on September 20 formally announced his candidacy, with the Klan as his major issue.

For six weeks father and son crisscrossed the state in the family Dodge, often accompanied by Sallie. During that time Bill put several thousand miles on the Dodge and listened to his father make the same speech more than one hundred times. But those miles and speeches were not enough—Paulen won decisively. White's supporters did claim a victory of sorts: he had called attention to Klan bigotry and garnered support for several key anti-Klan Republicans on the regular ticket. Later, though, Bill questioned both his father's effect and the wisdom of such a campaign. In his centennial address he remembered

> the morning after election, the Eastern Seaboard press was hailing William Allen White for having swept the Klan from Kansas. Back home we had another view. . . . We had a Klan-endorsed mayor, and had elected a Klan-endorsed sheriff. And

my father had lost his own county—the deepest humiliation
a politician can have. . . . We in the family knew that it had
been a bone-crunching defeat, that in the State, the County
and the City, all had been lost save honor and that, as practical
politicians, it would take us several years of hard work to pick
up the pieces of this Noble Victory and stick them together
again.[5]

But at the time Young Bill was such a maverick that he voted
for Progressive Robert M. La Follette for president, despite the
Gazette's endorsement of Calvin Coolidge.

Although Will had lost, he was not much out of pocket, because
he was adept at garnering free publicity and had been fed and
housed by friends along the way. In fact, that is how Bill met his
future wife, Kathrine. During a stopover in Ottawa, Kansas, they
were introduced one evening by Jack Harris, elder son of the editor
of the *Ottawa Herald* with whom the Whites were staying. She
was the daughter of a neighbor, Peter Klinkenberg, a local druggist.
A Kappa Kappa Gamma at the University of Kansas her freshman
year, she was attending Ottawa University that fall. The next day
the Whites drove on to another set of speeches, with Bill apparently impressed by that introduction, because Kathrine was a guest
on several special occasions the next year or so at the White home
in Emporia. But then they became more distant, she taking a job
out of state and he traveling to Europe.

With Will's gubernatorial campaign over, Bill returned to his
desk at the *Gazette* and to reading for his deficient final exams
at Harvard. After Christmas he went back to Cambridge where
he wrote acceptable general exams in history and literature, then
passed the final oral exam.[6] William L. White was now officially
a graduate of Harvard College. On the strength of that success
he lingered in the East several weeks but by mid-February had
returned to his reporter's job in Emporia. Later that year, in
November, he took two weeks off to journey east again, first to
Cambridge, where he attended the Harvard-Yale football game,
a dance at the Hasty Pudding Club, and a dinner with the
Lampoon staff, then to New York City, where he checked into the
Harvard Club for a week of theater. He had earned that break

by moving over to circulation manager and reorganizing the paper's delivery routes, thereby increasing its circulation.

Because Young Bill had settled energetically into his duties, Will followed through with his promise to send him on a European trip after a year or two back in Emporia. But like most small-town businessmen, Will was accustomed to trading-out accounts. For example, a local haberdasher who advertised in the *Gazette* would pay part of his bill in cash, part with credit at his store. The Whites would then shop on that account, thus setting up a network of mutual business loyalties. But because Emporia supported only one daily newspaper, unhappy advertisers had only a small-circulation Democratic weekly, the *Emporia Times*, to turn to, which freed the Whites somewhat from the parochial pettiness of that business tactic. Whenever feasible, though, the Whites, and their employees when out of town on business stayed in chain hotels on advertising "due bills," essentially bartered accounts. So it was natural for Will to try to tap into that credit system for Bill's trip to Europe. He wrote Elbert Severance in New York asking if Bill could write travel accounts for the *World Traveler*, a magazine Severance's advertising agency handled, to be paid "in a due bill on any excursion or any steamer going over to Europe." For, he wrote, Bill "is keen to get over to Europe, and wants to pay his own way." Failing that, "anything you know about cheap tourist tickets, will be of great service."[7] Severance was unable to come up with an assignment but did find an inexpensive tourist-class ticket on the Cunard steamer *Corintha* sailing from New York to Naples on April 3 under charter to a posh Raymond-Whitcomb Mediterranean cruise. To help pay his way, Bill agreed to write travel letters home for the *Gazette*, a face-saving attempt at quid pro quo. Actually, both parents were pleased to send him, as Will's first letter to him on board ship indicates: "I just want you to know how happy Mother and I are that you are going. The whole idea of the trip was hers originally. She felt that it would do you a lot of good to see Europe just at this time of your life; that you need a sense of freedom from Emporia which such a trip would give you."[8]

Will published sixteen of Bill's letters, some of them three columns, but in the first and several others he interpolated

humorous remarks to temper his son's sometimes grandiose tone
and make him more palatable to the home folks. In his first letter,
for example, Bill described the passengers' shipboard routine: "At
6:30 it is time to go down to our stateroom. When I get down
there, I find that the steward has changed the studs from my old
shirt to my clean shirt and laid out my dinner coat and trousers
on the bed, with the pumps carefully placed on the floor beside
them." His father commented: "The family reading this wonders
if the young man bought a flower on Mother's day for the stewards.
Probably not. The family also wonders if the steward sometimes,
looking down the aisle toward the cabin, does not see a gangling
pair of hairy knees under a flapping shirt, and over a pair of
passionate silk socks, and hear a sad voice wailing: 'Say, where's
my black tie? Who swiped my collar button? There's a button off
my pants,' or some such lugubrious incantation."[9] In his fourth
letter Bill described the squalid Casbah of Algiers: "Trickling over
the worn cobble stone steps of this miserable Algerian thorough-
fare, which was more a nightmare panorama than a street, was
a slimy rivulet across which we stepped gingerly. Even with my
cane I could scarcely keep footing on the greasy slimy stones."
Will could not let the cane pass in silence; it had become a too-
long-suffered personal pain: "The family here desires to remark
that this cane business is a touch which will queer the young man
in the Fourth Ward if he ever springs it here. In Emporia we want
no three legged youths."[10] But Bill was generally aware of his
audience and tailored his narrative accordingly, sometimes with
hometown allusions.

After the monthlong cruise terminated in Naples, Bill stopped
for several weeks on the island of Capri because he found it relaxed
and inexpensive. There he worked on a suntan and a rudimentary
knowledge of Italian. Then he loitered through Rome, Florence,
and Venice, with one eye on his budget, one on the picturesque,
and both on Italy's new Fascist government. But his political
commentary, while keen, was often youthfully cynical: "Following
the best traditions of dictators, the people of Italy are kept amused
with frequent parades, festivals, holidays and band music. They
seem to accept it as a satisfactory substitute for self government.
And after all, if they prefer to run shouting after a flag than to

vote intelligently, it is their own affair. I suppose the thing will eventually end in a smash."[11] From Venice the first week of July he caught a train for Paris, where he called on several journalist friends, former Kansans in residence there. Among them were Robbins ("Bob") Herrick and his wife, Meriam, recent graduates of Washburn College in Topeka. Bob, a fellow Phi Delt, worked for the Paris edition of the *New York Herald Tribune*; as a first cousin of Myron T. Herrick, then United States ambassador to France, as well as a prominent Ohio Republican and longtime friend of Will White's, he immediately invited Young Bill to several embassy functions.[12]

Fluent in French, familiar with the city from his 1919 stay, and happy to be with friends, Bill enjoyed his time in Paris. He was especially interested in the overthrow of Prime Minister Aristide Briand that July and the resulting free fall of the franc. But it was time to return home. His father had written that he badly needed him back "to help reorganize the business end of the office."[13] So he returned tourist class on the Cunard liner *Berengaria*, docking in New York on August 6. He visited the Severances, the Pembertons, and his aunt Jessie briefly, hosted a dinner for a small group of classmates at the Harvard Club, then caught a train for Emporia, arriving home on August 12. He was back at his desk the next day.

He had been gone five months, picking up a basic command of Italian and, as he originally wished, impressions unencumbered by YMCA strictures. As if to endorse his independent viewpoint, the *New York Evening Post* reprinted parts of two of his published letters in mid-August. Unfortunately for his sense of self, both were bylined "William Allen White, Jr., in Emporia, Kans., *Gazette*."[14] Due in part, perhaps, to the *Post* bylines, Bill was discontented after his European trip with his dependent role at the *Gazette*. He wanted somehow to launch out on his own. Mulling over possibilities, he decided there was a market for a regional rotogravure weekend newspaper insert aimed initially at a south-central plains audience. Such a magazine-like section, printed by a special photomechanical process something like today's offset lithography, would include not only many photographs but also feature articles, short stories, and book reviews. His father agreed to go along with the project, partly because Bill could promote it and still work at the *Gazette*. But in backing him, Will did not realize how much energy Bill was to invest in that scheme.

At intervals during the spring and summer of 1927 he was out of town trying to line up support for this project. In April he was in New York City to work the family's network there for potential advertisers and to attend the annual Associated Press dinner to sell his insert to regional editors or publishers present. In May and June he canvassed advertisers and dailies around the Kansas City and Wichita, Kansas, marketing areas and negotiated with a Memphis, Tennessee, printer who wanted to set up a rotogravure plant in Kansas City. During the first part of July he was back in New York City trying to land several national advertisers, then the last week of July he called on the larger dailies in Oklahoma.[15] Though advertisers seemed interested in his proposal, he could not get any significant accounts without firm newspaper contracts and circulation figures. Editors were polite but noncommittal. By the end of August Will wrote his New York brother-in-law, Bob Kane, that "Bill is hitting some bumps with his project but I have great faith that it will work out."[16] It did not.

In late September while again in New York trying unsuccessfully to sign up advertisers, Bill developed a nervous stomach that could not retain food. Early in October his father came to New York on business, joining him at the National Arts Club. Concerned about Bill's symptoms, he insisted Bill consult a doctor, who treated him for an intestinal infection and ordered bed rest. But after three weeks Bill had lost over thirty pounds with no alleviation in sight. At Sallie's suggestion Will brought him home, then sent him on to the Mayo Clinic in Rochester, Minnesota. There the staff recognized his symptoms as an anxiety disorder and treated him with regular exercise, diet, and rest.

Toward the end of December he was well enough to return home, where at the traditional Christmas dinner for the *Gazette* staff Will announced that his son was now associate editor." Then, or soon afterward, he also promised him a quarter ownership in the newspaper, as if to assure him the new title was more than a gesture.[17] Just after Christmas, at his parents' insistence, Bill joined them and the Victor Murdock family, old friends and publishers of the *Wichita Eagle*, on a ten-day Florida vacation. Back in Emporia in January he formally abandoned his rotogravure project to concentrate on the *Gazette* as its new associate editor, for him a welcome move out of the business side to the editorial. But he did not totally forget that scuttled project and futile attempt at independence. Later, in the 1950s, when he revamped the typography and format of the *Gazette* to award-winning status, he added an eight-page weekend photo supplement, an echo of the rotogravure scheme.

Calvin Coolidge chose not to run again for president in 1928; even before that Will had backed Secretary of Commerce Herbert Hoover for the Republican nomination, having suggested editorially as early as 1920 that he was presidential material. In July 1927 the elder Whites, while Bill was in Paris, gave one of their renowned dinners at 927 Exchange to introduce Hoover to a group of Kansas editors as part of an effort to sell him to midwesterners as a rural Progressive. However, at the national convention, in order to maintain a position in state politics, Will supported the favorite-son candidacy of conservative Kansas senator Charles Curtis. Hoover won on the first ballot, Curtis accepted the vice-presidential slot, and Will happily wheeled in under their banner. But when the Democrats nominated New York governor Al Smith, a Tammany-backed politician whom White had praised in a 1926 *Collier's* sketch, Will's wagon broke a spring, and gave him and his son a jolting ride to the polls. For Smith on pragmatic grounds supported repeal of the Eighteenth Amendment; White for deeply felt moral and social reasons staunchly upheld national Prohibition. To him that became the one issue of the campaign. In a July 7 *Gazette* editorial, nearly as intemperate as his 1896 diatribe against the Populists, Will accused Smith of voting as a young New York assemblyman against legislation to control liquor, gambling, and prostitution in saloons, a record that "would have damned him deeper than the slag-pits of hell" in any state other than Tammany-controlled New York.[18] Will repeated that attack in a Kansas kick-off campaign speech July 12 carried by the Associated Press. Smith countered that White's charges were based on false information supplied by fanatical Prohibitionists. Though his data were indeed secondhand, Will continued injudiciously to attack Smith's voting record. Bill, in a deleted passage from his afterword to his father's autobiography, wrote: "I felt it was unfair and I tried to dissuade him. I could not: he was tremendously in earnest."[19] But Bill probably did not protest immediately because he had just returned from a two-week jaunt to Boston and New York and had not yet realized how intemperate his father had become.

Will and Sallie were to sail on August 2 to Europe for two months on a magazine assignment. Apparently stung by widespread press criticism, he decided to go to New York early so he could check for himself Smith's youthful voting record, with Sallie joining him later. There he persuaded the Republican National Committee, through its director of publicity, his longtime Kansas ally Henry Allen, to hire two researchers to review Smith's assembly votes, then he repeated his charges July 28 with documentation. In that press release he proclaimed: "No Klansman in a boob Legislature, cringing before a kliegle or a wizard, was more subservient to the crack of the whip than was Al Smith— ambitious and effective and smart as chain lightning—in the Legislature when it came to a vote to protect the saloon; to shield the tout and to help the scarlet woman of Babylon, whose tolls in those years always clinked regularly in the Tammany till."[20] The day after he released that invective, his old friend Walter Lippmann, a prominent journalist and political insider, took him aside and convinced him that Smith had voted honestly against the bills in question because they were too loosely written. Two days after that, July 31, White withdrew the charges "in so far as they affect [Smith's] votes on gambling and prostitution" but renewed his attack on Smith's "position as to the saloon."[21] He and Sallie then sailed for Europe with Democratic newspapers declaring that he had retracted his charges.

In the midst of this election-year tempest Young Bill manned the *Gazette*'s editorial desk to referee the state and Lyon County August primaries and worked in local campaigns as Republican chairman of Emporia's Fourth Ward. It was he who suffered from

the slings and arrows of outraged Democrats while his father was
in Europe. And he did not suffer gladly. In a long letter to his
father in Paris giving the results of those primaries and reporting
office gossip, he slipped in this outburst: "Just before you sailed,
you used a very inept phrase to the Associated Press reporters.
You said you were starting for Europe 'with a chunk of money'
which was bad, and as dumb a thing to say as anyone could think
up. I caught it the minute I saw it in print. It came right after
the Al Smith retraction and your mail is now flooded with letters
from damn fools who think that the retraction of vice charges
was bought."[22] Much later, in his centennial reminiscence, he
reshaped the cause-effect timing of his father's New York City
outburst to stress his mother's absence during this "crisis" and
his father's need for her "steadying influence." Such a reconstructed memory suggests how pained he was by that instance
of his father's reactionary behavior and by his own embarrassed
efforts at damage control from his father's desk at the family
newspaper.[23]

By April 1929 Bill had earned enough on the *Gazette*, both in
real and psychic income, to take another trip to Europe. This time
he made his own travel arrangements, buying a round-trip third-
class boat ticket for $182. According to his father's public announce-
ment of that voyage, "he went to investigate the cost of traveling
for the average man."[24] Budget would be a primary concern.

Before boarding ship in New York he stopped by the offices of
Time magazine to say hello to Kathrine Klinkenberg, who worked
there as a copy editor. About a year before, when she was home
for a visit, they had renewed their acquaintance.[25] In fact, Bill's
father had Kathrine on his mind when he sent his son a letter
early in June with a packet of office mail, for he wrote, "Jack Harris
tells the story of your romance [in the *Chanute* [Kansas] *Tribune*]
which I am sending herewith. It seems to be confirmed by rumor
and public opinion in these latitudes, and luck to you."[26] That
item in Harris's personal column teased Bill about his falling
beyond salvation for a blonde University of Kansas Kappa just
before his "round dolorous face" gazed "sorrowfully at the
retreating American coast from the porthole on 'Q' deck of the
Ile de France."[27] The Whites had tried unsuccessfully over the

years to get Bill interested in several "safe" Emporia girls. Will seems
to have been concerned about Bill's rumored out-of-town romance,
though Harris had reported the item in a hyperbolic, bantering
tone. In the same letter to his son, referring to the family troubles
of a prominent elderly Emporia banker, Will exclaimed, "Lord,
Bill, when a man marries, he makes about the only decision he
makes in his whole life." And he warned obliquely that the
banker's troubles reveal "a fundamental fact about men, that their
sex choice is their only moment of free will."[28]

Bill left New York harbor April 19 on the luxury liner *Ile de
France*, one among its over three hundred mostly Eastern European
steerage passengers. But he did not keep to steerage. A seasoned
traveler, he bribed a steward to let him spend his days on the first-
class decks. A week later he landed at Le Havre and caught a
train for Paris. There he called on Russell and Connie Barnes.
She was a friend of Bill's from University of Kansas days and a
granddaughter of John Ingalls, three-term United States senator
and prominent Gilded-Age Kansas Republican. Her husband was
European correspondent for the *Detroit News*, her younger sister,
Sally, a close friend of Kathrine's. Knowing Bill was traveling on
a limited budget, they steered him toward a disreputable but cheap
hotel near their apartment and let him use their bath.[29] After
a brief stopover in Paris he left for the Mediterranean coast, where
he settled in for an indefinite stay at a pension in the small French
fishing village of Bandol, about ten miles from Toulon.

As before, Bill agreed to send letters home for *Gazette*
publication. His father printed twenty-four of those letters May
20 through September 5, the last the day he stepped off a Santa
Fe train in Emporia. They are significantly better than his travel
letters three years before. This time he worked seriously at
perfecting his writing; in them are the voice and techniques of
his later best-selling narratives. His tone is more consistently self-
effacing, and he places more reliance on background details,
characterization, and patches of dialogue to evoke mood and
convey message. He views scenery with an eye to fresh, precise,
concrete images, and he strictly limits editorial comments,
especially about politics. True to his announced intention, he
sprinkles his narrative with travel tips about lodging, food, and

prices. As if in recognition of his son's stylistic maturity, Will this time interpolated no derogatory "humorous" remarks but simply set each letter with a straightforward introductory paragraph under the same running head as before, "The Odyssey of Young Bill."

Bill stayed in Bandol two months because it was "exactly the kind of quiet poky little place" he wanted for a while, "probably the cheapest place in France."[30] In early July, bored with the village and uncomfortable in the increasing heat, he bought a used two-seated French racing car from a broke American journalist, Jed Kiley, to tour the coast, then head across the French Pyrenees to Bordeaux and Paris. But the frustrating legalism of French bureaucracy delayed documentation of the sale for more than a week. Finally, with a packet of signed and stamped registration cards plus a Michelin guidebook beside him, he motored quickly through villages and countryside until, just over the mountains, he met another nemesis, a mechanical breakdown. A sheared spring shackle, a collapsed universal joint, and a shattered dynamo stranded him by turns until, pressed for time, he sold the car to a mechanic in the village of Barbezieux and caught a train for Paris, about three hundred kilometers away.

For Bill had promised to meet Harold Trusler, then his best Emporia friend, at the St. Lazares train station on August 7 to act as translator for him and his wife and another Emporia couple and to show them around Paris. After nine days in Paris with those hometown friends, Bill caught the French liner *DeGrasse* from Le Havre, again third class, docking in New York on August 26. He stayed a week to serve as best man at the wedding of a fellow Kansan and Harvard classmate, Webb Wilson, a New York bank executive, and to see Kathrine. He also called on Arthur Krock, then Sunday editor of the *New York Times*. The elder White had sent Krock a sample of Bill's travel letters and a letter of introduction in which he wrote: "I think Bill could do some work for the Times out in this western country. He is rooted here, of course; Managing Editor of the paper and also as you know editorial writer and interested as I am in politics and in this mid-western life."[31] Though that meeting elicited no immediate assignments, the Sunday *New York Times* would carry five bylined interpretive pieces by Bill about Kansas economic conditions in the fall of 1931.

Back home early in September, Bill found himself a local celebrity. *Gazette* subscribers had followed his letters with interest, and newspapers around the state had commented favorably on his "Odyssey," often with one or two extracts.[32] Then the Sunday *Kansas City Star* carried on September 15 a full-page feature interview by him of a former German lieutenant he met in Bandol who at the Battle of Argonne had faced the American Thirty-fifth Division, made up of Missouri and Kansas national guardsmen.[33] It demonstrates even more clearly than the letters that on this trip he had found his narrative stance, one in which he selects an interesting person to interview, then lets him tell his own story in his own apparently artless way. Of course, he achieves that effect only by compressing and focusing the tale with painstaking care. That was the only freelance piece he placed from the trip. Monday, September 9, he was back at the *Gazette* organizing school correspondents and looking for a new Lyon County reporter. That fall, using movie film he shot during the trip, he gave a travelogue before civic clubs in Emporia and several nearby small towns. But interest in European travel "for the average man" waned after the stock market crash in October. Disintegrating economic and social conditions now claimed attention.

Gazette editorials in 1930, many undoubtedly from Bill's typewriter, focused on collapsing world markets, inadequate federal responses, rapidly increasing local unemployment, and statewide hard times. Both Whites called for political action. On the state level Bill had pushed for several years for revision of the property tax structure to incorporate new graduated income and inheritance taxes and thus bring about a broader, more equitable base. But at the biennial sixty-day legislative session early in 1929 his call was blocked by a business-dominated, standpat Republican majority. With economic conditions growing rapidly worse, in 1930 Young Bill decided to run on that tax issue as Republican candidate for the Forty-sixth Legislative District, which comprised the eastern half of Emporia and of Lyon County.

He easily won the August primary and in November bested his Democratic opponent by carrying large majorities in Emporia's Second Ward and Fourth Ward. Though the Democrats won the governorship and defeated his father's old friend Henry Allen in a bid to remain a United States senator, Bill's cousin "twice removed" Roland Boynton, a young Emporia attorney and protégé of the elder White, was also elected state attorney general on the Republican ticket. Once elected, and before the late January start of the next biennial legislative session, Bill launched a signed editorial campaign for tax reform. In partnership with Ed Rees, representative for the neighboring Forty-seventh District and floor leader of the House, he led a successful fight to submit an income tax proposal to the people in 1932, which the electorate then accepted. Though Young Bill did not run again for the legislature, he did work for implementation of that tax reform within Republican party councils and personally lobbied for it at the next legislative session, backed by newly elected Republican governor Alf Landon, another of the elder White's "boys." At the end of the term, March 25, 1933, the *Kansas City Star* in a front-page article subheaded "Success of Kansas Session Partly Due to W. L. White" praised his efforts, observing in part: "On the firing line in the last week of the income tax battle in the legislature, an outstanding representative of a new type of leadership appeared in Kansas. He was W. L. (Young Bill) White of Emporia, quiet mannered editor, who applied the laws of logic and sound reasoning through the medium of an impressive personality, while the bickerings and mutterings of the deadlocked legislators echoed through the halls of the state house."[34]

This was high praise from the area's dominant newspaper and an indication of a side of Bill White not widely known today, buried in the political trivia of the state's archives. But one cannot appreciate the full range of his activities and associations while at the *Gazette*'s editorial desk from 1924 to 1934 without recognizing his close connection with the liberal half of the state Republican party. The last part of that decade he was himself a force among his state's young Republicans and was thinking of running again for office when circumstances intervened. Later, when he became publisher of the *Gazette* after his father's death, he roiled state and local political waters with the occasional editorial stone, usually tossed from New York City. And throughout most of his life he was interested in national politics, attending, since the age of sixteen, most national conventions. Indeed, in

the 1950s and 1960s he worked behind the scenes to help determine which presidential candidate appeared on the Republican
national stage. In that too he was his father's son.

On June 17, 1930, Bill turned thirty. Single, living at home,
and working in the family business, he felt the sands of time
trickling past and captured that mood humorously the next day
in an editorial headed "Finis." Both in style and attitude it well
represents W. L. W. at that time:

> The writer of these lines has just passed his thirtieth birthday,
> and duly celebrat[ed] that event, not with feasting and revelry,
> but in fasting and gruesome meditation. Gone forever are the
> gilded twenties, even the memory of the 'teens is fading fast,
> and ahead lies a doleful and lugubrious land of wrinkles, falling
> hair, flattened arches and fatty degeneration of the heart muscle.
>
> As the body, weathered by time, relentlessly falls into decay,
> its steady decline will undoubtedly be matched by equally
> profound modifications of the mind. With astigmatism and
> shortness of breath will come a settled conviction that bar
> associations are better fitted to select judges than the people
> at the polls.
>
> As acidification of the bloodstream steals on apace, and the
> deposit of calcium hardens the artery walls, there will probably
> come a comfortable acceptance of the divine right of property
> to rule. Still later, as neuritis bends the back, hobbles the step
> and palsies the hand, will come horrid nagging fears,—of
> Bolshevism, municipal ownership, double taxation and a third
> party.
>
> Lastly, as the four varieties of pneumococci cluster in the
> tissues of the lungs and the cellular structure of the liver finally
> breaks down, and cheyne-stokes breathing sets in, there will
> come back only the words of the Preacher, the son of David,
> King in Jerusalem, when he said:
>
> "Then I looked on all the works that my hands had wrought
> and on the labor that I had labored to do; and behold, all was
> vanity and vexation of spirit, and there was no profit under
> the sun: for what can man do that cometh after the king? Even
> which hath already been done."

> That time is not yet, but at 30 the zenith is already past, the
> golden sun is paler, already the shadows lengthen apace. Is it
> only a coincidence that old-time newspapermen used to put at
> the end of every story, to signify its final conclusion, the
> symbol—30?[35]

The preacher in *Ecclesiastes* did indeed sum up Bill's dilemma:
"What can the man do that cometh after the king?" As an
Emporia editor whatever he did appeared but a reflection of his
father's achievements. That was especially true of his first
syndicated article, a well-written descriptive piece about a 1931
plane crash thirty miles southwest of Emporia that killed Knute
Rockne, the Notre Dame University football great. That widely
distributed article was bylined William Allen White. Yet Will was
ill at the time, suffering from nervous exhaustion complicated by
Ménière's syndrome. As the economic depression worsened, he
had grown increasingly frustrated with the lack of meaningful
political action on both state and national level. That had
contributed to a physical collapse toward the end of March that
sent him and Sallie by the last week of April to New Mexico and
then Colorado for what became a six-month rest. As usual, the
Gazette carried no announcement of the elder Whites' departure;
Bill simply moved over to his father's desk next to the newsroom,
and Walter Hughes continued managing the business side.

On the morning of March 31 the Gazette received a phone call
from its correspondent at Strong City, a small town twenty miles
west, that a plane had crashed south in the Flint Hills. Bill notified
the Associated Press, then he and reporter Lee Rich jumped in
the *Gazette*'s Model A Ford and headed for the scene, picking
up the local coroner along the way.[36] When they returned late
that afternoon, John Wheeler of the North American Newspaper
Alliance (NANA) had wired Will, a regular contributor to that
major syndicate, asking for a 1,500-word "descriptive dramatic story
aeroplane disaster filing early."[37] Fresh from the scene, Bill wrote
the story, cabled it collect, and the NANA released it the next
morning under his father's name. Wheeler immediately wrote Will
in care of the *Gazette*: "I understand that your son wrote [the
Rockne story], but that you agreed we could sign it by your name,

which we did."[38] Apparently, Wheeler wanted to go with a headliner. A week later, as if to make amends, he wrote Will, "We have had a lot of compliments on this story. I think your son did an excellent job."[39] But no one other than the staff knew it was by the son. Headed "How a Viking Died" when the *Gazette* carried it unsigned on the editorial page, it deserved the many compliments. It clearly demonstrates that Bill was no longer a journeyman at his trade, that in fact under pressure he could write a "descriptive dramatic" piece as well his father could, perhaps even better. For example, Bill concluded his commentary in two sentences that impressively fused his primary structural images throughout—the loneliness of the crash scene and the impassive sympathy of the cowboys who discovered it:

> So died the great Viking of football on a high hill overlooking a prairie, at the crossroads of the old forgotten stage road and the new highway of the air, and at his bier keeping vigil on the hill top stood, not the Four Horsemen of Notre Dame, but four sun-tanned horsemen of the plains forcing back from the tangled wreckage a gaping curious crowd.
>
> Swiftly and painlessly he passed from a land of far horizons into a horizon without bounds.[40]

Buoyed up by the success of that piece, the Kansas legislative session now behind him, Bill decided to go to New York toward the end of April, about the same time his parents left for New Mexico. While in New York, he planned to send enough copy back to the *Gazette* to keep the editorial page functioning, and he did, including several signed commentaries about the effects of the depression on the city.[41] He left Emporia armed with a letter of introduction from his father to John Wheeler, which read: "This will introduce my son Bill who wrote the piece about Rockne's death on which he used my name. I want you to know Bill. He has been writing editorials for the Gazette that have been credited to me off and on for eight or ten years, even while he was at Harvard. I want you to take a look at him and some time see if you can't find some writing that he can do. He is managing editor of the Gazette and we need him here, but we can let him go off and on as he can find something better to do."[42] That letter suggests Bill went east to check out the freelance market. But in reality he left for New York intending to marry Kathrine Klinkenberg, if she would have him, and bring her back to Emporia, an intent his parents knew about but did not quite approve of.

Within a fortnight of his arrival he and Kathrine were married in a small private ceremony on April 29, 1931, at fashionable Saint Thomas's Episcopal Church in Manhattan. She seemed truly fond of Bill and was to prove a loyal wife; together they built a strong marriage lasting forty-two years, until his death, though they did experience their full share of marital vicissitude. Back in Emporia Sallie sat quietly beside Will White, sharing his work, monitoring his style, and taking active part in the community. Kathrine, though, was to stand uneasily behind Young Bill. She was uncomfortable with the town. She shared his aspirations and would give him the occasional shove toward "higher" aims. It was she who eventually pushed him into the national arena. There, while he shadowboxed with his father for separate recognition, she tended his corner, ready with bandages, advice, and encouragement. His success in that fight was to a considerable extent due to her. Later, after the death of the elder Whites, when she returned to Emporia for extended stays while Bill oversaw the *Gazette*, she did not gladly suffer the naive or the obsequious or the stupid. And that contributed to much hometown unease— for her, for Bill, and for sundry citizens. So who was this young woman who became such a force in his life?

Kathrine Klinkenberg was a tall, attractive blonde who had worked off and on for nearly five years in New York City for *Time* magazine. She was a native Kansan, born July 9, 1903, in Cawker City, a village in the north central part of the state, the elder child of Peter and Frances Buckner Klinkenberg. Her father ran the town drugstore. When she was five, he sold out and moved to Ottawa, Kansas, to become a salesman for the McPike Drug Company. There in 1911 her brother, Royle ("Buddy"), was born. With that birth her father transferred his medical ambitions and much of his attention to his son, with the result that Royle eventually became a successful cardiologist, and Kathrine had to give up her childhood dream of becoming a physician. In fact, as the older child, a daughter, in a patriarchal Dutch family, Kathrine was expected both to help at home and to put in long hours at the drugstore her father bought in 1915. Her daughter remembers her recounting "how hard she worked as a little girl . . . how she hated housework" and how as a child she "determined never to grow up to be a drudge."[43]

A product of the Ottawa public schools, Kathrine enrolled as a freshman at the University of Kansas in 1922 and joined Kappa Kappa Gamma sorority. She dropped out her sophomore year, took several courses at the local, Baptist-affiliated Ottawa University, then transferred for one term to the University of Wisconsin. She returned to the University of Kansas but left without a degree in the spring of 1926 because of financial problems.[44] For about then her parents separated. Her father sold his Ottawa drugstore and rejoined the McPike Drug Company, transferring to Kansas City; her mother moved to Lawrence, Kansas, to be housemother for Kappa Alpha Theta sorority.

On leaving the university, Kathrine took a job as traveling secretary for Dr. Otto H. F. Vollbehr, a well-known German collector of incunabula (books printed before 1501). With an eye to finding an institutional buyer, he was exhibiting his unique private collection at major American libraries in 1926 and 1927. But when he returned to Europe in the fall of 1927, Kathrine ended up in New York City job hunting. Briton Hadden and Henry Luce had just moved their upstart weekly news magazine, *Time*, back from Cleveland, Ohio, to small offices at 25 West Forty-fifth Street, the same building that housed Harold Ross and his equally brash *New Yorker*. Hadden and Luce needed another clerk-typist when Kathrine by chance knocked at their door looking for editorial work. Hired as a typist, she soon moved up to utility rewrite editor and eventually settled in as a research editor, filling in as vacation relief to run the gamut from sports to aviation.[45]

Known as "Klink" to the *Time* staff, she attracted the attention of fellow employee John O'Hara, the novelist, with whom she and Noel Busch, who was to become a senior Time-Life editor, shared an office for several months. Harry Ferguson, for many years Washington correspondent for the United Press International, reminisced in a 1973 article for the *Atlantic Monthly* about his introduction to O'Hara at that time and his attraction to Kathrine: "Two blondes shared an apartment on East 34th Street. One of them was named Kathrine Klinkenberg, a Viking who was five feet seven inches tall and one of the most stunning females I have ever had the pleasure of gazing upon. O'Hara was her slave." Ferguson was dating Kathrine's roommate, whom he identifies only as Elizabeth:

> Around 11 o'clock one night, Elizabeth and I walked into the apartment after a frugal dinner in an Italian restaurant. Klink was sitting in an overstuffed chair. O'Hara was sitting on the floor cradling a pint milk bottle which I subsequently learned was filled with bathtub gin. Klink performed the introductions. . . . The pint milk bottle made the rounds. The atmosphere mellowed; the three-way conversation sparkled. I say three-way because Elizabeth sat in silence. . . . Shortly after midnight Klink adjourned the meeting. She gave O'Hara a kiss on the cheek and gave me a pat on the head.[46]

Clearly Kathrine could hold her own with the boys in New York City. According to Sally Ingalls (Baronesa Ostman van der Leye), Kathrine's University of Kansas classmate and longtime friend, Kathrine as a young woman could be very sharp in both wit and tongue. Abrupt, strong-minded, and somewhat aloof, she had few women friends. In her men friends she was most attracted to those with brains, humor, and a sense of honesty.[47] In a reminiscent obituary her daughter alluded to O'Hara's courting of her mother, remarking, "John O'Hara, in an eloquent letter, proposed marriage to my mother, and years later I found the letter, and sold it for $5 at a school fair, much to my mother's horror."[48] During that time Kathrine had another serious suitor too, an unidentified wealthy oilman, whose proposal she also turned down after being a guest at several weeklong parties aboard his yacht off the Florida Keys.[49]

That was the twenty-seven-year-old woman Bill White asked to marry him in April 1931. At first she demurred because she did not want to come to him owing money. Then Luce kindly offered two months' extra salary "as a retainer in case you get tired of the matrimony racket and want to come back to work."[50] That sum was enough to clear her debts and sustain her dignity. But Kathrine left *Time* magazine and New York with mixed feelings. Living on her own in the city at the onset of the Great Depression had been tough and unsettling. She barely made expenses commuting in 1931 from a cheap apartment north of Harlem River. According to Bill in a letter to his parents just after the wedding, when he asked her to marry him, her wardrobe consisted of two nightgowns, two dresses, one suit, a coat, and two hats; according to their daughter he was not exaggerating to enlist his parents' sympathy.[51] Still, during the latter part of the Jazz Age, Kathrine found New York exciting, her associates witty, and her work often interesting. That was the era of the New York speakeasies, which often catered to a well-acquainted, friendly clientele of young professionals, including New York journalists, remembered today as a mostly masculine, hard-drinking, sociable crowd. Among them a bright, attractive woman such as Kathrine would have received pointed attention.[52]

At work she was usually confined to her desk, sometimes until late at night, but office practices were flexible, reflecting the flamboyantly rebellious spirits of coeditors Hadden and Luce. After Hadden died in February 1929, Luce instituted tighter fiscal controls but still preserved the magazine's free-wheeling editorial style and office insouciance. And he occasionally assigned Kathrine to an outside story. In the spring of 1929, for example, he sent her and John O'Hara to interview Kansas-born Amelia Earhart, then aviation editor of *Cosmopolitan* magazine, who took Kathrine alone on a flight over New York City when an inebriated O'Hara failed to show up. And in the late summer of 1930 Luce sent Kathrine to Europe for three months to interview several wealthy English brewers for an article in his new business monthly, *Fortune*.[53]

When the stock market plummeted in October 1929, so did the Jazz Age, its detritus making hard times in New York City even harder to bear. In the spring of 1931 Broadway lights still reflected off glossy fenders of chauffeured limousines, but Bill reported in the *Gazette* that "a friend working on one of the larger magazines" told him "everyone was hanging onto his job with his teeth and there was a constant stream of applications for every opening."[54]

That friend was Kathrine. She too may have been worried about her job, but apparently it was secure. Two days after the wedding Bill wrote proudly to his parents: "The boys at 'Time' were in horrified consternation when she left. Her boss cried. Do you remember the closing lines of 'The Front Page' where the managing editor bids good-bye to the star reporter? Well, just as Kathrine was leaving the office, Editor Luce called out after her 'The son of a bitch stole my watch!' and then called me up over the phone to explain what a grand girl I was getting."[55]

Emporia, with a total population of 14,067 as counted by the 1930 census, had nearly 1,000 able-bodied unemployed in the fall of 1931, according to the *Gazette*, with no work in sight. Not only were times tough but the town itself could be stodgy almost beyond endurance, especially for someone like Kathrine, who had escaped to New York City. In Emporia Prohibition was a way of life, and blue laws were strictly enforced—even the three movie theaters closed on Sunday, in deference to the thirty-one churches. During the other six days those theaters could only show films previously approved by a state board of review, which of course allowed no scenes depicting the consumption of alcoholic beverages. The town's businessmen could not slip into a speakeasy for a quick pick-me-up; they had to settle for a fountain coke at Morris's Drug Store.

The best public dining was at the Blue Room in the eight-year-old, seven-story Broadview Hotel, the tallest building in town. There was a Harvey House hotel and restaurant near the five-year-old Santa Fe passenger depot, and the old Mit-Way Hotel had a popular businessmen's cafe. Newman's Department Store, under new management, continued to offer lunches for the genteelly fashionable in its second floor tearoom. In the fall semester of 1931 the normal school had an enrollment of about 1,300 students, and the College of Emporia had about 350; both colleges sponsored sundry cultural events.[56] And the Woman's City Club offered its members a curriculum of self-improvement courses, in addition to Bible study. The town's feminine pecking order went back three, sometimes four generations, with a comfortable sense of family and conformity understood fully only by those who have grown up in a small town, as had Kathrine.

The elder Whites were used to benign interference both in the moral life of the town and in that of their son. Kathrine received a foretaste of such well-meant meddling when, from New Mexico and on short notice, they changed the couple's honeymoon plans. Bill wired his father that they intended to go to Bermuda for two weeks. His parents replied that New Orleans, Louisiana, would be just as nice and less expensive because they could use a due bill at the St. Charles Hotel. Bill wired back, "Kathrine tired overworked needs two weeks in fresh air on beach suggested Bermuda herself so I did not show her your telegram would you mind awfully if we planned this trip ourselves."[57] But his parents' argument about expenses prevailed, and the young couple honeymooned in New Orleans and Biloxi, Mississippi. On Sunday, May 17, the newlyweds arrived in Emporia on the Santa Fe to be greeted by friends with an unusually sedate two-hour charivari at 927 Exchange.

With Bill's parents in New Mexico, Mabel Finney, wife of banker and telephone executive Warren Finney, assumed the role of doyenne to introduce Kathrine to the Emporia social circles appropriate for the daughter-in-law of the town's famous editor. But resentment by some who thought Bill should have married a local girl complicated Mrs. Finney's task. And from the outset Kathrine did not fit in well, for at least three reasons. First of all, she resented Mabel Finney's too obvious patronage. Second, Kathrine was bright, strong-willed, and outspoken, qualities that did not endear her to potential small-town peers. Third, though a Kansas girl, she had become acclimatized to New York manners and to holding a full-time, highly competitive job. Inadvertently, sometimes intentionally, she violated the unspoken mores of Emporia's matrons, both young and old.

In *What People Said*, his later roman à clef about the Finney bank-bond scandal, Bill recounted his wife's initial reaction to Mabel Finney. In that account Athena is Emporia, Liz is Kathrine, Junior Carrough is Bill; and the Norssexes are the Finneys:

> When Liz and Junior arrived in Athena after they were married, the first people Liz met were the Norssexes. The Carroughs were out of town, and because the Norssexes were their best friends in Athena they had asked Junior and Liz over to dinner. Liz

came home sputtering. Mrs. Norssex, she said, was a stern
version of the Old Lady from Dubuque in the *New Yorker*.[58]

Several pages later in the novel, in a passage still vividly
remembered by some older Emporians, Liz tells Junior about an
afternoon gathering she attended just after their arrival in town:

> "This morning one of the girls who called telephoned me and
> said she was having a little something at four o'clock for her
> cousin who is visiting. So I put on my blue tweed suit, and that
> off-cherry sweater we got in Bermuda that you like the neckline
> of so much, and my ghillies, and I went. And, darling, it was
> so *wrong* of me."
> "I bet you looked fine."
> "I did—but not in Athena."
> "What did they have on?"
> "Costumes."
> "What's a costume?"
> "That's what I call them. Sometimes you see pictures of them.
> It's something that isn't a suit or it isn't a street dress or it isn't
> a dinner dress or it isn't an evening dress. It's between a street
> dress and a dinner dress, but it isn't either one. . . . Prancing
> around in those costumes, they had such a kept look. As though
> they were all being kept by the same wholesale tobacco importer
> in the West Seventies."
> "I'll bet you looked nice and simple and elegant."
> "No, I didn't. Not in Athena I didn't. I looked insulting. As
> though I thought their party was a low-grade weenie roast.". . .
> "Well, get yourself a costume."
> "But I don't want a costume. Why should I spend money for
> a special creation so I'll look right eating angelfood cake with
> marshmallow frosting at four o'clock in the afternoon in
> Athena? Darling, . . . promise that I won't have to spend my
> life with a lot of women eating cake in the afternoons and
> playing bridge. . . . Because it's such a whory life, darling."[59]

With that attitude Kathrine found married life in Emporia dreary,
much as Sinclair Lewis's Carol Kennicott did in the *Main Street*
village of Gopher Prairie.

Contributing to Kathrine's alienation was having to live as "a White," something Bill had grown up with. For example, much of that summer they stayed at 927 Exchange, with Bill acting editor of the *Gazette*. To commemorate the Fourth of July, Emporia traditionally presented a patriotic program at Soden's Grove, a large park at the south edge of town, with political speakers introduced by the town's editor. Bill was to introduce Congressman Homer Hoch, who in turn was to introduce William Culbertson, the current minister to Chile and a former Emporia boy. Unfortunately for Bill's peace of mind, another of Emporia's own planned to attend: the flamboyant Belle Livingston, adopted daughter of John Graham, founding editor of the *Gazette*. In her day she had been a famous New York showgirl and then one of Europe's most glamorous courtesans.[60] Down but not out in her early fifties, she returned to New York and opened the speakeasy Salon de Thé, soon the city's most fashionable. Raided occasionally as a formality by the New York police, her club was closed early in 1931 by federal agents, and she was sentenced to thirty days in old Harlem jail. Released to a crowd of reporters amid the whir of a Pathé newsreel camera, she left New York to motor cross-country to Reno, Nevada, where she planned to open a new club, the Mundane Bohemia. In Kansas City on the morning of July 4 she announced her intent to set up an open bar that afternoon on the lawn of her hometown "friend" William Allen White, an outspoken upholder of the Volstead Act.

Belle, in truth, did not know Will White, for she had left Emporia in 1891 at age sixteen, four years before he bought the *Gazette* from her father's successor, W. Y. Morgan. But she did know how to use publicity, and her threat sent Young Bill scrambling both to cover the story and to save his absent father from embarrassment. Fresh from New York herself, Kathrine must have been both amused and bemused by the problem Belle posed when the *Kansas City Star* called Bill just after lunch asking him to cover the story.[61] An anonymous *Gazette* "Reminiscence" relates the comic results:

> The call came as the Whites were about to leave for the Grove, so Belle could be expected at about 3, in the middle of the

Fourth of July speeches. . . . [Bill told *Gazette* reporter Whitley Austin to interview Belle if she showed up and also told Bertha Colglazier, the White's housekeeper:] "If a middle-aged heavy-set woman tries to get in the house or opens up a bar on the lawn, send her packing."

At about 2:30 p.m., the sky over Olpe [a village ten miles south] turned purple. Twenty minutes later, as the Whites drove up to the house to close its 48 windows, they saw Bertha pushing a large woman off the porch into the storm. They rescued the woman—Mrs. [Congressman Homer] Hoch—and took her inside to wait for the rest of the party.

Nothing more was heard of Belle that night. But at the office next day, Mary Hughes [in charge of the classifieds] talked and talked and talked. For Belle—a schoolmate of long ago—had called Mary, invited her to the Broadview Hotel and told her the story of her life.[62]

By August 12 Bill and Kathrine were in Moraine Park, Colorado, to see his parents before going on to New Mexico for a short vacation. From Santa Fe and Taos Bill mailed several long descriptive travel letters back to the *Gazette* to brighten up its editorial page in his and his father's absence. The elder Whites would stay more than another month at their mountain cabin as part of Will's convalescence. From Moraine Park Will wrote Henry Haskell, then managing editor of the *Kansas City Star*, about "the smart young amazon who has captured [Bill]"—not an auspicious description of a new daughter-in-law.[63] But that is also how she struck many of the townspeople. Later, Will grew fond of her, sometimes addressing her in letters as "Tinker," her family nickname. Sallie, however, maintained a polite distance, at least in their correspondence.

When Bill and Kathrine returned home the first week of September, they set up housekeeping in the upstairs unit of a duplex owned by the Whites at 1003 Exchange, across Tenth Street from 927 Exchange. As Kathrine remembered that choice, Sallie insisted they live close because "Father was not well." Yet, "it was a pleasant apartment—high ceilings, fireplaces, good woodwork—but we were too close to have any kind of independent life."[64]

For, like Grandma White earlier, they were family and as such were assumed participants at Sallie's famous dinners, especially when there were guests. Those dinners, according to Kathrine, were "usually at 6. There were never drinks but the food was great. Too great with mounds of whipped cream it seemed, biscuits, soufflés, cake, pie and such. . . . We were expected to be present but it left us little time of our own. . . . When anything unusual seemed to be going on at our house, Bill's father would call to ask what was up. Much of this was because little goes on in a small town, but we did feel devoured."[65] Nevertheless, they lived across the street at the beck and call of the elder Whites for more than two years, until Kathrine's health, or ennui, sent them back East indefinitely. Of course, others saw the young couple as fortunately placed. Jack Harris in the *El Dorado Times* reported,

> This is the way a former El Dorado flapper-wife describes the new wife of a Kansas newspaper man whose father is an illustrious author: "She's a knockout in her clothes and a grand cook and she's having the walls of her new house [the duplex apartment] done in antique gold, the woodwork in black and one bedroom's woodwork in aluminum and the house is going to have a copper bath tub, Italian furniture, oriental rugs and everything else in it is 'hot stuff.'"[66]

In the summer of 1931 Bill initialed several analytical editorials, written from a local perspective, that countered President Hoover's assurances that prosperity was "just around the corner." On July 22, for example, Bill asserted that conditions were becoming desperate for Emporia's many unemployed. For "they face the winter of 1931 with their credit exhausted, borrowed up to the limit, and with the outlook for work blacker than it has been at any time since the depression started." And he called for a community effort to provide jobs through public improvement projects, and soon. That fall the Sunday *New York Times* carried four "special" commentaries bylined "W. L. White" about Kansas economic and political conditions, commissioned by Arthur Krock, who remembered Will's letter and Bill's visit several years earlier. Late in life, in a reminiscent letter to Krock, Bill wrote, "You have no idea how delighted I was to get that first job—a kid sitting out here in Kansas—that got my nose above our prairies and out into the National horizon." In those *Times* commentaries he not only reported the human costs of the spreading depression but also tried to puzzle out monetary causes and effects, a topic he returned to from time to time the rest of his life.[67]

In December Kathrine came down with the flu, which developed into pneumonia. The family physician, Dr. Frank Foncannon, put her in the hospital for nearly a month, then suggested she go someplace warm for the rest of the winter because he suspected tuberculosis. Remembering the fate of Sallie's brother Milt, the Whites followed that advice.[68] By the end of January Bill and Kathrine were in Mexico City; there through a family friend they rented a house in Taxco for several months, complete with three servants. Bill sent back several bunches of editorials to spell his father and in April ten long travel letters, much like those from Europe, and as before the *Kansas City Star* reprinted one.[69] In May Bill took Kathrine to a clinic in San Antonio for a thorough checkup, then home, much to the relief of his parents.[70]

When Will covered the national political conventions that summer for the NANA, Bill accompanied him. Though much impressed by Franklin D. Roosevelt's acceptance speech, Will campaigned for President Hoover's reelection, mostly out of friendship; Bill held his tongue publicly, not announcing his support of FDR until after November. But both father and son pushed the state Republican ticket headed by their faction's candidate for governor, Alf Landon, and including Will's second cousin Roland Boynton, up for reelection as attorney general. Dr. John Brinkley, a quack who prospered from well-advertised goat-gland male-rejuvenation surgery, ran again as an independent candidate for governor and split the electorate. Bill's only initialed editorial of this period vigorously attacked Brinkley as an agent of the oil companies and praised Landon for his program of tax relief, the proposal Bill had helped pass at the last legislative session. In the election Kansas went for Democrats Franklin D. Roosevelt and Senator George McGill, but Republicans took the statewide offices. Bill did not run again for the legislature, but Lyon County Republicans selected him as their state committeeman.

David Mulvane, state standpat Republican leader, died just after election day, which threw open his post as national committeeman. With Landon as governor-elect, Will was sure his faction would take that position. But John Hamilton, youthful heir to Mulvane, had mended fences that year by supporting Landon. So at the state Republican committee meeting in December, to promote party harmony, Landon sponsored Hamilton for the post and asked Bill White to nominate him, which he did. Apparently, Landon had not checked with the elder White, undisputed leader of the Progressive faction. In a December 21 editorial Will grudgingly supported Hamilton's selection, but he spoke through gritted teeth while his hands hovered over a big stick. He started out by observing that "Mr. [W. L.] White is now in New York City or on his way there and the opinion of this paper is not dictated or controlled by him in this particular matter. Therefore in endorsing the work of the state Republican committee in nominating John Hamilton, the *Gazette* will assume that Mr. White acted . . . in the interests of harmony among the younger Republicans of Lyon County and of Kansas." That shift in the Byzantine alignment of Kansas Republican politics, underscored by this half-stifled outburst from an old bare-knuckled Bull Mooser, was too much for the *New York Times*. On December 26 it chortled: "Now White père is a mossback and young Bill speaks for the Young Republicans. . . . It took [old Bill] some time to learn to love John Hamilton and the rest of the die-hards. It is hard work now, but he does it. Apparently, young Bill fled to New York to avoid parental wrath. He was perturbed unnecessarily. Old Bill ratifies young Bill." Will did acknowledge the joke on him in the *Gazette* on December 31, but still it was not easy being the son of "old Bill," even though the father had a sense of humor.[71]

When Bill got back from New York, his first initialed editorial comment was somber and had nothing to do with Kansas politics; instead he warned: "Don't go east, young man. Stay where you are. Let the big neon signs on top of the Broadway buildings flash and glitter. They reflect on the lines in front of the Sixth Avenue unemployment agencies, which stretch a block and a half, with policemen standing to keep the jobless in line."[72] But that caution may not so much represent his recent view of the city as it did a new sense of his own responsibilities. For after Walter Hughes had died early that fall, Will had "promoted" his son to business manager, placing him truly second in command at the *Gazette*. To Bill the duties of that position were more than worrisome. Like his father, he knew all the operations of the paper, but he had no aptitude for or, perhaps truer, no sustained interest in the minutia of business. Kathrine, later, handled the daily details of their personal finances and after Will's death tracked the business accounts of the *Gazette*. So Bill now tried what for him was temperamentally impossible, to cover Walter Hughes's vacated position, in the slough of the Great Depression, with advertising revenues and circulation figures off and falling.

As one sign of hard times, Emporia had its very first bank robbery late that winter, with Bill nearly getting shot. Five armed men from Wichita robbed the Citizens National Bank the morning of March 1, 1933. They had parked their stolen Buick just across from the *Gazette* building. Drawn from his desk by the bank's ringing alarm, Bill was standing at the corner of the block when the bandits drove by. Just then a store clerk from across the intersection emptied a .44-caliber revolver at the Buick, with Bill in the line of fire. Fortunately, he ducked behind one of the pillars marking the entrance to the Kansas Power and Light building as several bullets ricocheted by. The *Gazette* did not record his close call in its welter of details about the wounding of several citizens, the killing of one of the bandits, and the capture of another. But, of course, it was stylebook policy not to mention any personal movements of the Whites, even one this spontaneous, without approval.[73]

In February 1933 Will had interviewed Herbert Hoover at the White House for a long interpretive article in the *Saturday Evening Post*, which ascribed his chief failure as president to an inability to mobilize public opinion. In striking contrast, FDR dramatized leadership in his sober inaugural call for immediate action amid a banking crisis and in his reassuring first "fireside chat" three days after Congress passed the Emergency Banking Relief Act. With such words and actions FDR soon captured Will's unofficial loyalty, especially after the appointment of Harold Ickes, an old Progressive party crony, as secretary of the interior, and Henry Wallace, son of another former Bull Mooser, as secretary of agriculture. So the *Gazette* backed most of FDR's programs in 1933. But in truth that was more Bill's doing than his father's, because the editorials that spring that most strongly support the New Deal carry the initials W. L. W., a sign that the son was speaking on his own.[74]

On May 31 the elder Whites sailed for Europe. Will went to cover the London economic conference for the NANA. Mary Jane Finney, nineteen-year-old daughter of Warren and Mabel, accompanied them. Many hoped that conference would revive international trade by stabilizing world currencies so that importers and exporters could forecast costs. But that June Congress took the United States officially off the gold standard, which scuttled any meaningful monetary agreement in London. At the conference, though, Will became acquainted with FDR's new secretary of state, Cordell Hull, which was the start of a mutually beneficial friendship, one that would later dramatically affect Bill.

Initially, the Whites planned to return to Emporia in late summer, but once in London they decided to tour Leningrad and Moscow for several weeks to see the results of Russia's First Five-Year Plan. From there Will mailed several sympathetically critical interpretive dispatches to the NANA, which distributed them widely because of their topicality.[75] Still accompanied by Mary Jane, the Whites then traveled via Warsaw and Vienna to Italy, where they toured for a month. They finished with a Mediterranean cruise, then on October 19 arrived back in the United States after five months abroad. Bill had urged them to stay longer because the Finney bank-bond scandal awaited them at home, though they had not told Mary Jane that until they had docked in New York.

On May 26, just as the elder Whites left Emporia for the harbor in New York, Kathrine entered Newman Memorial Hospital suffering from abdominal pain. Dr. Foncannon diagnosed an ectopic pregnancy. Emergency surgery did not go well; infection set in, complicated by phlebitis. So that summer she lay in the hospital for six weeks, then had to stay around home several months more with one leg elevated. Bored by her hospital stay, she was grateful to Ronald Finney, Bill's boyhood chum, for his entertaining visits. A busy Topeka-based financier whose many statewide business interests seemed to flourish despite the depression, Ronald had a vibrant boyish charm and an aura of the unexpected that relieved the tedium of a Kansas summer. For example, one night, as a surprise, he climbed through Kathrine's ground-floor hospital window with a jar of caviar and a bottle of champagne in a bucket of ice.[76]

He and his wife, Winifred, daughter of John and Jennie Wiggam, both prominent Emporia citizens, entertained conspicuously that summer at his in-laws' former home, a large two-story house with a tennis court and a swimming pool, both new. Bill and Kathrine, even when she was well, did not mix much with the fast set "Ronnie and Win" ran with, but they did regard them as close friends and visited back and forth. Ronald had over the years grown to respect Bill's reserved studiousness, though he himself was a flamboyant extrovert, a plunger who picked up the tab and always seemed to have mysterious business deals working. In contrast to most staid Kansas businessmen, he lived extravagantly. For example, that spring he had bought for $25,000 cash the celebrated 101 Ranch Real Wild West Show, bankrupt and stranded in Ponca City, Oklahoma, with 200 animals and 125 people. He sent it on to the Chicago World's Fair with much fanfare. Though he often flew his own plane around the state to conduct business, he also owned a small fleet of automobiles, with a 1932 Pierce-Arrow touring car as the showpiece. In short, he was Emporia's Jay Gatsby. And Bill was to become Nick Carraway, his chronicler and final defender.

In *The Great Kansas Bond Scandal* Robert Bader presents a well-documented, dramatically written history of the Finney bank-bond scandal, of its many participants and its widespread political ramifications.[77] Bill traced some of those same events from his and Kathrine's perspectives in his novel *What People Said*. The following account is but an overview of the details and chronology of that scandal insofar as they explain the quandary Bill found himself in that August while his parents were traveling toward Italy from Russia.

Monday morning, August 7, 1933, Sardius Brewster, the United States district attorney for Kansas, met with Gov. Alf Landon by appointment to tell him that Ronald Finney had stolen or forged about $400,000 in municipal bonds to use as collateral at the National Bank of Topeka and several Chicago brokerage houses. The bonds were held by the Kansas School Fund Commission in a vault supervised by State Treasurer Tom Boyd, who had refused federal agents access to them. Presumably, by physically holding such investment paper, the state insured the safety of its school funds. Dismayed, then furious, Landon ordered Boyd to open the vault and threatened him with martial law when he resisted. The governor was deeply embarrassed because, just five days before, he had spent the evening in Emporia with Warren and Mabel Finney, Ronald's parents, and with Young Bill White and his wife, well-known friends of Ronald's.

Warren himself was prominent in Republican politics and had been the third-largest financial contributor to Landon's gubernatorial campaign. Both in 1930 and 1932, Finney had fought publicly for the state income-tax amendment, which was the cornerstone of Landon's campaign to put Kansas on a sound fiscal basis in spite of the depression. John Hamilton, whose election to Republican national committeeman Landon had recently arranged in order to increase his political base, was the Finney family's lawyer. And the state attorney general, a fellow Phi Delt and close friend of Ronald's, was Roland Boynton, who at that critical moment was in California visiting his mother, Will White's first cousin.

Federal agents, not state, had initiated the investigation; within hours that would be known, with Democratic and standpat Republican newspapers immediately raising a furor. Unless Landon acted vigorously and without apparent favor, his campaign for fiscal integrity and his own reputation for honesty would be undermined. Late that afternoon he directed the county attorney of Shawnee to issue an arrest warrant for Ronald Finney. The next day Ronald surrendered to Shawnee County authorities, to be released on a $25,000 bond signed for at the courthouse by his father, Warren. Warren Finney then went to the capitol building to appeal to the governor for time to get his own fiscal affairs in order, but by then special examiners had found some of the counterfeit bonds in the three banks he controlled. Landon ordered those banks padlocked and thoroughly investigated, starting that very night. Soon further revelations fueled a public firestorm blown red-hot by stories of Ronald's outlandish spending.

On August 10 Shawnee County officials arrested Leland Caldwell, Ronald's office manager, whose fingers did the actual forging. And that same day, in a dramatic gesture, Landon put the treasurer's office under martial law and posted state militiamen to guard its records and vault. By August 12 investigators had traced $926,000 in counterfeit bonds and warrants; the figure ultimately rose to $1.25 million, a huge sum to Kansans during the Great Depression. On August 15 Landon directed the county attorney to arrest State Treasurer Tom Boyd on embezzlement charges. By chance, on that day, the first meeting of the new legislative council was scheduled. It was a bipartisan fact-finding group picked from both houses to prepare for a special session already planned for that winter. From that council came an ad hoc committee to investigate the involvement of state officials in the spreading scandal and report its findings to the scheduled special session. Eventually, the committee would recommend impeachment of Attorney General Boynton and State Auditor Will French; State Treasurer Tom Boyd escaped that fate by resigning.

On August 15 Roland Boynton returned to Topeka from California. He immediately conferred with the governor, then the next day with District Attorney Brewster. Alarmed by Boynton's reluctant admission to Brewster that Ronald Finney had paid him extraordinary returns on a $400 investment, Landon immediately appointed a special counsel, thereby removing Attorney General Boynton from the investigation. On August 24 Ronald Finney was arrested again by Shawnee County agents on new charges and jailed when he failed to make $50,000 bond. Then on August 28 Lyon County Attorney Clarence Beck, a close friend of Young Bill White's, arrested the elder Finney in Emporia for bank embezzlement and fraud.

In the absence of his father, Young Bill found himself caught in the vortex of a Kansas political tornado. The Finneys turned toward him as the scion of Emporia's Great Oz, nearly as capable of manipulating public opinion, at least in Emporia, in order to calm the storm, perhaps even save them from it. To their dismay, he was no magician's son but an experienced newspaperman who stalwartly guarded his and his father's professional integrity while doing all he honestly could to help the Finneys.

From the outset he ran wire-service news copy. And his first *Gazette* commentary came early, on August 9, an unsigned half-column editorial headed "State Treasury Scandal." In it he carefully reviewed the situation as it was known, yet named no names. As examiners continued to discover forged bonds in the Finney banks, Bill ran that as straight news with all the details, to the discomfort of the elder Finney. Through August he continued to carry the scandal as a breaking news story, with both wire-service copy and local items. But his editorial commentary was sparse. On August 12 he published a short piece supporting Landon's actions headed "Proud of Him," which upset the Finneys because in it he wrote, "No innocent bystander or victim of circumstances need fear anything from Alf Landon. No friend who is criminally involved need expect one single drop of mercy from him."[78] On August 17 he repeated his support of Landon: "His actions prove that he is a citizen of Kansas first and a Republican politician only secondarily." But in reaction to the appointment of a special counsel, he specifically defended his hapless cousin: "There are in the statehouse today many men of high integrity whose reputations will be temporarily smirched simply because their official duties brought them into contact with the principals in the bond scandal. One of these is our cousin Rollie Boynton now sitting in the attorney general's office, pardonably annoyed by the rocket's red glare and bombs bursting in air."[79]

Then on August 25 he ran a long editorial entitled "A Friendship," a painfully personal account of his and his parents' relationships with the Finneys. For they had asked him the day before to help make bond for Ronald's second arrest. Bill could not refuse, though he knew his signature on that bond would tie him to the scandal and end his thoughts of running again for political office. He also knew it would call into question his journalistic objectivity. A straightforward declaration of conflicting obligations, that editorial was his last *Gazette* commentary directly about the Finneys during all subsequent court actions:

> The undersigned knowingly and deliberately violated an old unwritten law of the newspaper world yesterday when he announced his willingness to sign an appearance bond for Ronald Finney. His liability under the bond, had it been made, would have been limited to $5,000 and would have constituted no obligation against this newspaper or against his father's property.
>
> Yet no newspaperman should ever sign a bond in court proceedings to which he is not a party. If he does the public is apt to decide, and generally with reason, that he is taking sides in the case, and, because he has friends involved, his newspaper will print only part of the facts, burying the uglier ones, if he prints them at all, deep under layers of powdered sugar and whipped cream.
>
> As against this is the close personal friendship between the Finney family and that of the editor of this paper, for more than two decades. This friendship, as Emporia knows, includes few business contacts, as its editor has for the most part reinvested his profits in his business, with a few ventures into Emporia real estate. . . .
>
> Under ordinary circumstances the social relations and personal friendships of a newspaperman are matters in which the public has no concern. But yesterday morning the junior editor of this paper, in the dingy basement courtroom of the Shawnee county courthouse, signified his willingness to obligate his worldly goods so that his boyhood friend, Ronald Finney, accused of a major crime, might remain at liberty at least until a court has heard his defense. The readers of this paper have a right to know just what this obligation of friendship is and how far it extends. It should not influence either the editorial policy of the paper or color the news, as these duties of a newspaperman take precedence over any obligation of friendship he may have. . . .—W. L. W.[80]

On September 6 Bill made another unusual gesture; he closed the *Gazette*'s Wailing Place, its letters-to-the-editor column, to any comments about the Finneys.[81] But he did feel an editorial obligation to Rollie Boynton, whom he continued vigorously to support.[82] And he publicly defended a family friend innocently touched by the scandal, Ronald Finney's brother-in-law and New York "market informant," political publicist David Hinshaw, who had married Winifred's elder sister. A former Emporia boy, he had worked closely with Will White in the 1912–16 Progressive party; a Quaker, he was a confidant of President Hoover and Will's primary contact with that administration.[83] Another of Ronald's market informants under misplaced suspicion was Harold Trusler, Bill's best friend, an Emporia grain dealer and broker who in 1933 was working in Chicago for a commodities firm. In fact, it was Bill himself who in bull session analyses of financial conditions had unwittingly convinced Ronald "to get into the beans and bellies future markets," according to Whitley Austin, a former *Gazette* reporter who at the time was working as a lobbyist in Topeka for a group of farm organizations.[84] Bill indeed had conflicting loyalties and obligations.

Fortunately, the late Walter Hughes had saved the Whites from any significant financial entanglement in the Finneys' collapsing banking empire; for unlike his boss, Hughes had not trusted the elder Finney.[85] As *Gazette* business manager he had placed only a token account in Finney's Emporia bank. Though Warren and Will often co-chaired civic fund-raisers, such as the annual push for the YMCA, Hughes also kept Will out of Finney-backed speculations, which was not difficult. Will had learned fiscal caution early on, in 1902 and 1903, when he got himself into several shady speculations and nearly in legal trouble.[86] But in 1927 he had arbitrated a contract dispute between Warren Finney and Southwestern Bell, which had bought several of his phone companies and agreed to keep him on as their general manager.[87] The elder Finney's trial began in Emporia on October 9, two months before his son's in Topeka, but it was adjourned until late October, because his lawyers insisted the absent Will White could verify Finney's claim of wide legal latitude in handling Southwestern Bell funds. That distressed Young Bill because it focused attention on his father.

In fact, after Warren was arrested on August 28, both he and his wife pressured Bill to call his parents home so they could use

Will's considerable influence in an increasingly desperate defense. To the contrary Bill wrote his uncle Lacy Haynes asking for his help in urging the Whites to stay in Europe: "[The Finneys] are apt to ask all kinds of god damned crazy, unreasonable and embarrassing things, and I can turn them down where Father might impulsively get himself into trouble by trying to help them. . . . He is very fond of the Finneys personally, and I don't want to put him to the mental strain which all the necessary refusals of help would mean."[88] Bill also wanted to shield him from the unrestrained glee of his political enemies, especially from his adversaries at the oil-company-subsidized *Kansas City Journal–Post*, which in Will's absence had smugly attacked his son.[89]

But standing in as target for the real or feigned outrage of standpat Republicans was not great fun. Nor was patiently deflecting the Finneys' unreasonable expectations. So with relief and some apprehension Bill met his returning parents in Kansas City the morning of October 23 to prepare them for the onslaught. Will's general response was that of baffled pity. He wrote Erwin Canham, Washington correspondent for the *Christian Science Monitor*, to explain that "I knew [Warren Finney] as a fine, public-spirited, generous, intelligent, courageous and sometimes cantankerous man. But like all bankers, he was leading some kind of a double life [and seems] doomed for the penitentiary. . . . I was summoned by both sides of the case as a witness. . . . The trial started Monday. It is all sad and breaks my heart."[90] Will's appearance at that trial was of little legal help to Finney. In spite of its earlier adjournment because of Will's absence, the court ruled his testimony about the Southwestern Bell agreement inadmissible, though he was allowed to testify as a character witness.

With Will's return the *Gazette* remained closed to any editorial commentary about the Finneys, though as straight news the paper published the proceedings of the trial nearly verbatim, to counteract charges of a "White wash."[91] Instead, Will turned his energies to defending Rollie Boynton, a defense rendered difficult by Rollie's bemused, easy-going temperament. In a letter to Gwen Behr, Rollie's sister, Will sputtered, "I have tried, Bill has tried, Lacy Haynes has tried to get Roland to . . . fight for *himself*."[92] Nevertheless, that fall both Whites worked hard for him, Bill on the editorial page and Will on the political front, calling in political due bills and issuing others.[93] But they failed to quash a House resolution on November 25 to impeach him.

Earlier, an Emporia jury found Warren Finney guilty. On December 2 he was sentenced to from 3 to 50 years in the Kansas penitentiary on each of twelve counts, to run consecutively; indomitable, he appealed immediately to the Kansas Supreme Court.[94] Then on December 11 Ronald Finney's trial started in Topeka. For nearly two weeks the prosecution presented an exhaustively detailed case, with Finney's attorneys stalling for a plea-bargain. The state was to conclude on December 23, but on that day in Judge Paul Heinz's chamber, and with his concurrence, prosecution and defense agreed to a guilty plea for a minimum sentence of 15 years, to be pronounced after Christmas. But at the sentencing Judge Heinz, a Landon appointee, reneged on the agreement, to the protests both of the chief prosecutor and the defense, and sentenced Ronald to a minimum of 31 and a maximum of 635 years, the second longest sentence in state history. Immediately after Finney's plea, newspaper commentary statewide had called for a lengthy prison sentence, even life. Bill White came to believe that Alf Landon, reading his political future in those newspapers, pressured Judge Heinz to break his promise and thus calm public opinion. Bill summarily and permanently lost all loyalty to Landon. But not so Will White, who supported him in 1934 and 1936, or Lacy Haynes, who became Landon's presidential campaign manager.

The Whites had yet to fight the impeachment trial of Roland Boynton, which began January 8, 1934, before the Kansas senate. After two weeks of debate the senate voted on the four charges proffered by the House. Because two-thirds were needed to convict, Roland was acquitted, though a majority had voted against him on one charge. But he and the Whites had won a Pyrrhic victory: his political career was over, Will had spent much political capital, and Bill was sick of Kansas politics and hometown ties. The criminal proceedings were not yet over. During January and February 1934 Topeka juries convicted both former state treasurer Tom Boyd and Leland Caldwell, Ronald Finney's faithful aide. With that the Landon administration rested its cases, but Kansas did not, as the Finney affair loomed prominent in the election campaigns of 1934. And Young Bill White never let it rest, even after Ronald gained parole in 1945.

Chapter Three

Back East in Search of an Identity, 1934–1940

Early in March 1934 Bill and Kathrine left Emporia for New York City. Bill wanted to take a long break from Emporia and his job to write a novel based on the Finney scandal. Both perceived a crude, hypocritical vigilantism among the Kansas populace and were revolted by the politics necessary to respond to it. They were also concerned by Kathrine's phlebitis and continuing gyne-cological problems and planned to seek better medical advice. Little family correspondence from the next eighteen months survived, and what did are mostly Western Union telegrams or night letters. Even the elder Whites sometimes seemed unsure about Bill's whereabouts and activities, though he remained on the *Gazette* payroll during those months. For example, at the outset, Will sent a worried cable to his sister-in-law Jessie Kane, March 20: "Bill should be at National Arts [Club]. If not there wire us. All well here starting East for New York April seven."[1]

The family had planned to get together in New York that April, but instead Bill and Kathrine booked passage to Bermuda, where she had wanted to honeymoon. This time Will cabled them: "Don't postpone trip to Bermuda for us. We eager Kathrine try sunshine."[2] From Bermuda, Kathrine wrote her in-laws on April 24: "I'm fatter & my insides are fine & the leg even goes better. . . . Bill is working quite consistently. . . . I don't hear much writing going on—it's largely floor walking so far but he isn't in the least discouraged."[3] Several days later Bill wrote his parents: "I'm unbelievably stale. When I think how little I've written since the death of Walt Hughes, I can begin to understand. But I'm getting better. . . . Now of course, always, there isn't any reason why I can't return to Emporia at any time. That's always understood and if anything begins to bother you, let me know."[4]

After little more than a month in Bermuda, where they at first intended to rent a house long-term, the younger Whites returned to New York for a week. From there Bill telegraphed his parents, "Landed Arts Club temporarily."[5] Then on May 20 Bill telegraphed that they were in Baltimore, Maryland, where Kathrine consulted a gynecologist, a Dr. Emil Novak, who was on staff at Johns Hopkins University.[6] In a June 1 telegram to Baltimore the elder Whites queried, "Anxious about Kathrine."[7] Several weeks later, in a letter to Edna Ferber, Will wrote: "Bill and his wife are at Chatham, Massachusetts. She must be in the East where she can conveniently be under observation from time to time in the Johns Hopkins Clinic. We know very little else about what they are doing."[8] No other available information exists about their whereabouts that summer.

In August Will went to the Mayo Clinic for prostate surgery. Bill may have returned to Emporia then to help out, for on August 15 the *Gazette* carried a long W. L. W. editorial analyzing the coming congressional elections and endorsing the Republican candidate for representative from the Fourth District as a man who would work with President Roosevelt. That was Bill's first initialed editorial since February 13. Another appeared August 24. Later he mailed copy back from the East Coast, mostly unsigned, to spell his father, and that, of course, may have been the case here, because several other long W. L. W. commentaries appeared that fall in the *Gazette* when telegrams place him back

East. On September 12 Bill wired his parents that he and Kathrine were in Boston for an indefinite stay.[9]

At this time Kathrine became the patient of a well-known Harvard-connected internist, Dr. Maurice Fremont-Smith, whose brother Frank was a psychiatrist at Harvard Medical School. Maurice became her longtime physician and counselor, but a brief note from Kathrine to Bill's parents from Boston postmarked only 1934 suggests that initially she may have consulted both brothers. She wrote that she had met a nurse who so admired William Allen White that she could not believe Kathrine was his daughter-in-law: "She idealized you always and somehow a flesh and blood daughter had never been in the picture—she didn't add that a nutty one was too much for her—she was too nice to."[10] Whatever the medical situation, by the end of September Bill and Kathrine had settled at the Brattle Inn near Harvard Yard in Cambridge. Will in a letter November 9, 1934, to his cousin Mrs. Louise Quackenboss wrote: "Bill has been with his wife in the East looking for health. . . . She seems to have found a doctor in Boston who is helping her and Bill left her in the hospital yesterday and is on his way home."[11] But if Kathrine were at a hospital, it must have been as an outpatient. For her in-laws telegraphed her Thanksgiving greetings at the Brattle Inn and sympathy that her doctor was on vacation in Vermont.[12] By Christmas Bill was back in Boston with Kathrine.

At any rate, over the next six or seven years she and Bill both sought medical counseling with Dr. Maurice Fremont-Smith, then psychiatric, she with Dr. Carl Binger and he with Dr. Sandor Rado, then both with Dr. Gerald Jamieson, and later he with Dr. Ruth Brunswick—all prominent Boston or New York clinicians. On the East Coast in the late 1930s that was socially acceptable, even fashionable, if one could afford it. But most small-town Kansans in the 1930s regarded anyone under psychiatric care with grave suspicion, just as they spoke of cancer in shamed whispers and obliquely referred to a hysterectomy as "female trouble." Will and Sallie White were intelligent, sophisticated citizens and knew the breadth and depth of such prejudice. Each had suffered at least one serious nervous breakdown. And Will was a friend of Dr. Karl

Menninger, the internationally known Topeka psychiatrist, who himself underwent analysis in 1939 and 1940 under Dr. Brunswick. Though usually supportive of Bill's and Kathrine's pursuit of such counseling, the elder Whites were also extremely circumspect. For Will dictated nearly all his business and much of his personal correspondence; letters addressed to him either at the paper or to 927 Exchange usually ended up on a secretary's desk. So references to psychiatric care in the available family correspondence are for the most part indirect or coded as "singing lessons" or "music teachers." And contributing to difficulties in interpreting that correspondence was Bill's syndrome of projecting his own emotional problems, ultimately diagnosed as manic-depressive, onto Kathrine, which Dr. Brunswick was eventually to recognize and address.[13]

For the first several months of 1935 the younger Whites stayed in Cambridge at the Brattle Inn, with Bill mailing editorials back home. January 23, for example, Will sent his son a Western Union night letter about office matters, ending with "Your editorials widely copied. Keep em coming. Dearest love to you both."[14] That close was unusually warm; his standard sign-off to Bill was "Affectionately." But he had reason to be more forthcoming because Bill and Kathrine were thinking about staying in the East. In a night letter on February 11 Will wired: "We are eagerly waiting news of your final decision. Both send love to you two."[15] The decision seemed to be to return to Emporia. In a March 15, 1935, letter to his brother-in-law Bob Kane, Will wrote: "Bill is home. Kathrine is getting along fairly well. They are looking for a site on which to build a house, and I hope they can find it."[16]

But in mid-May Bill accompanied Kathrine back to Boston; apparently she left angry at both his parents and him, for his father sent him a brief letter May 21 which ended with "Don't hurry. Give Kathrine every break."[17] That was followed a week later by a telegraphed night letter that began, "Worried about Kathrine wire us about how she is don't hurry don't worry give her every chance."[18] As Kathrine remembered the situation much later, in some notes written after Bill's death, it was not her emotional volatility that was the issue: "It happens in 1935 when Bill's salary was $35 a week we wanted to buy a house of our own. That was when Bill went to his father to remind him that he had always been told a fourth of the paper belonged to him and that he wanted to use it to borrow some money. When Mr. White answered that he knew he had always said this but now felt that to give Bill his share would be 'like cutting a baby in two' we decided to leave."[19] Whatever the catalyst, by late spring Bill had decided to stay back East. In his centennial speech about his father, he remarked: "My father didn't oppose my leaving, but it was equally clear he didn't want us to go. That he felt somehow that he had failed. And maybe he also feared that I would fail, which he didn't want to happen, for he was very proud of me. I had the feeling that maybe I was pretty good. But so long as I stayed in Emporia, how would anyone find it out?"[20]

Certainly, at the time Will was proud of his son's recent editorials to the *Gazette*, especially his widely copied humorous "Prayer for Rain," published April 27, 1935, just after the worst Kansas dust storm of those drought- and heat-afflicted depression years. The next day came a half-inch of rain, with much more following. Three weeks later his father telegraphed him in Boston: "floods receding Rotary wanted to wire you to pray for drought everyone delighted with success your petition rains still coming."[21] That praise did not change Bill's decision; he was job hunting. On July 10 he wired his father from Washington, D.C.: "Probably home in 4 days Myer job looks best . . . he wants me by August Fifteenth."[22] Walter Myer had been on the faculty at Kansas State Teachers College from 1915 to 1925. Encouraged by his friend Will White, he left Emporia for Washington, D.C., where he founded the Civic Education Service, which published several nationally distributed scholastic newsletters. On August 1 the *Gazette* announced: "W. L. White, business manager of The Emporia *Gazette*, will resign next week to take a position as managing editor of the weekly *American Observer*, published in Washington, D.C. . . . The *Observer*'s circulation of 120,000 is almost exclusively in schools and colleges, where its editorial comments and analyses of news events supplement text books."[23] Actually, starting with the September 9 issue, W. L. White appeared on that newsletter's masthead as an associate editor, along with Paul D. Miller.

That decision behind them, Bill and Kathrine proceeded to house hunt in Washington, where FDR's depression-born alphabetical agencies were pulling in the young and talented, making housing tight. Temporarily they stayed at a women's country club in Bethesda, Maryland, but soon rented a small house in Georgetown and sent home for their furniture and their Scottish terrier, Sandy. Will wrote his son on August 13, "We have adjusted ourselves to the situation. But of course we do miss you and Kathrine. We want to hear from you; hear all that you are doing."[24] Two months later Will later wrote a cousin, Mrs. Ella Peterson, in a reflective mood: "Bill and his wife are in Washington. Bill has a good job there making much more money than he was here, and he wanted to get out and try his wings. He is 35 and he has a right to taste life on his own responsibility outside of my shadow. Of course I was sad about it, and still am, but I know and Sallie knows that it is best for Bill. Maybe he will come back to Emporia. . . . I don't know."[25] That fall he and Sallie accepted an invitation to tour the Philippines and then China on behalf of the Rockefeller Foundation. They left town in mid-October and were gone for four months, leaving the *Gazette* with no White in charge but in the hands of its staff, most of whom had worked there for years.

In Washington Bill quickly found friends—some were former classmates at Harvard, some displaced Kansans, some journalist acquaintances of Kathrine's or his, and some connections of his father's. He immediately joined the National Press Club, where, for example, he ran into the writer from whom he had bought the racing car in France in 1929, Jed Kiley, who took him and Kathrine to a party given by Drew Pearson, the columnist, who became a lifelong friend.[26] Both Bill and Kathrine were excited about being at the center of New Deal politics, among people who were witty, liberal, and sometimes even socially uninhibited.

Bill stayed with the *American Observer* for little more than three months, his name last appearing on its masthead on November 25. Then he moved on to the more prestigious *Washington Post*, whose conservative Republican publisher, Eugene Meyer, another friend of his father's, hired him to fill an editorial slot starting the first week of December. But after less than a month, Meyer moved him off editorial to news beats, then by the end of January

1936 fired him. At the time, Bill was quite bitter about his treatment at the *Post*; in an autobiographical note published by *Esquire* the next year, when that magazine excerpted a chapter from his novel-in-progress, Bill wrote that Eugene Meyer hired him because he

> felt the paper could use a fresh, western view of the national scene. . . . My fresh, western view coincided, not with what the *Post* thought a fresh western view ought to be, but (as it later turned out) with the election results from that part of the country. So at the end of three months I was fired for inciting to riot, speaking without a permit, marching without a flag, disturbing the peace and dignity of Mr. Meyer, and for demonstrated incompetence in every department of the paper.[27]

Actually, Bill was only at the *Post* two months. Five years later, in an interview by Robert van Gelder for the *New York Times Book Review*, after the extraordinary success of *They Were Expendable*, Bill saw his *Post* experience as part of a pattern, a burden he had to carry as the son of William Allen White:

> "You can't imagine what it is like," he said, "to be the son of a man like that unless you have lived through it. What I mean is newspaper publishers who weren't quite sure of themselves and were wishing that they had someone like William Allen White to make decisions for them would think to themselves, 'Why, he has a son,' and they'd hire me. They'd feel fine then, thinking they had William Allen White around the place. The trouble was that I'm just the son. I am another guy. I'm not for people such as Landon when they want to be President. So after a little while these publishers would hear that I was saying things that weren't solid Republican and they'd feel betrayed. They'd feel that I had gotten them to hire me under false pretenses. So I'd have to move on.'[28]

Whatever the reasons or rationalizations, Bill was out of a job by February 1936. So he and Kathrine went back to Emporia for a week or two to confer with his parents. On February 24 Will wrote a worried letter to his sister-in-law Jessie, who planned to visit the younger Whites in Washington: "Kathrine will be home when you get this. Bill ten days later—maybe. Whatever you see whenever you visit them, for Heaven's sake write us. Kathrine has been especially fine about details, but I would like to have your point of view."[29] When Bill got back to Washington, he went job hunting. On March 25 he wired his parents: "Probably going to work for Winant in research department of social securities." But that message did not please, because when he was home he had consulted them about several writing options, one a newspaper column for syndication, the other his erstwhile Finney novel. Will was out-of-town when Sallie received that telegram, so she wrote a note to him on the back and sent it on. The note voices her worry about her son and her distrust of Kathrine's judgment:

> Perhaps he feels he *must* go to work. If he wants to write maybe you better wire him he can have the 5 or six thousand needed for year, & that you are mailing 2000 today. Also urge he not go to work till he is entirely up to it.
>
> She [Kathrine] will be urging him into a job before he is up to it, if it comes into her head, and he should know he need not feel compelled to take a job just to live for a while—this is a suggestion to you. Feel he should know just what he can expect from us before he commits self to job.—SLW.[30]

Bill did have rental income from Grandma White's house at 923 Exchange, which he had inherited, and the duplex unit at 1003 Exchange, which was now his. And at this time Will apparently honored his promise of quarter ownership in the *Gazette* and started paying Bill that share of the profits.[31]

So Bill did not go to work for Winant; instead he tried his hand at a daily column, sending his copy to the *Gazette* for publication and taking samples around to editors. But most large daily newspapers in 1936 were conservative, and that did limit his potential market. From the Senate press gallery on April 27 he dashed off a note to his mother: "I wrote a couple of letters today trying to peddle my stuff—one to the Louisville *Courier-Journal* and the other to the New York *Post*. Both are liberal papers. I don't think the *Herald Tribune* would be interested—I'm too far to the left."[32] And he also told her he was having "a hell of a belly ache caused I think by listening to Senator Vandenberg

explain all afternoon how consistent he is." His "belly ache" was
a return of the psychosomatic intestinal upsets first occasioned
by his 1927 rotogravure scheme. In a letter on May 6 he wrote
his parents: "It may be that I'll have to knock off here and do
the novel. Although I don't want to. Between belly aches I'm
having a swell time. . . . But what I now plan to do is to start
for Boston this week end and see Dr. Fremont-Smith two or three
times next week and I think a week should see me through it."[33]

His initialed five-days-a-week column had started April 6 on
the editorial page of the *Gazette* under topical heads datelined
Washington. After a month he named it "A Washington Note-
book" and continued it in the *Gazette* until June 13, then starting
June 15 his father's syndicated convention coverage for the NANA
took over the editorial page. As in the past, father and son together
attended both national conventions, watching Landon capture
the Republican's dubious prize in Cleveland, Ohio, and Roosevelt
sweep to a second-term nomination in Philadelphia. After the
conventions Bill gave up his attempt at marketing a column and
returned somewhat reluctantly to his novel.[34]

From Boston on July 4 he wrote his parents that he had "combed
all possibilities for a job during the summer in Washington and
failed to find anything." So he and Kathrine sublet their Washington house for July and August and headed for New England.
He intended to get a room on the seashore and work there at
the book while Kathrine, her mother, and Esther Kane (his Aunt
Jessie's sister-in-law) shared a small summer cottage elsewhere. He
explained in that letter, "When I get stuck and confused and
perplexed Kathrine reacts very hard to it and is afraid she'll blow
up under it, and this in turn reacts on me and we're off in a whirl.
Both of us want to get the book written and both want to stay
out of a whirl so it's a question of getting us all settled where
there will be an irreducible minimum of whirling."[35] Then in the
late fall, after the novel was roughed out, Bill planned to work
for the *New York Herald Tribune*, where he had an open job offer
from publisher Ogden Reid. But after returning to Washington
at the end of August, discouraged because he was far from a
completed rough draft, he wrote his parents he thought he would
take the *Herald Tribune* job immediately. His father replied on

September 2 with a Western Union day letter: "Please and double please don't leave your house or at least take another job until you finish that book ready for printer. Out of sad experience . . . let me warn you that book once abandoned is ten times more difficult to finish."[36]

Bill took that advice, to stick with the book while staying in Washington. But toward the end of September he wrote that "our landlady leased our house out from under us"; they had to be out by October 1. Because Bill would most likely take a job in New York after he finished the novel, they decided to apartment hunt there, where they leased a floor in a brownstone on East Forty-ninth Street. "But," Bill continued, "it won't be ready until about the end of November."[37] Back in Washington they stored their furniture, sublet a friend's small apartment for six weeks, and established a routine. Bill continued plugging "away steadily at the book" and Kathrine advised absentee voters on behalf of the Women's Democratic Committee, after refusing its request for a press release.[38] But the move to New York was unsettling; their apartment was not ready as promised. By late November, though, they had settled in, with Bill back on the novel and happy about the defeat of Alf Landon in the elections.

That winter, through Kathrine's friendship with the journalist Ben Stolberg, Bill and she gravitated toward a circle of Trotskyite writers called the Chelsea Gang after the old Hotel Chelsea on Twenty-third Street near Seventh Avenue, where Stolberg and several other members lived. At cocktail parties there the Whites became acquainted with members of that group, such as the editor Suzanne La Follette, the critic Edmund ("Bunny") Wilson, and his future wife, the novelist Mary McCarthy.[39] More important, through that group Bill met and became a lifelong friend of the novelist John Dos Passos, whose work he had long admired and whose later political evolution to conservatism was much like his own. Kathrine and Katy Dos Passos were mutual friends with Helen Augur, an impassioned freelance journalist and biographer, and Sheila Hibben, food editor for the *New Yorker*.[40] Bill also joined the Players, a theatrically oriented social club at 16 Gramercy Park South, next to his father's favorite, the National

Arts Club. Actually, he and Kathrine socialized with a variety of people that first year in New York. For example, at a party Kathrine gave for his thirty-seventh birthday, they juggled three groups of guests. As he wrote his parents,

> We had on the left (Stalinist) Maurice Hindus, . . . Joris Ivens Duch (communist photographer who has just come back from Spain . . .) and Hope Hale, whose husband is—or was till recently Claud Cockburn, New York correspondent for the London Times who resigned to join the communist party and is now publishing a communist weekly in Madrid.
>
> Then to balance all these C. P. members (Stalinists) we had about an equal number of Trotskyites—Ben Stolberg, members of the Trotsky Defense Committee. . . .
>
> Then we invited—to keep them separate—a large preponderance of Capitalists—Art Tully [stockbroker, Harvard 1924] and Oliver LaFarge [novelist, Harvard 1924] and Mary Fraser of Time Mag and Dan Longwell of Life Mag and Dave Hulberd of Time and Frank Norris of Time and Bill Stroock [a lawyer] and his wife (I met him in Washington when he was Justice Cardozo's secretary).[41]

The younger Whites obviously enjoyed the social diversity of New York City. And Bill enjoyed teasing his father about such far-left friends, because Will would usually react humorously, at least for the record. In a letter to Alf Landon on April 21, 1936, for example, Will recounted his efforts to push Landon's presidential candidacy in Washington. In sounding out the opposition, he reported, "I talked before two or three groups of young New Deal radicals, newspapermen, Bill's friends, who think Bill and Kathrine are rich because they wash occasionally."[42] Sallie, however, was more liberal politically than her husband and less whimsical personally. Not a professional Republican, she sometimes marked the Democrat side of her ballot and even, through John Dos Passos, quietly contributed to the Loyalist cause in the Spanish Civil War. In Emporia, though, a public statement of sympathy for the Spanish Loyalists in 1938 got a young history instructor fired from Kansas State Teachers College.[43] So the teasing value of such a party list was lost on Sallie; her letters to son and daughter-in-law reveal a more pragmatic, more domestic mind than Will's, with fewer quizzical reactions.

The first winter in New York for the younger Whites was one of discontent, as Bill struggled with his novel and Kathrine with him. Using rewrite skills honed at *Time* magazine, she edited his rough drafts in an attempt to move him along; prone to exhilaration or depression when under pressure, he sometimes overreacted to her suggestions, which in turn triggered fretfulness on her part. And as the national economy plummeted again that winter, she worried about money and their reliance on his parents. As a result, so he reported, they would again end up in a "whirl." Early in February 1937 they consulted the psychiatrist Dr. Carl Binger, who accepted Kathrine as a patient and referred Bill to Dr. Sandor Rado. After some advisory correspondence with the elder Whites, Bill and wife went into analysis, with significant financial and moral support from home. Such family obligations were a way of life for all the Whites. Bill in turn cashed in several insurance policies that year to be able to help Kathrine's brother, Buddy, finish medical school.

By the end of March Bill had completed a fair copy of the novel. His father wired him congratulations and advice: "Overjoyed novel is done. Take your time tinkering. Instead of dallying with music teacher [the psychiatrists] why don't you and Kathrine take that money and go to Europe for six weeks or two months. Rest will do you more good than considering the caprices of your psychological intestines."[44] They were able to take that travel advice by late summer, but first Bill had to find a publisher and a job. With the novel in readable form, he interested the literary agent Bernice Baumgarten in it. She was an aggressive member of the well-established firm of Brandt and Brandt and at that time agent for John Dos Passos. Bill wrote his parents he was heartened by her reputation "as a hard-headed girl . . . with excellent literary judgment."[45] Bernice suggested a number of revisions, though, before targeting a publisher. But she began her campaign immediately by sending several excerpts off to magazines as short pieces of fiction.

Convinced Bill could become a good property, Bernice opposed his working for the *Herald Tribune* because, as he reported to his parents, "it would give me neither the leisure to write nor would it leave me any ideas to write about, because the day-to-day grind would leave me completely dry." Instead, she introduced Bill to the poet Russell Davenport, the new managing editor of *Fortune* magazine, who wanted to lift its style by hiring more "creative" writers at a thousand dollars a month, with the added inducement of three to six months off to work on their own stuff. Bill liked that feature, he wrote his parents, but better yet, "it's a job I get on my own merits—because of my ability as a writer as attested to by my own agent. Nobody is hiring me for my name or my father's name. Because on Fortune they don't sign names to articles. . . . And I'll be content to write any tripe Harry Luce wants and come to any fallacious conclusions which he desires, if I know that I have six months of the year in which to be myself and write my own slant on things."[46] Davenport hired him initially for three weeks in July as a freelance to rewrite a botched story for the next issue. Pleased with that work, he offered Bill a six-month trial slot starting October 1, which he accepted. Then the first week of August Bernice asked him to stop tinkering with the novel and let her show it to Viking Press, their first choice. She urged him to take a break and then, if necessary, return to the book fresh. Both his and Kathrine's analysts were to be on vacation that August and September. So Bill took his agent's and his father's earlier advice and used his July paycheck from *Fortune* to book tourist class tickets for Europe, sailing from New York on August 11 to return September 9.

That was a welcome holiday. He and Kathrine spent several days in London, a week in Paris to attend its 1937 International Exposition, then a final week in Saint-Jean-de-Luz, a small French sea resort near the northern border of Spain. There Bill ran into Claude Bowers, American ambassador to Spain, who was with Owen Wister, the novelist, and his son, whom Bill knew at Harvard. A staunch supporter of the Loyalists, Bill welcomed that chance to talk with Bowers and several others in his party about the Spanish Civil War. But, otherwise, Bill and Kathrine spent much of their time at Saint-Jean swimming or lying on the beach in the company of the younger Wister.

Back in New York in September Kathrine wrote her in-laws, "We had a beautiful trip." But while they were gone, she reported, their landlord had started a remodeling project on their brownstone and during the upheaval their apartment was ransacked and robbed. Furious, they broke their lease, and she went apartment hunting while Bill conferred with his agent and the editors at Viking Press about the novel. After several days of negotiation, Viking accepted it for spring publication and advanced him five hundred dollars. Kathrine soon found a triplex in another brownstone on East Fifty-fourth Street.[47] They moved there that October after Bill started his job at *Fortune*.

For the next six months he was one of Henry Luce's stable of writers for that chic business monthly. Before taking the job Bill checked with his friend John Chamberlain, who was an editor there from 1936 to 1938. Bill wrote his parents that John told him "in the average menstrual cycle of Fortune the first week or ten days are placid, and then the pace of work picks up and toward the end of the month you find you are working until midnight three or four nights in the final week."[48] The routine suited Bill, who found in it time to give his novel a final revision. But he did not find writing anonymously in harness as easy a pull as he first thought. He was especially bothered by the imperiously intrusive second Mrs. Henry Luce (née Clare Boothe) when he worked on a "café society" article for the December issue. Calling her a "perfume counter queen," he described her interference to his father: "The last three days she broke loose in the story like a wild brahmin cow, hooking metaphors out of sentences right and left, and inserting in our Café Society list five or six names of pals of hers, including Condé Nast and a couple of other guys she used to room with."[49] Much later, after Bill had established himself as a best-selling author and moderate conservative and she was a two-term congresswoman, they became good friends.

He also had trouble writing to order. Without great enthusiasm he wrote a story on the condom industry for the February issue.[50] Assigned next to do a "beauty parlor" study of Alfred P. Sloan, Jr., of General Motors, a staunch Liberty Leaguer, he could not

capture an adequate tone of subdued adulation, so he complained
to his parents, and had to hand the story over to another for a
complete rewrite. He believed he worked best with industrial
analysis, but Davenport did not agree. Thus Bill continued to
work on assignments in which he had little interest, with the result,
he wrote his parents April 6, that "last Wednesday I was canned
from Fortune. . . . They didn't like my stories, they wouldn't take
my suggestions as to the kind of stories I could do for them, and
. . . they told me gently but firmly, that we'd better call my six-
month trial a failure."[51]

For Bill that loss was greatly tempered by the publication on
April 1 of his novel *What People Said*. Viking Press had sent
advance copies out in March and reported an enthusiastic initial
reception from booksellers and potential reviewers. Its aggressive
promotion, plus Bill's many connections, soon brought widespread
reviews. To his nervous relief those were generally positive, and
to his pleased surprise *Time*, the *Saturday Review of Literature*, and
the Sunday book sections of the *New York Times* and the *Herald
Tribune* gave him top billing. Henry Canby reviewed it in the April
newsletter of the Book-of-the-Month Club, which offered it as
a substitute for that month's selection, as it would for seven of
Bill's thirteen books. His father vigorously promoted it in Kansas.
And to keep from competing directly with his son he held off
publication of his own long-awaited scholarly biography of Calvin
Coolidge, *A Puritan in Babylon*, until November. Because advance
orders for the novel came to nearly 10,000 copies, Marshall Best,
Bill's editor at Viking, optimistically predicted early in April a
year's sales of 40,000 to 50,000. With royalties at $400 per 1,000
Bill was euphoric.

But *What People Said* did not make national best-seller lists,
though initially it sold well regionally, being first in fiction for
several months in Kansas City. Final sales figures were a decided
disappointment for Bill, about seventeen thousand copies—good
for a first novel, but far fewer than had been expected. And after
the first spate of reviews little more was said about it, though
Harold Strauss in the *New York Times Book Review* had asserted
that W. L. White "stood squarely in the great American tradition
of realism, shoulder to shoulder with Frank Norris, Dreiser and

Lewis."[52] By contrast, within a month after its November publication his father's book about Coolidge was in a fifth printing,
with historian Charles Beard rating it as one of the most interesting
histories of the decade.

The reason why *What People Said* did not meet its publisher's
sales forecast was that as a work of fiction it did not sufficiently
engage the reader's imagination. For it was Bill's attempt, in the
guise of a 1930s social problem novel, to explain the white-collar
criminal actions of Warren and Ronald Finney in depression-
scarred Kansas, counterpoised against the sordid career of a local
petty crook he knew, the Union School bully Tracey Brown. In
a letter much later to Truman Capote praising *In Cold Blood*, Bill
alluded to his own first book as similarly based on actual events:

> I started out to write a fictional account suggested by a criminal
> case which I knew very well in my home state, but I immediately
> found that I was having difficulty making fiction out of it. So,
> after scratching my head for a couple of weeks, I finally decided
> to write a first draft of the thing, just as it happened, on which
> I would base the fictionalized second and final draft.
>
> But the trouble was, that when I tried to make it into fiction,
> I discovered that anything which was not true somehow rang
> hollow, and the truth was far more interesting than anything
> I could invent. In the end, I contented myself with only changing
> the names.[53]

A portion of that first draft exists and is indeed a dramatized
journal of those 1933 events with real names. In fact, subsequent
name changes and stylistic editing of that portion are in Kathrine's
hand. From other extant manuscript portions it is clear that Bill
did significantly revise the Tracey Brown (Buck Warn) story,
changing both events and characterizations to avoid libel suits.[54]
But the Finney (Norssex) main plot is a straightforward, sensitive
job of reportage.

Most of the events of *What People Said* are seen through the
eyes of Junior Carrough, the Oxford-educated, mild-mannered
son of Charles Addington Carrough, widely respected Progressive
Republican editor of the *Athena Sun*, the small-town "Oklarado"
daily. A reluctant observer and minor participant, Junior reports

how he and the townspeople react to the unfolding events of a major statewide bank-bond scandal that involves close friends of the elder Carroughs, Charles and Fran (Will and Sallie White) and the younger, Junior and Liz (Bill and Kathrine). Those friends are Isaac and Ida Norssex (Warren and Mabel Finney), Lee and Henny Norssex (Ronald and Winifred Finney), and Willie and Babs Tatlock (Roland and Betty Boynton). The novel begins with Junior's return from two years as a Rhodes Scholar at Oxford, which have profoundly but quietly changed his view of the town and its people. His thoughts about that change bring a flashback to 1912 when Isaac Norssex moved his family to Athena (Emporia) from nearby Elm Valley, after he bought the local power and light company.

Junior then traces the development of Isaac and Ida Norssex's friendship with his parents and the Norssexes' subsequent rise to local civic and business leadership. In doing so he explains the fellowship between him and their son Lee, while both families spent their summers at Rusty Gun Lake in the Colorado Rockies. He also traces the history of easygoing Willie Tatlock, orphaned son of a former employee whom the Carroughs virtually adopt. Uncle Charles sends Willie to the state university and on through law school, then when he returns from the war, helps him establish a practice in town and run successfully for public office. Another relationship Junior narrates, but uncomfortably, is that between him and the school bully, Buck Warn (Tracey Brown), son of a railroad section foreman. After a year in reform school, Buck joins the navy and returns from the war a genuine hero. He marries a local girl but drifts from job to job and town to town for years until hard times force him home to insist on Junior's polite but hesitant help. Buck's story underscores the main plot at a lower social level, as his search for acceptance and easy money puts him behind the wheel of a bootlegger's Buick and ends with a state trooper's bullet through his chest.

The main story, of course, literally follows that of the Finney bank-bond scandal, with about equal focus on Isaac's and Lee's actions and motives, with ancillary attention to Willie's naive involvement. Part of that plot concerns Jake Tranforse (Alf Landon), the governor, as he carefully extricates himself from the political quagmire of the scandal. The theme of the novel is Junior's need to understand why the principals act as they do. Implicitly throughout, he poses to himself and his readers questions of motive, but the answers do not add up to simplistic exempla. Instead, true to the social-problem genre, Bill conveys ambivalent indictments of what he views as an essentially materialistic culture in its social, political and economic reward systems. Following its real-life prototype, the novel concludes with Lee in the penitentiary for twice the term he expected, with Willie unfairly impeached, with Isaac resolutely committing suicide assisted by his wife, Ida, and with the people of Athena crassly gossiping about the denouement.

In adhering so literally to the facts of the bond scandal and to their sequence, Bill straitjacketed his imaginative prerogative to reorganize events. Yet the reviewer in *Christian Century* praised *What People Said* for just that actuality: "Considered for what it is, the book is magnificent reporting. It reveals the facts of life in a small prairie city, as that life is really lived."[55] But the reviewer for the *Springfield* [Massachusetts] *Republican* regretted that "Mr. White did not organize and present his excellent material with greater regard to effective literary standards. . . . There is too much lost motion in his—prevailingly formless—method."[56] The court of time has sustained the latter opinion. The book is an interesting period piece of fictionalized sociological analysis, but it does not captivate readers, for too many characters and too much case history diffuse our attention. That said, as a roman à clef it did give many Kansans several months of fun comparing personal indexes, but that of course was not Bill's reason for writing a 614-page novel.

Instead, in that book Bill tried to combine John Dos Passos's tone of panoramic, clinical objectivity with Ernest Hemingway's technique of laconic dialogue, in a minimally sketched dramatic context, to satirize middle-class midwestern mores. But because of that tone and structure we do not get sufficiently inside the characters. Strauss in a caveat to his favorable *Times* review observed that Bill's novel "is cold and dry and underwritten; the suspense of its underlying narrative, which could have been made really exciting, is weakened by the indirection of its method."[57]

The narrator creates much of that problem; he is an ill-disguised W. L. White, a somewhat bemused, mildly superior, essentially passive observer, a subservient "junior." By selection and implication he quietly indicts human nature, small-town provincialism, and economic conditions as reasons for the foibles of the principal characters. But in that persona he is unable to grab his reader by the lapels and pull him into the story to "experience" the events, which is the chief rhetorical failure of this historical report qua novel.

Buoyed up by the reviews and initial sales of *What People Said*, and rendered more introspective by his ongoing "music lessons," Bill did not react so emotionally to his being fired from *Fortune* magazine as he had from the *Washington Post*. Instead, in a letter to his father, he reasoned out what sort of writing job he could realistically work at best: "I've been thinking down to a pretty fine sharp point along these lines; the place which will be the best for me in the long pull, is where I can write about what I know best and am most interested in under my own signature. . . . I think experience can teach me something here, and it is this—that when I've tried to do someone else's act, it's fizzled, and when I've sat down and thought it out for myself and sweated it out alone, it's clicked. So I think I'm a lonely-sweater—just on the basis of the record.[58] Realizing that, and more confident in himself now as a writer, he decided to follow his agent's advice to freelance the magazine market. So he set up an office address with another freelance writer on East Forty-fifth Street and tried his hand at several magazine short stories.

Earlier that spring he and Kathrine happened across an abandoned 103-acre farm near Frenchtown, New Jersey, across the Delaware River from picturesque Bucks County, Pennsylvania. Known as the "old Johnson place," its eighteenth-century, ten-room house was just off the Frenchtown-Flemington Road, about a hundred yards beyond and above a cascading, graveled stream. Though sound, the farm house had no electricity, no functioning well, no plumbing, was overgrown with brush and littered with mud-dauber nests and raccoon scat. Undaunted by its lack of amenities and the debris, Bill and Kathrine were enthralled with its potential as a weekend retreat. For it was "about an hour and

45 minutes from New York by car and about an hour by train," Bill informed his father. So in June they bought it, putting up $2,100 cash and assuming a $1,400 mortgage. They then took out a federal housing loan to bring in electricity, drill a well, and put in plumbing. Delighted to take a break from the hustle of the city, they spent most of their weekends that summer and fall in overalls proudly cleaning out, painting, and supervising basic repairs to the house.[59] For twenty years they were to own that farm, using it as a quick escape from the city.

But in 1938 Bill could not long escape his need to earn a living, because that purchase and a backlog of psychiatrists' fees absorbed what he had earned from his novel. Bernice had no luck placing the several pieces of short fiction he had written, so he asked his parents to stake him another year in New York, to which they quickly agreed, and he turned to writing magazine features, a genre with which he was in truth more comfortable. Fall and winter 1938–39 his agent did place two lead articles with *Scribner's*, long sketches of two figures important to the shaping of current public opinion: Pare Lorentz, the documentary filmmaker, and Joseph Connolly, director of the Hearst news empire. She also placed commentary pieces with several other well-established magazines.

Concerned about expenses late the summer of 1938, Kathrine tried to sublet their New York apartment for that winter and to find instead a smaller, less costly place, but that did not work because times had become even tougher. According to Michael Emery and Edwin Emery in their standard history of American journalism, the years 1937, 1938, and 1939 were "the blackest years in the history of American newspapers," with "one-third of salaried employees in the newspaper industry" losing their jobs.[60] No wonder Kathrine continued to worry about Bill's carelessness about finances and his easy reliance on his parents. Unhappy about that pattern of financial dependency and feeling a need to reaffirm her own self-worth, she asked friends at *Time* magazine if she could return as a part-time backup researcher. They agreed and over the next two years she filled in as an editorial assistant at *Time* and *Life* when and where needed. The occasional, part-time job helped her "get my bearings," she later told her in-laws, and gave her a sense of security and purpose during a most difficult period, because Bill as a syndicated columnist and European war correspondent would be out of the city or out of the country many of those months. Yet professionally and personally he depended during that time on her continued presence in New York.[61]

Bill soon recognized his work as a freelance was uncertain at best. In September 1938 he turned down an offer to be director of the Federal Writers Project in New York City at one hundred dollars a week because he decided he could do as well on his own. But he had to hustle. In a November 28 letter to his parents he wrote: "This magazine stuff keeps me working un-evenly—hard at times, but each week—and even each day—there is considerable slack. And I've been thinking hard of utilizing it by trying to develop a tri-weekly newspaper column for eventual syndication which would run parallel with my magazine stuff. Would you mind my trying it out in the Gazette to see how it goes?"[62] Early in March and later in April 1939 his father was twice back East, the second time to attend to duties as president that year of the American Society of Newspaper Editors. Apparently, he and Bill talked over that syndication project then, and Will agreed his son could again use the Gazette as a springboard. On Monday, May 8, 1939, two days after Will returned home, Bill's commentary headed "Take a Look" first appeared on the Gazette's editorial page. For two weeks Bill experimented with format and frequency, mailing copy from New York, then starting Monday, May 29, he sent it daily through July 7. He worked hard on those commentaries because he had agreed with Charles Lounsbury of the Des Moines Register-Tribune Syndicate to offer the column free that month to subscribers to see if it would sell.

Determined to place his column this time, Bill wrote his parents on May 31 to ask both for their advice: "I'd like more criticism on the column from both of you, and more detailed. What columns are readable and what ones are dull?"[63] Then in a letter to his parents on June 5 Bill reported receiving a note from Lounsbury "quite unexpectedly because the trial month has only been going two weeks—in which he says: '. . . usually I don't care much about superlatives, but I do want to say that I think the stuff has been swell.'" Bill went on to comment that "for about 4 years I've been trying to find one kind of vehicle for my writing which would make me self-supporting on a decent income. . . . Now if . . . it looks as though it might turn out to be this column, I think I ought to nurse the project along in its infancy."[64] And he wondered if the column would be more likely to sell under its New York dateline, which would mean scrapping plans for his return to Emporia that summer to oversee the *Gazette* while his parents vacationed for a couple of months in Colorado. However, the *Register–Tribune* Syndicate could not sell "Take a Look" during that month, its New York origin notwithstanding. By July 1 Bill was in Emporia and after a week had dropped the column.

He resumed it in the *Gazette* on Wednesday, July 26, with an Emporia dateline and from a clearly midwestern perspective. For he had secured a New York newspaper base, with his views from Kansas as the gambit. His opportunity came when his father's longtime close friend the columnist Franklin P. Adams (F. P. A.) took his August vacation from "The Conning Tower," now carried by the *New York Post*, and suggested to his feature editor, Ted Thackrey, that he use Bill's "Take a Look" as temporary replacement. A kindly man, Adams did not forget the son of his old friend when he saw a chance to give him a leg up. Elated, Bill wrote his mother in Colorado, July 22: "My column starts in the New York Post August 1. . . . I don't know what they will pay me and I don't care because it will get attention from the other New York editors."[65]

Another break came when the trade weekly *Editor and Publisher* reported the vacation replacement in a paragraph on August 19. Though wrong in details, the notice did suggest the marketing angle Bill wanted to give his column, that it presented the New York views of a Kansas transplant with roots still embedded in the Midwest. For according to the trade weekly, "It's common for a small town newspaper to publish a column written in New York, but the New York *Post* is reversing the order and is printing daily a column written in Emporia, Kan. [by] W. L. White, of New York."[66] When F. P. A. resumed his column Friday, September 1, the *Post* announced that W. L. White would continue to contribute "an occasional column."[67]

September 1, 1939, Germany invaded Poland. During August Bill's column under its Emporia dateline interested a wide audience

because he provided in those anxious days a liberal internation-
alist's view from America's heartland, the stronghold of isolationism. For example, in his August 25 column, the day after Hitler
and Stalin announced their signing of a nonaggression agreement,
Bill invited his readers to "walk down the main street with me
and watch the war fever rise in a midwestern town as Hitler
mobilizes. Before the Russo-German pact most of them were saying
we should stay out. Some of them still say this." Bill then reported
eighteen interviews of people on the street and concluded: "More
think we should get in either now or soon. Fewer believe we can
or should stay out."

Events moved swiftly. On September 3 Britain and France
declared war on Germany, and the debate over America's future
role waxed hotter. Ten hours after that declaration a German U
boat without warning torpedoed the British passenger liner
Athenia. A faculty member from the teachers college in Emporia,
Irene DuMont (Mrs. Charles Hendricks), was rescued from the
sinking ship, and several other faculty and students soon afterward
returned from England under blackout conditions on the British
liner *Aquitania*. So the war immediately became personal for Bill's
townspeople.[68] The *Register-Tribune* Syndicate quickly reacted to
the popularity of Bill's commentary from small-town Midwest,
now authenticated by appearance in a major New York daily, and
began another campaign to line up subscribers. On Monday,
September 11, "Take a Look" reappeared in the *Post*, then
continued on a mostly five-day basis.

During that month American interest in the war intensified.
On September 21 President Roosevelt called for repeal of the 1935
Neutrality Act, which embargoed the sale of arms and ammunition
to nations at war, and asked that it be replaced by a cash and
carry policy. Five days later Clark Eichelberger, New York–based
director of the Union for Concerted Peace Efforts, phoned William
Allen White in Emporia to ask him to head the ad hoc Non-
Partisan Committee for Peace through Revision of the Neutrality
Law. Secretary of State Cordell Hull had recommended the elder
White because he was a widely respected midwestern liberal
Republican and an adept publicist. Reluctant at first to take on
that task at age seventy-one, after two days of indecision Will was

persuaded by New York friends of his importance to the committee and agreed to head it. Undoubtedly, his son, convinced that American intervention would eventually be necessary, added his voice to theirs. Though he was still in Emporia, Bill already planned to sail to Europe to report at firsthand what "the common people in the country districts of war-torn Europe think," according to later publicity releases.[69] He wanted to capitalize in his column on his topical appeal as an unusually worldly American small-town Farm Belt voice.

To help his son, the elder White wrote his friend John Wheeler of the NANA, Will's own syndicate of many years' standing, to interest him in distributing Bill's column airmailed from Europe. Wheeler wrote back expressing mild interest, but by then the *Register–Tribune* Syndicate had contracted to back Bill's European wanderings as its "roving reporter columnist" and by the middle of October had picked up about twenty-five tentative subscribers for him, including eight large-city dailies. Will then wrote Wheeler to report that agreement and thank him for his interest.[70] But Will's involvement in his son's project did not stop with soliciting syndicate support. On October 3 he wrote Cordell Hull, secretary of state, to ask that he expedite Bill's passport application, delayed by red tape, and furnish letters of introduction to "whoever is in charge of the embassies in London, Berlin, Rome and Paris and of the Legations in Switzerland and Holland."[71] He also wrote Sir Frederic Whyte, head of the British Ministry of Information, to ask that he intervene to waive a war-imposed visa restriction and allow Bill to travel to England after stopping in Germany.[72]

By the end of the second week of October the Whites and their wives were in New York City, with Bill preparing for departure and Will hard at work on his committee's public relations blitz. Bill arranged with Ted Thackrey of the *Post* that Kathrine, who was to remain in New York, would receive and edit his dispatches and that Thackrey would act as liaison with the managing editor of the *Register–Tribune* Syndicate, Henry Martin, in Des Moines.[73] On Tuesday, October 17, Bill left New York for Naples on the SS *Rex*, a nearly empty Italian passenger liner, with his wife and parents seeing him off. His mother reported that leave-taking for the *Gazette* and commented: "It's all a new venture but it's in

the hands of a skillful and experienced syndicate. If Bill can get
his part of it through to New York, they attend to everything else.
But the hazard of war cannot be forecast. . . . Events and luck
alone will guide the adventure after Italy."[74]

Bill had written enough copy in advance to continue his column,
as carried in the *Gazette* from syndicate boilerplate, through
October 28, datelined New York. After a ten-day hiatus the *Gazette*
resumed it dated "Aboard SS Rex, Oct. 18 (By Airmail)" and
continued carrying it with sundry datelines on a nearly daily basis,
except when it was delayed by censorship or by wartime disruption
of the mails or by travel, until Bill dropped it on September 30,
1940. The files of the *Gazette* furnish the most complete and
accessible run. After he returned, ill and depressed, from Europe
in the middle of May 1940, the number of newspapers carrying
the column had fallen from a one-time high of over fifty to less
than half that, and by the end of September to only several, though
the *Post* carried it regularly as a column through August and
occasionally in September as a special.[75] Thus all references here
to "Take a Look" are to the *Gazette*.

From Naples he dated his first dispatch October 27. The next
day he was in Rome, where he stayed nearly two weeks, then
caught an overnight express train to Berlin, arriving there on
November 8 and checking into the Hotel Bristol, where he roomed
with fellow correspondent Joseph C. Harsch.[76] In Italy, true to
his announced intention, he wrote about impressions picked up
from the general civilian population, from anonymous hotel guests,
other journalists, Italian businessmen, fellow train passengers—
whomever he could strike up a conversation with. But he had
to send his material to New York by airmail because cable
permission was difficult to obtain and rates were prohibitively
expensive. As a result the syndicate almost immediately dropped
the date from his dateline, retaining only the place, to allow
Kathrine more freedom to cut and extend the column to give it
continuity. And she soon found that necessary because in Berlin
Bill ran into censorship and mail restriction problems, which
delayed his dispatches.

To compound her difficulties German officials would not grant
him cable privileges for several weeks, though he presented valid

press credentials. On November 14, for example, he wrote Kathrine: "Have no idea what you or my family or the newspapers are doing or if my stuff is getting through. It is absolutely forbidden here for foreigners to wire out any kind of a message, which is the reason I haven't been able to let you know I was finally in Germany."[77] At last, on November 25, he received a three-week-old cable from Kathrine forwarded from Rome, and that day he finally got permission to send cables, but only for brief press messages to the *New York Post*. Nevertheless, he had continued mailing his impressions of the European situation as perceived by the average German, written with careful irony to get as much past the censors as possible.

At the end of November, under the pretense of greater efficiency, the Nazis started requiring that press commentary in English be translated into German for censorship then retranslated, typed, and mailed by the German Propaganda Ministry in its own envelopes. Kathrine received nothing for a while; then nine columns arrived in a bunch in sometimes oddly simplistic prose. Yet even under those conditions Bill managed irony. At the end of one of those columns, in which he reported the tearful tale of a Polish Jew whose relatives had been separated and sent to labor camps, he observed that "the German viewpoint . . . is that Jews are a cunning people who lie about Germany to play on the maudlin sympathies of the weak-minded liberal democracies. The Germans themselves are a strong people who never cry, except about the unbearable humiliation inflicted on them by the Versailles Treaty. As a weak-minded democratic liberal I used to cry about these humiliations myself, but now since I am getting the viewpoint of new Germany I also am getting strong, so I do not cry about them any more."[78] Once out of Germany his tone became unambiguous. When he reached Stockholm, he wrote that the Swedes

> disdain to use the fact that they are blond as the basis for a cheap racket. . . . [They] believe, as we do, that race is important only if it can produce a large number of intelligent, kindly, hard-working, cooperative, cheerful and sensible individuals. . . . And after seeing the Swedes, I have become very tired of hearing the Germans bellyache around about how Germany has been

robbed and Germany has been kept down and Germany is oppressed, so, therefore, Germany must go out and rob and keep down and oppress a lot of other people.[79]

In Berlin Bill ran into William L. Shirer, who was broadcasting from there for the Columbia Broadcasting System (CBS) radio network, and they quickly became friends. Shirer's wife and baby daughter were living in Geneva, where his wife, an Austrian citizen, was less vulnerable. Shirer arranged for Bill to fill in for him for a week starting Monday, November 27, while he visited his family. White wrote his own separate commentary for CBS, which he had to clear with German censors in advance of broadcast, but he got by with enough Kansas understatement to convey his distaste for the Nazis. That, and a good radio delivery, impressed Paul White, a fellow Kansan who was news director for CBS in New York.

Thursday, November 30, the Soviet Union invaded Finland. Shirer returned to Berlin that weekend, and Bill left Monday, December 4, for Helsinki to cover that war for his newspaper syndicate, with Kathrine fretting in New York about mail delays and no backlog. On Wednesday, December 6, Shirer telegraphed Bill in Stockholm, at Paul White's request, asking him to cover Finland for CBS. Bill agreed because it gave him a much-needed communication link with New York. As Shirer recalled in his memoir *Twentieth Century Journey*, "He proved a happy choice. His broadcasts, especially from the front, where the outmanned and outgunned Finns were stopping the Russians cold, were very moving, and one on Christmas . . . from the frozen, snow-covered Finnish trenches was memorable."[80]

That was his Christmas Eve broadcast, "The Last Christmas Tree," which won the National Headliner's Club award for the best European broadcast of the year—the radio equivalent of a Pulitzer Prize. Robert Sherwood, the playwright and a speech writer and confidant of FDR's, wrote Bill's father on December 29: "[I have] been listening to your son's voice as often as I could—and have read his remarkable reports every day in the Post. . . . [His] broadcast description of Christmas in an advanced post of the Mannerheim line was a superb piece of composition. . . . —he really is visualizing the imponderables, the deep essentials, and not bothering with the spot news."[81] In fact, that broadcast was an important catalyst for Sherwood, who had been stewing all fall about the future of Europe, because Bill's commentary inspired him to write the Pulitzer Prize–winning drama "There Shall Be No Night," a passionate statement about Finland's brave but doomed resistance. For unlike the prelude Spanish Civil War, the political and moral issues of the Russo-Finnish fight quickly became clear to most Americans, who from its start sympathized with the Finns.

Throughout 1939 the CBS radio roundtable "Today in Europe," anchored by Elmer Davis or Paul White in New York, had attracted a wide national audience, and Bill's sympathetic, sometimes exciting broadcasts from Finland increased it. Soon after arriving in Finland, for example, he reported a routine Russian air bombardment of a small town near the front, then added:

> The foregoing words were written before I got to the studio. But I think the events of the last few minutes deserve a little comment. We drove half the night to get to this microphone, arriving long after midnight in bitter zero weather with half-frozen hands and feet, driving through darkened streets looking for the place where this broadcast was scheduled. Suddenly there was a tremendous bang, and we didn't have to be told what that was. We jumped out of the car, caught the acrid smell of powder smoke, and discovered that we were exactly in front of the building we were hunting for. We found the studio with all lights out and the staff huddled in the downstairs corridor with a couple of soldiers with fixed bayonets guarding the door. No, they said, this time it is not bombs—the Russians are shelling this place with long-range heavy artillery. Then there was another bang, and we hurried upstairs by the light of our electric flash lamps, where I am writing these last lines. So if this broadcast concludes with a loud crash, you will know that the Bolsheviks have scored a direct hit.[82]

Bill's radio reports from Finland became widely popular, earning him a featured spot January 6 in the article "The Dials of War" in the magazine *Cue*.[83] That was nearly a year before Edward R. Murrow's now better-remembered CBS broadcasts went out under air bombardment in London.

Meanwhile Bill's newspaper column lagged more than six weeks behind his movements. In Finland he broadcast with a censor by his side, and his column too was subject to review. Unlike in Germany, though, once he got his dispatches cleared, he posted them himself from Helsinki. But for over a month his airmailed dispatches somehow did not get through, and Kathrine ran out of copy on January 12 with his last posting from Stockholm, just before he flew to Finland. Bill sent duplicates by ordinary mail, but his syndicate had to suspend "Take a Look" for a week until they arrived. With Bill's voice on CBS usually coming in clear over an improvised system of phone lines and short-wave hookups, his syndicate was embarrassed by the delay. In December Kathrine had written her father-in-law that "Ted [Thackrey] says that if Bill gets to missing but stays on the air the papers will squawk that he's sold out to radio."[84] Will was proud of his son's broadcasts and published notices of them in the *Gazette*, but as an old-time print journalist he had little regard for radio spot news, though he recognized the appeal of the new medium. On October 15 he had himself given a nationwide speech over CBS on revision of the neutrality law, and his committee had distributed a recording of it to all unaffiliated stations.

Throughout the 1930s the powerful American Newspaper Publisher's Association had fought a rearguard action against radio news. The Associated Press, for example, refused to sell its wire service to CBS or the National Broadcasting Company (NBC) until 1940. *Editor and Publisher* in its January 13, 1940, issue analyzed news coverage of the Finnish front and named all American reporters there, except Bill for CBS and Warren Irwin for NBC.[85] And in January 1939 several local businessmen had put radio station KTSW, a Mutual Broadcasting System affiliate, on the air in Emporia, a form of competition the editor of the *Gazette* had quietly tried to block.[86] Will was concerned that Bill's newspaper column, carried by major dailies across the country, would lose customers as a result of his availability on radio. Kathrine, however, wrote her father-in-law that Bill's broadcasts "were making the sale of his column much easier—and moreover [CBS] enables him to get places that he couldn't get to or afford to get to otherwise. Everyone wants him to keep it and I am sure

his radio audience is much the greatest in the country. He's
running close to [H. V.] Kaltenborn at his height."[87]

Bill stayed in Finland nearly two months, not leaving until just
before the Soviets launched their massive final attack the first week
of February, though CBS urged him to get out sooner.[88] He had
written his first column in Helsinki on December 11, but not until
January 19, 1940, were subscribing newspapers able to start his
Finnish columns, thirty-two of which were datelined from Helsinki
or Viipuri, sixteen from "Somewhere in Finland." In the latter
he reported his visits under extreme winter conditions to the two
main fronts, that at the Mannerheim line and that above the
Arctic Circle. At both fronts he came under Russian fire. "And
this," he wrote,

> although I'm a bit ashamed to write it, is the most fun of all,
> provided of course that you do not get killed or hurt, or that
> no one you know does, or that it does not come so often that
> your nerves go to pieces, and you cringe inside a little when
> you hear one even a long way off.
>
> But leaving all these out, the danger in being shelled, or in
> dodging a belt full of machine gun bullets, is like the most
> exciting moment in the best ball game that you have ever
> watched, or like a very tense moment in a card game.
>
> Because, as in cards, keeping alive in war requires not only
> plenty of skill but also some luck.[89]

As he observed in his next column, much like Ernie Pyle later,
"Around wars . . . you get to be a fatalist and are content to make
the best of the world as you find it."[90] That sort of honesty, early
in 1940, made up part of Bill's appeal.

But his Finnish reports ran well behind events because of airmail
delays. In late February the Scandinavian countries refused passage
to a combined British-French expeditionary force meant to relieve
the overwhelmed Finns. Starving, with nearly 60 percent of its
army dead or wounded, Finland could not counter the new
Russian offensive and sued for peace. March 12 it formally accepted
Russia's terms. But Bill's newspaper commentary written before
he left Finland did not conclude until March 15.

From Helsinki Bill went first to Stockholm, then by night train to Oslo, where he ended his February 5 broadcast with the somber comment: "Tomorrow night I will bring you more about Norway and these other little Scandinavian democracies who are still sitting on the fence just as the now-extinct American wild pigeon used to sit there, as the hunter walked along with his club and bag. Of course America is also a democracy sitting on the fence, but it's a long fence, we're at the very end of it, and so our turn won't come soon."[91] From Oslo he took a ferry to Copenhagen to try to get back into Germany, which after a week rejected his visa application. Shirer in a 1942 blurb about Bill for the Book-of-the-Month Club wrote: "The Nazis at that time did not officially like what White said about the Finns and Russians, and one day I was told he could not come back to Germany, nor even pass through on his way home—a Verbot for which I envied him."[92] While in Copenhagen, knowing he would be under tight censorship if allowed back into Germany, Bill wrote a series of ten columns about the Russo-German pact to give Kathrine a much-needed backlog. In retrospect she thought that that series, which she started on March 18, received more attention than any of his other copy from Europe.[93]

Unable to return to Germany and frustrated by his isolation in Denmark and the general stalemate throughout Europe that winter, dubbed the "Phony War" by the isolationist United States senator William E. Borah, Bill left Copenhagen for Amsterdam on February 14. Believing he had now established his column and working as but a stringer for CBS, he was thinking of returning home. He was also bothered by Paul White's continued attempts to temper his open criticism of Nazi Germany; for example, White had wired him in Copenhagen in cable shorthand: "Strongly recommend against any publicity German order. Also your unmentioning when next you broadcast as twould tend make suspect future broadcasts stories exother belligerents."[94] Ignoring the implications of that advice, Bill made CBS broadcasts from Amsterdam on February 20 and 21 that were critical of German war aims, then Thursday, February 22, left for London.

There he received the following telegram from his father: "Syndicate growing expect fifty papers soon Desmoines anxious you stay long as possible. We agree."[95] Though he filled in a week on CBS for Edward R. Murrow from February 26 to March 1, while Murrow recovered from a bout with pneumonia, Bill felt increasingly uncomfortable in England because of the complacency of many upper-class Britons toward the Nazis and the weakness of Neville Chamberlain's continuing leadership.[96] "Take a Look" was still running six weeks behind his movements, with the first column from England not appearing until April 11. He was in that country for several weeks, but the syndicate sent out only seven pieces datelined London, each politely critical. Possibly, Kathrine held back the more splenetic when she ran them, for the British, with Winston Churchill then in the Cabinet, had just responded to Adolf Hitler's April 9 invasion of Norway with the Home Fleet and a small expeditionary force.

Sometime in the second week of March Bill left London for Amsterdam and then Paris, where he substituted several days for Eric Sevareid on "Today in Europe." But by March 21 he had definitely decided to return to New York because his father cabled him as follows: "Syndicate most unhappy about your return. We think it tragic mistake. Syndicate selling you now in fifties running close to [Eleanor Roosevelt's] My Day acclaim wide and significant. Syndicate feels all it has spent building you up would be lost if you return. Martin asked me to beg of you to stay and go to Balkans."[97] His father had two reasons for sending that cable. First he had been told by Cordell Hull that the State Department believed the next war would be a Russian invasion of Romania. The *Register-Tribune* Syndicate had been promoting Bill as its roving correspondent who was writing "a brand new idea in columns," an interpretation of the common people of Europe "in terms we Americans understand and believe."[98] Believing the rapid success of Bill's column was due in large part to that European angle, especially his coverage of the Finnish war, Will had tipped Henry Martin about Hull's prognosis. Both agreed Bill should head to Romania for a possible scoop.

Will's second and more important reason was private. Sometime in 1939 Will corresponded with Kathrine's psychiatrist, Dr. Binger, who suggested her reports about Bill were not trustworthy. She believed Bill in financial difficulties overseas and under increasing emotional distress. While in New York City that winter, Will made an appointment with Dr. Gerald Jamieson, another well-reputed psychiatrist, to consult him about Kathrine's view of Bill and Bill's own emotional health. Jamieson in turn conferred with Dr. Binger and Bill's former psychiatrist Dr. Rado, then met with both Will and Kathrine. Will came away from that interview more suspicious than ever of Kathrine's mental integrity. He inferred from Dr. Jamieson's rather guarded advice that what Bill really needed was to stick with a project until he had achieved undeniable success, in order to bolster an ego battered by his father's fame. Even a writer for the *Kansas City Star* observed at the time: "Young Bill White, whether he would admit it or not, has chafed at the position of being Young Bill to Old Bill, particularly in that cozy way where he would be accepted as happy to bask in a handsomely won glory. Indeed, he has not been happy."[99] So Will with the best of intentions, from his perspective, ignored Kathrine's view that Bill should come home and urged his son to stay in Europe to establish more firmly his career as a newspaper columnist.

Unfortunately, what Bill had not yet told his father was that Paul White of CBS had asked him to return to New York by April 3 to spell Elmer Davis as anchor for "Today in Europe." CBS offered to pay his expenses back from Paris plus one hundred dollars a week and to send him on a lecture tour to every city where it had a big affiliate. Bill happily accepted, but only if the network cleared the offer with his syndicate. Apparently, Thackrey of the *New York Post* readily agreed but not Lounsbury or Martin in Des Moines, and Bill was actually under contract to them. Kathrine did not know enough about the offer to convince her in-laws of its validity and worth.

Assuming his syndicate had agreed with CBS, Bill caught the American liner *Washington* at Genoa for New York. On board ship, en route in the Mediterranean, he received a wireless message from Martin that it was "imperative" he "get off the boat and go to the Balkans." When the *Washington* anchored for unofficial but required clearance at Gibraltar, Cordell Hull, at the elder White's urging, had arranged for British officials to escort Bill off the ship. It sailed on, and Bill from Gibraltar cabled CBS in London to that effect. Murrow cabled back: "View your change of plans Columbia now dropping you from payroll. New York office immensely disappointed syndicates behavior. . . . Office takes position Columbia been badly treated."[100] But no more so than Bill. He cabled Thackrey at the *Post*: "Tell syndicate as result their lightning alterations have been fired by Columbia thus ending carefully built up radio connection invaluable to future. Imperative syndicate official call immediately on Columbia giving sensible reasons if one exists for sudden plan change and costly both to me and Columbia."[101]

His father, trying to expedite Bill's visas and passage to the Balkans, cabled him in care of the American consulate in Gibraltar on March 28: "Can I help with Hull. What about cash. Glad to help. . . . Stuff going splendidly more than fifty papers really splendid reception. Don't worry."[102] Two days later, more disingenuously, he cabled Bill in Trieste on his way to Bucharest: "Mixup nobody's fault. Unknown to Paul White syndicate been selling you successfully as Balkan correspondent. Over fifty papers. Your homecoming plans unknown to syndicate. Both understand now. If after surveying Balkans no important story develops you might notify syndicate rearranging plan so that Columbia and syndicate can synchronize. Stuff going big."[103] But Columbia and the syndicate were unable to "synchronize." Bill did broadcast for CBS several times from Paris after his return from Romania and later, the next winter, from London during the blitz, but only as a stringer.

In April Kathrine sent her father-in-law a six-page letter explaining her perspective about his and the syndicate's interference. The New York *Post* had wanted Bill

> home for a long time. Now they have the Chicago Daily News foreign service for just a little more than they pay Bill—so they really don't need him as a European man. . . . [Henry] Martin wired Ted [Thackrey] after you had been there something to this effect: "Don't let Kathrine influence Bill to come home. . . ."
> At Ted's suggestion I called Martin, explained that I had done absolutely nothing about it—was going to do nothing about

it to influence Bill. I told him Bill's side financially . . . [and] asked him why he was so stony about it. He said that you agreed with him. . . .

The syndicate people talk airily about a $30,000 per year billing. However Bill has received from them exactly $1219 as of March 9. Up to Dec. 16 when he went on the Columbia expense account he had spent $3000 just getting around. He is not extravagant and was budgeting carefully. I have some of those records. Without Columbia he not only could not have gotten what he did but it would have taken another $5000 to swing this trip. The Balkans will cost every cent the syndicate is making for him. . . .

Bill didn't have to choose between radio and the column. Radio was working hand and glove with Bill and the column.[104]

As Kathrine recalled those events years later in some notes she made after Bill's death, her bitterness at her father-in-law's interference was still apparent:

One of the big oil companies was so impressed by the work he did [in Finland] that they offered to sponsor the CBS news program (and the news program was struggling then) for 26 weeks—but only if Bill was brought back to act as anchor instead of Elmer Davis. . . .

The elder Whites said nothing to CBS, to Bill or to me. Instead they went to Des Moines where they talked Bill's syndicate into ordering him to the Balkans where they, the elder Whites, believed the war would soon break out. (They told us later that Cordell Hull agreed.) . . .

In May of 1940, Bill finally got home, broke and broken. His parents who had been proud of his broadcasts took the position that they had meant what they did for his own good because he was a newspaper man, not a radio man.[105]

In this memorandum, about thirty-five years after events, Kathrine did confuse a few details; for example, Bill was to coanchor with Davis and for but an initial twelve weeks. But her account does indicate how much she resented that parental interference. Later in those same notes she wrote that "Bill cannot be understood—

that his career or lack of it—cannot be understood without some knowledge of what his parents, his often dear parents, could and did do."

At the time Bill did not know to what extent his father had influenced the actions of the syndicate. So before leaving Gibraltar he wrote his parents his view of why the column was selling so well: "The reason this column has been good is that I have, up to now, been able to go where I see the story, write it as I pleased, and leave when I feel there is no story for me. I feel that way about Europe now. . . . I think the whole trip has been badly bitched. . . . From here on out the focus of American opinion is going to shift from Europe to the political conventions, and I timed my return to ride the crest of this interest."[106]

As both he and Kathrine predicted, when he got to Romania about April 4 there was no story; Russia in fact did not seize Bessarabia until June 28. And his columns did not get through but were stolen by Romanian postal workers for the stamps.[107] Then the morning of April 9 Hitler moved instead through Denmark and Norway. Later Kathrine filled in with six ersatz columns datelined "Paris (by wireless)" and prefaced with this explanation: "Because of the invasion of Norway and Denmark Mr. White has interrupted his trip to the Balkans to send the following and succeeding dispatches on events in the North."[108] Those were followed by five columns datelined "SS. Saturnia en route to Trieste," then five mailed from Gibraltar before he boarded the *Saturnia*. Only then did his column carry five commentaries ostensibly from the Balkans—three datelined Budapest and two Bucharest—but those did not start until May 17, four days after he had returned to New York.

Disgusted with his syndicate, finding no story in the Balkans, short of funds, and homesick, he had left Romania the third week of April headed for Paris. There he suffered the recurrence of his psychosomatic intestinal troubles. As Kathrine wrote her in-laws just after his return: "In Paris he had a sort of nervous collapse and couldn't do anything. He was furious at the syndicate and still is."[109] Anticipating his return and realizing how depressed he was over missed opportunities and resulting money problems, she had written his father May 10 asking for a secret loan of two

thousand dollars in two installments to clear off some debts and
present him with a good financial picture: "Then I think he'll
be in a position to fight his way through wherever he has to."[110]
His father quietly sent the money to Kathrine, knowing his son
was as yet unaware fully of his own collusion with the Des Moines
syndicate.

By May 3 Bill had recovered sufficiently to take the boat train
from Paris to Genoa where he boarded the USS *Manhattan* for
New York. The morning of May 10, while he was somewhere near
mid-Atlantic, Hitler commenced his blitzkrieg through Holland
and Belgium. So Bill docked May 13 in New York City having
twice missed the very story his father and his syndicate had sent
him to the Balkans to find, at the cost of his CBS connection.
His column datelined New York began May 25 on the German
invasion of France; it carried this preface: "W. L. White arrived
in the United States at a critical moment in world history after
having touched every warring European nation except Poland.
No other American newspaperman has done this. White begins
today his first articles on what events abroad may mean to our
own social, economic and political future." That presented a brave
face to subscribers, but he knew he had missed the main chance,
both with CBS and now with his column. Kathrine wrote the
elder Whites on May 21: "The syndicate men have been here and
Bill . . . got them to apologize to Paul White. Maybe now with
some time and effort that can be patched up. Bill thinks it's pretty
impossible to try to do without . . . the radio connection. . . . The
Post began again this week on new stuff that Bill is writing as
he goes—but it is all such a lot of work to do over."[111]

He tried to capitalize on his European experiences with speeches
booked by the independent Columbia Lecture Bureau, the first
on May 24 in Bangor, Maine, where the *Daily News* carried his
column. Then the first week in June he made a lecture swing on
his way to Emporia, speaking in Cleveland, then in Pittsburgh,
Pennsylvania, then Louisville, Kentucky, where he was sponsored
by the *Courier-Journal*. On June 7 he spoke before an overcapacity
crowd of nearly five thousand townsfolk in the auditorium of
Emporia's new civic building, followed by speeches in five other
sizable Kansas towns, capped by a final talk on June 19 at the

Kansas City municipal auditorium. But those speeches did not give him the national exposure a CBS-sponsored tour had promised.

Meanwhile, late in May the British scrambled to rescue the Allied Expeditionary Force from the beaches of Dunkirk. By mid-June the Germans had occupied Paris and the Italians had belatedly declared war. Deeply worried early in April by Hitler's invasion of Norway, Will White had begun a series of consultations with Clark Eichelberger and others in New York and in Washington, D.C., to plan for a new lobbying effort to be named the Committee to Defend America by Aiding the Allies, later known simply as the White Committee. A week after Hitler invaded Holland, Will as chairman sent telegrams from Emporia to prominent citizens across the nation inviting them to join him in that new effort. He received immediate widespread support. By the time Bill reached Emporia, his father was once again directing a nationally significant publicity campaign. And the son found himself, as usual, watching from the sidelines, but aware now that his father had lost him the CBS job.

Bill returned from Europe thinking his and America's attention would shift to the upcoming presidential campaign; events dictated otherwise. Though he datelined most of his columns that summer from the Midwest, they were about Europe and the war. He did cover the Republican convention in Philadelphia in late June and the Democratic convention in Chicago in mid-July, but the real issue on his mind—and on the minds of his readers—was American foreign policy. Concerned about America's reluctance to support the Allies, he wrote "As I Saw It" for the *Yale Review* and "Coming Home" for *Cosmopolitan*, both articles about his recent experiences of German chauvinism. He also contributed the chapter "I Saw It Happen" about the war in Finland for the book *Zero Hour*, a polemic against appeasement by six contemporary American writers.[112] And mincing no words in his columns, he was for immediate and vigorous intervention on the side of the Allies. For example, in "Take a Look" for July 31 he analyzed the meaning of "realism" as used by isolationists and pointed to the "realistic" possibility of the British fleet, like the French, falling into German hands if America did nothing to help. He ended that column by declaring: "The particular kind of 2-bit astigmatic realism which

England practiced during the 1930's has brought her to the brink
of disaster. So let's get sentimental and stand by our friends while
we have a few left, and do a few favors for England if we expect
any in return. And I'll bet you Tiny Tim's crutch against a
machinegun that the pay-off will be bigger in the end."

After his return from Europe "Take a Look" soon regained its
snap but not its subscribers, lost during the Balkan-caused slump.
For a change of pace he covered the Wendell Willkie campaign
in Iowa the first week of August, but he was both bored and
depressed to be covering politics-as-usual while democracy in
Europe died. He confessed that personal unrest in his August 23
column: "The chances that I may presently be in England could
not yet be called reasonably good. But they may improve, and
I hope to get there, and wish very much I were there now." But
to get to England he had to jump two major hurdles. First, he
had to find transport from a neutral United States into a now-
forbidden war zone. Second, he had to get out of his contract
with the *Register-Tribune* Syndicate, which did not want to gamble
a second time on him abroad. He cleared both within a month.

In his final column, September 30, he announced, "It's all very
mysterious, but I'm leaving tonight for . . . London, so it is
necessary to wind up this column's affairs and give it a decent
Christian burial." *Life* magazine later revealed the mystery in the
six-page article "Atlantic Crossing on U.S. Destroyer" by William
L. White. On September 3 FDR had traded fifty overage destroyers
to Britain for English military bases in this hemisphere. The White
Committee had been instrumental in persuading the public to
support that exchange. Not surprisingly, Young Bill managed to
get a berth on one of those destroyers, the former USS *Madoz*,
sailing from Halifax, Nova Scotia, with a British crew during the
first week of October.[113] His new press assignments were reported
by *Editor and Publisher* on October 12: "He will cover the second
winter of the second world war from England for North American
Newspaper Alliance. White, who plans to stay abroad for several
months, will write articles for *Reader's Digest* and gather materials
for a book in addition to cabling articles to NANA. He was
released to NANA through an agreement with the Des Moines
Register and Tribune Syndicate."[114]

With that trip to an England under bombardment Bill finally stepped out of the now darkened shadow of his father, who personally had nothing to do with those press arrangements. Impressed by Bill's coverage of the Russo-Finnish war, DeWitt Wallace, publisher of the *Reader's Digest*, contracted with Bill through Carl Brandt, head of Bill's agency, for six articles about Britain under siege. But Bill's primary contract was with John Wheeler's NANA, which gave him press credentials, cable privileges, an expense account, and syndication in more than fifty newspapers. Wheeler did not write the elder White until September 30 to tell him he had signed his son, who asked that his stories be sent free to the *Gazette*. Will wrote his thanks on October 3, then on October 26 wrote again asking "confidentially and frankly, how the stories are pleasing the folks. As a proud father it seems to me the boy is telling an intelligent story of what is happening in Great Britain but proud fathers aren't so smart."[115] That "boy" was forty years old; and Will was smart enough this time not to interfere with his son's plans.

Chapter Four

The *Reader's Digest*, the War, and the Passing of a Sage, 1940–1945

Bill cabled his first NANA dispatch from London on October 12, the day he arrived. Actually he had landed near Glasgow, Scotland, but because of British censorship could not report that. As his destroyer neared England, it picked up a downed Royal Air Force (RAF) crew of five and put in at the nearest British port with military hospital facilities. In that first account he gave his impressions from the long train trip to London of an English countryside virtually untouched by war. His second story, also dated October 12, gave his initial assessment of the London Blitz:

> On my first afternoon in London I gazed at St. Paul's high, carved altar smacked flatter than a boarding-house pancake this morning by a number of massive stones from the great arch above, each about the size of a shetland pony, which had been dislodged by a German bomb. . . . The absolute, rock-bottom wholesale cost to the Nazi government of manufacturing that bomb and delivering it F.O.B. to St. Paul's altar could not be

less than $10,000 in reichmarks. The amount of military damage it inflicted on the British empire I would generously estimate at something less than eight Canadian cents. But it has deeply angered England![1]

In general that was to be the tone of most of his dispatches—the irrational, inhumane waste of the Nazi attacks versus the resolute response of the British.

His topics were limited because Wheeler, he wrote his parents, "doesn't want any interpretive articles, which he calls 'editorial,' and only wants trips and stuff about the airforce and things like that."[2] And that was what Bill gave him. During the nearly four months he was to be in England and Ireland, the NANA syndicated thirty-six of his reports, from one-half to two columns long, mostly about the blitz, British morale, and the RAF. Bill also fulfilled his *Reader's Digest* commitment of six pieces. His first submission was the December 2 destroyer article, which, as standard practice, the *Reader's Digest* "planted" with *Life* magazine, complete with photos he had taken, then reprinted in a shorter version in its January issue. Two others were cabled "originals," unusual then for the *Digest*, both in the March issue—"A Day of Sweeping Mines off Dover" and "London Fire, 1940," a dramatic eyewitness account of the worst incendiary raid of the blitz, Sunday night, December 29.[3] Early in December Bill also filled in a week from London for Edward R. Murrow on the CBS evening news program. Murrow had flown to neutral Portugal for an emotional reunion with Bill Shirer, who was on his way home at long last from Berlin, sick and depressed by the course of the war.

From firsthand observation and from interviews of both civilian and military authorities Bill soon became convinced that Britain could survive only if the United States entered the war. In his NANA report datelined November 1 he compared Britain's naval position in April 1917, just before the United States entered World War I, to its much more desperate position late in October 1940, when in a single week it lost 200,000 tons of shipping, mostly to German U-boats.[4] To his father he wrote, "I don't see how they can win in the long run unless we actually get in, and for our sakes, the sooner we get in the better."[5] But Will knew how prevalent isolationism was in the Midwest and also knew his appeal as chairman of the Committee to Defend America by Aiding the Allies lay in his not being too far ahead of his midwestern readers. Yet many committee members on the East Coast had come to his son's conclusion. Thus the policymaking group of the White Committee, based in New York, decided that month of November to advocate repeal of the Neutrality Act and adoption of some form of the Lend-Lease program, soon to be announced by FDR.

That greatly troubled Will. When he heard that Roy Howard, president of Scripps-Howard, planned to attack the committee's policy change in his influential newspapers, Will wrote him disavowing the change, then permitted him to print the letter. That caused such an uproar within his own committee that Will, depressed by the arguments for a more aggressive stance, tired at age seventy-two of the struggle, and worried about Sallie's ill health, resigned as active chairman on January 3 and as honorary chairman on April 3, actions hailed by such groups as America First, to his discomfiture. In London, not fully aware of his father's fatigue and moral struggle, Bill gave an interview to a Scripps-Howard *Chicago Times* reporter, just after Will's letter came out, in which Bill said the reports probably "will prove to be half truths circulated following a high-pressure interview with my father. So strongly do I feel that both convoys and repeal of the neutrality act are essential to proper aid for Britain, that I have requested and received official permission to telephone my father informing him of my views and reasons."[6] That newspaper interview embarrassed Will further. When the *Times* phoned him for a follow-up statement, he uncharacteristically refused to comment, except to say, "Bill is entitled to his own opinion." As soon as the son understood the context of the controversy, he wrote his father an apology.[7] Young Bill, even as a successful foreign correspondent in war-torn England, remembered he was still perceived by many Americans as but the son of William Allen White, prominent voice of midwestern moderation. After his return home, however, with his father off the committee, he felt freer to voice his own fervent interventionism.

Before he left New York in October, Bill had agreed with Kathrine to find a couple of British war orphans to bring back.

They had considered adoption off and on since her ectopic pregnancy but had put it off because of his uncertain job prospects and their unsettled life together. But now they had a home at their Frenchtown farm and he had a name for himself as a journalist. From London he wrote his parents: "I'm trying very hard to locate some good kids here for adoption—I've got it mostly lined out now but selecting the kids and then getting them home. My best bet now looks like making arrangements with the Red Cross here to get some kind of . . . authority to come back with the kids on a British boat—they, still being British subjects, could travel on it but I, as an American, am debarred by the neutrality act."[8] The story of that search and return makes up the narrative thread of his second book, *Journey for Margaret*. Through the National Adoption Society he found two war orphans, ages four and three, whom he calls John and Margaret in the book. Unfamiliar with children, he turned to Anna Freud, daughter of Sigmund Freud and herself an expert in child psychology, who had set up a nursery-clinic for war victims in Hampstead, a London suburb. There he placed the two for evaluation while he tried to find transport back to the states.

That proved nearly impossible. Like Bill Shirer, he discovered the only route out of Europe to the states in December 1940 was through Portugal, which had at that time nearly ten thousand refugees who were also trying to leave the continent, most aiming for the United States. He could not get a visa into Portugal without a confirmed and paid-for reservation out, either a flight on a Pan Am Clipper or a berth on a ship of the American Export Line. He finally got a Clipper reservation for December 14 and thereby his visa but then could not get a place until late January on one of the British Imperial Airways flights to Lisbon, which had backlogs of nearly one thousand reservations, because that was the only way into Portugal from England. He deferred indefinitely the Pan Am reservation. To fill part of the wait he went to Dublin for about ten days to assess Irish reactions to the war. Not until January 28 was he able to fly to Lisbon from the English port of Bournemouth on a small, eight-passenger seaplane.[9]

To book another seat was impossible, but he did obtain permission to take a child on his lap instead of checking luggage.

Under the circumstances he chose to take the girl because she was lighter—just under the luggage weight restriction—and, according to Anna Freud's tests, brighter.[10] They landed in Lisbon only to find the earlier Pan Am reservation voided. Kathrine tried her best from New York to get another commitment from Pan Am, and his father asked Cordell Hull once again to intervene on Bill's behalf. But Pan Am would offer only a tentative place the following week. Then Bill managed late Saturday afternoon, February 1, to get a single cabin aboard American Export Line's USS *Excalibur*, sailing from Lisbon at 6:00 P.M. After a mad scramble to get the child—a British "belligerent"—an exit visa, he boarded ship just as it cast off. They docked at Jersey City, New Jersey, on February 10.

Bill returned to find himself named by the Merchant Tailors Association one of America's twenty best-dressed men of 1941. In itself that fact is unimportant, except it does indicate his public visibility as a war correspondent. Recognizing that as an asset, Kathrine worked with the Columbia Lecture Bureau while he was still in England to line up speaking engagements. Such lectures had become an integral part of the increasingly strident national debate about the war, and they drew large, earnest audiences. For example, Leland Stowe, foreign correspondent for the *Chicago Daily News*, returned home through Lisbon the same week as Bill, and with the same conviction that America must enter the war against the Nazis, and soon. Stowe spent most of the spring of 1941 lecturing across the United States, determined to deliver his message that America had "no other road to freedom," the title of his best-selling book that fall about his 1939–40 war experiences. Unlike Stowe, Bill White did not have the push in 1941 for such a long lecture tour, nor did he write so polemic a book. But he did travel as far as Texas that spring to speak his convictions, and that fall his own book, *Journey for Margaret*, implied the same thesis. He also argued his father into active editorial support of FDR's policy of Lend-Lease, writing him in a tone of authority new to their correspondence: "I hope very much before you say much publicly on the subject of convoys that you come back here—or rather to Washington—and find out what is actually going on out in the Atlantic."[11]

On his return, his primary task, so Bill told a reporter for *Editor and Publisher*, was to put together the book he had in mind when he left for England.[12] Much of it was topical material without a long shelf life—excerpts from his NANA reports and magazine pieces. Bernice Baumgarten had interested Knopf in it, based on a tentative outline, so between speaking dates Bill wrote as continuity a long (44,000-word) narrative about his search for the children. But both his agent and Knopf's readers thought that account too lengthy and too sentimental. Several versions later Knopf was still dissatisfied and Bernice frustrated. Then Marion Ellet, editor of the *Concordia* [Kansas] *Blade*, "blows into town," he wrote his parents, "and I let her read it. She said there was a lot of good stuff in it but the thing which grated was the intrusion of 'my' thoughts—my various sentiments and night thoughts on the subject of being a father. . . . And I think she is completely right and has put her finger on exactly what all the other readers were objecting to, only they couldn't say the right words to make me see it—they only made me mad."[13] Following her advice, he cut the narrative by two-thirds, broke it into chapters to be sandwiched in between his war reports, then framed it with a brief introduction and denouement.

Because of those several rewrites, he did not get the final manuscript to Knopf until early July; that firm then rejected it as not following the original outline, though Bill thought he had a commitment and had announced the book in the *Reader's Digest* as forthcoming by Knopf. The novelist Christopher Morley, an old friend of Will's and fellow Book-of-the-Month Club judge, then read the manuscript and recommended it to his brother Frank, head of the trade division of Harcourt, Brace. In his later review for the *Book-of-the-Month Club News* Chris Morley wrote, "This book says more to me than anything yet published about this war. This is not America First but Margaret First."[14] Frank agreed with his brother, signed it for Harcourt, Brace in August, and arranged for an early November publication, in time for the Christmas trade.[15] Helping to promote it was the *Reader's Digest* cut of the book's orphan story in its November issue, prefaced by the note "a new book, *Journey for Margaret*, soon to be published by Harcourt, Brace."

With the book behind him Bill thought of the future. John Wheeler urged him to start another column but, Bill wrote his parents, he "won't guarantee anything and it looks like a gamble. So . . . I think I'll sit down this summer and try to turn out a play about Europe. It's a long chance, but if it should click it would pay infinitely better in money and in reputation than a column."[16] That idea did not click; instead he went back to magazine freelancing and wrote a long analysis of British politics for *Town and Country* and three substantive articles for the *Saturday Evening Post*.[17] One of those was something he had tried in 1929 but not since, an extended interview as narrative dialogue, a genre to become his distinctive stock-in-trade. Entitling it "The Norse Travel Again," he reported his story almost exclusively as interviews, in Norwegian-flavored English, of three young men who escaped their occupied homeland to join an air squadron of their countrymen near Toronto, Canada. As a technique these self-effacing interviews work: they provide a well-focused, colorful narrative, with the linguistic effects contributing to the verisimilitude. The principals seem to tell their own stories artlessly in their own words. Yet he achieved that only after much hard work, selecting and condensing from tablets of notes and making many censorship changes so as not to reveal any harmful facts to the gestapo. Bill's father, in response to praise of that piece by Frank Motz in the *Hays* [Kansas] *News*, wrote: "I am awfully glad you like Bill's Norwegian story. . . . The boy is acquiring a good narrative style, something I have never been able to do as well as he. I think I can beat him at editorial but he certainly has got me licked seven ways for Sunday as a story teller."[18]

In a flush of enthusiasm over Bill's earlier "mine-sweeper story" DeWitt Wallace had written Carl Brandt, head of Bill's agency: "May we completely surround the person of Bill White with a circle of ten-foot-high stakes? He's more exciting than a 7-alarm fire."[19] But Wallace did not follow up on that note until after Bill's book and the *Saturday Evening Post* articles came out. Then December 12, 1941, at a Friday luncheon meeting with Brandt and Bill, he offered him a "roving assignment" to write for the *Digest*, with a retainer of $1,250 per month and a minimum of ten submissions per year. He was also free to work on things not "in the province" of the *Digest*. Aside from his 1924 decision to return home to work for his father, this became the most important business agreement of Bill's life. It brought him an enviable blend of security and freedom.

It also brought him a huge, essentially middle-class audience, because several years after he signed on, the *Reader's Digest* became the largest-selling magazine in the United States, with a circulation of about nine million in 1945; and twenty years later, after establishing its many international editions, it became the largest magazine in the world, with a total circulation of twenty-five million.[20] In thinking back fifty years later on the New York publishing world of 1941, Lambert Davis, Bill's editor at Harcourt, Brace, recalled that "the *Reader's Digest* and the Book-of-the-Month Club were the two most important non-book-publishing organizations in the book-publishing world. To get a *Reader's Digest* digest was a big, big help, and to get a Book-of-the-Month Club choice was the equivalent at that time of getting a TV version out today."[21]

In the November 1942 issue Wallace listed W. L. White as a permanent "roving editor" on the *Digest* masthead, where his name remained for over thirty years, until his death in 1973. Such roving editors were not editors but staff writers who lived and worked where they chose under "first refusal" contracts with the *Digest* to write on subjects they themselves often suggested. It was Wallace's idea that, in his words, "given the security of a monthly stipend, most writers would do a better job. They would have the financial means to take the time to go scouting for article ideas, to explore the possibilities of an article, and to make sure that what they wrote was the last word, as of that time, on that particular subject."[22] He chose the first three writers in 1940, then expanded to twelve in 1942. As one of those original twelve, Bill felt free over the years to report directly to "Wally," whom he came to consider a close friend, a confidant, even a father figure.

After Bill arrived in New York with "Margaret," whose real name was Barbara and who turned four years old just after their arrival, Kathrine took on much of the parenting. By April Bill was able to write his mother, who was then at the Mayo Clinic: "Barbara is apparently all settled down. She raises hell in her own way now and then, and I think it's an improvement that she feels secure enough with us to be able to raise the hell. But for the most part it's all very placid and sunny and lots of fun. . . . And I wish again you could get back and see her."[23] Finding their apartment on Fifty-fourth Street no longer large enough, Kathrine spent most of her time at the farm that summer. So that October, when their lease was up, they rented a full brownstone on West Twelfth Street, in the heart of Greenwich Village. Then the day before Thanksgiving 1941 they "formally adopted Barbara in front of Surrogate Judge Foley at the Chambers Street court," so Bill announced to his parents.[24]

Meanwhile, *Journey for Margaret* came out November 14, with an advertising blurb by Bill Shirer, whose own *Berlin Diary* was leading the best-seller lists. He wrote: "Bill White has made many journeys in this war. The 'Journey for Margaret' was the best. . . . [For] it brought us a gem of a book, a book about war-scarred Margaret . . . and the war that scarred her." The reviews were similarly positive. Typical was that by Ralph Thompson in the *New York Times*: "[White's] account of how he found [Margaret] and brought her back is the unique part of his book. It might have been badly sentimentalized; it is handled delicately and beautifully. For the rest, there are excellent first-hand descriptions of the familiar England at war, its aviators, seamen, soldiers and civilians."[25] *Life* Magazine in its December 8 issue ran a four-page photo feature of "Margaret" at home with the Whites. Yet in spite of the reviews, and the publicity, the book did not make the national best-seller list. It did do better than *What People Said*, and it was more readable. Bill's uncle Lacy Haynes, for example, wrote him that he was delighted with the new book because in it "you had lost all your cynical touch; it was a kindly, sympathetic . . . piece of work."[26] But the timing was off and competition tough. The Germans had invaded Russia in June, pulling public attention away from England, and trade lists already featured books by several popular war correspondents. Then the Japanese attack on Pearl Harbor on December 7 abruptly ended the fierce national debate over entering the war, which this book was implicitly a part of. Metro-Goldwyn-Mayer (MGM) bought the movie rights just after publication and had it rewritten into a brief screenplay that changed many of the narrative details. Starring Robert Young, Laraine Day, and Margaret O'Brien, the film was released in December 1942. As poignantly provocative war propaganda, it became a box office hit, with the *New York Times* ranking it number two in its list of the year's ten best movies.

Early in 1942 Bill, in examining his new role as a father, belatedly recognized how much of a burden Kathrine had borne during the six or seven years he had struggled to establish himself as a writer. Since 1936, often against her advice, he had not kept a job long but instead had borrowed from his parents, for living expenses as well as psychiatrists, while trying to write on his own terms. Over that time his parents had come to believe, from his own rationalizations to them and from correspondence with Dr. Binger, Kathrine's psychiatrist, that she was irrationally dependent on Bill and unduly suspicious of others. They seemed to ignore his own pattern of psychotherapy. In retrospect Bill thought that Dr. Binger had intentionally misinformed them to cover up his misdiagnosis of Kathrine—that it was Bill, not she, who was emotionally troubled. Thus the elder Whites had lost confidence in her and her reports about Bill and his activities, which contributed, for example, to Will's unfortunate intervention at Gibraltar in 1940. With a daughter to look out for, with a new recognition of Kathrine's longtime support, and with his mother ill and both parents in their seventies, he decided he had to address what he saw as an unfortunate, unacknowledged alienation within the family, caused in part by his own lack of stability.

The success of his NANA and *Reader's Digest* materials gave him the self-confidence he needed to confront the problem. Early in May 1942, after several months of reviewing old letters and rethinking the past, with the perceptive help of Dr. Brunswick, Bill and his father got together in New York to clear up those several years of misunderstanding and to put their financial affairs in better legal order. Afterward, Bill wrote his mother how thankful he was that this "barrier between us has been finally removed."[27] The family rapprochement seems to have boosted his morale further, because the next several years were to prove his most productive.

In reply to a friendly inquiry from fellow editor Frank Buxton of the *Boston Herald*, Will wrote on March 19, 1942: "You ask about young Bill. . . . He is working for the Reader's Digest [and] will have a lot of stuff coming out this year. At the moment he has an article in the Survey-Graphic. . . . Of course he wants to go to Europe. But he has a wife and a child now and it is pretty hard."[28] Instead of chasing overseas, Bill picked up war stories at home, which, with his many personal contacts and bolstered by his *Reader's Digest* position, proved highly successful. Within the next two years he published two best-selling books and seventeen popular magazine pieces, not counting *Digest* reprints. For example, the *Survey Graphic* article his father mentioned to Buxton appeared in both the April issue of that magazine, under the title "Negro Officers: 1917 and Now," and the *Reader's Digest*, condensed and retitled "The Negro in the Army." As published in either magazine it is a tightly written, sympathetic account of the training of black officers for black troops. But the original manuscript was a much longer, more acerbic attack on the army tradition of segregation, indicative of both Bill's lifelong sympathy for blacks and an ironic iconoclasm that sometimes got him into difficulties.[29] But the *Digest* staff thoroughly vetted his suggested topics and edited his submissions to fit the essentially conservative, simplistically optimistic tone of the magazine. DeWitt Wallace wished "to inform, inspire and entertain" with articles of general appeal written for ready apprehension. Those standards shaped much of Bill's subsequent magazine output.

Bill's magazine pieces for 1942 and 1943 focused on the war effort in the United States—on coastal defense, on military readiness and training, on transport, on weapons production. Bill got the topics from military public relations personnel, many of whom he knew as journalists in civilian life. And they facilitated his gathering of impressions and data by arranging for him to take a training flight or participate in a submarine escape exercise or join a shake-down cruise of a new aircraft carrier. They were especially eager to do that after the extraordinary success of *They Were Expendable*, his story about an American PT boat squadron caught in the Japanese conquest of the Philippines. It originally appeared in the September issue of *Reader's Digest* as a thirty-five-page special feature. Then Harcourt, Brace published it the second week of September as a 205-page book. The Book-of-the-Month

Club hurriedly offered it as an alternate choice for October in a unique supplement to its September newsletter, complete with a pictorial sequence, a profile of White by Bill Shirer, and a laudatory summary-review by Chris Morley, which ended, "One is sorry for those" few Americans who will miss reading it. Other reviewers were even more emphatic. For example, Stephen Vincent Benét in the *Saturday Review of Literature* declared it "a tale of gallantry, hardship, action, ingenuity. Simply and forcefully told, it ranks with the great tales of war."[30] And Frank S. Adams in the *New York Times Book Review* found it "so engrossing that few who begin it will be able to put it down until they have finished its action-packed pages."[31]

The first book designated "Imperative" by the newly formed Council on Books in Wartime, it thereby secured the cooperation of all major American publishers in advertising and distribution. That award inspired *Life* magazine to run a seven-page photo feature of the story in its October 26 issue. With sales in the United States over 850,000 hardcover volumes, it became an all-time national best-seller, staying seven months among the top ten nonfiction books listed by *Publishers Weekly*. MGM negotiated for the movie rights and lined up Spencer Tracy to star in a 1943 release. But because of legal difficulties, MGM did not shoot the film until 1945 and then with a considerably revised script and with Robert Montgomery, John Wayne, and Donna Reed as stars. Yet the film story still proved popular, for when the movie came out, the *New York Times* ranked it tenth among the year's ten best films.

What gave Bill's story such immediate and enduring appeal? When asked that question nearly fifty years later, Lambert Davis, Bill's former editor, offered two answers. First was the timing. The sneak attack on Pearl Harbor stunned the country into unity overnight. But aftershocks continued relentlessly as the Japanese swept across the Philippines, an American commonwealth, only to end with the humiliating surrenders of Gen. Edward King on Bataan on April 9, 1942, and Gen. Jonathan Wainwright on Corregidor on May 6. Astonished and chagrined by those military disasters, the American people hungered for firsthand accounts of that action but wanted them palatable. *They Were Expendable* gave them realism with heroism. Second, Davis said, "as adventure the book had everything; it fit the formula to a tee." It had novelty, youth, clear-cut villains, a David-versus-Goliath conflict, action, suspense, sexual romance, and a final fast-paced sequence with a last-minute rescue.[32] Moreover, it told of the escape of flamboyant Gen. Douglas MacArthur, in the autumn of 1942 the home front's man of the hour. It also had the audacity to criticize haphazard defense efforts and give the public some insight into the United States Army-Navy rivalry that was to mar the early years of the Pacific war. And it was cleverly written: four young navy officers told their tales in their own words, vividly and directly. For the navy it was a public relations coup; for Bill a fantastic hit.[33]

Those young officers were from Motor Torpedo Boat (MTB) Squadron Three, which arrived in the Philippines the previous fall with six boats and had fought to the last one. When brought back to the United States in May 1942, they were given ten-day leaves before reporting for their next duty. Both Lt. John Bulkeley, commander of Squadron Three, and Lt. Robert Kelly, second-in-command, were from New York City. But when they arrived home, they were immediately taken in tow by the navy's public relations department and dragged through a schedule of public appearances—a ticker tape parade, speeches, war bond rallies, and press interviews.[34] Corregidor had just fallen, and the navy urgently needed heroes. As part of that publicity campaign, the navy contacted the *Reader's Digest*, because of its large circulation, to offer it first chance at their story. Intrigued, DeWitt Wallace sent Bill to check it out.[35] After a brief interview with Lieutenant Bulkeley, Bill immediately sent Wallace a five-page analysis in which he wrote: "I don't know what of Philippine material is being offered you, but none of it could be so good as this potentially is. . . . I suggest that you assign me to spend a week or so going into this material, and then writing it just as tightly as I write any Digest article."[36] Wallace quickly approved and Bill interviewed Bulkeley more extensively in Washington, D.C., where FDR was soon to present him with the congressional Medal of Honor. Then for a week he interviewed Lieutenant Kelly and ensigns Anthony Akers and George Cox at Melville, Rhode Island, where they had reported to a new PT boat training center.

He soon concentrated on Kelly because, so Bill told an
interviewer for the *New York Times*, he

> had the flair, and the first afternoon I recognized this and said,
> "The first thing we must think of is structure, because if we
> don't get structure into this story we can't work it right.". . .
> Then I said that there were three lines, three themes, that we
> had to stick to. 'The first is this—you started with six boats and
> in the end there was only one. Now there is a clear line—what
> happened to each of these other boats and what were you doing
> when you heard what had happened to them? That's the first
> line. The second line is that you started out thinking that you
> were winning and then you learned bit by bit that you were
> losing, and finally realized that you had lost. And then the third
> line—I think that should be the story of the girl.

The girl was the army nurse Lt. Beulah Mae Greenwalt, nicknamed
"Peggy," a friend of Kelly's captured by the Japanese on Corregidor
and not released until February 1945. During that week of interviews
Bill filled lined tablets with abbreviated penciled notes that he later
typed out on cards. Then, he told the *Times* interviewer, he "rented
a ten-buck-a-week room at the [Hotel] Brevoort as a working place,
and set up a work table, and spread out the notes . . . on the bed.
. . . [The manuscript] ran to about 44,000 words and I wrote fast
on it, finished it in ten days. . . . I seem to have hit the mood
of that moment, of the moment that it appeared. You can't repeat
on things like that, I suppose, but it is swell to do it."[37]

Much like his earlier "The Norse Travel Again" account, in this
book Bill essentially removed himself as narrator, except for a brief
foreword and an introductory frame. But here he sets up a more
dramatic dialogue, as if the four officers were telling their collective
story together in the give and take of one long sequence, with
Lieutenant Kelly taking the lead. While providing for several
perspectives, the story is unified by its focus on the experiences
of one man, Kelly, whose observations are often salty and
irreverent. Through him Bill introduces Peggy, the nurse, who
becomes a friend to Kelly when he is treated at the hospital on
Corregidor for a badly infected hand.

The story begins when Lieutenant Bulkeley gets word by phone at the Cavite Naval Base near Manila of the attack on Pearl Harbor. Two days later the Japanese bomb Cavite, but by then the six boats of MTB Squadron Three have scattered to become the navy's first line of defense along the shores of Luzon, attacking Japanese cruisers, transports, and landing barges to sink about one hundred times their own tonnage, despite sabotaged gas and no repair parts. As the Japanese close in on Manila, the four surviving boats snatch General MacArthur, his family, and staff from Corregidor in a daring night run to Mindanao, to be airlifted to Australia. Then in the chaos of defeat, with but one battered torpedo-less boat afloat, the narrators take different routes to the last American airfield in the Philippines and escape surrender, leaving Peggy and thousands of other Americans behind as "expendables."

In a letter to Edna Ferber on July 21 Will reported his and Sallie's surprised reception of Bill's new book, which they had known little about, and proudly quoted fellow Book-of-the-Month Club judges:

> We had finished up the quota of books for the Book-of-the-Month when one came rolling in by air mail, special delivery. . . . And when we opened it up, by George there was the proof of Bill's book. . . . The day of the meeting I got this telegram from Chris Morley, Dorothy Canfield and Henry Canby: "Unanimous is our intention to take the book you did not mention; gosh, Bill, that boy can write. We chose the book by W. L. White.". . . And if it goes—well, he will be in the good money. Bill has never been in the good money. He has had two books that got swell notices but the cash register kept ringing up "No Sale," at least not very big sales, not enough to buck him up. And we are so happy about it Sallie and I. It has been a long time since we have had anything cheer us up.[38]

Though Bill was too busy early that summer to write his parents, Kathrine wrote them regularly with domestic news about Bill and Barbara, the farm, various family members, and their cook, Alice. She reported that after Bill finished the *Expendable* story and cleared it through navy censorship, he was off to Washington to follow up several other leads for the *Digest*. Then October 20 she wired them: "Barbara seriously injured Sunday near farm in rented car with driver. Weak door catch gave way sucking her out. Complicated operation later New York hospital."[39] Though she mended quickly, Bill and Kathrine were, as one result, especially sensitive to MGM's attempts that fall to use her and the family in publicity for the film version of *Journey for Margaret*, to be released in December. As Kathrine explained in a letter to her in-laws, she and Bill wanted to shield Barbara but "had to be careful not to upset the balance so that the vague, faint, thin chance of still doing the Expendable movie wouldn't be hurt."[40]

Negotiations for those movie rights were further complicated December 12 by a story in the *Kansas City Times*, the morning edition of the *Star*, reporting unattributed Washington gossip that Lieutenant Kelly had refused to sign a movie release without a disclaimer that "the injection of Peggy into the story of M.T.B. squadron 3 is entirely fiction." Seemingly unaware of negative reactions, possibly because he had himself fictionalized a love interest in his World War I account *The Martial Adventures of Henry and Me*, Will reprinted the *Times* piece that afternoon in the *Gazette*. Bill was furious and fired off a telegram to his father, exclaiming: "Terribly unfortunate that you reprinted Kansas City Star's damaging story saying I faked part of Expendable's narrative. Will presently write my own correction but must first salvage what I can from chaos created by such libelous matter being reprinted in paper bearing my name on masthead."[41] Bill had good reason to be angry: the report attacked his integrity as a journalist by asserting "the trouble is—so the story here goes—that Young Bill gave his imagination a free rein in injecting the love interest in his best seller."[42] Both *Reader's Digest* and Harcourt, Brace had promoted the story as unvarnished truth, or as Chris Morley put it, "the unsparing account of what Mr. White calls America's Little Dunkerque, told without benefit of cosmetics."[43] The Peggy of the story did sue MGM later for invasion of privacy in its rewritten screenplay and eventually won a small settlement. But in answer to a recent inquiry about the truth of White's portrayal of her, she replied that the book itself was "quite accurate."[44] Of course in 1942 she was in a Japanese prison camp at Santo Tomas, Manila, and unreachable. Thus, in spite of Bill's angry denials, that gossipy report created doubts about his honesty—doubts that called into question his self-effacing interview technique and later lent credulity to accusations of dishonesty in his *Report on the Russians*.[45]

At the end of October, encouraged by the sensational success of *They Were Expendable*, Bill picked up an idea for a similar story from fellow *Digest* editor Paul Palmer about Army Air Force Maj. Frank Kurtz, a B-17 pilot who took part in the doomed air defenses of the Philippines and the Dutch East Indies. Then, after escaping to Australia, he flew commanding Army Air Force Lt. Gen. George Brett's plane the Swoose, a battered B-17D that had survived the Japanese attack on Clark Field and many subsequent bombing missions of its own. Bill wrote Wallace on November 4, 1942: "I have had several days with [Kurtz] and, frankly, the story looks as good as, if not better than, the Expendables looked after my first three days with them."[46] Eager to balance negative publicity as its offensive in New Guinea sputtered and the navy and Marines held on to Guadalcanal, the army flew Bill late in November to Panama, where Brett and the crew of the Swoose were newly stationed. Bill interviewed them, then when he got back to New York wrote Paul Palmer at the *Digest* that "I've got some fascinating dope and material which, in my opinion, is better than *They Were Expendable* but which also presents a much more difficult job of organization and writing."[47]

He was certainly right; the book proved much more difficult, for he was frustrated not only by the lack of inherent structure but also by the inconsistencies of army censorship. Not until after a considerable fight did he get the War Department's stamp of approval on the second half of the manuscript, which the first half had received with only minor changes. But the second had been turned over to a different reader who heavily blue-penciled all "profane and vulgar expressions" attributed to officers and in an accompanying memorandum called for elimination of all "controversial matters" and criticism of "military superiors." Finally, Bill appealed to an old friend of his father's, the journalist Herbert Swope, who was then special assistant to the secretary of war and who intervened to save that half from evisceration.[48]

The *Digest* published the narrative as a sixty-nine-page continued story in its April and May issues, then Harcourt, Brace issued it on June 3 as the 273-page book *Queens Die Proudly*.[49] Because of the censorship battle and the rumors about his integrity as a narrator, Bill wrote a brief foreword including a disclaimer to protect his sources and a guarantee from Lieutenant General Brett that the incidents described were historically correct. Having learned from Lieutenant Kelly's second thoughts about his and Peggy's roles in *They Were Expendable*, Bill was careful to clear this manuscript with all principals and obtain signed releases. He even checked with navy lieutenant commander and congressman Lyndon Johnson, whom he depicts humorously when the crew of the Swoose gets lost and has to make a forced landing with a load of fellow dignitaries in the Australian outback.[50]

The principal narrator is Frank Kurtz, a former Olympic high diver, who begins the story as a pilot in the Nineteenth Bombardment Group, thirty-five B-17Ds sent in October 1941 to Clark Field in the Philippines. The others are Margo, his wife; Lt. Harry Schreiber, navigator; Sgt. Charlie Reeves, bombardier; Sgt. Rowland Boone, gunner; and Sgt. "Red" Varner, crew chief. As with *They Were Expendable* Bill begins the story with a brief introductory frame, then lets the narrators take over, telling in an extended dialogue their tales of sorrow and courage as the Japanese roll over the Philippines and the Dutch East Indies early in 1942. Kurtz begins with the bombing of Clark Field about half a day after Pearl Harbor and the loss of his crew and plane, Old 99. Kneeling near his burnt-out B-17, beside the body of "Tex," his copilot, he promises that so long as he is alive Old 99 and its crew will be flying in formation with him. Margo then breaks into the story to provide the "feminine" touch, the pathos of her helpless waiting at home in Omaha, Nebraska. After the disaster at Clark, Kurtz flies to Del Monte in the Philippines, where twelve planes from the Nineteenth Group escape being hit. Harry Schreiber next tells of a bombing mission by five of these fortresses against a Japanese flotilla along the Luzon coast and the loss of two planes. Del Monte becomes untenable and the planes are sent to Batchelor Field near Darwin, Australia, to continue flying nearly impossible long-distance missions into the Philippines. Soon they are sent to Dutch-held Java and Borneo, with Kurtz taking over one of the fortresses. From those closer bases they continue to hit Japanese shipping with only ten crippled planes operating from defenseless fields.

In January sergeants Reeves and Boone arrive in Java along with six B-17Es, a new model with a tailgunner. They tell of other reinforcements that did not make it and then of their bombing assignments and successful battles with Zeroes, Japanese fighter planes, while Kurtz pulls desk duty as liaison with the Dutch military. From that vantage point he describes the desperate last days and fall of Java in March. What is left of the Nineteenth Group retreats again to Australia, where Kurtz becomes pilot and air aide to General Brett. After two months of flying military brass from Melbourne to bases in northern Australia and trying to persuade them to establish a defensive airfield at Buna in New Guinea, General Brett, his plane the Swoose, and its crew are ordered home. On the long trek back Kurtz imagines Old 99 flying home next to him. Then Margo receives a phone call from her husband in San Francisco and her months of anxiety end.

Most reviewers were positive, but not all. Several were bothered by Bill's subsumed voice and sentimental tone. All agreed, though, that *Queens Die Proudly* was an exciting story, and it became an immediate best-seller. *Publishers Weekly* carried it for two months as number five among the nonfiction top ten nationwide, and that without its being sent out as a primary book club choice, though listed as an alternate by the Book-of-the-Month Club. Harcourt, Brace ordered two extra printings, to a total of about 80,000 copies. Then sales dropped off precipitously, for it ran into stiff competition that summer with other books about the Pacific theater, such as Richard Tregaskis's *Guadalcanal Diary* and Ted Lawson's *Thirty Seconds over Tokyo*.

Just after completing the book Bill checked into Roosevelt Hospital "with what the doctor said was a mild case of nervous exhaustion" that had brought back his former intestinal troubles, so he wrote Wallace.[51] But he was soon out and about, working ironically enough on an article about battle fatigue with Col. William Kennard, who had been chief flight surgeon of the Army Air Force in the Far East on December 7, 1941. And he was busy with the details of a potentially lucrative NBC radio contract. Sponsored by the Goodyear Tire and Rubber Company, he was to host a dramatized "Service Story of the Week" for one thousand dollars each. His agent, Carl Brandt, had signed him up for fourteen weeks, starting April 20, and Bill was delighted to be back on the air and for that much money. But because he insisted on editorial control both over his script and the story selection, the arrangement lasted only three programs. He refused to host a fourth because, from his point of view, Goodyear, contrary to its promises, had commercialized the stories and exploited his connection with *Reader's Digest*. Bill and his agent then negotiated with NBC for a similar program with a different sponsor, but to no avail.

For his parents' fiftieth wedding anniversary on April 27 Bill and Kathrine had planned to go to Kansas, where he would broadcast over a leased wire. But while in New York earlier that month, both his parents came down with the flu. Will's recovery was especially slow, so they celebrated their golden anniversary in New York at Roosevelt Hospital. After they returned home, Will wrote his son to ask him to explain the hospital charges. Bill replied that the account was actually less than he expected but "if you need to borrow any money from me, to help you over the hump on these hospital expenses, just let me know."[52] Bill now was earning much more than his father; after so many years of borrowing from him, making that gesture must have given quiet delight. Earlier that year Will had learned that the owners of the Emporia radio station, KTSW, were willing to sell, and he suggested it to Bill as an investment. Though tempted, he decided at that time not to make an offer, after noting its considerable losses. Still, that year from New York he kept a weather eye on the *Gazette* and its competition because his father's health was becoming more problematic.

But as a proud father Will still had the energy late that spring to embarrass his son. When *Queens Die Proudly* came out, Will suggested his son personally send signed review copies to regional newspaper editors. Bill wrote him that

> it's perfectly all right for you to send out your own books. You, for the past 30 years have become a kind of patriarch . . . [but] the boys are still trying to decide whether I am a flash-in-the-

pan or maybe a reasonably permanent fixture in the American
literary scene. . . . You have made the very pardonable error
of confusing me and my position with you and your position.
But something which would be in every way in good taste,
applied to your books, is bad taste when applied to mine and
will continue to be for a good many years.[53]

Though now earning more, Bill had no illusions about his and
his father's relative public standings. And he knew that in spite
of his current success he too could be considered surprisingly
expendable. For that June, while Carl was ill and hospitalized,
Bernice Baumgarten on behalf of Brandt and Brandt wrote Bill
to terminate their agent-author contract. In the past she and he
had had several heated arguments, and there was residual
dissatisfaction on both sides. After trying unsuccessfully to patch
things up, Bill wrote Wallace asking him to suggest another agent,
if indeed one were necessary, given their exclusive contract and
his relationship with Harcourt, Brace.[54] Wallace advised Bill to
work always through an agent, which he subsequently did.
Kathrine, though, took over most of the accounting details
previously handled by Brandt, which proved a felicitous decision.

In "My Day" for June 13 Eleanor Roosevelt reported that
"William White, the son of our old friend, William Allen White
of Kansas," accompanied her to Norwalk, Connecticut, to
substitute for Norman Cousins as moderator of a town hall forum
at which she spoke, "and the whole evening went on with real
interest on everyone's part."[55] Her interest was piqued on the train
back when she and Bill talked about the difficulties of sons with
famous fathers, a subject he felt "very strongly" about, so he wrote
her afterward.[56] A month later while working on a story about
aerial reconnaissance, he had a chance to interview her eldest son,
Col. Elliott Roosevelt, who had commanded the Third Photographic Group in North Africa and flown a number of reconnaissance missions. Following White House policy, War Department
censors struck out any reference to Elliott in the story. Bill
persuaded *Reader's Digest* to delay publication so he could appeal
to Mrs. Roosevelt but had to wait until late September, when she
returned from a tour of the South Pacific. The article appeared

in November, not naming Elliott but "so worded that he could easily be identified," as Bill had requested.

Then in the spring of 1944, for a story explaining how American military government functions in occupied territory, Bill interviewed an officer just back from Sicily, the former Hearst editor John Boettiger, who had married FDR's daughter, Anna. During that interview Bill dined at the White House with Boettiger and his mother-in-law, and their conversation returned to problems faced by the Roosevelt sons, especially since Kansas Republican congressman William Lambertson had recently accused the president of shielding his sons from frontline duty. Afterward, Eleanor wrote her close friend Joseph Lash that Bill had "rejoiced my soul expounding his theory on a Society for the Sons of Famous Fathers, motto, 'You are following in your Father's Footsteps,' Vice President Jesus Christ."[57] As the charter member of this mythical society, named the "Sons of God," Bill empathized with her worries about her sons—after all, he had lived in the shade of a famous father all his life—and Mrs. Roosevelt responded to his sense of humor. Subsequently, he and Kathrine became friends with the Boettigers and attended a family dinner with Mrs. Roosevelt at the White House later that year. When Bill went to Russia late that spring, she commissioned him to find out informally how the Russians would react to a visit from her.[58]

In general, though, the spring and summer of 1943 were frustrating for Bill; in addition to the NBC fiasco and the disruptive break with his agent, several promising stories did not jell. One featured the crew of a Mitchell medium bomber named the Hell Cat, which had just returned from North Africa after fifty missions. Before Bill could complete his interviews the crew members were sent around the country on a war bond drive. Kathrine too found the summer depressing. Barbara and she stayed mostly at the New Jersey farm, where, so she wrote her mother-in-law, it rained nearly every day; and New York City was hot, dingy, and crowded with people preoccupied with the war. At the end of August Bill took her to Mexico City for a break and sent Barbara with their cook to stay with Kathrine's sister-in-law, Eileen, and her children in Florida. But Bill had to cut their Mexico vacation short to get back to Washington to try to save his flight surgeon story, which had run into censorship problems. Their hurried return proved fruitless: even with his personal connections he could not get enough of the story through the War Department to interest the *Digest.*

After his bout with the flu in April, Will White never fully recovered. On October 12 the Associated Press reported that he was on his way to the Mayo Clinic for a checkup, having "been kept at home much of the time in recent weeks by illness."[59] The day Sallie phoned Bill with the diagnosis of cancer, Kathrine wrote her: "We are so sorry—and you are so far away. Bill will probably be there before you get this letter as he is taking the first plane he can get all the way through on."[60] He got to Rochester in time to talk with his father before he underwent abdominal surgery. Afterward, in the recovery room, Bill and his mother learned Will had at best several months to live. While still in Rochester, Bill wrote his uncle Lacy: "Just before he went on the operating table (he didn't expect to come off alive), he told mother and me that there were only two things in his life left undone. First, he had hoped to be able to finish his autobiography. . . . Secondly, he said that, even more than the book, he had wanted to see Ronald Finney free, now that he had served ten years."[61] Bill took over both projects, the Finney one first because Ronald was eligible for a third executive clemency hearing in December.

Freeing Finney was more than filial duty. Both Bill and his father corresponded with him regularly. Kathrine and Bill had first suggested, then encouraged what became for Ronald a successful career, writing pseudonymously for trade journals, and when in Kansas, Bill occasionally visited him at the penitentiary.[62] Will had editorially supported Ronald's first two pleas for clemency and for the second had enlisted the aid of an old ally, Justice William Smith of the Kansas Supreme Court. But despite that support Gov. Payne Ratner had denied both applications. Now with a new governor, Andrew Schoeppel, and a new state parole attorney, Judge Schuyler Bloss, the Whites mounted a vigorous effort with the help again of Justice Smith.

That Thanksgiving Bill, Kathrine, and Barbara joined his parents in Emporia for two weeks, returning to New York in time for him to speak on December 8 before four thousand delegates to the

Second War Congress of the National Association of Manufac-
turers on the topic "Tokyo Is Expendable," as part of an afternoon
panel on war aims.[63] But by December 12 he was again in Emporia
working the White political network on Finney's behalf. On his
way he stopped in Kansas City to enlist the support of Roy Roberts,
managing editor, and Henry Haskell, editor, of the *Star*, and to
confer with its Kansas editor, his uncle Lacy. Will, though weak
and in pain, wrote identical letters to thirty Kansas newspaper
editors, friends who would respond to his personal request not
to criticize the upcoming Finney hearing. Bill did the legwork.
At Judge Bloss's suggestion Ronald drafted, with Bill's help, a
statement of remorse and an explanation of what had happened
to the money, insofar as he knew. And Bill arranged a meeting
between Governor Schoeppel, Mabel Finney, and himself a few
days before the hearing to give the governor their view of the
broken 1933 plea bargain.

At the December 16 hearing Bill appeared before Judge Bloss,
together with Mabel and an attorney, to testify about Ronald's
repentance and his writing career. Then to cover all bases, just
before leaving for New York, Bill sent a grudging letter to Alf
Landon asking for his support, not as a favor to him but to his
father: "I do not ask you for favors for the same reason that I
do not [write] checks on a bank where I don't keep an account;
we have a mutual friend who got into trouble doing that. . . . You
might do this if father asked you to, but I have not suggested it
to him, because on the other hand you might not."[64] Landon
replied that he was sorry "but the tone of your letter makes it
impossible for me to discuss the Ronald Finney matter with you."[65]
Bill was not to forget that. His reply to Landon suggests quiet
fury: "[You] say you are sorry my letter's tone keeps you from
discussing Ronald's case. I didn't ask you to; we both know the
facts. I showed you how you could do what I feel is a decent
honorable thing which would also be most helpful to father.
Clearly you didn't want to do it."[66] But Landon did hold his
tongue publicly, and to Bill's relief, on January 21 Governor
Schoeppel commuted Ronald's sentence of 31 to 635 years to a
sentence of 18 to 36, making him eligible for parole in February
1945.

Just after the hearing Bill wrote Wallace asking that he not be given a new *Reader's Digest* assignment because he needed time "to straighten out my father's business affairs. He grows a little weaker each day, and I don't see how he can last many more weeks. This naturally brings up a number of problems around the management of the Emporia Gazette in which I can help him and my mother."[67] Bill's only extant report of his reaction to his father's death the morning of January 29 he wrote much later, in his centennial address:

> Suddenly at four o'clock in the morning it happened—the nurse running in to tell us that [father] was gone. . . . So now, being of a newspaper family, a chip, if you like, off the old Sage of Emporia block, I found myself hastening to the phone to call, not the undertaker, as any sane family would, but the A.P. and the U.P. Both, I knew, had brought up to date their biographical sketches. Four o'clock would be just right to start moving them out on the main trunk wires, so that the Sage of Emporia's last big story could get full-dress treatment and page one play in the papers across the land. Only after I had hung up did I remember the undertaker. Stupid, isn't it? My father would have laughed.[68]

Any less calculated but more personal response Bill seems, characteristically, to have kept to himself. For when he again wrote Wallace he focused on practical, not emotional considerations, confiding that "my father's affairs are in very bad shape and it will take several weeks to straighten them out. His estate consists largely of the Emporia Gazette and he left one of those nice old fashioned 1880 wills (completely ignoring the present war time estate and inheritance taxes) . . . my job for the present is to . . . see what can be done to save the paper as a healthy unit."[69] And he was reading the manuscript version of his father's autobiography, which he had promised to edit. Before Will died he had dictated six pages of instructions about arranging and completing the book, which he had under contract with Macmillan, his longtime publisher. Essentially he had brought it up to 1923; beyond that he had only previously published reminiscent pieces that would require considerable rewriting if they were to be used.

But after the eulogies of the funeral, held in the chapel of the College of Emporia, after the pageantry of the interment at Maplewood Cemetery, which on a bitterly cold day drew eighteen hundred people, and after the acknowledgment of hundreds of telegrams and letters of condolence, Bill turned also to consideration of his own life, absent his father. Keeping the *Gazette* meant much to him; not only did it assure his mother a comfortable income but it contributed to his own sense of identity and security for his family. As he explained in his February 29 letter to Wallace,

> while I don't intend for the next ten years to live in Emporia, I have very important roots out in that country which I should not sever because it is a typical country town in an average rural state where I have grown up with the people. Occasionally going back there to share with them a common interest, I got a kind of calm and sensible perspective on the nation as a whole, what it wants and where it is going, that I get in no other way.
>
> If my plans work out I intend to operate the Emporia Gazette at long range—going back there an occasional week or so every season to keep in touch with it and with the people.[70]

Bill certainly did not intend to pick up Elijah's mantle as *Gazette* resident editor and leading town booster; he had worked too hard to establish himself back East. Besides, he liked the excitement and anonymity of New York City, at least that is what he confided to an old Cambridge friend in 1943: "[New York is] a curious and very frightening place, viewed from a distance, but after you've lived here for a month or so, it becomes as comfortable and homelike as an old pair of shoes. . . . Most of all, you can have either plenty of privacy or plenty of fun, whichever you happen to be looking for. By chance I like privacy."[71] Young Bill, now in early middle age, realized that privacy would be impossible if he moved back to Emporia, and self-definition difficult.

So toward the end of March 1944 he was again in New York, eager to pick up a *Reader's Digest* assignment. He knew the *Gazette*, ably edited by Eugene T. Lowther, required little attention from him that spring, especially with Sallie determined to watch over

it from 927 Exchange. John Wheeler had asked him to take over
his father's contract to cover both national conventions in Chicago
for the NANA, but they did not start until the end of June.[72]
Meanwhile, in the *New York Times* he read that Eric Johnston,
the charismatic liberal Republican president of the United States
Chamber of Commerce, had just accepted an unusual invitation
from Joseph Stalin to visit Russia for several weeks that spring.
Stalin, so it developed, wanted to lobby Johnston for long-term
American credits after the war. Bill immediately wrote Wallace,
who was vacationing in Arizona: "I would like to go along. What
do you think of it? Certainly they would let him see everything
that they would ever let anybody see and I would bring back the
material to publish at a time when everybody in this country . . .
would be vitally interested in Russia."[73]

During 1943 Wallace had become a fan of Johnston's as a
vigorous, liberal spokesman for American business and had
become concerned about Russia as an anomalous wartime ally
and enigmatic postwar power. As a result the *Digest* featured three
articles that year by Johnston explicating American capitalism and
commenting on its postwar potential. And it published four
articles about Russia, two briefly extolling the Soviet war effort
and two rather critical leaders. The first of those was by Wendell
Willkie, an excerpt from a chapter of his forthcoming book *One
World* with the title "Life on the Russian Frontier," which ended,
"We must learn to know Russia [because] . . . she will not be
ignored in the world after the war." The other was an "original"
by roving editor and well-known philosophical radical Max
Eastman entitled "We Must Face the Facts About Russia."
Essentially an editorial, it was an earnest, hard-hitting plea that
the Soviet government be recognized as a ruthless dictatorship.
Then early in 1944 the magazine again carried a story sympathetically depicting the Russian people at war.[74] Against that background Bill's proposal for a unique "color story"—that is, an
informal account of his impressions from that trip—won Wallace's
immediate approval. Now Bill had to persuade Johnston to accept
him as a travel companion and the Soviets to grant him a visa.

Johnston eagerly agreed, Bill reported to Wallace, because "he
has on his hands a very minor boom for the Republican

nomination for President, which he doesn't take seriously, but he is keenly interested in the suggestion that perhaps he would be made Republican key-noter at the convention and privately I think he would welcome the chance to have his name kept before the public in the next two or three months, which is why he is keen on taking me along, if it can be arranged."[75] Though the Soviets consented to Johnston's bringing along a secretary and an aide, they were not so keen on his choosing a *Reader's Digest* roving editor as that secretary, especially one who had covered the Finnish side of the 1939–40 war and who was on record in his newspaper column as an anti-Stalin Progressive. But Johnston assured the Russian ambassador that such a writing assistant was vital to him. After checking with Moscow, the embassy issued Bill a visa. To legitimize his status further, he secured credentials as a war correspondent through John Wheeler, with an agreement to file NANA dispatches from the Soviet Union, as he had from England in 1940.[76] To that end he packed a United States Army officer's uniform with the insignia of a brevet major, a correspondent's privilege. A Chamber of Commerce public relations aide named Joyce O'Hara, an eccentric hypochondriac, also accompanied Johnston. The army would fly them free to Tehran and back as VIPs, but while in the Soviet Union Johnston insisted they pay all their own expenses. Intrigued by the trip, Wallace authorized a $4,000 travel advance for Bill.[77] On May 15 Johnston, O'Hara, and White left Washington for Tehran via North Africa on a crowded army C-54.

By the time they reached Casablanca, Johnston was suffering from sinusitis, which grounded them for nearly two weeks before a physician would approve a flight to Tehran. Because Johnston's hopes for a national political role had faded, he did not have to get back to Washington until July 12, so he simply extended the trip. But that delay scuttled Bill's plans to cover the national conventions.[78] They arrived in Tehran the same day as Averell Harriman, the American Ambassador to the Soviet Union, on his way back to Moscow from consultations in Washington and London. The next day he took them with him in his converted B-24 Liberator. Though they landed in Moscow on June 2, Johnston's promised interview with Stalin was put off inexplicably by the Soviets until the night of June 24.[79] So for three weeks they waited. At first their official hosts, the People's Commissariat of Foreign Trade, gave them standard factory tours around Moscow and treated them to theater offerings and formal banquets. But after D-Day in Normandy, June 6, which the Soviets welcomed as establishing their Western Allies' often promised "second front," Johnston and his party felt increased official warmth. They were taken on a private steamboat trip up the Moscow Canal and along the Volga River, with a band, operetta stars, and selected members from the American press corps. Soon the Red Army arranged for them, and some of that press corps, a several-day trip to the Finnish front via Leningrad, which gave Bill the unusual opportunity to cover that front from the other side. And the Office of Foreign Trade worked out an itinerary for a unique two-week tour, after Johnston's now-scheduled interview with Stalin, of new industrial areas well beyond the Urals, some not yet seen by American eyes.

In Moscow Johnston and O'Hara stayed at the American Embassy, but Bill managed to get in at the Metropol Hotel, where most of the foreign press were staying. In his book *Report on the Russians* he explained he did that to "ear-bite," which "is a technical newspaper term for a correspondent who comes to a foreign city for a short time and pumps the regular correspondents or diplomats there for the rich fund of information and background, which it has cost them years to collect, and some of which they can't write and stay where they are." He then asserted that "my conscience is fairly easy about biting ears here because I can answer their eager questions about America, and because, when in the past I've been stationed abroad, I've always let traveling reporters bite my ear for helpful information."[80] Perhaps, but some of those correspondents—Alexander Kendrick, Harrison Salisbury, and Bill Lawrence, for example—viewed him after his book came out as an opportunistic visiting fireman who took advantage of them. At the time, though, he was accepted as an experienced fellow correspondent deserving of sympathy because the Soviets would not grant him cable privileges.[81]

Becoming frustrated while Johnston waited in Moscow for his appointment with Stalin, Bill grabbed a chance on June 21 and 22 to go along on an overnight press trip to the new United States

Army airbase near Poltava in the Ukraine, built for American
shuttle bombing from Italy across Romania and Germany. Poltava
being the site of a famous Russian victory over the Swedes in 1709,
the Soviets, as a matter of pride and xenophobia, had not allowed
the American army to bring in its own radar, coordinated anti-
aircraft guns, and night fighters. But they should have, for the
Soviets had only visually aimed gun batteries, so German bombers
destroyed forty-nine B-17s on the ground that night and damaged
twenty-one others, killing two Americans and thirty Soviets in
the process. Bill and his fellow correspondents witnessed the raid
in pajamas hunkered down in shallow trenches. The next morning,
before being airlifted back to Moscow, they inspected the damage
unhampered by dazed Soviet officials, but Bill was the first allowed
to report that disaster, nine months later in a chapter of his book,
as cleared by army censors in Washington.[82]

At his evening meeting with Stalin, Johnston asked if he could
invite four of the Moscow-based American press corps along on
his tour beyond the Urals, a request previously denied by the
Soviet Foreign Office. Stalin agreed, so the next morning two
Soviet-built DC-3s were ready for the group, one a VIP version
for Johnston's party, including Bill, the other a military transport
for the four extra correspondents and a censor. Those four,
endorsed by their peers, were Richard ("Dick") Lauterbach of Time-
Life, Harrison Salisbury of the United Press, Robert Magidoff of
the Associated Press (AP), and Bill Lawrence of the *New York
Times*. They flew to three wartime industrial evacuation centers:
first to Magnitogorsk, about 800 miles southeast of Moscow; then
northeast 250 miles to Sverdlovsk; then east 500 miles to Omsk.
At each they stayed overnight after a day of factory tours, an
official banquet, and an evening concert. From Omsk they then
flew 400 miles further east to Novosibirsk, capital of the huge
province of Siberia.

Here they stayed several days as guests of Michael Kulagin,
dynamic Communist party boss of that province, whom Bill later
compared to Jimmy Cagney and characterized as a perfect
Tammany politician. At the end of their stay there, before they
headed southeast about 1,000 miles to Alma-Ata, Kulagin
presented Johnston with a fortune in gems—nearly fifty diamonds,

rubies, and emeralds—as a "personal" gift. Johnston felt seriously embarrassed by such a blatant bribe, but Kulagin vehemently insisted he accept it, out of "friendship." Bill, experienced in Kansas politics, came up with a face-saving solution. Though he did not include this episode in his own account of the trip, both Salisbury and Lauterbach focus on it in theirs. According to them, White suggested that Eric give the gems back just as they left, with the explanation that as a good Republican he could not break party discipline, which forbade acceptance of such a gift without official approval. If he accepted them, he would be in serious trouble back home. After some hesitation, Kulagin, who understood well the concept of party discipline, took back the gems. In retrospect, Salisbury thought Kulagin's gift a clumsy attempt, directed from Moscow, to take care of Johnston, because of his previously noncommittal stance during the trip.[83]

After Alma-Ata, the group flew west to Tashkent, just north of Afghanistan, from where the four correspondents made their way back to Moscow, and Johnston's party, having covered an immense stretch of the Soviet Union, flew back to Tehran. There they caught an army transport back to the United States, arriving in New York on July 12, as Johnston had determined. Unfortunately, the Associated Press photo of their arrival shows Bill in a correspondent's army uniform. The Soviets used that photo, after *Report on the Russians* came out, to accuse him of deception. They claimed that because he had worn the uniform during the trip, they thought him a military aide and under strict government control. He replied that he wore his uniform home only because, in contrast to his civilian clothes, which he had in fact worn throughout Russia, it was relatively clean. But such accusations and recriminations did not come until later, after the Soviets turned his Russian color story into an American cause célèbre.[84]

Immediately on his return, Bill wrote a mildly critical commentary about the Soviet war effort for the NANA, a piece he felt he owed John Wheeler. The commentary, released July 18, caused Ambassador Averell Harriman to warn Johnston by cable "that since White entered the Soviet Union as a member of your party, what he writes in consequence of the visit will be considered by Soviet officials as being approved by you." Johnston sent a copy of that cable to Bill "for your information," then criticized the Soviets himself in a Seattle speech, in which he declared that while in Russia "'never before did I realize the importance of our freedom, our standard of living, our habeas corpus, our Bill of Rights,'" because it is a land where "'civil liberties are only a vague promise.'" Later, when Bill's book came under harsh critical attack, Johnston moderated that stance and publicly distanced himself from White.[85]

After writing the NANA piece, Bill then ghosted a first-person account for Johnston of his interview with Stalin, to be carried by the *Reader's Digest*, and helped him with a feature article about his Soviet trip for *Life*.[86] Finished with those by the end of July, Bill took Kathrine and Barbara for a fortnight break to the New Jersey seashore, where he started work on his own story, assuming it would flow easily from his notebooks; it did not. Work in New York City that August proved impossible: the weather was miserable and their living accommodations in disarray. While Bill was in Russia, Kathrine happened on a bargain housing buy, a solid but somewhat dowdy brownstone on East Sixty-sixth Street, part of a restricted neighborhood of twelve houses overlooking a private park called Jones Woods, about six blocks from Bloomingdale's department store. The house became their New York base for the rest of Bill's life.[87] But before moving, Kathrine insisted on renovating and redecorating. The lease on their Greenwich Village brownstone was up at the end of October and the best short-term city rental she could find late that wartime summer was a small, two-room apartment at 21 West Sixteenth, in the Garment District. So while Kathrine handled those matters, Bill settled in at their New Jersey farmhouse for what was to become a nearly three-month struggle to turn his notebooks into a coherent, book-length account.

His only professional break from that struggle was at the end of September, when he took several days off to write a feature article about the combat death of the fighter pilot son of Joe Falls, a longtime *Gazette* pressman, for the Christmas issue of *McCall's*. Entitled "Little Joe's Star" and bolstered by hometown photos, the article proved a touching story about the family's reception of the news and the inherent dignity of their grief.[88] In contrast his Russian story did not flow as quickly. In his notebooks he had mistaken or misspelled many Russian names. And some of his more personal impressions of Soviet society had to be checked for accuracy or backed up by data. He soon realized he needed a good research editor. Fortunately, he had married one, and she came to his rescue.

With Kathrine's steadying help he managed to produce a workable draft by the end of October. Both felt pressured to get it written because rapidly changing wartime conditions would soon date his narrative. And he had to get back to Emporia to help his mother settle his father's estate and sort out the business end of the *Gazette*. Wallace planned to run cuts of Bill's account in the December and January issues of the *Reader's Digest*. So Kathrine vetted the manuscript while Bill was still writing it, then after he left for Emporia, she went over it again paragraph by paragraph with Alexandre Barmine, a former Soviet army officer and diplomat who had defected during the 1936–37 purges.[89] After sending that version to the *Reader's Digest* for condensation, Kathrine worked closely through November and much of December with Lambert Davis at Harcourt, Brace to get the manuscript ready for book publication. Meanwhile, in Emporia Bill responded by mail or phone to their queries and had the final say on all substantive revisions.[90]

He was glad to be nearly done with what had proven an onerous task. But even in Emporia Russia was still uppermost in his mind, for just after he arrived home he published in the *Gazette* a signed editorial explaining that he planned to vote for FDR for a fourth term, because "if the President is reelected, I think we will arrive at some kind of friendly compromise with Stalin over European governments and boundaries." Though the *Gazette* itself officially supported Thomas E. Dewey, Bill wrote that Dewey "by refusing all compromise . . . might bring either an immediate war [with the Soviets] . . . or be forced back into the isolationist position of some of his early supporters." To Bill's delight the president sent him a note of thanks soon after the election.[91] By the end of December much of the Russian book was in initial galleys and Kathrine and Barbara were in Emporia, to be with Sallie and Bill the first Christmas after Will's death.

While sorting out *Gazette* financial matters, Bill had hoped to start editing his father's autobiography and had begun reading the manuscript closely with his mother. But thunderheads gathered over the *Reader's Digest* December installment of his Russian report. The first distant flicker appeared December 9 in Moscow's official newspaper *Pravda* in a commentary by the Soviet journalist David Zaslavsky, who charged Bill with violating Soviet hospitality and trust by writing a book that was "the usual stew from the Fascist kitchen with all its smells, calumnies, ignorance and hidden anger." This was reported in a number of American newspapers.[92] A similar bolt came later from the *Canadian Tribune*, a Toronto-based equivalent of the *Daily Worker*, which in a full-page feature on December 30 interviewed Raymond Davies, a Canadian Broadcasting Company correspondent just back from Moscow, about the January *Digest* installment. Headed "Davies Unmasks W. L. White as Liar," it concluded with Davies thundering that "Bill White has smeared his father's name in the gutters in which wallow all fascist swine. The Germans will be only too glad to use it for their propaganda as they have done with other *Reader's Digest* articles." Both Bill and Kathrine had anticipated a squall from the Soviets, but not one damning him for defaming his late father's name.

For a while, early in December, Bill worried about rumors that Sen. Joseph F. Guffey planned to accuse the *Reader's Digest* before the Senate Foreign Affairs Committee of harming the Allied cause by excerpting Bill's *Report on the Russians*. But Wallace checked his Washington sources, then wrote Bill not to worry, that "everyone continues to say that your article was one of the best the Digest ever published." Wallace also advised him not to "let anyone talk you into revising or modifying the book."[93] Unexpected by Bill, then, was Bennett Cerf's blast on December 30 in his influential "Tradewinds" column carried by the *Saturday Review of Literature*. Though Cerf had access only to the two *Reader's Digest* cuts, he predicted that White's forthcoming book would be one of the worst of 1945 and that "it is precisely such prejudiced and deliberately angled reports as his that make Soviet officials and censors so eternally suspicious of the foreign journalists quartered in their midst."[94] Pique, not public spirit, seems in part to have motivated that attack: in 1942, after the Allies had warily embraced the Soviets, Cerf, as head of Random House, proposed a wartime moratorium by commercial publishers on books hostile to the USSR, an agreement quietly encouraged by the State Department and honored informally for nearly three years by the trade. Now, with the war in Europe entering its final stages, Harcourt, Brace proposed to break that moratorium with the full version of Bill's *Report on the Russians*, a move that many in the trade regarded as a legitimate challenge to both Cerf's "authority" and State Department interference.[95]

The real tempest was still to come, though, brewed up at a distance by the Soviet government, which had no conception of an independent, free press and which, as a result, reacted with paranoia even to the threat of published criticism in an important "friendly" country. The war, of course, intensified that reaction, so much so that Bill's essentially analytical *Reader's Digest* accounts triggered the scurrilous *Pravda* and *Canadian Tribune* attacks. However, those were but preliminaries to an extraordinary four-month campaign to stop publication of the book or, failing that, thoroughly to discredit it. For American Communists had learned from Bill's fellow correspondent and friend Dick Lauterbach, who had gone over the uncut manuscript with Bill and Kathrine in October, that the book version would have not only a more critical tone than the *Reader's Digest* condensation but would also cover additional and, for the Soviets, more discomfiting topics. Afterward Kathrine reviewed the history of Lauterbach's involvement for Bill Stroock, the Whites' lawyer and old friend. She wrote that after first reading the manuscript and essentially approving it—except for the secondhand references to slave labor, the panic of Moscow, and the Katyn massacre—Dick "was always cooperative when changes were made later for I made a great many in Bill's absence and invariably checked with Dick to be sure the balance was not destroyed. Then—for a few weeks I could not reach him. When he called again he was entirely different." Of all the Moscow correspondents Bill knew, Kathrine wrote Stroock, "Dick was the only one who had read the book or to whom Bill talked at all."[96]

The Soviet storm against Bill had an American cloud cover, the National Council of American-Soviet Friendship, which had state branches, a New York headquarters and a paid staff. The council had developed from a Soviet-backed wartime public relations effort, an annual Congress of American-Soviet Friendship, organized in 1942 by Dr. Corliss Lamont, Bill's Harvard classmate and a longtime Soviet apologist. Joseph E. Davies, former American ambassador to the USSR, served as honorary chairman, backed by eighty prominent American sponsors, including, ironically enough, Bill's father. Lamont was executive chairman, as he had been during the 1930s of a similar organization, American Friends of the Soviet Union. But before invoking the authority of the council, the Communists apparently tried personal intimidation. During December Kathrine received a number of anonymous letters and local phone calls at 21 West Sixteenth, their unlisted temporary apartment, demanding that Bill withhold his book because it was impolitic and unpatriotic. And those continued after her return from Kansas in January.[97]

Next the Soviets tried a direct appeal. Under the aegis of the council, Dirk Struik, a professor of mathematics at the Massachusetts Institute of Technology (MIT) and chairman of the council's Massachusetts branch, wrote to both Harcourt, Brace and the *Reader's Digest* to argue that "the publication of such a book . . . would only help to increase the misunderstanding which exists in our country concerning the Soviet Union and for that reason would be a negative contribution to the cause of American Soviet friendship."[98] Then he led a Massachusetts delegation to New York to call on Donald Brace to urge that he not publish the book. According to Lambert Davis, Bill's editor, Brace told them the book would be published and showed them the door.[99] Understandably bothered by such tactics, Bill later ran into Corliss Lamont at the offices of Harcourt, Brace and, uncharacteristically for both men, got into a shouting match about publication of the book.[100] Later, Lamont wrote Bill to deny that he was personally trying to block publication.[101] But as executive chairman of the council, he undoubtedly countenanced the next phase of the campaign.

Raymond Henry Davies, the *Canadian Tribune* contributor, together with Ella Winter, widow of the muckraker Lincoln Steffens and a prominent American Communist, drafted a petition against White's forthcoming book that Edwin Smith, executive secretary of the council, cabled in February to the Anglo-American Correspondents Association in Moscow asking for its endorsement as a body.[102] The petition, as rewritten by John Hersey in Moscow in an effort to make it more palatable to fellow correspondents, read in part: "For Americans seeking understanding on the basis of real knowledge of Russia, in the hope of finding a common ground for living at peace with our neighbors, White's book must rank as a highly biased and misleading report, calculated to prolong the oldest myths and prejudices against a great ally, whose sacrifices in this war have saved us incalculable bloodshed and destruction."[103] The association met and voted against endorsement. No Moscow correspondent, of course, had seen the book; none had seen even the December issue of the *Reader's Digest*, including David Zaslavsky, the *Pravda* commentator who had opened the campaign.[104]

Yet sixteen correspondents later signed that petition individually, several quite reputable—such as John Hersey, Alexander Kendrick, and Quentin Reynolds—others clearly biased—such as John Gibbons of the *Daily Worker*, and Ella Winter and Raymond Davies, the original authors. Toward the end of February the council sent the petition, along with an explanatory letter, to every source to whom Harcourt, Brace would likely send review copies. And the private war of intimidation escalated, with someone breaking into the Whites' weekend farmhouse retreat early in March to search through Bill's files and take some of his papers. Then about a month after the mid-March publication of Bill's book, the National Council of Soviet-American Friendship issued a slickly printed and illustrated thirty-two-page brochure entitled "The Truth About the Book the Nazis Like." The council sent copies on consignment to all booksellers of note, asking them to stock it, priced at fifteen cents, next to Bill's book, if they still wished to carry the book.[105]

What had Bill done in this book to elicit such an extraordinary campaign? To answer that, we need to go back about five years, to August 24, 1939, when in his "Take a Look" column Bill addressed the plight of American Communists after Stalin signed his nonaggression pact with Hitler. For Bill wrote, somewhat sympathetically, "Stalin's reasons, from the point of view of Russian nationalism, are no doubt sound. But his American followers are not Russians. They felt that in trusting him they were giving their loyalty not to a foreign power but to an international beacon light of truth and freedom. It is a bitter hour for those who, in hope of making a better world, made to the cause the ultimate disastrous sacrifice—independence of mind."[106] Such independence of mind was precisely what Bill had during his trip with Johnston through the Soviet Union. Though under contract to *Reader's Digest* and NANA, he functioned very much as a freelance, in that each had but a "first option" on either his newspaper or his magazine pieces. The *Digest* did advance him travel money, but as a roving editor that did not obligate him or the magazine to publish. So from the outset Bill could record his observations unencumbered by the need to follow any orthodoxy, to flatter an uneasy ally, or to protect his visa or correspondent's certification. The resultant independence comes across early in the book.

For example, on the flight from Tehran to Moscow Harriman's plane dipped low over the ruins of Stalingrad, awful symbol of Soviet resistance, where early in 1943 Marshal Georgi Zhukov captured Hitler's Sixth Army. But Bill was not dutifully impressed by the sight. In the book he wrote: "It is, of course, hideous. But I have become used to ruins, starting with the blitz over London in 1940. If you coiled Stalingrad up and set it down in the ruins of London, there would still be plenty of room for Stalingrad to rattle around."[107] Such impolitic iconoclasm marked his tone throughout. In stance he exemplified the unabashed, outspoken American abroad. Thus he wrote that in the Red Army the "old czarist military caste lines between officers and men have been vigorously revived." As a result "there is more saluting in this socialist army than in any other in the world, except possibly that of Mexico, which in dress this army curiously resembles."[108] And his reaction to heavy-handed Russian hospitality, with Johnston's group pursued by an official caterer with cases of vodka and tins of caviar, became a litany of half-humorous complaint that impugned such official feasts as vulgar and false, when set against a backdrop of wartime sacrifice and misery. But Bill was truly an uninvited guest, just along for the ride, so his tone or stance comes across at times as rude rather than humorous, especially when he compares the Soviet Union to a "moderately well-run penitentiary," whose inmates are uniformly shabby.[109]

But tone was not the chief reason for the crusade against his book. It was not how but what he reported. Outside the reach of Soviet censorship, Bill told of that censorship and of a police state in which a citizen could "disappear" at any time. He emphasized the importance of American industrial aid to the Soviet war effort and in contrast reported on the disorder and inefficiency of most Soviet factories, though he did acknowledge the effect of dislocations caused by the war. In addition to narrating the events of Johnston's visit, he reviewed both the Russian and German accounts of the Katyn Forest massacre, the slaughter of ten thousand Polish army officers either by the Soviets in the spring of 1940 or the Germans in the fall of 1941. He was openly skeptical of the Soviet version, which blamed the Germans. And he reported a circumstantial account of widespread panic in Moscow in October 1941 as the Germans approached the city, a reaction opposite to the official Soviet claim of intrepidity.[110]

Later in the book he just as purposely focused on another topic Soviet censorship had ruled off-limits, political prisoners. At Magnitogorsk during the Ural tour, in an auto caravan on the way to a big steel plant, Bill was startled when his car turned aside for a long column of ragged women marching disconsonantly along the road four abreast under armed guard. Clearly, the women were forced laborers, a fact studiously ignored by his escort from the People's Commissariat of Internal Affairs (known as the NKVD— Narodny Kommissariat Vnutrennikh Del). A fellow correspondent nudged Bill and asked quietly: "'Did you see what I saw?'" He replied "'Yeah,'" then commented: "Every writer who approaches even a minor theme is confronted first with the problem of selection of material, and secondly with the decision as to which incidents shall be expanded, and which he should merely chronicle, and the foregoing is a case in point."[111] Unwilling just to chronicle that sight, Bill later placed in Omsk a simulated conversation about prison laborers with two American mining engineers working for the Soviets in Siberia. At the airport hotel late at night he claimed he could not sleep and wandered down to grab a cigarette in the lobby, where he happened on the two waiting to catch a plane. There, presumably, they told him about their own experiences of the Soviet's extensive and brutal use of forced laborers in Siberia. Actually, he had that story from three American engineers in Moscow but dramatized it thus in Omsk to cover identities, which was to bring about accusations of dishonesty from fellow correspondents after the book came out.[112]

At the same time, he was touched by the patriotism and simple friendliness of the workers he met officially. Again at Omsk, but this time for real, he and Dick Lauterbach met a few of those same workers unofficially. During intermission at that evening's concert, he and Dick wandered off to look for a water fountain to offset the many champagne toasts at the obligatory banquet. A friendly NKVD officer led them to a fountain at a nearby open-air dance pavilion. There the two Americans forgot the concert for a time to talk and dance with girls from factories they had toured that day, who tried out their English and German phrases on Bill and spoke elementary Russian with Dick. After a while, he turned to Bill, as Bill recorded the conversation, to say, "'I suppose so few foreigners come through here that these people haven't learned it's dangerous to talk to us. A thing like this could never happen in Moscow.'"[113]

The Soviets found this narrative pastiche of objective reporting underscored by suggestive skepticism particularly dangerous. For while Bill observed that in 1944 the Russian people fought heroically under the most adverse of conditions, he also disclosed that the USSR was still inescapably totalitarian, still suffering from the cause and effects of the 1937 purges, still more Asiatic than European. Though not categorically hostile, he often questioned Soviet social and political assumptions. More immediately, he also questioned Soviet postwar intentions, and concluded: "I think those intentions will turn out to be friendly. However, if we move our armies out of Europe before the continent is stabilized, and if disorder, bloodshed and riots then ensue, the Russians will move into any such political vacuum. After all, they are not stupid."[114]

Between the Yalta conference of early February 1945 and the Potsdam conference of late July, most Americans assumed a friendly USSR would cooperate willingly with the Allies in reestablishing a peaceful world. But Soviet intransigence that spring at the San Francisco conference to organize the United Nations raised doubts about such cooperation. After Japan's surrender on September 2, the Soviets were newly established in Manchuria while remaining, unlike the United States, fully mobilized in Europe. Many Americans then, if they had not already, began to question the friendliness of this touchy wartime ally. Significantly, review copies of Bill's book came out in February, just after the Yalta conference, with publication in mid-March, when Americans in general still "patriotically" trusted the USSR. Because of that attitude, Bill's condensed, moderately iconoclastic accounts in the *Reader's Digest* evoked enough curiosity about the forthcoming book that Harcourt, Brace received advance bookstore orders for 48,000 copies and planned two more printings of 25,000 each. Then came the many hostile reviews. Soon a whirlwind of controversy overtook both the book and its author.

In January and February Bill remained in Emporia to work with the *Gazette* after Kathrine returned with Barbara to New York City. Then early in March he met them at Melbourne, Florida, where Kathrine's sister-in-law, Eileen, still lived.[115] On March 16, just after the first negative reviews appeared, Lambert Davis wrote Bill that he applauded "wholeheartedly your decision to [vacation] in Florida. There will be plenty of people to uphold you, and it is the wise as well as the dignified thing to do to let them carry the ball at the outset."[116] But neither Davis nor Bill anticipated the extraordinary critical turbulence that followed.

Editor and Publisher in its March 31 issue covered that phenomenon in four separate pieces, which together give succinct insight into the critical reaction. One was a four-column article by Dwight Bentel headed "White's Book Creates Reviewer Furor," which he based on a survey of seventy-five reviews that ran three-to-two against. His article observed that

> not for years had a new book kicked up such a commotion in the literary columns as White's "Report on the Russians," a "brightly written and racy"—or "smart alec"—account of his travels in Russia with Eric Johnston, president of the U.S. Chamber of Commerce.

> Book reviewers across the country were in a dither, alternately blowing on their spectacles and beating on their typewriters in the production of such a flurry of diverse opinions as is rarely seen even in the book columns.[117]

The rest of the article was a series of stridently contradictory quotations from selected reviews. Next to that article *Editor and Publisher* ran a sidebar commentary headed "William Allen White Wouldn't Have Done It? But He Did." It began:

> Several of the critics who lambasted W. L. White's "Report on the Russians" . . . reproached White, Jr., with the "betrayal" of his great and famous father, William Allen White of the Emporia *Gazette*.
>
> "You shouldn't have done it, Bill," they said in effect. "Your father wouldn't have done it.". . . [But, to the contrary,] White, Sr., did a three-week tour of Russia in 1933 with Maurice Hindus and several other correspondents. He later wrote, in the *New Republic*: ". . . I am merely . . . a competent middle-class witness who on the whole, as an average American, has wished the Russians well. I still do. I think the Russians are mad. I believe they cannot possibly succeed until they cure their madness, and I am as sure as I can be that Communism as a philosophy won't hold water. I feel that it is not a creed that men may long live by."
>
> Then follows an unfavorable comparison of the Russian standards of living and justice with those existing in Emporia. . . .
>
> And did William Allen White raise a howl of protest from various literati with this writing? He did.[118]

Also in that issue *Editor and Publisher* included its own decidedly critical review, which described the book as "readably facile, unfortunately quick-see, and distortingly prejudiced." Then on its editorial page the magazine staunchly defended Bill's freedom as an American journalist to report his own impressions: "God forbid that the time ever come when an American newspaper man, having visited a foreign country, can't write fully and freely of what he saw—or what he thought he saw—because he will 'harm America.' That a foreign country manifests a certain touchiness about things written of it doesn't indicate the need for a change in a basic principle of American democracy."[119]

For *Editor and Publisher* that paradoxical coverage of a book's reviews was most unusual, but so was the campaign against the book. The National Council of American-Soviet Friendship had cleverly aimed its attack first of all at reviewers, with most receiving a copy of the petition alleging that *Report on the Russians* was biased, inaccurate, divisive, and intentionally misleading. After targeting the literary establishment, the council then focused on American book buyers with its illustrated pamphlet denouncing Bill and his book. But the campaign caused some to come to his defense. For example, Norman Cousins, editor of the *Saturday Review of Literature*, published a generally positive review of Bill's book by Louis Fischer, then followed that with commentary by five other reviewers, each from a different perspective. In a prefatory note Cousins justified the unusual roundtable feature "because of the arguments that the book has generated, as well as the importance of the subject itself."[120]

At first such controversy seemed to help sales, with *Report on the Russians* among the nonfiction national top ten for five months, from March through July, according to *Publishers Weekly*. But the final sales total of about 85,000 hardcover copies did not meet Harcourt, Brace's initial expectations. The campaign did discredit the book for many readers, with some librarians, for example, refusing to order it because it was "dishonest and unpatriotic."[121] And the campaign significantly affected both Bill's personal and professional life. Twenty-four years after publication Bill replied to a note from Lambert Davis reminiscing about their work together on the book: "I certainly remember those days but I don't wake up laughing about them, for that period was a pivotal one in my life. During it I lost about half, or better, of my New York friends and replaced them with a number of new ones. Still this is a shock and an up-rooting."[122]

Not only did the public attacks on his journalistic integrity continue through the summer, alienating him from many associates, but so did the personal letters.[123] Though many wrote to support his stand or his point of view, many chorused the Soviet lines of attack, including the scurrilous. For example, Stella Gonser, a

Chicago school teacher, wrote him patronizingly: "Why all the bitterness, the petty faultfinding, the inconsequential recordings, and, yes, the satisfaction the writer seems to take in whatever makes imperfection in Russia? Surely, it cannot be due to personal frustration in life. Your father's photograph showed a handsome man, and he very probably picked him a pretty wife. By all the rules you should be well-favored, well-regarded, sufficiently loved."[124] Or, more abusive, United States Army Capt. Wilbur Van Horn, Jr., wrote: "You are not a chip off the old block, just a mere splinter. Pardon me while I go and vomit."[125] To all such letters Bill sent a form acknowledgment, simply saying, "I am sorry we do not agree."

While he maintained a public stance of stoical indifference to both published and private attacks, the various invidious allusions to his late father hurt. The March issue of *Soviet Russia Today* contained the most egregious of those in an "open letter" to Bill by Raymond Davies, who had helped author the petition. Assuming the role of sadly aggrieved friend, Davies offered such observations as "You know, Bill, I think your dad, one of America's great exponents of liberty, must be restless in the great beyond reading your words. Why should he not be restless? Have you not dragged the honored White name through mire?"[126] Barely acquainted with Davies, Bill wrote Professor Watson Kirkconnell of McMaster University, at that time president of the Canadian Authors Association, asking what he knew about him. Kirkconnell replied that he was a well-known Canadian Communist whose Russian family name was "Davinsky" and who first as "Roy Davis" then as "Raymond Henry (or Arthur) Davies" had been a party-line journalist in Toronto since the mid-1930s.[127] As the result of such inquiries, Bill soon recognized that much of the criticism of his book and most of the personal attacks resulted from a calculated Communist campaign to manage American public opinion. A published reply on his part would be fruitless, he concluded, until events proved that campaign a failure. Eighteen months later in the *Saturday Review of Literature*, he was indeed able to say to those critics "I told you so," but with such heavy-handed irony that he revealed how much they had hurt. After detailing his version of the unfairness of the criticism, he noted ruefully, "The moral is, never try to tell people on the day before Christmas that there isn't any Santa Claus. Let them find out for themselves."[128]

The various attacks against *Report on the Russians* did not entirely preoccupy Bill that spring. Sallie White at age seventy-five was in increasingly frail health and could no longer supervise the family newspaper. So Bill began to edit the *Gazette* in absentia. When he left Emporia in March, he had arranged that the city editor airmail a copy to him daily. That started what became a long-standing practice when he was in New York of his airmailing back to Ted McDaniel, city editor, then managing editor, a close critique, often augmented by a phone call.[129] An interviewer once asked Ed Shupe, a *Gazette* reporter from 1947 to 1959, if Bill were "mainly editor in name." Ed replied that Bill

> checked that paper over every day from stem to stern, and in the mail the next day would come back [a copy covered with red marks]. Usually he would get on you about maybe something you didn't cover in the story or maybe even the grammatical construction of the story—he was great on that. . . . If you said something in an article that was controversial or in any way other than straight reporting of facts you better be sure you had somebody to attribute it to because he would say, "Who said this?" "Where'd you get that?" Things like that. He'd pick up everything; he really would pore over those things.[130]

For example, in a three-page, single-spaced transcript addressed to Ted McDaniel of a telephoned critique from Frenchtown, appended to a dictated editorial, Bill humorously but pointedly criticized a story by Ed Shupe:

> I enjoyed Ed Shupe's golf story on page 14 but have a couple of criticisms. I felt that the beginning and the end of his story was, for the most part, unnecessary wind and that the solid and interesting facts were confined to column 2, column 3 and the first part of column 4. The trouble with his lead was that he was trying to be literary but gave the reader no facts to go on not already known to every Cretan until he introduced the Eatons at the bottom of column one, where the story really begins. After that it went along smoothly and factually and the

whole thing was excellent until the final paragraph where he again succumbs to the lure of literature and hauled in poor old Mother Nature, that badly overworked little woman, to help him end the piece in a burst of sunset glory. Now, from the literary standpoint a piece like this certainly should be well organized which means that it should have a good ending. But the way to achieve this is to save for the very end the most revealing fact or significant incident or startling statistic in the story, and close crisply with that, rather than to drool all those mushy and factless sentences at the end, like sweet sorghum mash falling out of a cow's mouth.[131]

For nine years, from 1945 to 1954, when he spent most of a year in town, Bill ran the *Gazette* as an active but mostly absent editor-publisher. He did not usually write for the editorial page, unless he was in Emporia, though he did supervise that page closely and sometimes gave assignments. On special occasions he would dictate an editorial from New York. When FDR died on April 12, for example, Bill phoned an editorial for the next issue in which he warned that the Yalta agreements were illusory, that Roosevelt "goes at a time when, though our victory is sure, that free peace for which it was fought seems far away; at the very moment when, over the roar of the battle it becomes clear that solemn promises made to him may be worth little." Bill concluded with a prayer that Harry Truman "this honest, earnest, unpretentious citizen of Lamar, Missouri, may make a success of the peace, having back of him our loyalty and God's guidance, both of which he will sorely need."[132] In the spring of 1919, as a young man about Paris, Bill shared his father's hopes for a "just and lasting peace" through the Treaty of Versailles with its League of Nations covenant. Then at home in 1920 he had observed his father's dismay as the Senate rejected such an "entangling alliance." Thus in the spring of 1945 he worried about the enigmatic aftermath of the war, about America's resolve to broker a peaceful, democratic Europe in the face of Soviet imperialism. That worry would underscore two of his next three books.

Bill and sister, Mary Katherine White, 1910.
(Courtesy of White Memorial Library,
Emporia State University)

Bill and father in portrait pose, ca. 1914.
(Courtesy of White Memorial Library,
Emporia State University)

Bill and father in New
York City, 1916. (Courtesy
of Barbara W. Walker)

Bill in SATC private's
uniform at the University
of Kansas, 1918. (Courtesy
of Barbara W. Walker)

Bill at the University of Kansas, winter 1919–20. (Courtesy of Barbara W. Walker)

Bill and father in the garden of the New York National Arts Club, 1924. (Courtesy of White Memorial Library, Emporia State University)

Bill with parents as he boards the Italian liner *Rex* in New York City, October 1939, to cover the war in Europe. (Courtesy of Barbara W. Walker)

Bill, supervised by Finnish censor, broadcasting from Viipuri, Finland, December 1939. (Courtesy of White Memorial Library, Emporia State University)

Bill with parents on side porch of 927 Exchange after his return from Europe, June 1940. (Courtesy of Barbara W. Walker)

Bill in London during the blitz, winter 1940–41. (Courtesy of Barbara W. Walker)

Bill and Kathrine with daughter, Barbara, at their New Jersey farm house, 1941. (Courtesy of Barbara W. Walker)

Will and Sallie White in front of 927 Exchange, ca. 1942. (Courtesy of White Memorial Library, Emporia State University)

Eleanor Roosevelt with Bill at a town hall forum, Norwalk, Connecticut, June 1943. (Courtesy of Barbara W. Walker)

Cover of pamphlet attacking *Report on the Russians,* issued by the National Council of American-Soviet Friendship, March 1945. (Courtesy of Kansas Collection, Spencer Research Library, University of Kansas)

Bill in Moraine Park, Colorado, August 1947. (Courtesy of Barbara W. Walker)

Herbert Hoover and Bill at dedication of Jo Davidson's bust of Will White at Peter Pan Park in Emporia, July 1950. (Courtesy of Barbara W. Walker)

Bill at father's *Gazette* desk, ca. 1954. (Courtesy of White Memorial Library, Emporia State University)

Emporia *Gazette* building, 517 Merchant, in the 1960s,
before Bill and Kathrine remodeled it. (Courtesy of
Barbara W. Walker)

Bill interviewing John Dos Passos in Catfish television
studio, November 1964. (Courtesy of Barbara W. Walker)

Bill delivering his "Sage of Emporia" speech at the University of Kansas in honor of his father's centennial, February 1968. (Courtesy of Barbara W. Walker)

Chapter Five

A Search for Peace and a Story, 1945–1951

Early in May 1945 Bill and Kathrine moved into their own refurbished brownstone at 160 East Sixty-sixth, where John and Katy Dos Passos were their first dinner guests. "Dos," having himself been the target of a "Stalinist gang-up" earlier, had written Bill a letter of sympathy late in April; he replied with an invitation to the "new house . . . because it would be nice, in all this, to see some smiling faces other than Herbert Hoover's." Dos Passos's 1939 novel *Adventures of a Young Man* portrayed an idealistic American Communist betrayed by the party in the Spanish Civil War for being politically "unreliable"; it triggered a left-wing critical furor that dismayed Dos Passos and left him permanently disenchanted with the "New York intelligentsia."[1] In spite of the implications of that invitation to Dos, Bill did not become immediately estranged from his New York Progressive friends. January 24, before most public attacks on his book, the American Civil Liberties Union (ACLU) at its celebratory Twenty-fifth Annual Meeting elected him for a three-year term to its seventy-member national committee, an honor even though the group functioned mostly as a figurehead. Living in New York City, a friend of both Roger Baldwin, ACLU executive director, and Morris Ernst, its general counsel, Bill was able to take an unusually active role in committee activities. Because of that sustained interest, regardless of the previous Communist-led attacks on his credentials and integrity, the ACLU elected him in 1948 to its thirty-member board of directors, where he served until 1956, when he returned to its less active national committee, on which he served until his death. Like Dos Passos, Bill did become a political conservative after personal disenchantment with American Progressives. But he did so gradually, while remaining a staunch libertarian. Through the McCarthy era at least, he kept an open mind and retained a number of prominent politically liberal friends.

In June 1945 Kathrine wrote her mother-in-law that "Bill's gone to Washington about a Pacific story—something about submarines that doesn't interest him greatly . . . the navy wants him to go to Guam but he doesn't think too much of it." He was casting about for a new *Reader's Digest* assignment and not having much luck. During that Washington trip he met with several senators and representatives who were interested in his view of the Soviets, such as Clare Boothe Luce, a member of the House Military Affairs Committee, and Karl Mundt, a member of its Foreign Affairs Committee and later Richard Nixon's principal ally on the House Un-American Activities Committee (HUAC). And, as arranged through Charles Ross, a friend and the new White House press secretary, Bill spent a private half hour on Saturday morning, June 16, with President Truman, who in July would meet with Stalin at Potsdam.[2]

Such Washington contacts were exhilarating, but Bill failed to land a story. Earlier in New York, at the end of March, he had run into George Moorad, just back from seven months as a Moscow correspondent for CBS. In Romania, Hungary, and Poland, Moorad had witnessed the Red Army as a merciless army of occupation, which Bill thought a timely story. But he had no luck selling it to the *Digest*, though a year later Moorad published those experiences in his book *Behind the Iron Curtain*, with an introduction by W. L. White. Nor did Bill fare any better with an interview story he wrote early in April of Army Lt. Ted Ellsworth's experiences as a German prisoner of war liberated by the Russians when they swept through Poland. It did not emerge from War Department censorship until late July and then, as Bill wrote *Digest* editor Burt MacBride, "with the guts clawed out of it and with a note saying that the deletions were necessary because no officer on active duty could be permitted to say anything which would be considered even as an indirect reflection on any of our allies."[3] Bill agreed with MacBride's decision that the story was no longer interesting or timely.

But that July the War Department did arrange for him to interview Army Capt. Howard Chappell of the clandestine Office of Strategic Services (the OSS, forerunner of today's Central Intelligence Agency, CIA), who had helped direct partisan resistance forces behind German lines in northern Italy. From that interview Bill wrote the story "Some Affairs of Honor," which, after its bumpy ride through War Department censorship, he sent at the end of September to the *Reader's Digest*, where it appeared in the December issue as "a condensation from the forthcoming book by William L. White."[4] But such a book did not come forth. In reply to Chappell's January inquiry why not, Bill explained: "As the Digest was going to press, my feeling was that I might get out a fairly small book which would combine several stories of the war's end, yours among them. . . . However, before I could get to work on this, I had to spend several months working on my father's unfinished autobiography which is now just about to go to press."[5] The autobiography was a convenient excuse; he simply did not have a book. Both Moorad and Ellsworth had decided to write up their own stories, and censorship restrictions on two other OSS stories he had in mind limited their interest. Thus editors at Harcourt, Brace were unenthused. As Bill explained in answer to a later inquiry from a *Digest* reader, his publishers told him "that they did not think that in 1946 people would be interested in this type of book on the war."[6]

That shift in the market became a significant problem for him. He had made his name with interview stories about the war; now the war was over. For two years, from January 1945 to January

1947, he placed only the story "Some Affairs of Honor" with the *Digest*. But factors other than market contributed to that hiatus. For whatever reason—unresolved grief over his father's death, reaction to the critical attacks on the Russian book, the new demands of editing a daily newspaper in absentia, or the angst of being a political Cassandra—his symptoms of depression returned, causing him again to enter psychotherapy.[7]

Bill did spend part of the fall of 1945 getting his father's autobiography ready for Macmillan. In July he had engaged Morris Ernst, who was Edna Ferber's lawyer, to help with details of its sale. For at that time Bill tried to interest Wallace in it as a *Digest* book selection, but Wallace begged off. In October Bill spent several weeks in Emporia, conferring with his mother about the *Gazette* and his editing of the manuscript.[8] Meanwhile, Macmillan enlisted Francis Brown, an editor for the *New York Times*, to suggest sizable cuts in the manuscript to tighten the narrative line, only some of which Bill later accepted. In the manuscript Will had traced his life up through the spring of 1923, but he had not had time to bring continuity to his story after 1917 nor to review the manuscript as a whole, which ran close to two thousand typed pages. So he left his son written instructions clarifying the chronology of events from 1918 through 1923. And he continued that chronology more generally through the 1920s and 1930s, with suggestions where in his personal papers and published commentaries Bill could find the materials to complete the account. Will assumed his son, with the help of Sallie, would weave those materials into a coherent narrative from 1923 on through the formation in 1940 of the White Committee. But to do so required of Bill the combined skills of a researcher, copy editor, and ghostwriter, plus a selfless dedication well beyond filial duty.

Bill did edit the manuscript for repetitions, factual errors, loose syntax, and minor lacunae, but he did not continue the story in the sequential depth his father had suggested. Early in December, when he was reviewing galley proofs, Bill wrote his father's old friend the novelist Dorothy Canfield Fisher, who had read the edited manuscript version for tone and authenticity, that he had come up with a "tentative solution" for finishing the book, a problem that had puzzled him: "I want to make it as completely as possible in his own words, a mosaic of what he thought about the Ku Klux Klan, Calvin Coolidge, the Al Smith campaign, the D.A.R., Herbert Hoover, the N.R.A., the New Deal in general, Wendell Willkie, Franklin Roosevelt, the war, our various gallant allies, the outlook for peace after the war—all of this in direct quotes from him, and with nothing from me except transitional sentences."[9] And that is precisely what he did, making no attempt to continue the story as narrative. Instead he appended a postscript chapter quoting his father on a few outstanding public events or figures after 1923. Several years later, in reply to a friend who praised him for "revising" that autobiography, he wrote: "You give me too much credit. . . . My job was purely a pedestrian one with the exception of one rigid discipline: to allow him to tell his own story in his own way—it was his life, not mine."[10]

Macmillan published Will's autobiography on March 4, 1946, with an initial printing of 400,000 copies, because the Book-of-the-Month Club had chosen it as a principal selection. It became an immediate best seller and remained on the national top ten nonfiction list for seven months. Then in 1947 Columbia University awarded Will White his second Pulitzer Prize, posthumously, this time for biography, his own.

In 1945 Bill also completed the other unfinished task he had taken over from his father, the release of Ronald Finney from prison. In February Bill and Sallie attended Finney's parole hearing in Topeka to counter any possible last-minute protest. They succeeded. On February 19 Finney emerged from the state penitentiary at Lansing a free man, to leave Kansas almost immediately for southern California, where his wife, Win, lived with their two children. In September he traveled east to stay with Bill and Kathrine for several weeks, first at their Frenchtown farm then in New York City, where he followed up leads as a freelance writer before returning to California.[11] The battle to free Finney had further embittered Bill toward the liberal wing of the Kansas Republican party. Afterward, when William G. Clugston, one of the Whites' erstwhile standpat opponents in Kansas journalism, wrote that it was the Kansas Progressives who had finally freed Ronald Finney, Bill reminded him that "no Kansas progressive gave a good god damn what happened to Ronald except my father and me."[12] About a year after that parole, Win divorced Ronald. By 1948 he had remarried and had settled near Gardiner, Oregon, writing for various trade journals, as in prison. True to his promise to his father, Bill kept in frequent touch with Finney until his death in Florida in 1961.

On January 24, 1946, Alfred Dashiell, managing editor of the *Reader's Digest*, wrote Ruth Shipley, director of the passport service, asking her to supply Bill White with whatever State Department documents were necessary for a tour of twenty European countries, some under Soviet control. By the end of February Shipley had not issued Bill a passport, so he wrote John Wheeler of the NANA asking him to write her and Secretary of State James Byrnes, saying that you hope "to get me visas to those countries of Eastern Europe which are more or less under Soviet jurisdiction."[13] Then early in March, just after publication of his father's autobiography, Bill flew to Emporia to see his mother and check on the *Gazette* before leaving on his European trip. From Emporia, March 9, he wrote Secretary of State Byrnes directly to ask for his help in securing those visas. Bill told him he was to be gone for about three months and on his return planned to write "a book on the general situation." The only American reporters granted visas to those countries, he complained, were those "carefully screened by the Russian foreign office." So he needed Byrnes's help because "I have criticized, not these governments, but Soviet foreign policy, and I have vigorously supported our democratic American foreign policy."[14]

This time Bill was lucky. Tom Blake, also of the Harvard class of 1924, was Byrnes's special assistant, and he made immediate arrangements for Bill to see the secretary, who had also been approached on Bill's behalf by Arthur Vandenberg, chairman of the Senate Foreign Relations Committee. Within several days Bill had his passport updated for Western Europe and special visa requests forwarded by the State Department to the Washington consulates of European countries under Soviet control. But none honored those requests. Nevertheless, he sailed for England on March 20. The apparent urgency, coupled with a disregard of realistic possibilities, testifies to Bill's state of mind at that time. He had entered a manic phase that lasted until well after his return to the United States. His psychiatrist, Dr. Brunswick, had died unexpectedly in January, and he needed her tempering influence. Soon after his return, on Kathrine's emphatic insistence, he became a patient of the psychiatrist Dr. Marianne Cris for several years, then transferred to Dr. Robert Knight.[15]

From London Bill cabled Herbert Hoover, then in Warsaw on a fact-finding relief mission, asking him to push his various visa requests with Soviet authorities. The next day Bill obtained entrée into Poland, but by serendipity, not influence. Poland's London consulate was not yet under strict Soviet control, and a young woman there routinely stamped his passport because he was a credentialed journalist. Obtaining no other visas, Bill left for Warsaw. Though he sent Wheeler several dispatches from there, subsequently released through the NANA, no accessible personal correspondence survives from this period.[16] In fact, Bill may not have written any because in a business letter to Morris Ernst on April 26, Kathrine noted that "Bill seems to have lost himself in the crowd in Poland. I don't know just when he will be back."[17]

After several weeks in Warsaw he moved on to the American sector of Berlin, where he stayed at the American Press Club for a month or more. He was back in New York City by June 12, for he wrote Wallace from there about paying Werner Asendorf, a German journalist he had hired in Berlin to be his chief "research scout." Educated at the University of Oregon, Asendorf had been a reluctant attaché to Joseph Goebbels's propaganda ministry in Berlin in 1939 when Bill first met him. Early in July Asendorf forwarded a collection of anecdotal accounts about life in occupied Germany to Bill in New York through Charles Arnot, a mutual friend working in Berlin for the United Press. Then during that July and August Bill spent most of his time working on a first draft of his report on Poland and Germany.

But at the same time he did not neglect other concerns, one of them the *Gazette*. That August his old friends Jack and Sid Harris, brothers who together owned a chain of small-town Kansas newspapers, bought a 95 percent interest in the Emporia radio station, KTSW, and applied for an FM license. Bill thought he and they had an understanding not to invade each other's territory, so when he heard about their purchase he immediately wrote Jack to ask, "What are you up to with that Emporia radio station? As you know we have been watching that situation for some time and as you also know . . . we are temporarily over a barrel due to estate problems and inheritance taxes."[18] Next he wrote his uncle Lacy asking him to find out what was going on and to monitor the situation. In a follow-up letter to his uncle, a veteran newspaperman, he explained his concern, an explanation that confirms Bill too was a veteran:

> When [KTSW] was owned by a group of fellows in Emporia, none of [whom] had a majority of the stock, it didn't greatly matter [who controlled the station] and I had always figured that I would pick it up cheap from them, come the next depression.
>
> The Harrises are an entirely different kettle of fish. It is also true that when a newspaper in a town the size of Emporia does not own its own radio station, the value of that newspaper is seriously affected because, in case of any kind of a row, it is very easy for the radio station to start a competing newspaper. . . .
>
> I don't want to get into a position where someone else has me by the short hair even though that short hair is held in a tender grasp of hands as loving as those of the Harris boys.[19]

Bill was hard at work writing his report on the postwar situation in Europe, but he could not ignore a commercially threatening situation in Emporia. He knew small-town journalism well and knew he had to protect his interests. Fortunately for their long-standing friendship, Jack Harris again assured him in confidence that he and Sid had bought into the Emporia radio station only to move it to Topeka as part of a larger takeover attempt. Later, in the spring of 1947, after that Topeka deal had fallen through, the Harrises offered to sell the station to Bill for what they had paid for it. But after extended negotiations Bill turned them down because the several minority stockholders wanted him to match an offer by another small-town newspaper chain, headed by the brothers Robert and George Reed.[20] Afterward, he wrote his uncle that the Reeds "have paid such a fantastically high price for this dog that it becomes a very dubious property, and one which I may be able to buy cheap in a few years."[21]

In September 1946 Bill sent the manuscript about the Polish part of his trip to his friend Llewellyn ("Tommy") Thompson, head of the Division of Eastern European Affairs in the State Department. After talking with Thompson about his reaction to it, Bill wrote Wallace that "Tommy says that . . . the Polish story will start to break in the latter part of December when, according to the Yalta agreement, they are scheduled to hold free elections there."[22] With that prediction in mind Wallace turned the manuscript over to *Digest* editor Thomas Hard, who had done the cut on *Report on the Russians.* Greatly condensed, "Report on the Poles" appeared in the December issue as "part of W. L. White's book on Poland and Germany, which will be published this winter." Soon after forwarding that manuscript to the *Digest,* Bill wrote Lambert Davis that he was sending him "two hunks of copy," one a 14,000-word preface about the Versailles treaty, the other the uncut manuscript about Poland of about 70,000 words. Still to come was a longer German section.[23]

But Bill did not complete the German unit that fall. He was distracted in part by problems at the *Gazette,* in addition to the issue of the local radio station. Most of the staff wanted wage increases because of postwar inflation. Rather than increasing wages piecemeal, Bill introduced at that time an incentive plan under which employees got a supplementary percentage of the gross business, which figured out to a bonus of about 15 percent. Also, because of a newsprint shortage, in September he had to reduce the paper for several months from a norm of ten or twelve pages to one of six or eight, and to do the same again the next fall. As a matter of principle, when the paper was thus shortened, he increased the proportion of news and editorial to advertising. That brought letters of protest from local display advertisers, which White answered diplomatically but firmly.[24]

He was also distracted by his delayed response in the *Saturday Review of Literature* to the critics of *Report on the Russians,* by his several answers to resulting letters to the editor, and by health problems both he and Kathrine were experiencing. For in November he had a flare-up of his psychosomatic intestinal troubles and wrote Lambert Davis early in December that "I have been sick for about 3 weeks and my work has been delayed."[25]

Davis replied that "there is no loss in our not being able to do anything now, as your name is big enough to carry the book in the trade. We will simply wait until it is in and then be prepared to push it through as rapidly as possible."[26] But for Bill the German section did not go at all for a while.

Just after Christmas 1946 he and Kathrine traveled to Florida to spend several weeks with Herbert Hoover on a yacht fishing off the Keys. There Kathrine became seriously ill and had to enter a Miami hospital. When she had recovered enough to travel, Bill took her back to New York then on to Boston where she had surgery in February for a uterine tumor. Though the tumor proved benign, she came down with a postoperative infection from which it took her nearly a year to recover because one of the drugs used to treat it gave her arsenic poisoning.[27] One indication of Bill's concern for her health was that while in Boston to be near her, he researched and wrote a magazine article about uterine cancer entitled "Killer of Women," which the *Reader's Digest* placed first in *Ladies' Home Journal*.

Early that spring he accompanied her back to Florida for a month of recovery in the sun.[28] During this time the Whites hired a companion from a company called Proxy Parents to stay with Barbara in New York City. Barbara seized that opportunity, at age eleven, to switch herself, without parental permission, from the Walt Whitman School for Girls, which she disliked, to the Nightingale-Bamford School, both private. She was to remain happily at the latter through high school.[29] Leaving Kathrine in Florida and an intrepid but recalcitrant Barbara in New York, Bill flew on to Emporia where he spent nearly six weeks working with the *Gazette* staff and negotiating unsuccessfully for the radio station. But by the end of May both he and Kathrine were back in New York.[30]

Those events delayed completion of his commentary about postwar Germany, so much so that the Polish section lost its timeliness. He continued to work on his German commentary early that spring, supplemented by conversations with Herbert Hoover, who had toured war-devastated Europe extensively, and bolstered by confidential information from columnist Drew Pearson. Among others, he enlisted his father's old friend Anne

McCormick, Pulitzer-Prize-winning European correspondent for the *New York Times*, to review and criticize the manuscript before turning it over to Harcourt, Brace.[31] The book did not come out until mid-July 1947 and then only as *Report on the Germans*, without the Polish unit and with the original prefatory section, "Wilson's Peace and Ours," rewritten as a lengthy afterword. To Bill's disappointment, Wallace decided not to place a cut of it in the *Digest*.

Report on the Germans garnered many notices, but most reviewers came to much the same conclusion as Robert Lasch in the *Chicago Sun*, who thought the book "readable but superficial and not very original."[32] The first part, headed "These Are the Germans," consists of eleven chapters in which Bill tells the stories or records the conversations of about two dozen people he met or heard about on his fact-finding trip to Berlin. Chief among them is the German journalist Albrecht Schultz, pseudonym for his hired scout Werner Asendorf. The others range from Friedrich Neumann, an unreconstructed Nazi, to Mrs. Sophia B., an elderly Jewish *hausfrau* who had escaped the holocaust, to a group of German men clustered around the bar of a small *bierstube*. Bill uses his trademark interview technique to make each speak as a separate persona. The underlying message of their accounts is that most Germans were bemused victims of the Nazi regime, as much beguiled by Hitler as was Chamberlain or Stalin. Thereby Bill argues against the proposal of Henry Morgenthau, Jr., former secretary of the treasury, that Germany should be punished by transforming its industrial base into a weak agrarian one. Bill portrays that as not only immoral but also politically stupid, given the postwar intransigence of the Soviets. Such anecdotal argument, however, seems too discursive and subjective to be sufficiently convincing.[33]

The second part of the book, "Wilson's Peace and Ours," is a four-chapter commentary based on Bill's memories of the 1919 Paris Peace Conference, with its historical lessons, as compared to the postwar situation in 1946. Coherent and often perceptive in this essay, he argues that Anglo-American insistence during the war on an unconditional surrender forced the Germans to fight on to total destruction, thus creating a power vacuum in central Europe that drew the Soviets to the banks of the Elbe River. For him the dangers of the present peace lay in the American government's misplaced faith in Soviet intentions, as shown by too free a Lend-Lease program to Russia, too many concessions to Stalin at Tehran and Yalta, and too rapid a demobilization of American military forces in Europe.

A prewar "interventionist liberal," Bill laments the failure of the United States to accept Wilson's League of Nations. But now after this war, he views Europe pragmatically in terms of power politics, as did the French conservatives in 1919, though early in 1946 he had signed on as a sponsor of the World Federalist organization formed to support the United Nations.[34] Given the reality of the European postwar situation, he argues that a strong democratic Germany is absolutely necessary to deter Soviet totalitarianism. But such a Germany, he concludes, cannot rise above "the parched stubble of Mr. Morgenthau's goat-pasture." Though subsequent events confirmed that analysis, the book itself gives the impression, as one reviewer remarked, that Bill "had a lot of random notes lying around and decided to knock them together between covers."[35] Yet he was in earnest about the topic, and in the 1950s came to hold the revisionist view that the United States should not have entered the war until several years later, if at all.[36]

In the summer of 1947 Bill turned his attention to a problem much closer to home. In May a New England college student, Albert Johnston, Jr., son of a small-town New Hampshire physician, had met the award-winning film producer Louis de Rochemont at his Newington, Connecticut, home, where a group of students had gathered to discuss the role of blacks in films. Moved by that discussion, Albert told de Rochemont afterward that not until he was sixteen years old had he known he was black, that to work in New England both his parents had "passed." Intrigued by the dramatic possibilities, de Rochemont interested Bill in the story. That June he interviewed the boy, his parents, and siblings, then wrote much of their story while vacationing at his parents' cabin in Colorado during July and August.

Sallie White did not join the family in Colorado, and Kathrine, unhappily, had to spend much of her time there resting to regain her health. So in the mornings Bill would work on his story, then go horseback riding or fishing with Barbara. Reexploring Estes Park through Barbara's young eyes, Bill had a memorable time. But enforced idleness only deepened Kathrine's dislike of the Colorado retreat, so they vacationed there only two weeks the next summer, and never again.[37]

Back in New York by the end of September, Bill finished the Johnston story in time for a cut to appear in the December issue of the *Digest* under the title the "forthcoming book" *Lost Boundaries*.[38] But changes at Harcourt, Brace delayed publication. At first Bill worked with Lambert Davis, but then was shifted over to Eugene Reynal, an old friend and Harvard classmate, who replaced Davis as trade editor late in 1947. As a result Harcourt, Brace did not release *Lost Boundaries* until March 1948.[39] Though but a brief ninety-one-page book, it was widely and favorably reviewed. The title, *Lost Boundaries*, metaphorically suggests its didactic theme. For it is the story of Albert Johnston, Jr., who suddenly found himself lost between the white, upper-middle-class New England world he grew up in and the, to him, totally unknown world of the American black. A Harvard-trained radiologist, practicing in Keene, New Hampshire, his father had patriotically applied for a naval commission just before the war only to be rejected when the navy discovered he was one of two blacks in his class at the University of Chicago's Rush Medical School. When he interned at the Portland, Maine, General Hospital, everyone there assumed he was white, so in order to keep the position, he had to pass. His wife, who was even lighter than he, had already passed to keep a job in Boston. Stung by the navy's rejection, Dr. Johnston, having had several drinks, told his eldest son, for the first time, that he was black, on both sides of the family.

At first Albert Jr. seemed more intrigued than bothered by that revelation, but during his freshman year at Dartmouth College the fall of 1941, he became so nervously morose his father pulled him out for treatment by a well-known black psychiatrist, who could find nothing wrong. With the start of the war, Albert Jr. decided to join the navy as a hospital orderly. But increasingly anxious that, like his father, he too would be exposed, he suffered a nervous collapse and was given a medical discharge. He then decided to see what the other side was like by looking up relatives in Cleveland, Chicago, and finally Los Angeles. There he stayed with an aunt, enrolled at the University of Southern California (USC), and began dating a black doctor's popular daughter. But in his aunt's community he encountered social and racial attitudes new to him. For at USC he passed as white, which alienated his aunt and black friends; thus he found himself again defensive, again an outsider, unsure and unhappy. So he went back home to New Hampshire, where he slowly regained self-confidence and enrolled at the state university, yet again did not declare his race. But there at a social problems seminar Albert Jr. for the first time publicly spoke up to say he was black, and could contribute personally to the dialogue, an act that reestablished his boundaries.

Reviewers were uniformly positive, with most making the same sort of comment as Richard Watts, Jr., for the New Republic, who wrote that "Lost Boundaries is a short book, but within that brief space [W. L. White] has written a masterpiece of insight, intelligence and unsentimental compassion."[40] Louis de Rochemont planned to film the story as an MGM feature movie, but because the House Un-American Activities Committee had attacked the Hollywood Ten the previous fall, in the summer of 1948 MGM and other major studios began to drop plans for "'message' pictures like hot coals," according to Variety, and that included Lost Boundaries.[41] Finally, de Rochemont financed the film himself and released it the summer of 1949 to a limited number of independent theaters through Film Classics, a small East Coast distribution company. Starring the then-unknown Mel Ferrer as Dr. Johnston, the movie was not a commercial success but did win the best script prize at the Cannes Film Festival the next year.[42]

In mid-October 1946 through friends at the New Leader, then a weekly socialist tabloid, Bill met Leon Volkov, a lieutenant colonel in the Russian air force who had just sought political asylum in the United States. Volkov wished to interest the Reader's Digest in a book about his experiences as a Soviet citizen. Six weeks later, after Bill had recovered from his psychosomatic slump that fall, he introduced Volkov to DeWitt Wallace who, after consulting Max Eastman, another Digest roving editor and anti-Communist liberal, advanced the Russian one thousand dollars for expenses in return for right of first refusal.[43] By the fall of 1947 Volkov had managed to put together three magazine pieces, carried by the *Saturday Evening Post* in January 1948 under the title "Stalin Thinks I'm Dead." Actually they were ghostwritten by Kenneth Crawford of *Newsweek* and published under the pseudonym Vasili Katov.[44] But Volkov found a book beyond his and Crawford's abilities. So he urged Bill to write a book-length narrative of his life as a Russian air force officer, which Bill agreed to do but only after Harry Scherman, founder of Book-of-the-Month Club, seconded Volkov's request.[45] For the first six weeks of 1948, though, Bill worked on a North African combat story, interviewing a number of tank commanders who had taken part in that campaign. But it did not fall into place. In an eleven-page lack-of-progress report to Wallace he explained his problem was narrative structure, that he could not find a "central theme or character around which interest could be built."[46] But with Volkov he had such a character and, with Wallace's approval, he buried himself in that account, which became the book *Land of Milk and Honey*.

First he interviewed Volkov intensively then put together a coherent narrative from his point of view, under his pseudonym. Both the book and the first *Digest* cut came out in January 1949, with a second and longer excerpt in May. But the story posed two problems for Bill. First, Volkov's extended family and many old friends were still in Russia. Though Harcourt, Brace advertised the book as "the completely true, fresh and vivid narration of Vasili Katov, Red Air-Force Colonel," Bill had actually altered places, personal names, and chronology to prevent Soviet retaliation. Second, he did not wish to turn out just another war adventure book from the critical perspective of a Soviet deserter. Instead, as he first described the account to Wallace, he intended to present through Katov the story of a "child of the revolution," one born in 1914 who remembered nothing of czarist times, who did not realize he was living "under a dictatorship until after the war when, with the Soviet Army of occupation, he entered Europe and became familiar with it."[47]

Most reviewers understood Bill's intention, but they did not agree he had achieved it, especially as his own anti-Soviet stance was so well-known and some data had been purposely obscured.[48] For Bill announced in the preface that he had, "in order to present an essentially true story of living people, to alter some unimportant facts such as their names and other dates and places which might identify them." But that makes it, as Philip Mosely remarked in the *Yale Review*, "difficult for the reader to know what role in selection and emphasis has been played by the American collaborator."[49] In the preface Bill also announced his thematic purpose, that whether the war with Russia continues hot or cold or turns to peace, America needs to understand the new, exclusively Soviet generation as represented by Vasili Katov and why to him the United States, not the Soviet Union, had become the Promised Land.

The first chapter tells of Vasili, still in Russian uniform, arriving in New York City and reacting naively, confusedly, to things American. Then the narrator flashes back to Vasili's childhood in Moscow, as the younger son of a factory worker and living with his parents, a brother, two sisters, and a grandmother in a seven-room apartment with two other families. In high school he falls in love with Golya, the bright, pretty daughter of a well-educated engineer, and she with him. But then his father dies, his older brother has already left home, and Vasili must support his mother and sisters. He works hard at a factory job, joins the Komsomol, a Communist youth organization, and attends night school. But he gradually stops seeing Golya because she has gone beyond him to literary studies at the University of Moscow. Then after four years at the factory he achieves admission to the Moscow Technical Institute to study aeronautical engineering. There he makes friends with a small group of intellectuals from professional-class backgrounds, who are in secret opposition to party policies of forced industrialization. The next year those friends simply disappear during the purges of 1935 and 1936. But his friendship with the group has initiated a habit of critical observation that causes him silently to continue questioning Soviet policies. As a result the narration develops a cumulative context of rationalized criticism that prepares us for Vasili's decision, when the opportunity arrives, to turn his back on the Soviet Union.

After graduation Vasili becomes an engineering test pilot for an airplane factory near Moscow. Soon he heads a testing section of ten, including his oldest friend, Boris, whom the NKVD pressures to submit secret reports concerning his boss, Vasili, which he does, but only after consulting him. Boris also introduces him to Elena, a blonde history major at the University of Moscow. When Nazi troops invade Soviet territory, Vasili and Elena pledge to marry after the war. After his factory moves out of Moscow, Vasili joins an air force squadron assigned to the southern front, where he is twice wounded and hospitalized. Then as the Germans fall back, he takes part in the Soviet occupation of Romania and Hungary, which have standards of living and culture much higher than those in Russia. That startles him. With the war over he returns to Moscow to try to work things out with Elena, who for wartime favors has kept company with her former boss, a married man. Promoted to lieutenant colonel, Vasili welcomes an opportunity to forget Elena and fly Russian detainees back to the USSR from Paris. But there he is further disillusioned by a comparison of Soviet and Western European values and by the reluctance of fellow Russians to return home. Suddenly he and other officers in his group receive NKVD orders to return to Moscow. But the plane carrying them crashes and burns. Vasili manages to bail out and, realizing he will be assumed dead, walks away to a new identity.

Because of changes in both the domestic and international political climates, this second Russian book by Bill received many and rather gentle reviews, in spite of the intentional alterations to the story. And as usual for a book by Young Bill White, the *Book-of-the-Month Club News* reviewed it as an alternate choice. In fact, the only "nasty review," from Bill's point of view, was that by Harrison Salisbury, who in the *New York Star* of January 9, 1949, praised it as a "swell writing job" but questioned its inherent honesty and, by implication, Bill's.[50] While Bill obviously selected events for maximum critical effect, especially when during the war Vasili comes across his first love, Golya, forced to become an NKVD "escort," those selections seem well within a writer's rhetorical license, assuming that writer honest. And he was. To Robert Littell, one of the senior editors at *Reader's Digest*, Bill sent a four-page letter listing the major factual changes he had made in the narration to confuse Soviet authorities.[51] The list upholds his claim in the preface that the changes were immaterial to the theme, that this is "an essentially true story."

Sometime early in 1948, apparently pleased by *Lost Boundaries* and concerned that Bill might return to Emporia as full-time editor of the *Gazette*, Wallace changed his payroll status. He moved him from "independent contractor" at $12,000 per year to "employee" at the same retainer, plus the advantages of a pension plan worth a third again as much, a 10 percent yearly bonus, social security, and term life insurance of $45,000.[52] Of course, as a roving editor he was still paid by the article and for all business expenses.

Bill had indeed been thinking of a return to Emporia. The previous fall he had written his uncle Lacy that he was "preparing to devote a lot more time to Emporia," that he and Kathrine had "spent a number of hours driving around town looking for a building site or a house which we could buy" but that "everything seemed fantastically overpriced."[53] Soon afterward, back in New York, he became involved in his project with Leon Volkov and in due course came to realize he had to stay East to remain viable as a *Digest* contributor. In a letter to George Moorad about *Land of Milk and Honey*, he observed in a personal aside that "I know that I can't work in Emporia on anything serious when I'm trying to run the Gazette. But that may be because I am a congenitally lazy bastard and because the Gazette is more important to me than anything that I try to write about at the time."[54] So for the next four or five years he continued to focus on his *Digest* commitments and let E. T. Lowther and Ted McDaniel run the newspaper, under his supervision.

For the Whites, after the turmoil of the Communist-inspired personal attacks in 1945, life in New York City was once again fun, as were weekend escapes to their Frenchtown farm. Kathrine enjoyed the aesthetic sophistication of the city and both of them appreciated its tremendous variety of personalities and ethnic groups, its cultural events, restaurants, and nightclubs. For example, Billy Rose, the famous theatrical producer and nightclub owner, was one of their numerous show business friends, and they frequented his Diamond Horseshoe Club. They also dropped in often at such fashionable night spots as El Morocco, the Stork

Club, and 21. And in March 1948 Herbert Hoover and Robert Littell, a fellow *Digest* roving editor, successfully proposed Bill for membership in the Century Club, an old, very exclusive private club of literary, journalistic, and political figures, to which his father had proudly belonged. To Bill that membership meant much more than just social acceptance by an important group of the eastern establishment, though such acceptance was especially sweet because the Century had decisively voted him down just after publication of *Report on the Russians*.[55] Actually, he already belonged to the New York Harvard Club, the Players Club, and the Dutch Treat Club (which he described once as a "misnomer for a literary-radio-magazine lunch club, which I'd say takes in the top guys in the field").[56] Membership in those clubs he found useful for scouting stories for the *Digest*; they were tools for his trade, not just badges of social prestige. He knew, as did his father before him, the importance of access to influential people.

Another sign of his reacceptance by former New York associates, and of changing times, was old-line Progressive editor Freda Kirchwey's telegram to him in the summer of 1948. In it she asked him to serve, along with the poet Archibald MacLeish and other literary notables, on an ad hoc committee to support her militantly liberal magazine the *Nation* against a subscription ban by the board of superintendents of the New York City schools, which he did with vigor.[57] And as a member of the ACLU board of directors he enjoyed in the fall of 1948 the irony of supporting his old enemy Corliss Lamont's reelection, even though that Harvard classmate helped lead the Communist attack on *Report on the Russians*. As he wrote Lamont gleefully:

> My position on what [the Nominating Committee] should do was that, since your status in relation to the Communists was now exactly what it had been for a good many years, and since during those years the Civil Liberties Union had considered you a reasonably valuable officer, it was therefore outrageous that, simply because public opinion had changed, they should now heave you to the wolves. I am, of course, heartily on the side of the wolves, but I don't like people with rubber knees

who bend before storms of public opinion, and it seems to me
that you have shown both consistency and courage, even
though this goes along with a deficiency in horse sense.[58]

The year 1948 was a presidential election year and Bill, son of
his father, could not be left out. During the spring and early
summer, though working on Volkov's story, Bill commented on
preconvention national politics in a series of *Gazette* editorials
he sent from New York. The first was a thoughtful two-column
analysis of Harry Truman, whom he commended for "having done
a good job in the White House" but who, he predicted incorrectly,
would go down to defeat not only because the country was tired
of the Democrats but also because "that common man" had the
"courage to stand up for human freedom both in Alabama and
Czechoslovakia." Then after two editorials about the political state
of the nation Bill wrote four two-column editorials analyzing the
major Republican contenders, Thomas E. Dewey, Harold Stassen,
Robert Taft, and his own choice, Arthur Vandenberg.[59] He then
attended both party's conventions in Philadelphia, within commuting distance from his Frenchtown farm, this time not as a
syndicated columnist for the NANA, as he had contracted in 1944,
but in his role as a small-town Kansas editor.

At the state level Bill had a personal impact on the elections
of 1948, for he initiated the reluctant retirement of Arthur Capper,
the eighty-two-year-old United States senator from Kansas, and
in doing so got back at his real target, former governor Alf Landon.
Because of state factional politics, Landon had backed the aged
Capper in his decision to run for reelection. Landon did that in
opposition to an intraparty enemy, former governor Andrew
Schoeppel, who had announced his candidacy for the United
States Senate as part of a state leadership fight.[60] Though Senator
Capper had been a Kansas ally of his father, Bill despised Capper's
rigid prewar isolationism and what he had come to see as the
senator's always-safe political opportunism. So he supported
Schoeppel in his senate bid. In one of his last acts as governor,
Schoeppel had helped arrange Ronald Finney's parole, and Bill
was grateful for that, even though Schoeppel was a standpat party
foe of the Progressives, Will White's old faction. In the fall of 1947

Kansas Supreme Court Justice William Smith, another enduring ally of Will White's, wrote an impassioned plea to Young Bill, invoking his father's "progressive spirit," not to support Schoeppel. Bill explained his position emphatically to Smith: "Let's first go into this matter of my father. Often we agreed, but quite often we didn't, but one thing which I intend to copy carefully from him is his attitude toward his own father which is accurately reflected in his autobiography. . . . Every now and then some of the old-timers would start hollering that some of his performances were causing his father to revolve in his grave, but he paid no attention to this, and I intend to follow his example."[61]

And so he did. For that spring Bill wrote a bittersweet *Gazette* editorial that drew state and national attention both to Capper's age and Landon's factional motives. Captioned "Kansas Grouches," the editorial shows Bill in his maturity as a newspaper commentator, a skillful rhetorician masked as a western humorist, whose remarks deftly draw blood together with laughs. To read that editorial in full is to appreciate W. L. W. as a local editor:

> Senator Arthur Capper, who is universally beloved by Kansans, is now a very old man. The term of his service to our state dates back even before the memory of most of those who will vote in the next election. Arthur Capper had already arrived in the United States Senate two years before the writer of these lines got his first pair of long pants.
>
> During every one of those years, including 1948, Arthur Capper has served us in the Senate efficiently and well. But during the recent ones it has been at a terrible cost to himself.
>
> The duties of a United States Senator cannot be performed efficiently even by a vigorous young man in an ordinary 8-hour day. Arthur Capper has fulfilled them, but in the past few months this has cruelly taxed his understandably failing strength. Only because he has given of this with great selflessness can it be said that during the senatorial term which he is now completing, he has been as useful to Kansas as he was during his first, so many decades ago.
>
> Now all his friends who, in this situation, have no personal axes to grind, and who wish to see his political career end, not

in humiliation but in the high honor it deserves, have been unanimous in recent months in assuring him that the time has now come when he can lay these heavy burdens down.

Why, then, is he running for another term which, in the highly improbable event that he serves it, would keep this frail man in that heavy harness almost into his nineties?

Of one thing you can be sure. It is not, as is now being whispered around Kansas, an old man's vanity. For Arthur Capper is today the same gentle and unselfish little Quaker that he has always been. He would not be running today if he were not being whipped into harness by those who tell him that it is his duty to stay there.

In the past Arthur Capper's real strength has lain not only in the wisdom which he has devoted to his senatorial duties, but to the fact that no one was closer than he to the Kansas grass roots.

Arthur Capper knew not only every politician but the plain people as well, with the result that although he got bad advice by the barrel, he could sort and reject it. The trouble is that most of Arthur Capper's old-time friends whom he could trust are now under the sod, with the tragic result that the time may come when the Senator's ear is no longer at the grass roots, but can be stuffed with tumbleweed and fox grass by various statesmen who may well believe what they are telling him, but whose first interest is not the true welfare of Arthur Capper.

You can be sure that today nobody in the Capper organization either in Topeka or in Washington, those who know and love him best and have been helping him in his struggle, are trying to push him into this. That also goes for his Kansas friends, with, so far as we can make out, only one exception. That exception is Alf M. Landon. Why?

Alf has just one reason for urging Arthur Capper to make the race, and this is that he has worked himself up to the point where he firmly believes that the heavens will totter and the Republic will crumble if former Governor Andrew Schoeppel should get to the United States Senate. But why should Alf want to risk the health and the fine reputation of Kansas's most beloved political figure in a grudge-fight such as this? Anybody who asks this question obviously knows nothing about Kansas agriculture.

Because out here we raise the biggest political grouches in the world. The little lovers' quarrels among our statesmen may be bunion-size to start with, but under the gentle rains of April and the warming sun of May they thrive and flourish until, by the time they are ready for harvest in the August primary election, a Kansas political grouch is redder than a carbuncle, and with a central core of hatred harder than a railroad spike and bigger than a watermelon.

In further defense of Alf Landon, it should be pointed out that his particular grouch against Andy Schoeppel is no sudden mushroom growth. It started many years ago, early in Schoeppel's first administration, over some minor matter of patronage in which Andy may well have been wrong, or probably did not give Alf's views the respectful consideration they deserved. But from this small beginning Alf has nursed and with loving care cultivated his grouch until it is already at least as big as the grouch which Clyde Reed took into the Kansas primary campaign a few years back, this being up until now the biggest Kansas political grouch of all time, and having richly deserved the prizes it won at all our county fairs.

Now, whether or not Alf Landon's grouch is already bigger and juicier than Clyde Reed's former prize winner is not for us to say. Final judgment should be passed only by qualified experts from the State Agricultural College. Alf has, however, every reason to be proud of his, and it is certainly big enough to explain everything he does in the current political year.

The fact remains, however, that on the whole we prefer the way that Clyde handled his grouch to Alf's performance to date. Because Clyde Reed did not involve anyone else. He was certainly as mad as Alf is now—maybe even madder—but when the time came to settle scores and to take his revenge, he did not hide behind anybody else's reputation, but had the courage to risk his own. He got into the fight as a candidate himself—cussed out his enemies for the dastardly two-headed double-crossing miscreants that they were, said his say, hollered his holler, yelled his yell, smote his opponents hip and thigh, got smitten himself on the same well-callused organ, and then retired with dignity and the honors of war, a wiser if not a sadder statesman, to the more quietly contemplative atmosphere of the United States Senate, having gotten the whole thing out of his system.

And we feel that Alf should follow Clyde's fine precedent. Even if Arthur Capper should ultimately decide not to run, we also think that it would be a mistake for Alf to move Payne Ratner, or any lesser figure than himself, in as a substitute. Because after all it is his grouch and not Payne's. Furthermore it is, as we have said, a grouch of massive proportions, and there is no point in sending a boy to do a man's work.

It is a job which only Alf Landon can and should do for himself. So let him come out from among his tall white columns in Topeka, don his stainless steel armor, straddle his three prancing radio stations, and take his grouch to the voters.

Objection will instantly be raised that this is impossible because Alf Landon is now politically dead, having been appropriately butchered at the recent state convention, his hide nailed to the barn door and his carcass already jointed and packed in the pickling barrel.

But this is an exaggeration. True, his hair was mussed up, his shirttail pulled out, and his nose slightly bloodied. But he is hardly in a state to be admired as a triumph of the embalmer's art.

Because the thing that keeps us believing steadfastly in the Resurrection and the Life is not so much our constant reading of the Scriptures as watching Kansas Republican politics. Always, after every such ruckaboo, the victorious statesmen joyously pronounce the vanquished politically dead forever, and gleefully roll the stone into its place before the sepulcher. And then, miraculously, we see these stiffened corpses invariably flip the pennies from their eyelids, scramble out of their satin-lined coffins, mount their political machines, and peddle gaily off toward the next election where they presently are up to their old orneriness.

So it certainly will be with Alf Landon. Furthermore, he has already been pronounced politically dead three times: once at the beginning of his career when Prairie Oil and Gas beat him for precinct committeeman in his home town of Independence, again when he ran for President and still again at the recent state convention.

It will thus be seen that Alf Landon has so far lost only three of the nine political lives guaranteed to every Republican statesman under Article XII of the Lecompton Constitution of our state. Of the six which therefore remain to him, Alf Landon can surely afford to sacrifice one in airing his grouch against Andy Schoeppel.

But most important of all, it would enable him to join with all of Arthur Capper's other true friends in assuring the Senator that the time has now come when he may with dignity and honor lay down the heavy burdens of office, step out of the shafts, and lie down in green pastures beside the still waters, so that, in the peaceful years which will remain to him, he will enjoy that rest which he has so richly earned.—W. L. W.[62]

That editorial created so much comment that Bill had to cover himself with a puckish "bread and butter" letter to Wallace. For about a month later Bill wrote him that

you may have seen . . . an Associated Press story to the effect that an editorial of mine in the Emporia Gazette induced Arthur Capper to withdraw from the Senatorial race. . . . Actually I haven't been in Kansas a single day since last November and the whole Kansas uproar was stirred up by an editorial I mailed out to the Gazette from New York some time ago.

This is only to reassure [you] . . . that whenever I find it advisable to remove any United States Senator I always am careful to do this after working hours and not on company time.[63]

Yet when former Emporian Willard Greene wrote him to praise the Capper editorial, Greene suggested that "it will not carry the weight that such an editorial in the Gazette would have carried a generation ago. W. A. made New York listen when Emporia spoke, but few people have the gift of making Emporia listen when New York speaks—about Kansas politics. . . . The undivided and unquestioned loyalty of 'Old' Bill and Sallie White to Kansas was a very important factor in W. A.'s influence."[64] Bill replied, in apparent candor, that if he moved back to Kansas now, "I should have to drop my work here which supports my family. The income from the Emporia Gazette . . . is at present just about enough to support my mother comfortably."[65] In point of fact Bill was at that time earning a base salary of about five thousand dollars a year from the *Gazette* in addition to receiving income from local real estate investments, such as nearly two thousand acres of pastureland he and Kathrine held in neighboring Chase County. That of course could not maintain the lifestyle he had become accustomed to as a *Reader's Digest* roving editor. But that does not count the profits going into the *Gazette* account he held jointly with his mother.[66]

Late in August 1948, after he had finished the manuscript of *Land of Milk and Honey*, the family vacationed for two weeks at Moraine Park, Colorado, for the last time.[67] Then Kathrine took Barbara back to New York and school while Bill stayed behind in Emporia until mid-November. He stayed in part because his mother at age seventy-eight was becoming forgetful, and he needed to see after her and the *Gazette*'s business affairs. And he stayed to vote, thereby maintaining for tax purposes his legal residency in Kansas, which he did from then on, and which eventually required him to live nearly six months of each year in Emporia, to Kathrine's sometimes open dismay.

Back in New York toward the end of November he scouted several stories for the *Digest*, but none of those efforts made it through the editorial process. Then in January 1949 Paul Palmer, a senior editor to whom Bill was close, suggested he follow up a tip the magazine had received from a soldier of fortune in Paris calling himself "LeMan." The tipster claimed that the Russian NKVD in an elaborate clandestine operation was supplying Israel with planes and pilots in the ongoing Palestinian war.[68] Bill was interested in that story, for he had followed the Palestine problem closely throughout the 1948 United Nations debates. In fact he had written two lengthy *Gazette* editorials in the spring of 1948, in his self-appointed role as Emporia's occasional schoolmaster, to explain the Palestine question in a historical context from both Jewish and Arabic points of view.[69] Yet he urged caution on Palmer: "I don't need to remind anybody on the Digest that I have been accused in the past of prejudicially lying about the Russians; and it would do neither the Digest nor me any good if I got involved in another highly controversial subject with a weak or vulnerable witness to back up what I feel is an essentially true story—as well as an important one."[70] First he wanted to know who this LeMan was. Within a day Palmer had a telegram from Paris identifying him as Hans Alexander Lehmann, a Swiss pilot who had formerly worked for the Israelis; he had references from two reputable *Christian Science Monitor* correspondents.[71] Still Bill was skeptical, but the story was hot, and they decided to move on it. So he flew to Paris where he interviewed Lehmann. Favorably impressed, Bill then flew on to Palestine to check out the story.[72]

Once again Bill was in a war zone, but this time one with no clear-cut villains or lines of authority or borders or even armies. He did find, though, the usual stonewalling, censorship, spies, and partisan hyperbole. After four weeks with the Israelis he could verify with certainty only about 20 percent of Lehmann's story, that indeed "there had been a three-way deal between Israel, Czechoslovakia and Russia" to supply arms to Israel by means of American dollars. But he could not verify the operational details. Frustrated by both Jewish and British authorities in his various attempts to find out more about "Alaska Airlines," a charter firm that seemed to cover clandestine Israeli air operations, he gave up, realizing, so he later wrote Lehmann, that he simply could not gain access to anyone significantly involved.[73]

Nevertheless, he wrote Paul Palmer, he had traveled Israel from the

> Sea of Galilee in the extreme north, clear down to Akaba, which is at the tip end of the Negev Desert on the Red Sea—filling notebooks methodically as I went, just as I have done when I traveled in Russia, Germany and Poland. After this month, I managed to get permission to pass through the lines in Jerusalem into the Old City which is held by the Arabs and, in spite of the fact that I had that Jewish visa in my passport,

talked my way up to Amman, the capitol of Transjordan, then
over into Beirut (capitol of Lebanon) and thence to Damascus
(capitol of Syria) where, incidentally, I got an interview with
Colonel Zaim (the new military dictator).[74]

Without having confirmed Lehmann's story, but with material
for ten to twelve potential stories of his own, or even a book, he
returned to Paris to wind up several interviews there. When he
reported to Wallace at the *Digest's* offices in Pleasantville, New
York, they mulled over the possibilities of a book and the inevitable
storm it would evoke, because Bill had become openly sympathetic
to the Arabic point of view.[75] Just before meeting with Wallace,
he wrote Paul Palmer, on leave in Maine: "It is a book which I
am not frantically eager to write for I realize that it would cause
both me and the Digest about two-thirds of the trouble which
we went through with *Report on the Russians*. But, for exactly the
same reason, I feel that someone should write and print such a
book now as a public service to our country—and I happen to
be the unlucky devil who has the material for it!"[76] But to write
just a war story would be problematic because Israel had signed
armistice agreements with Egypt, Lebanon, and Jordan that spring.
So Wallace first asked Bill to solicit two articles by knowledgeable
American Jews, one for Zionism and one against. This he did,
with Rabbi Abba Silver's "The Case for Zionism" and Alfred
Lilienthal's "Israel's Flag Is Not Mine," which appeared side by
side in the September issue under the heading "Zionism and
American Jews."

At the end of June Bill attended the twenty-fifth reunion of
his Harvard class. He had happily anticipated it for more than
a year because he had been asked to give one of the principal
addresses. After the reunion, which proved a triumphant occasion
for him, his class nominated him to run for the Harvard Board
of Overseers. Bill then settled in at his Frenchtown farm and
proceeded to work up his controversial Middle East materials. As
he remarked at the time to his father's old friend, former secretary
of the interior Harold Ickes: "You may think, my friend, that in
your time you have handled your share of hot stove-lids, but I
would like to assure you that until you have tackled this particular

subject, you are an innocent and trembling virgin on the subject of hot stove-lids."[77] By mid-August he had outlined twelve possible stories, five from a Jewish view, seven from an Arabic, complete with a ten- to twenty-page précis for each. Those he sent to Wallace for comment or approval, then he flew to Emporia to see his mother, who had fallen on July 29 and broken a hip. He stopped long enough to see that she was comfortable after her August 22 release from Newman Hospital, then flew on to California to join Kathrine and Barbara, who had spent three weeks at his cousin Gwen Behr's ranch near Victorville, California. On his return to New York, Bill immediately checked in with Paul Palmer at Pleasantville only to learn, over the inevitable *Digest* editorial luncheon, that his suggested stories were considered too hazardous. As Palmer explained further in a letter, only the "one on the Arab refugees" offered possibilities that "perhaps, at some time in the future, we shall want to do something about." Meanwhile "Wally feels that we can find plenty of other things for you to do."[78] After all that work Bill was understandably disappointed.

With his Middle East trip and materials deemed unusable, he flew back to Emporia for about two weeks to see his mother again and to put their business affairs in better order. He had discovered that she had spent the then large sum of $32,000 to remodel a house she owned two doors down, at 913 Exchange, for Bertha Colglazier, her faithful housekeeper. Sallie had some vague notion that Bertha could keep boarders after Sallie was gone. That uncontrolled expenditure highlighted a significant weakness in the family business arrangements. Sallie and her son held the *Gazette*, its building, and other family real estate in a simple partnership, with an agreement that he would gradually buy out her share. But in the event of her death, that dutifully equitable arrangement would be for him a tax disaster. So he began the legal process of changing their partnership into a corporation, after consulting his uncle Lacy, who agreed it seemed "fair and sensible."[79] As soon as he had worked out some of the legal details and had reassured himself that his mother, now confined to a wheelchair, continued to be well looked after by Bertha and a shift of nurses, he returned to New York and to the new *Digest* assignment Wally had promised.

Gen. Dwight Eisenhower told Wallace at a lunch during September 1949 about the importance in breaking out of Normandy of a tank-mounted hedgerow cutter developed in the field by an American soldier. Wallace thought that a good story and assigned it to Bill. He interviewed those involved, including generals Eisenhower and Omar Bradley, both of whom suggested he focus the story on Sgt. Curtis Culin, who had thought up the device. By the end of October Bill submitted his final version of that story, which the *Digest* ran in its February 1950 issue as "Sergeant Culin Licks the Hedgerows." It proved one of his most popular pieces.[80] Also that month Wallace assigned him to do a "citizenship" story of about 10,000 words on Bernard Baruch, the multimillionaire advisor to six presidents. Bill immediately started research for that, but soon asked if he could also cover the Alger Hiss trial, with credentials from Wheeler's NANA. "This case will grow in importance," he explained to Wallace, so "it is almost certain that eventually the Digest will have an important article on it and, because I knew both Hiss and [Whittaker] Chambers, . . . you have on your staff someone qualified to do this job."[81]

A year before, in the fall of 1948, Bill had closely followed newspaper accounts of HUAC's interrogation of Alger Hiss, a former Roosevelt State Department official. By that time Bill had become a staunchly anti-Communist moderate Republican, moving gradually to the right under the influence of his growing friendship with Herbert Hoover, still a leader among the Republican old guard. The Hiss case hastened that move. For Bill personally knew Whittaker Chambers, Hiss's principal accuser, as a knowledgeable but eccentric anti-Communist senior editor at *Time*, whom he had himself consulted during the Communist-led furor over *Report on the Russians*. Bill knew Hiss personally too; they had mutual friends at both the State Department and the Carnegie Endowment for International Peace, of which Hiss was president from 1947 to 1948. So the psychological and political ambiguities of the HUAC confrontation intimately engaged White's interest. Then that December Chambers produced his famous "pumpkin papers," microfilmed State Department documents, which convinced Bill, among others, that Chambers was the one telling the truth. The following fall, with the second Hiss trial pending, Bill simply could not stay out of it.[82]

To repay John Wheeler for furnishing him with press credentials, Bill wrote four published commentaries that month for the NANA. But scarred by the underhanded tactics the Communists used against him in 1945, he was in those reports an unabashed partisan, skillfully coloring them against Hiss.[83] In the middle of the trial, for example, Bill wrote Wheeler, "Whittaker Chambers and his wife were over to dinner last night and I think I have a swell exclusive lined up which will pack plenty of dynamite, being always mindful of course of the libel laws."[84] When the verdict went against Hiss, while some press accounts still questioned Chambers's honesty, Bill wrote a long letter to his old friend Henry Luce urging him as a necessary gesture of support and vindication to rehire "Whit," who had resigned from *Time* in December 1948.[85]

After Christmas Bill flew again to Emporia for several days to visit his mother, then eighty years old, and then returned to write up a three-part laudatory summary of Chambers's role as an informer from 1939 on entitled "The Story No One Believed." Congressman Richard Nixon, whom Bill admired and would come to know on a first-name basis, gave him a copy of Chambers's secret HUAC background testimony, with the understanding that he not quote from it. He interviewed other sources too, such as Allen Dulles, the former OSS top official who would be appointed CIA director in 1953. Then he sent his version to Chambers to check for accuracy and tone.[86] But Wallace went instead with a book condensation of Ralph de Toledano and Victor Lasky's dramatically written *Seeds of Treason*.[87] Bill then sent the manuscript to his friend Ben Hibbs, editor of the *Saturday Evening Post*, but he had just bought the rights to Chambers's partially finished autobiography. Bill's piece soon lost its timeliness and remained unpublished, but the narrative stayed with him, increasing his political conservatism.

At the same time Bill gathered materials for his Baruch story, with help from family friend Herbert Swope, a veteran Baruch associate. After interviewing Baruch he became intrigued by that private public figure and decided, with his permission, to expand the sketch into a book.[88] Wallace, though, early in March suggested that he do an anecdotal biography of Gen. Dwight Eisenhower as part of a widespread, behind-the-scenes campaign to arrange a "draft" for a 1952 Republican presidential nomination. Bill wrote Wallace that "unless you prefer otherwise, I should like to sit down and finish up that Baruch story before I start west on the Eisenhower job. . . . The Baruch material is ready to roll and . . . some of it is already on paper. It has been some time (due to various miscarriages on the Palestine material and the Alger Hiss business) since I have had a piece of any importance in the *Digest*."[89]

By early summer, then, Bill had finished a eulogistic biographical sketch of Baruch, which Harcourt, Brace issued as a 132-page account in September and the *Digest* as a 14-page cut in its October issue. Strictly speaking, it is not so much a biography as an uncritical outline of Baruch as uncanny financial genius, infallible industrial expert, and public-spirited but often unappreciated advisor to presidents. It is supplemented by two appendices presenting his plan as the American delegate to the United Nations Atomic Energy Commission for control of atomic energy. An anonymous reviewer for the *New Yorker* summed up most responses when he wrote that "White has done an able journalistic job, although he sometimes sounds as if he were about to nominate Baruch for president."[90] From a later perspective *Bernard Baruch: Portrait of a Citizen* seems unalloyed advocacy journalism and as such the least substantive of White's thirteen books.

With the Eisenhower biography Bill ran into a fundamental problem, given his technique of working from personal interviews. The general chose not to encourage a *Reader's Digest* public relations effort. Bill spent three weeks just getting in to talk with an aide, who told him that Eisenhower was too busy to see him. So he wrote Wallace to suggest instead an anecdotal approach through interviews with others: with Dwight's brother Milton, then the president of Kansas State University; with fellow army officers; and with well-informed war correspondents, such as John Gunther, "who happens to be a good friend of mine."[91] Wallace agreed, so Bill began gathering anecdotes and taking notes from published sources. But late in October Wallace postponed that sketch because he felt the time was not right and suggested several other topics instead, which did result in *Digest* placements in 1951.[92]

In fact, many of Bill's magazine projects miscarried during the 1950s for several reasons, but Emporia, its citizens, and the *Gazette* provided him with outlets for his energies, though local results often miscarried too. For example, from New York during 1949 through 1952 he directed two *Gazette* campaigns to improve the town, neither of which worked. Unfortunately, both contributed to a nascent local resentment of him as an overbearing absentee editor, an attitude that later caused him considerable trouble. One was simply quixotic, aimed at slot machines in such Emporia haunts as the Country Club and the American Legion hall. Influenced by the June *Digest* article "The Big Slot Machine Swindle," Bill first noticed them in Emporia when home in September 1949. He started his campaign against them with a *Gazette* editorial of October 3, in which he supported Kansas Attorney General Harold Fatzer's crackdown on gambling in the town of Parsons, but acknowledged that if "Kansas now wants gambling and slot machines it should say so at the polls, and then provide for an adequate tax so that the profits would go in large part to the state, rather than to individual or to private groups. But until then, slot machines should not be allowed to sneak in the back door via 'clubs' no matter how social or patriotic they may be."[93] He then planned a survey of 2,000 representative Emporia voters via postcards distributed by the *Gazette*. Those surveyed returned 1,033 cards, with a four-to-one majority against the slots. Responding to that poll, Lyon County Attorney Sam Mellinger dutifully closed them down early in 1950.

Emporia's socialites resented Young Bill's interference from New York. Harold Trusler, Bill's hometown best friend and president of the local country club, gave him some angry, straightforward advice at the start of the slot machine crusade:

> About the slot machines, I think you are planning to lose many friends and give your enemies a vulnerable spot unprotected by anything except WLW's skin. While you think you are an Emporian, there are not six Emporians who so regard you, and your best friends don't want your moral advice (on Emporia) as an export commodity from New York. Nobody wants a card poll on slot machines, and nobody gives a damn what you think

about slot machines, you having left Emporia 15 years ago. . . .
I wish you would spend a few days here and learn what goes
on. Your spies at the Gazette can't tell you because they mostly
don't know.[94]

Certainly, results of the postcard vote did not tell the real story—
that after World War II social attitudes had changed. Within
several years the town's various clubs had slot machines back in
operation.

His other crusade, saving the old Lyon County courthouse,
completely backfired. He was correct from the start when he
pointed out in an editorial of December 28, 1949, that the building
was structurally sound. Though constructed at the turn of the
century in heavy Romanesque style and jammed inconveniently
onto several downtown lots at the corner of Fourth and
Commercial, its interior could be remodeled, he believed, for much
less money into more usable space than the county would spend
for any modern "square cracker box." Moreover, he suggested,
the old courthouse "as she stands, her massive thick walls, her
impressive high ceilings and doors, give her a dignity and potential
beauty which few modern buildings have."[95] In 1943 Lyon County
voters had approved a pay-as-you-go levy to build a new
courthouse on a more spacious site. But by the fall of 1949 funds
had accumulated to little more than $200,000, and the county
critically needed better facilities. Some suggested an additional
bond proposal. Others petitioned the commissioners to buy and
remodel the late senator Preston Plumb's spacious, conveniently
located mansion instead of going into debt for a new structure.
Buying the Plumb House, in use for years as a woman's community
center, proved unpopular. But it was this suggestion that interested
Bill in the issue. For he replied to an inquiry about his attitude
toward that petition that "my general feeling on the Court House
business is that if it were mine, instead of spending about a half
million dollars putting up more masonry and concrete, I would
spend about $150,000 completely modernizing the present building
. . . for a fraction of the cost of a new building. Anyway that's
my private opinion on it."[96] Within a month that had become
his and the Gazette's public opinion.

In response to *Gazette* editorial pressure the county commissioners in 1950 sponsored a nonbinding referendum in which "the 'remodlers' won out in a land-slide majority of almost two to one."[97] Then in 1951 the *Gazette* backed special legislation to permit a countywide vote on a new courthouse, which unanimously passed the Kansas house of representatives. But it was bottled up in committee in the Kansas senate by a legislator friendly to the faction favoring a new courthouse. Biennial, the state legislature would not assemble again until 1953. When the county board early in 1952 came up with a plan to raze the old courthouse and build a new one on the same inadequate site, and called for bids, the *Gazette* sponsored another postcard straw vote, which ran six-to-one against.

In the November elections it supported a slate of board candidates pledged to block that plan. They won but could not take office until the start of the year, so the old board stubbornly proceeded with its plan to raze the courthouse. The *Gazette* then backed Clarence Beck, a local attorney and close friend of Bill's, who sought to stop further action by an appeal to the Kansas Supreme Court, which ruled for the old board. By the end of the year the lame-duck county board had torn down the old courthouse. Thus Lyon County had to pay for an unpopular, architecturally mediocre new courthouse in the same impractical downtown location, as planned and contracted for by the repudiated board.[98] Unfortunately, many Lyon County citizens thought Young Bill's outside interference caused the fight in the first place and resentfully, and wrongly, blamed him for their abominable new courthouse.

But Emporia was truly home to him and occasionally during this time elicited an editorial that transcended divisive local issues or state political fights to recognize a wider concern. Then his readers, sometimes reluctantly, had to acknowledge that they and their mostly absentee editor were fellow citizens of a larger community. Two eulogies from 1948, for example, demonstrate that he could on occasion rise above the common fray and force his readers to do so too. One was his obituary editorial for Rink Collins, a long-time *Gazette* printer killed by a drunken hit-and-run driver. The other was for Ruth Pemberton, a local interior decorator and the sister of Murdock and Brock, his New York "godfathers."[99] She had been disabled from birth by a severe curvature of the spine. Both essays are poignant commentaries that prove Bill could match or excel his father in controlled pathos; the one for Ruth suggests Bill could also demonstrate more intellectual steel:

> Usually from here in The Gazette office we get a sense of Divine Scheme, which is to say that if you wait long enough people eventually seem to get their just deserts, virtue being rewarded right here on this whirling globe, and the wicked, as in the case of Mussolini, being hoisted ingloriously upon meathooks, or getting their comeuppances in some fitting way.
>
> But there are times when sense and justice seem to be lacking and when Providence seems to have knocked off to go quail-hunting out among the spiral nebulae leaving the affairs of this world in charge of some substitute who is possibly well meaning, but whose competence is at least as doubtful as that of the late Harry Hopkins.
>
> Specifically, we have in mind the life and recent death of Ruth Pemberton, whose wistful, pain-lined face has been familiar to Emporia for almost six decades. The Creator first endowed her with the desire and instincts of every normal woman for love and a happy home with a husband and children. Then He gave her a curved spine which made any of this forever impossible. Also He gave her shrewdness so that she could not, even for a few years, deceive herself into thinking that she might have the things for which He made her yearn. So at her death she could not even look back with a sad smile at years when she had dared to hope.
>
> There are occasional people who "rise above" such afflictions and, somewhat because of them, reach an exemplary sweetness of soul. Why then did not Providence endow Ruth Pemberton with some unusual aptitude for sainthood, some extraordinary measure of selflessness, instead of giving her only the normal amount, plus a yearning for exactly that happiness which normal people have, but which was forever denied to her?

Of course it can be fairly said that here in Emporia we were kind to Ruth. Many people were unusually kind, out of pity. The trouble was that Providence, in addition to crippling Ruth, gave her a normal self-respect which made her resent pity. Then, just to make sure that she was spared nothing, she was also given the intelligence to see that some of the rather few pleasant things which happened to her, came largely for that reason.

The only kindness which she really trusted came from her brothers, Murdock and Brock. Probably the only happiness she really knew was a reflection of theirs. Since they were her flesh and blood she felt she had some right to thrill to their victories, to feel that their happiness in distant New York was almost her own.

For the rest, she spent those almost sixty years in her own private little hell of cold loneliness, watching her old crowd grow up, fall in love, pair off and drift away.

Perhaps it is only natural that this woman who was so starved for beauty should make it her occupation, and that, as a result hundreds of homes in this town are warm and soft and gay and pleasant because of her. But she gave us something still more important, a deep understanding which came out of her own tragedy. She had a boundless love for under-dogs. The outcasts, the defeated, the social rebels, the despised and rejected could always find warmth and generous understanding in Ruth Pemberton. Ruth knew.

It was her senseless torture that she, who had so great an eagerness for gaiety and beauty could have so little of it, that the things for which she longed should be so close that she could almost but never quite touch them, that she must stay just outside in the shadows listening and watching, as through a window, to the laughter, the music and the dancing, the fluttering confetti and the throbbing of the violins—a pale, pain-lined face pressed wistfully against the glass.

And why?

It is just possible (yet not very probable) that the rest of us may as a result be a little more grateful for that normal health and happiness which we take so much for granted.

But was it worth it?

When everyone gets back from that quail-hunt and all the big questions are answered, we may find out why such a moral lesson could not have been taught the rest of us in some way slightly less agonizing to poor Ruth. Meanwhile, thinking of her wistful loneliness, we look out into that great emptiness beyond the Big Dipper where the light-years go bending off into space and again ask, "Why? Why?"

As Man has always asked, and always will.—W. L. W.

In 1950 Kathrine and Barbara summered on Fishers Island, New York, essentially a seasonal community at the mouth of Long Island Sound, just off Mystic, Connecticut. The next year Bill and Kathrine bought a cottage there, the converted "diet kitchen and diet dining room" of the Mansion House, an old-fashioned summer hotel, and joined the local country club.[100] This cottage, rather than the cabin in Colorado, now became their regular summer retreat. But in July 1950 Bill flew back to Emporia to host Herbert Hoover who spoke at the delayed dedication of a commemorative bronze bust of Will White, cast in 1947 by the artist Jo Davidson, their mutual friend and fellow Century Club member. Paid for by the people of Emporia through subscriptions to a White Memorial Foundation, the bust had sat in storage for three years while the town argued over an appropriate location.[101] Bill, on principle, avoided the issue. Finally, on July 11, 1950, Hoover dedicated the bust on a site beside the lake in Peter Pan Park, fifty-two acres that Will and Sallie had given the town over the years 1928 to 1930 in memory of their daughter, Mary. Then toward the end of July Bill joined Hoover for two weeks at his very selective all-male "Cave Man" retreat at Bohemian Grove, near Palo Alto, California. That year's gathering became historically notable because it was there that Congressman Richard Nixon first met Gen. Dwight Eisenhower.[102]

Also in July 1950 Harvard alumni elected William L. White to a six-year term on the university's Board of Overseers. Of course, Emporians would have preferred that he, like his father before him, had been appointed to the more locally significant Kansas Board of Regents. But Bill fully appreciated the higher honor and took his duties as one of thirty Harvard Overseers seriously, meeting with the full board in Boston once every six weeks when back East and serving each year on departmental visiting committees, sometimes chairing them.[103] But perhaps his most valuable service to the board occurred during the behind-the-scenes debate in 1953 and 1954 in which it decided to reprimand yet retain physics professor Wendell Furry, a self-confessed former Communist party member who took the Fifth Amendment rather than testify against former party associates.

By refusing to fire Furry summarily, Harvard incurred the wrath of Sen. Joseph McCarthy, who in 1953 had accused the university of harboring scores of Communists, based partly on Furry's testimony at several investigative hearings. Bill led board opposition to Furry, arguing in letters to fellow board members that "a Harvard professor should have complete freedom to criticize the government or its policies or, indeed, our entire form of government provided his opposition is honorable, open and above-board." But, he wrote, "what we have in the Furry case is no issue of freedom of speech, but rather Freedom to Conspire." Bill believed Furry's refusal to testify about Harvard and MIT colleagues, fellow members of a secret Communist cell working together on a classified government radar project during and just after the war, betrayed his country and university. To Bill it demonstrated a misplaced allegiance to Soviet conspiracy, much like loyalty to the Mafia. He thought the board should not confuse academic freedom with "freedom to conspire" but should give Furry an ultimatum to tell the whole truth. At board meetings Bill articulated that side with quiet reason in a sometimes acrimonious debate. And when his side lost, he wrote Keith Kane, one of the board's principal supporters of Furry, "any differences between us are within the Harvard family. I shall support your decision even though privately I don't happen to agree with it, and will publicly defend it, should the need ever arise." Significantly, Bill's public voice carried some weight in that era of hysteria. He was a cold warrior through intellectual and emotional conviction, not political expediency or fearful conformity.[104]

In April 1950, just two months after Senator McCarthy had started his career of blanket accusations with a speech in Wheeling, West Virginia, Bill wrote Kansas senator Andrew Schoeppel a confidential seven-page memo about the Wisconsin senator, whom he thought had "behaved with fantastic stupidity. He shot off his mouth on the basis of a bunch of rumors, quite a bit of what he said was inaccurate, and then he found himself in the position of having to scurry around to collect the facts to back up his charges." And Bill found the people working for McCarthy "extremely inept," especially in their attempt to enlist Bill as a witness against Owen Lattimore, an academic analyst of Chinese affairs, "whom I have never laid eyes on." Unlike many at the start of that decade of cold war tension, Bill was openly anti-Communist and believed most party members Soviet agents who should be ferreted out. Rather than McCarthy, though, "the two men in Congress," Bill wrote Schoeppel, "who in my opinion have the experience and the skill to carry on such an important fight are Karl Mundt in the Senate and Nixon in the House."[105]

As the author of *Report on the Russians* Bill stood as a "credentialed" anti-Communist in 1945. By the end of 1950 he had also become a conservative Republican who was a staunch civil libertarian. As a well-known anti-Communist conservative during the McCarthy era, he sometimes lent support to possibly vulnerable but worthwhile causes or organizations. For example, he was an active board member in the 1950s of Freedom House, an influential but sometimes controversial civil rights organization. At the ACLU he acted to bridge the deep split in the early fifties between liberal and conservative board members. He was, for instance, appointed to the ad hoc committee that reviewed fellow board member Merlyn Pitzele's public charges of inaccuracy and misjudgment against an ACLU-sponsored report on blacklisting, *The Judges and the Judged*, by Merle Miller. The book was a formal response to such Red-baiting publications as the weekly newsletter *Counterattack* and the pamphlet *Red Channels*, which listed 151 alleged subversives in radio and television. Though Bill had originally voted to commission the report, he agreed with Pitzele that it contained inaccuracies that should not be ignored. In the committee he brokered a compromise recommendation that saved ACLU faces on both sides of the issue.[106]

Early in 1951 he was one of five founding directors of Radio Liberty, a sister organization to Radio Free Europe aimed specifically at the Soviet Union, both secretly financed by the CIA. Bill was elected treasurer of the enabling corporation, the American Committee for Freedom for the Peoples of the USSR, Inc., and continued a trustee until his death. That essentially titular post reflected the public value of his name. The CIA liaison for Radio Liberty was Frank Lindsay, formerly an OSS officer whom Bill had met in 1945 when working on "Some Affairs of Honor." Two fellow directors were anti-Soviet journalist friends, Eugene Lyons and Bill Chamberlin. Lyons in 1951 was also a roving editor for the *Digest*. DeWitt Wallace was a prominent supporter of Radio Free Europe; hence Bill functioned within a network of conservative postwar associates. Later, he wrote president-elect Dwight Eisenhower to recommend Allen Dulles as director of the CIA. In that letter he claims to "know this field fairly well," and to "have known [Allen Dulles] for years" as "one of the best analytical and planning minds of our time."[107]

As an unquestioned anti-Communist with numerous personal connections, Bill was sometimes able to defend or to mediate effectively for friends under attack. For example, he was a stout defender of physicist J. Robert Oppenheimer, of the Harvard class of 1925 and a fellow Overseer, who had told him in 1951 on a train between Boston and New York of a flirtation in the late 1930s with Communist causes and never invoked the Fifth Amendment in subsequent investigations, unlike Furry. Later, in 1954, when the Atomic Energy Commission conducted hearings about extending Oppenheimer's security clearance, Bill supported him publicly and suggested to Edward R. Murrow privately that he interview Oppenheimer on "See It Now," which he did for one of his more memorable programs.[108] And in the fall of 1951 Bill interceded with Federal Bureau of Investigation (FBI) Director J. Edgar Hoover and Secretary of Defense Robert Lovett, both of whom he knew personally, to get cartoonist Bill Mauldin, a close friend, fellow Century Club member, and outspoken liberal, a correspondent's visa to Korea, which had been delayed without explanation.[109]

In 1950 the Korean War, coming just after the Hiss case, propelled Bill further to the right. In an editorial on July 1, five days after North Korea had invaded South Korea, he characterized that peninsula as a "military booby-trap," which the "short sighted leadership of George Marshall and Dean Acheson" had tripped by not helping Chiang Kai-shek as the generalissimo fled to Formosa. "But now we are in a dilemma," Bill observed, because the Soviets "don't want war now, but are only feeling our muscle. If it is firm, they will withdraw, leaving us in the booby trap. If it is flabby they will shove us out, and this slap in the face will ring from Norway to the Philippines. Either way, how can they lose?" At the moment such cynicism was not popular, and his commentary evoked a number of protests.[110]

But by December, just after the People's Republic of China had intervened with its armies, he struck a common nerve in a follow-up editorial, "A Note on Wars." In it he asserted sardonically that Truman had rushed to the defense of South Korea so that "the unbearable vulgarities of Joe McCarthy would be drowned out by bugle and drum. Who then would dare say the Truman administration was not firmly anti-Communistic?" And he reflected growing cold war disenchantment with American postwar foreign policy, which, he believed, had frittered away our military superiority. For he asked,

> why, when we were powerful, did we not insist on free elections in Poland, in Hungary, in Rumania, in Jugoslavia, in Czechoslovakia, in East Germany, and in the Baltic states? Why did we sit stupidly by while Communist terror strangled freedom in all this vast, rich, civilized area and then, having stripped ourselves of arms, why do we suddenly begin to shriek for a free election in Korea, a backward country which, in all its three thousand years of history, never has had free elections nor seemed particularly to miss them?

Reminding his readers he had favored confronting Stalin five years before, he offered several guideposts for future American foreign policy. Among them, he insisted we should avoid concentrating "all our forces in one distant isolated spot," leaving only one American division in Europe "between Stalin's 300 divisions and the Atlantic," and "we should not be offended when a nearby ally [Chiang Kai-shek] offers help."[111] That editorial was widely copied, with the *Gazette* reporting on December 15 that "in recent years no editorial" in this newspaper "has brought greater response." That editorial, and subsequent ones during the next several months, placed Bill firmly in the China Lobby of such right-wingers as Henry Luce and Alfred Kohlberg, millionaire importer of Chinese lace and publisher of the anti-Communist magazine *Plain Talk*. And Bill's conservatism gradually expanded from international politics to inflationary fiscal policies to domestic social welfare programs, until toward the end of his life he seemed to many just a splenetic reactionary.[112]

December 19, 1950, Sallie White died at age eighty-one. Because of the recent family incorporation, her death created none of the legal and tax problems that his father's had. Nor did it affect the daily operations of the *Gazette* because she had relinquished any significant supervision three or four years before. Therefore, he and Kathrine stayed in Emporia for only a short while after the funeral to respond to local civilities and arrange oversight of 927 Exchange, which they kept, with its effects virtually untouched, as their Emporia home.

In February, leaving Barbara in school in New York, they once again accepted Herbert Hoover's invitation to join him for several weeks off the Florida Keys. Afterward, as if in return, Bill wrote "Story of a Smear," a selective retelling of the march the summer of 1932 on Washington, D.C., by about twelve thousand unemployed World War I veterans. Calling themselves the Bonus Expeditionary Force, they were seeking from Congress in those hard times a special veterans appropriation. On President Hoover's orders they were dispersed and their camp burned by troops led by Chief of Staff Gen. Douglas MacArthur. In recounting that Bill argues that the Communists cleverly used a previous police shooting of unruly marchers to denounce President Hoover falsely as "the murderer of American veterans." To the contrary, Bill asserts in an excess of disinguous zeal, "after General MacArthur and his tiny task force took over, there was not a single bruise." That assertion, of course, goes against objective historical accounts in which MacArthur's troops, backed up by tanks, used bayonets and tear gas against a disorganized, unarmed mob containing women and children.[113] The *Digest* planted Bill's apologia in the ultraconservative magazine the *Freeman*, financed quietly by Alfred Kohlberg, then ran it virtually uncut in December.[114]

Bill placed four other magazine articles in 1951 and spent two months in Emporia on the *Gazette*, from mid-August to mid-October. As usual, when home he regularly contributed editorial copy, this time thirty-one commentaries, many two columns, whose topics ranged from local to international. Also in eight issues starting September 29 he serialized former secretary of defense James Forrestal's diaries. He had "laid out considerable hard cash" to do so, he told subscribers, because the minority in Lyon County, "which decides elections by voting, not its narrow interests but what it earnestly believes are those of the nation, must have the facts if those votes are to be wisely cast."[115] An admirable purpose, of course, but an explanation that suggests patrician patronage, a tone not lost on Emporians. Old Bill White had often enough used his newspaper as a bully pulpit, but did so with a bluff, comic egotism that had not offended. Young Bill's tone too was humorous, but that did not hide his condescension. Perhaps part of that attitude came from his license not to give a damn. His *Digest* earnings freed him from the *Gazette*, and his *Gazette* income from the *Digest*. With three homes back East he was not confined to Emporia or to New York City but lived in several communities, each with different networks of friends and acquaintances. Now in the *Gazette* he could make his private opinions public, within the bounds of libel law and his own journalistic ethics, without the need to please his parents or DeWitt Wallace or to placate distressed Emporians.

Chapter Six

A Cold War Conservative Libertarian and an Award-Winning Small-Town Editor, 1951–1973

In October 1951 Bill assumed his role of small-town Kansas editor to help anti-Taft GOP forces draft General Eisenhower for the 1952 nomination. DeWitt Wallace, Herbert Hoover, and Kansas senators Harry Darby and Frank Carlson were part of the backstage drama. But it was Roy Roberts, publisher of the *Kansas City Star* and an old Eisenhower crony, who suggested that Bill write a *Gazette* editorial to urge Kansans to claim Eisenhower as a favorite-son candidate. By phone from New York City Bill dictated "Mud Creek to the Elbe" for the October 26 issue. In it he compared Eisenhower, "hand-whittled hickory," to Sen. Robert Taft, "too sour a pickle," in a "grassroots" call to Kansans to get behind their "son of the sod." The real call, of course, was to the general, then in Paris as supreme commander of the North Atlantic Treaty Organization (NATO).

But Eisenhower nearly took himself out of the race on November 4 in statements to reporters on arrival in the United States for brief government consultations that he was not interested in politics. Roy Roberts and Arthur Krock, then *New York Times* Washington bureau chief, outlined for Bill a three-page telegram that he rewrote and phoned to his secretary at the *Gazette*. From Emporia she sent it in his name as a well-known small-town midwestern editor to General Eisenhower in care of the Department of Defense. In it Bill told him if he did not give Kansas delegates an immediate, clear signal that he would accept nomination, they would go to Taft. The next day Krock wrote Bill: "That telegram was much improved from the original in the form in which it reached the General. And it is perfectly obvious that it had a sobering and correcting effect upon him, as witness his statement today on leaving for Paris."[1] Later General Eisenhower sent Bill in care of the *Gazette* a four-page letter marked personal and confidential that answered the telegram point by point and concluded "that, like any other loyal American, the knowledge that any thoughtful citizen considers me qualified for such a post fills me with feelings of the most intense pride, accompanied by equal feelings of humility. Coming from you, they have special value."[2] But he still did not commit himself publicly until April 1952.

That July during the Republican convention Bill was on Fishers Island working on the Korean medical story that became *Back Down the Ridge*, one of his more successful books. He was delighted with Eisenhower's nomination for president and even more so with Richard Nixon's for vice-president. In his enthusiasm he wrote Eisenhower "ordinarily Vice-Presidents aren't worth cutting up for catfish bait, but in my opinion, which is both humble and deeply pondered, yours is a dinger."[3] And he immediately wrote Wallace offering to do a piece on Nixon in time for the October issue, with a quick run to California for color and interviews. His good friend Herbert Hoover, Jr., one of Nixon's backstairs supporters as early as 1946, would be willing to help. But just at that time *Digest* Associate Editor Hobart ("Hobe") Lewis wrote Bill about a Russian refugee story the magazine had access to, asking him to look over a packet of enclosed materials about it to see if he were interested He was, so he stayed back East that summer.

Bill had an interest in military medicine, dating from his abortive 1943 flight surgeon story. For his Korean account he used Walter

Reed Army Hospital in Washington, D.C., as a base to interview doctors, nurses, and over thirty amputees back from the war. As narrative he focused on the stories of twelve wounded infantrymen, how they got "clobbered," what they did and said and felt as they were carried to a battalion first aid station and then transported back by a "meat wagon" or a "chopper" to a MASH (mobile army surgical hospital) unit. Several of the amputees he follows on to Japan and then the states. As in his other war books Bill takes the information given him, selects representative figures and anecdotes, then puts them in a carefully contrived narrative structure in which his characters seem to tell their own stories in their own words. In reviewing the book, Bruce Bliven in the *New Republic* acknowledged the effectiveness of that technique, writing, "William L. White is one of the most skillful journalists alive. He never tries to mastermind anything; . . . he prefers the small picture to the big one, and by concentrating on what happens to a few individuals, he often succeeds in conveying great events better than he ever could by painting on a broad canvas."[4] Dos Passos, just after the book was released, wrote Bill, "You've been working up this particular technique for a long time and now you've got it to a terrific point of clarity and simplicity so that there's nothing between the reader and the guy in the wheelchair."[5]

But this story differs in narrative structure from *They Were Expendable* or *Queens Die Proudly* in two rhetorically difficult respects: it has no central narrative figure to give it continuity, and the most significant dramatic events, the "clobberings," come at the beginning of each story. As a result, like King Lear, Bill gives the kingdom away in his first scenes. That he still commands interest indicates his sophisticated narrative skill. He does this by creating suspense, by raising the question of what happens to each soldier after he is carried "back down the ridge." This funnels attention to the frontline hospital, the new MASH units and their procedures, which he describes graphically step by step. As he explained to Louis de Rochemont in trying to sell him the story as a semidocumentary film, the book gives "a very detailed account of exactly how the packing house process operates on each wounded man in this front-line hospital."[6] Later, Gene Reynolds, producer of the long-running television series "M*A*S*H," wrote Bill that *Back Down the Ridge* was required reading for his writers, specifically because "it describes that medical operation with such accuracy and detail."[7] Though Bill overcomes a potentially anti-climactic or choppy story line, he does break narrative tone several times, which can bother the reader. For he calls attention to himself when he makes an occasional partisan comment criticizing American policy in the Far East and when he lectures the American public for not responding sufficiently to Red Cross blood drives. The *Digest* ran its cut in the February 1953 issue and subsequently in eight of its international editions.[8] Harcourt, Brace issued the book version on February 15, to numerous favorable reviews, but unlike his earlier war books this one did not make the national best-seller list.

After submitting *Back Down the Ridge* for *Digest* vetting, Bill spent nearly two months in Emporia, from mid-September to early November, monitoring the *Gazette* and the elections, both local and national. This was then the usual date for his annual commitment to his hometown. And he made use of the days. He wrote twenty-four *Gazette* commentaries this year, with subjects ranging from a local industrial development plan to Richard Nixon's "Checkers Speech" to the annual chicken dinner at Saint Joseph's Roman Catholic church in Olpe, together with endorsements in hometown vernacular of selected local candidates.[9] But such a flurry of W. L. W. editorials only called attention to his more usual absence.

On his return to New York City he started work on the Russian refugee story Hobe Lewis had suggested that summer. The Tolstoy Foundation, a nonprofit Soviet émigré organization, had approached the *Digest* with the offer of story rights about a small colony of Russians who had escaped from the Chinese province of Sinkiang. Encountering many hardships, they had fled across the Gobi Desert through Tibet to India then to the United States, arriving in New York in March 1952. The story was a gamble, though, having already been rejected as too diffuse by *Life* and the *Saturday Evening Post*. Intrigued by the challenge, Bill devoted several months to it, with considerable help from the *Digest*'s research department. He interviewed about twenty members of the group with an interpreter and dictaphone, then put the material on four-by-six-inch index cards, as was his wont. But he was unable, after trying various tacks, "to make it into a sustained narrative with any commercial value," so he reported to a representative of that group.[10] He did, however, become a nominal director in 1953 of the Tolstoy Foundation, and in the spring of 1954, at the suggestion of Eugene ("Gene") Lyons, who had become *Digest* general editor, wrote a forty-page character sketch of the Countess Alexandra Tolstoy, daughter of Leo Tolstoy and president of the foundation. But after four editors tried unsuccessfully to cut the sketch, it too remained unpublished.[11]

In the fall of 1952 Bill helped James Spadea, a good friend and a fashion magazine publisher, expand into newspaper syndication. They had been acquainted when students at Harvard but did not meet again until years later, at a dinner party hosted by George Sakier, whose wife, Kay, fashion editor for *Mademoiselle* magazine, was a friend of Kathrine's. The Spadeas lived in Bucks County, Pennsylvania, just a few miles from the Whites' farm at Frenchtown. As near neighbors with common interests and acquaintances, they gradually became close friends. When Spadea decided to start his syndicate with a column of independent commentary by best-selling authors, he consulted Bill and another neighbor, James Michener, the writer. Both encouraged him and both recommended the journalist Victor Lasky as editor. Ultimately, the column, "For the Record," edited by Lasky, appeared in sixty-five major newspapers and included over 130 contributors. During the ten years that the column ran, from 1953 to 1963, Bill placed an occasional piece in it but out of friendship refused payment; he also sent Spadea other pieces from time to time and used his syndicate for press credentials.[12]

For the November 1952 issue of the magazine *Freedom and Union* Bill upheld the affirmative on the question "Should the NATO Nations Form an Atlantic Union?" Isolationist and archreactionary Col. Robert McCormick presented the negative, but not content with that venue, he also hammered at Bill's argument in a lead editorial in his *Chicago Tribune*. Amused, Bill reprinted those magazine pieces in several January issues of the *Gazette*, framed in typical irony, followed by a copy of the colonel's editorial, which accused Bill of wanting "to sell out the United States to foreign domination." After commending McCormick's patriotism and often-addled sincerity, Bill admitted "Thus we stand, exposed and unmasked. We had hoped to inveigle this Republic into an Atlantic union in time to have Queen Elizabeth II brought over here to be triumphantly crowned sovereign lady of this land in Chicago's auditorium, with Colonel McCormick humbly bearing her train. Foiled in this we must now turn to other mischief."[13] Like his father before him, Bill was an endemic Kansas humorist who could not resist deflating the self-important in the pages of his newspaper.

But he did not find much humor that spring in the first scandal of the new Eisenhower administration. Soon after Wesley Roberts, a Kansas Eisenhower Republican and former state party chairman, had been named national chairman on January 17, newspaper charges forced a legislative investigation of his role in the state purchase of a fraternal lodge hospital that legal records suggested the state already owned. For arranging that questionable trans- action in 1951, Roberts had collected a fee of $11,000, 10 percent of the sale price. He had also lobbied for the deal without identifying his self-interest, in violation of state law. In the early stages of the investigation, in answer to an inquiry from Eisen- hower sent to Emporia, Bill as editor of the *Gazette* advised the president that the accusations against Roberts were not serious, then almost immediately had to admit he had been misinformed— that on checking from New York he found the situation indeed serious. When Roberts resigned as national chairman on March 27, Bill was embarrassed because he had been revealed to the president as an absentee editor unfamiliar with behind-the-scene politics of his own state.[14]

For about six weeks, from the last of April through May, Bill was in Emporia concentrating on *Gazette* business affairs in preparation for a nearly three month family trip to Europe. As usual, while home he commented about local matters on the editorial page, from the planting of curbside trees downtown to the firing of a nontenured professor at the teachers college, Dr. W. Lou Tandy. He had signed a petition protesting the conviction of eleven Communist party leaders under the 1940 Smith Act;

he was fired because he had identified himself on that petition with his professional affiliation, as had such signers as United States Supreme Court Justice Hugo Black. Bill was concerned both about Tandy's treatment and about the college itself, which he described to the chairman of the Kansas Board of Regents as "in pitifully bad shape," steadily losing enrollment under an "idiotic" temporary president and several previous "glad-handing mediocrities." In the editorial "Education vs. Concrete" he advised the regents "what we don't need and don't want here is a dynamic wind bag hired on the theory that he could go down to Topeka and back-slap the legislature into giving us more concrete. What we desperately want is a man of high academic qualifications, with dignity, standing and experience, and a background of real scholarship which commands respect."[15]

On June 12 Bill, Kathrine, Barbara, Mary Hyde (a school chum of Barbara's), and the family's 1950 Chevrolet station wagon sailed from New York to Europe, not to return until September 5. Landing at Southhampton, the Whites planned to tour parts of England, France, Italy, Communist Yugoslavia, Soviet-occupied Vienna, and Allied-occupied Germany. Bill carried correspondent's credentials and intended to stop at various *Digest* international offices to make contacts and pick up story leads. But immediately on arrival in Paris, Barbara ended up at the American Hospital for an emergency appendectomy, which kept them in that city for thirty days, then ten days to the Lido off Venice for her further convalescence. Because of medical expenses and the high cost of their unexpected stay in Paris, they decided to spend what was left of the trip mostly in Vienna, which had a more favorable exchange rate, with a weeklong auto jaunt back through Germany and Holland to board ship at Rotterdam. During that tour Bill wrote a series of two-column travel letters for the *Gazette*, starting with the June 26 issue, a series that totaled forty-nine pieces, with the last five functioning as a postscript, comparing Emporia to small communities in Europe. After his return to New York he loosely revised the first forty-five into a framed narrative, entitled it "Castles at 16" with reference to the two teenagers, and submitted it to the *Digest* for consideration as a book section. But it was turned down as "too much a collection of travel notes."[16]

Next Bill began work, with *Digest* editor Paul Palmer's approval, on two articles about "agriculture and industry behind the iron curtain." But then Wallace told him "he didn't think the Digest wanted anything more on the Commies from that end of the world."[17] Bill dropped those articles to take up, curiously enough, a suggestion by Gene Lyons to look into the life of white-collar workers behind the European iron curtain. Bill interviewed recent escapees then wrote a twenty-page article entitled "Smuggled Messages," which he submitted April 1954. *Digest* editors rejected that and his sketch of Alexandra Tolstoy at about the same time. He also worked on several other unsuccessful story ideas in 1953 and 1954. For nearly three years, from March 1952 to January 1955, the only piece Bill got in the *Digest*, other than the cut of *Back Down the Ridge*, was a four-page "unforgettable character" sketch about Harry Caldwell, a missionary in China. Though reprinted in seven international editions, at Pleasantville the sketch counted as but one brief article.[18] Such lack of success contributed to a sense of dissatisfaction apparent in one of the postscript travel letters to the *Gazette*, where he wrote: "Your editor, in his task of earning a living, for the time being must lead an unpleasantly nomadic life—flitting from region to region . . . [to] work for a magazine."[19]

Perhaps to break that syndrome, he began to concentrate in 1954 on redesigning the *Gazette's* typography and makeup, starting that summer when he replaced its old black, Gothic headlines with lighter, Jensen typefaces. Readability was his primary goal, or so he claimed in several explanatory editorials and straw votes of subscribers.[20] But in actuality, since studying needed back-shop changes in 1948, he had grown interested in the aesthetics of fonts, until that became even more of an intellectual passion than his hobby of coin collecting. To oversee this typographical project, Bill and Kathrine stayed in Emporia off and on more than seven months that year, with Barbara boarding part of the time in New York City to finish out her senior year at Nightingale-Bamford.

To readers of the *Gazette* the most obvious change occurred November 20, when Bill replaced the traditional Saturday comics insert with a four-page weekend pictorial section. Then, starting December 4, he ran the entire Saturday edition as a tabloid.

Because of back-shop problems, though, he dropped that tabloid format after a month but expanded the weekend photo supplement to eight pages on better quality newsprint. In some respects that was the belated realization of his 1927 rotogravure scheme and became a *Gazette* fixture until the month of his death. Usually its subjects struck a balance between local shots—of college students, Emporia industries, special community events, the man or woman of the week—and uplifting "photo studies"—of Venetian highlights, the ballet, classical Greek statuary, or Gothic architecture.[21]

In that mix of features the weekend edition reflected Young Bill's ambivalent attitude toward his hometown, that of unblushing booster and condescending patron. And whimsy underscores his ambivalence. For example, the first "man of the week," on December 14, 1954, was Ivor Rees, a local farmer who had in 1950 bought from the city the old Soden's mill dam across the Cottonwood River just south of town. At the time most townsfolk thought it a white elephant, not worth the $300 he paid for it, but he saw it as a flood hazard to adjacent fields and planned sometime to dynamite it.[22] In 1954, after several years of severe draught, Emporia had nearly exhausted its Neosho River water supply and had to impose extraordinary usage rules: no flushing except for solids, no baths in more than two inches of water. When the city tried to buy back Soden's dam for an auxiliary water source, Ivor priced it at $1,750, which city officials stubbornly refused to pay because it needed extensive renovation, although they planned a pipeline to the river reservoir costing over $100,000. Bill enjoyed the irony, if others did not. After that, the man or woman of the week became a serious and respected feature of the Weekend edition, most of the time.

Over the next several years Bill continued to collaborate with his staff to revamp typography and makeup. Whenever possible, he used white space for emphasis. He redesigned the *Gazette*, which had a stable circulation of about 8,500, to be read not from the newsstand but from the lap, by a subscriber. So he changed the news fonts to Corona and eliminated most column rules and lines. He worked to redesign standing heads and enhance photographic reproductions. And he started a wide column on the right-hand side of the editorial page headed "You Should Read" in which he published excerpts from current books or magazine articles he deemed important and required no or very low permission fees. By 1957 the *Gazette* had won honorable mention for its circulation class in the N. W. Ayer newspaper design competition. Pleased, Bill continued tinkering with its format.[23]

For Bill those months in Emporia during 1954 seem to have renewed his interest, or luck, in placing articles with the *Digest*. From January 1955 to February 1956 he placed five pieces, but one, "Ridiculous Waste in the Armed Services," in the April issue, caused him and others embarrassment. He based it on details from a report on military waste scheduled for release in March by the Commission on Organization of the Executive Branch of the Government, set up by Congress and headed by former president Hoover. Bill's close friendship with "the Chief" gave him exclusive early access. But internal disagreements about conclusions caused the commission to delay release by a month or more, well after the April *Digest* had gone to press. As a result that magazine published information not yet available to Congress, which caused the chairman of a House Armed Services Subcommittee to threaten Bill with an official inquiry. He made a quick trip to Washington to placate that congressman and others.[24]

The article also angered Secretary of Defense Charles Wilson, who thought it a partisan attack on his administration. Thus he nearly blocked a proposal that month by Undersecretary of State Herbert Hoover, Jr., and CIA Director Allen Dulles to ask Bill to write up a government white paper about the treatment of prisoners during the Korean War. They had just received a British government report about its prisoners and believed something similar from the State Department, if timely, would be useful for cold war purposes. The Korean War had ended in stalemate with the signing of an armistice agreement in July 1953. Repatriation of prisoners had concluded by early 1954. To be timely that report should be out in 1956, but that was impossible without Pentagon cooperation. To appease Secretary Wilson and his staff, Bill offered to do a follow-up piece for the *Digest* "based on the great progress they had made in clearing up the mess." Somewhat mollified, the Pentagon agreed to release its records to the State Department, which in turn gave Bill access to them. And in the November *Digest* his "New Look in Defense Spending" praised Wilson's efforts to impose sound business practices on the chaos of military procurements.

Another 1955 *Digest* piece "Should Unions Have Monopoly Powers?" marks his advocacy of right-to-work legislation, which pitted him against Kansas governor Fred Hall and caused him to write two later *Digest* articles on that subject. Bill was in Emporia several weeks during March and April, just after a right-to-work bill had passed both houses of the legislature and been sent to Governor Hall for his signature. Instead, he vetoed it and called for more moderate labor-management legislation. Bill was incensed by that veto, having become convinced the union shop had given labor leaders a stranglehold on American industry. In addition, Hall was a maverick Landon Republican, a lawyer, but the son of a prounion railroad engineer. He had won the governorship in 1954 largely because the public was fed up with the other Republican faction, which had tried to whitewash the Wesley Roberts scandal; thus Hall became the center of intraparty feuding. During 1955 and 1956 Bill wrote twelve *Gazette* editorials against the governor, who was defeated in his reelection effort in the August primaries. Unfortunately for the Republicans, though, such feuding cost them the governorship, for the first time since 1932, which went to George Docking, a Democrat whose family had summered near the Whites in Moraine Park when both he and Bill were boys.

Under the direction of her father, Barbara applied during her senior year to three of the Ivy League's "seven sisters" colleges—Radcliffe, Vassar, and Pembroke—but on her own initiative she also applied to Stanford University. California had first appealed to her when she and Kathrine visited Bill's cousin Gwen Behr in 1949; the lifestyle there seemed more relaxed and open, in contrast to the East Coast.[25] By May Barbara had decided to attend Stanford. Her decision delayed Bill's work on the Korean prisoner book because early that fall, after about a month in Emporia, Bill and Kathrine spent six weeks touring the West Coast, especially the San Francisco area, to get to know Barbara's choice better. Only then did Bill settle down in New York City to work on the book. Not until April 1956 was he able to submit the first half to the *Digest*. Wallace and several senior editors read it carefully to see if an article cut were feasible but decided not. When Bill submitted the second half in August, the same editors went over it with a possible book supplement in mind but again thought a condensation would not work. It was a sizable manuscript of nearly 550 pages, and its effect resulted from the cumulative impact of details and documentation. Besides, the *Digest* book editor wrote him, "Wally does not approve . . . because of the subject and the timing."[26]

Timing was a major problem. At first the State Department thought Bill could do the project in three to four months and the government could then pay him and issue it as an official report of less than a hundred pages. But after he began research, he found the materials more complex and interesting than he first thought. Because that would make for a longer, more time-consuming report, he suggested commercial publication, with the State Department endorsing it but not picking up costs. That suited the department. After he had finished, though, Harcourt, Brace turned it down, but Charles Scribner's Sons picked it up at the end of August for its late fall list. Unfortunately, Bill got into a six-month wrangle with a Col. Kenneth Hansen, then in the Office of the Joint Chiefs of Staff and formerly chief of Psychological Welfare for the Far East Command. With Defense Department approval Bill had interviewed Hansen about his role in the screening of prisoners for repatriation, and Hansen had lent Bill for his use an unpublished book manuscript about that process. When in September Bill asked Hansen to check the final manuscript for accuracy and sign a release, he accused Bill of "skimming" his manuscript "in Reader's Digest fashion, taking as much as possible of my color and many of my choicest anecdotes." And he threatened a lawsuit for damages because his own manuscript was being considered for publication.[27] Since some of Hansen's details were otherwise unavailable, Bill had a problem, for Scribner's would not issue the book until Hansen posed no legal threat. Bill revised the contested section by combing archive sources further and interviewing another key officer, Col. William Robinette, who had also screened prisoners. And he rewrote several crucial passages to meet Hansen's specific objections. Finally, Hansen signed a release in February, but *The Captives of Korea: An Unofficial White Paper on the Treatment of War Prisoners* was not published until mid-May 1957.

The book was about eighteen months too late. Though it received widespread positive reviews and Book-of-the-Month Club listed it as an alternative, it sold slowly because the public was no longer very interested in the Korean War.[28] Yet it was a substantial work: thoroughly researched, well-documented, written with skilled attention to continuity, illustrated, and indexed. As Gen. S. L. A. Marshall remarked in the *New York Times Book Review,* "White deals, in a semi-scholarly way, with prisoner of war problems. . . . Except for its passionate tone and tricks of continuity to preserve high reader interest, 'The Captives of Korea' might have been published as a government document."[29] Bill achieves narrative interest, those "tricks of continuity," by following at intervals the stories of six American prisoners, much as he did with the soldiers "clobbered" in *Back Down the Ridge.* But at the request of the Defense Department and out of respect for the prisoners' families, he uses only descriptive names and representative situations—the General, the Tank Lieutenant, the Artilleryman, the Doctor, the Ranger, the Lame Captain. He intersperses their stories with the real-life story of Paul Ruegger, head of the International Red Cross, who throughout the war tried fruitlessly to interest the North Koreans in the niceties of the Geneva Convention to be directed under Red Cross auspices.

The other narrative line follows United Nations treatment of its many prisoners. Here Bill sifts through a confusion of evidence to present a coherent and essentially objective account of the Communist-led riots at United Nations prison camps and propaganda battles over repatriation procedures. At the end more than half the Communist prisoners refused to go back—a total of 88,000 compared to the 21 Americans, 1 Briton, and 327 South Koreans who refused repatriation. Those figures underscore one of the major themes of the book, that the inhumane methods of the Communist side, with intensive interrogation and indoctrination backed up by torture, starvation, isolation, and death, often did produce false war crime confessions, but they did not "convert" prisoners to the Communist side. A corollary theme emerges from the background to the stories of the six unnamed Americans. Captured, half-trained, youthful conscripts, as many of the Americans prisoners were, can be so easily demoralized that they become informers or give up and die, especially when deprived of leadership and subjected to calculated brutality. But seasoned, well-trained troops who maintain lines of discipline, as did the Turks and the British, can survive such brutality with dignity. That theme culminates in Bill's endorsement of the idealism of the Geneva Convention, which assumes that, even in defeat and under imprisonment, every individual has an innate human worth that ought not be violated. If we as a free people do not continue to strive for that ideal, he concludes, "then let the Termite State take over, and All Hail the Coming of the Night." But that message reached only a few thousand because the book was not a commercial success and had not been excerpted in the *Digest*, with its approximately fifteen million American subscribers.

In Emporia on Saturday afternoon, June 22, 1957, Barbara White married Air Force 2d Lt. David Walker, whom she had met at Stanford. To have the wedding in Emporia was her decision. To make it the town's most fashionable ever was Bill and Kathrine's. Henry Luce sent a photographer to record the event for *Life* magazine, as a follow-up to its 1941 coverage of *Journey for Margaret*.[30] The *Kansas City Star* sent its society editor, Nell Snead. The reception was at 927 Exchange, in the house and its large side garden. The wedding itself was in the new First Congregational Church, about nine blocks away. At 5:00 P.M. Kathrine, in a gray brocade gown, and Bill, in top hat and cutaway, were ready to leave for the church and the 5:30 ceremony. A string quartet tuned up in the living room. Magnums of champagne in silver ice buckets rested by banks of glasses on linen-covered tables on the side porch and in the garden. But no cake! Kathrine, on the advice of her old friend Sheila Hibben, food editor for the *New Yorker* magazine, had weeks before ordered an elaborate wedding cake plus two hundred "little cakes in white and gold encasements" from the New York House of Blanche, a most exclusive caterer. At noon the express service admitted it could find no trace of House of

Blanche cake, so Kathrine had frantically phoned Emporia friends asking them to bake a cake, any kind of cake for the wedding. But as she left for the church there was none in sight, and Bill ordered the kitchen staff to assemble emergency hors d'oeuvre sandwiches.

When the wedding party returned about an hour later, they found on the dining room table an elaborately frosted, four-tiered, Emporia-made wedding cake covered with rosettes, topped by a bouquet of sugary white roses and flanked by a score of other cakes, all baked that afternoon. Nell Snead in the *Kansas City Star* reported that Kathrine, misty-eyed, could only murmur, "It's magic. How could these dear people do it?" At that moment her resentment of small-town life seems to have evaporated. Several days later, in a *Gazette* editorial, Bill reprinted the *Star*'s lively account of the cake crisis, then added background and the sequel, that two days later a deliveryman showed up with the crated wonders from the House of Blanche, which were firmly refused. Then, in the role of small-town editor as booster, Bill ruefully ended with "The moral? Trade at home."[31] For both him and Kathrine Emporia was now truly home, at least part of the time. As one sign of that, with Barbara married and Bill more involved with the daily operations of the *Gazette*, Kathrine in 1958 sold their Frenchtown farm, which they had in recent years virtually abandoned as a weekend retreat.

Because *The Captives of Korea* had taken so much of his time, Bill placed only two articles with the *Digest* from late 1955 through 1957. He did submit several others and had one, a "legal aid" story, accepted and paid for but not published. Normally, in their extensive correspondence DeWitt Wallace praised and encouraged him. For example, Wallace wrote after reading the final cut of "New Look in Defense Spending" for the November 1955 issue: "You are an Ace Reporter—and I wish we could have more of your articles in the RD."[32] But after the final editing of his next acceptance, "400,000 Boys Are Members of the Club," for February 1956, Wallace wrote: "Your inaccuracies have caused a lot of extra work, annoyance and expense, too. There seems to be a feeling here that you are the most careless Rover in your writing."[33] Bill's immediate response was a long, pained letter of rationalization, blaming the *Digest's* research division. Wallace's reply was one of humorous encouragement, designed to mollify his ruffled author.[34] But Bill's output, for whatever reason, slumped at this time.

After a year during which Bill placed nothing in the *Digest*, Wallace wrote: "Can't something be done to improve your RD production? . . . Won't you make a strenuous effort this year to make up for lost time?"[35] Bill did get an article in the October issue that year, but several other submissions did not make it to cutting. He was especially disappointed when three successive editors turned down his story about a former North Korean soldier who escaped to the West during the abortive 1956 Hungarian revolution. He had worked hard on that piece, but Gene Lyons wrote him, "It simply doesn't lend itself to handling for a boiled-down and unsophisticated magazine like the Digest."[36] Chagrined by his general lack of success, Bill returned three of his $1,000 *Digest* checks late that fall. Startled, Wallace wrote him: "Never before to my knowledge has a Roving Editor returned a monthly salary stipend—let alone three of them! . . . Something must be done to augment the satisfaction you derive from your Roving Editorship. To what extent does the Emporia Gazette interfere with your RD activities? And how can your dealings with the editors at headquarters be improved?"[37]

Wallace's last question highlighted a major problem Bill faced at the *Digest*; it had changed significantly since he had signed on in 1941. After the war the firm had grown like Topsy. A research division, multiple international editions, an advertising department, an expansive condensed book club, a phonograph record club—all were clear signs in the 1950s of such growth. Not so clear was the increased editorial redundancy. When Bill became one of the first roving editors, he reported directly to Wallace and only to Wallace. In 1957 "Wally" was sixty-eight years old. Though he did not officially retire until he was eighty-four, by 1957 he was delegating much of his initial editorial responsibility. While Bill remained one of "Wally's boys" and always felt free to consult him, he also reported to various senior editors during the 1950s, especially Paul Palmer and Gene Lyons, and then during the 1960s to Hobe Lewis, the managing editor, though that relationship did not work very well. Adding to the confusion of editorial supervision was an evolving process of final selection. Five top editors rotated the job of issue editor, who would choose from a pool of articles, selected or assigned by one of them or another senior editor. An assignment editor could be enthusiastic about a piece, even to the point of buying and cutting it for a targeted issue, only to have the issue editor decide not to include it, to the disappointment of both author and assignment editor. As a result Bill was sometimes encouraged by an editor to work up a piece, then have it rejected or, worse yet, accepted, cut, typeset, tentatively scheduled, then rejected.[38] In this he was not alone; most writers for the *Digest* endured that as standard practice, because the magazine accepted a much larger pool of articles than it used.

In 1958, though, Bill was far from disappointed: he placed five articles in the *Digest*.[39] The first, on right-to-work legislation, he had thought about for some time because of his clashes over that issue with Kansas governor Fred Hall. In the fall of 1957, to interview business leaders about that topic, he made a swing through the Midwest and the West, where a number of right-to-work votes were pending. In Phoenix, Arizona, he spent several days talking with Sen. Barry Goldwater, a kindred conservative whom he would later support for president and whose state had a right-to-work law.[40] Also of personal significance was the article on pay television. He had been interested in the potential of electronic media since his days with CBS. He still kept an eye on the Emporia radio station, as a competitor and possible buy. In 1958 the only television channel most citizens of Emporia could receive with clarity, even with an outside directional antenna, was a CBS affiliate, WIBW-TV at Topeka. Concerned about the quality of programming the network provided, Bill advocated in his article Federal Communications Commission (FCC) approval of a system of pay TV channels that would encourage local educational and public interest programs. Research for that set him thinking about the one-channel reception Emporia suffered and planted the seed for his plans in 1960 to expand *Gazette* coverage via his own cable TV business.

October, November, and much of December 1958 Bill and Kathrine toured Italy, after spending the summer in Emporia. Before leaving town he wrote Wallace that "it may well be that

I can pick up a few human interest stories which you can use. However, if I don't, then very certainly I intend to return to you monthly checks covering the time we are gone, as I have no desire to be lolling in Rome and Naples at your expense."[41] He returned with several story ideas but none interested Wallace, so instead Bill continued work on an article approved by Kenneth Payne, *Digest* executive editor, about the use of American surplus grain for meat production. The piece, "Let's Turn Our Surplus Grain into Meat," got caught in a *Digest* editorial tug-of-war. Bill had aimed it at the July issue; on Payne's recommendation it was cut, typeset, and so scheduled. But then Hobe Lewis sent it to one of their agricultural experts, who insisted in a detailed memo that its premise was wrong. Hobe then kicked the article over to a department editor, who sent it to the research division for an opinion, which got a reading from experts at the United States Department of Agriculture. They agreed with the gist of Bill's thesis, but the research division still asked him to write a memo further supporting his argument. This he did under protest, the several editors involved approved, and the article was rescheduled for August. But then the issue editor held it over because it conflicted with the book section. A new crop year that September changed its statistics, which could not be updated for several months, and it was dropped, to Bill's outspoken disgust.[42]

In June and July 1959, with Wallace's and Hobe Lewis's approval, Bill spent five weeks in England researching a story about the British economic recovery and the Labour party's continued loss of popularity in the face of a probable call for general elections that fall. Back on Fishers Island, he quickly wrote an anecdotal story predicting a Conservative victory and explaining why. With Hobe Lewis's editorial help he met the deadline for the October issue, which would be out before the elections that Prime Minister Harold Macmillan had just called early in September for October 8. Entitled "Socialism Fizzles Out in Britain," Bill's story was cut, typeset, and quickly sent through the research division, which questioned its premise but passed it. However, the issue editor for October left it out. The Conservatives won decisively. Bill's story thus lost its punch and fell immediately into *Digest* limbo. This time he was furious. From Emporia the first week of

December he wrote Wallace a long, purposely delayed letter detailing his complaints about such editing and enclosing "three checks which, though variously dated, represent the fact that I have spent most of September, October and November writing for the Gazette and cooling off."[43]

Writing for the *Reader's Digest* was no longer much fun because of such internal hurdles, with their implicit office politics. But writing for the *Gazette* was. On its editorial page he could argue for right-to-work legislation, comment about the Little Rock, Arkansas, school integration issue, mull over Chiang Kai-shek's desire to hold onto the Quemoy Islands group, or boom his Kansas City friend Harry Darby for a Republican gubernatorial nomination. Perhaps even more important to him, he could suggest whimsically that Emporia's huge elms protected it from recent tornadoes or declare that Florine Lostutter was the only woman in town who could still make sand plum jelly, both assertions, of course, eliciting letters of protest to the *Gazette*'s Wailing Place with tongue-in-cheek editorial ripostes.[44]

Bill's increasing focus on the *Gazette* over the preceding five years, and especially that winter and spring, paid off. Based on its March 14 front page, the *Gazette* won the Ayer Cup for 1960, first among 859 newspapers surveyed that day for excellence in typography, makeup, and printing.[45] The N. W. Ayer advertising firm, publisher of the semiofficial *American Newspaper Directory*, had run the contest since 1931, with the prestigious *New York Herald Tribune* winning the award nine times. Bill was justifiably proud because the *Gazette* was the smallest newspaper ever to win the cup; under his father it had never even received a mention. In his April 23 editorial "Our Beauty Secrets" he announced:

> We are all very happy around the Gazette office for it is not often that we or any other concern gets an award for being, not just the best in town, not just the best in the county, not just the best in the state, not just the best in our small-circulation class, but an award putting us at the top of the nation, including all papers—small, medium sized and large—for being the most readable and best-appearing paper in the entire United States of America for the year 1960.

And Bill continued its fame as a prime example of the art of printing. For example, the day of John F. Kennedy's interment he devoted the *Gazette*'s entire front page to printing the words of the Roman Catholic ritual read over the grave by Richard Cardinal Cushing. First came a Latin line set as Roman capitals inked a rich purple, "the church's color of deepest mourning," he explained later, followed by the English translation set upper and lower case inked black.[46] The unique and reverent dignity of that makeup caught the attention of editors nationwide. During the 1960s, therefore, that small daily continued to win typographical awards; it earned three honorable mentions in the Ayer competition and in 1968 scored first in class B (those with circulation under 10,000) in the Inland Newspaper contest conducted by Northwestern University's School of Journalism. Though Will White had made the *Gazette* famous through its editorials, under him it had won no beauty contests. In capturing the Ayer cup and the Inland award, Bill achieved, perhaps unconsciously, an objective he had aimed at for years: in the area of typography he had surpassed the journalistic achievements of his late father; the awards testified to that.[47]

In 1960 Bill decided to start a cable TV business in Emporia, a project he had been thinking about since his *Digest* article in 1958.[48] The concept seemed simple enough. From a receiving tower set on a high point outside town, he would send amplified signals via a cable network to local subscribers for a modest fee. He would offer four TV channels from Wichita, Hutchinson, and Topeka, which included the three major networks, plus a fifth channel for local TV programming, plus FM radio reception. With the legal help of Bill Stroock, the Whites' closest family friend back East, he and Kathrine set up a privately held CATV corporation whimsically named "Catfish." But they ran into several initial problems. First, the technology was relatively new and, to them, alien, which caused much anxiety and necessitated much research. Second, while they were able to negotiate in August 1960 a ten-year franchise from the Emporia Board of Commissioners, with another ten-year option, several commissioners were hesitant about granting such a monopoly to the town's one daily. Third, they had to set their own poles because of opposition from Kansas Power and Light and Southwestern Bell.

But by the fall of 1962, after building a tower, setting the poles, and stringing wire, Catfish was in operation. As vice president, Kathrine handled the finances and much of the management, which became increasingly more of a burden for her as the company grew to serve more than one thousand subscribers by 1965.[49] The *Gazette* staff were distracted too. Next to the newsroom Kathrine converted a twenty-by-twenty-foot space into a makeshift television studio where Ray Call, city editor, read a daily noon news summary, together with the society editor, Teresa DeLong. Before ending his day, Ted McDaniel, managing editor, prerecorded a summary of afternoon news for 6:00 and 9:00 P.M. broadcasts. On a weekly basis a one-hour woman's program followed the noon news, and students from the two local high schools and colleges presented news of school events. During the evening the staff conducted a weekly "town meeting" program, and Ray Call hosted a phone-in show. On an ad hoc basis the staff telecast special news bulletins or community programs, especially around election time, with candidates dropping in for interviews. But all that was strictly local, amateurish, noncommercial, public affairs programming. For example, when John Dos Passos visited the Whites in Emporia in the fall of 1964, Bill interviewed him for a special segment of the noon program, mostly about his relationship to Hemingway. On the air Bill urged him to be candid because they were "practically talking in privacy since this won't get out of Emporia."[50]

While Kathrine and the *Gazette* staff struggled with that cable franchise, Bill became involved in another book. In April 1961 the E. P. Dutton firm offered him a $10,000 advance to write the story of two B-47 Strategic Air Command (SAC) fliers whom the Russians had shot down on a surveillance flight over the Barents Sea, imprisoned, and just recently released. Four fellow crew members died in the attack. The crew had been stationed at Forbes Air Force Base near Topeka. One of the survivors, Capt. John McKone, was born and reared in Kansas. Interested in the down-home angle and the Russian connection, Bill took the contract with the understanding that the *Digest* had the right of first refusal for a magazine version. Bill interviewed the two crewmen and their families for a month. He also collected background by visiting SAC headquarters in Omaha and going on a B-47 SAC flight from Forbes to above the Arctic Circle. He assumed he could wrap up the writing in three to four months, but that proved as usual too optimistic.[51]

The story itself is brief. On July 1, 1960, a United States Air Force RB-47 took off from an air base in England loaded with sophisticated electronics and a crew of six, three of them technicians. It was to fly a standard surveillance loop around the Barents Sea above Finland to gather information about Soviet early-warning radar installations. But that was just two months after U-2 pilot Gary Powers had crashed near the industrial city of Sverdlovsk, 1,300 miles into Soviet territory. Nervous, the Soviet Air Force scrambled a jet fighter from its base near Murmansk on the Kola Peninsula to intercept the RB-47. Though the American plane was fifty miles out to sea, the Russian pilot thought it was over Soviet waters and headed inland. When it refused to respond to his signals, he shot it down.

Only the copilot, Capt. Bruce Olmstead, and the navigator, John McKone, survived to be picked up by Russian fishing boats and taken to Moscow's Lubyanka prison. There they were kept in isolation and interrogated for seven months in preparation, they were told, for a public trial like that of Gary Powers. But neither would confess to charges of espionage and insisted the plane was on a routine mission over international waters. The United States protested the incident strongly in the United Nations, supported by American and British radar records confirming that the RB-47 never strayed over Soviet territory. Then January 24, 1961, just after John Kennedy's inauguration, the Soviets released the two airmen as a gesture of goodwill toward the new president, who had pledged to continue Eisenhower's ban of U-2 overflights. Amid much press coverage John McKone and Bruce Olmstead returned to the United States.

For over nine months Bill worked on the manuscript, interrupted at times by business matters at the *Gazette* and Catfish and by six weeks in bed ill from a return of his psychosomatic anxiety symptoms.[52] E. P. Dutton released the book in May 1962 as part of its spring list but missed its previously targeted market, the 1961 Christmas trade. It did appear as a book section in the *Digest* and was also excerpted by *True, the Men's Magazine*, but the book did not recoup the advances paid by Dutton to Bill and the two fliers.[53] As usual, the *Digest* version was a focused, tightly controlled narrative. But the book itself needed better editing. In it the story goes limp about a third of the way through, with too many static interrogation sessions, too many anxious thoughts by the fliers and their wives, and too many verbatim letters from home with all their intimate trivia. Ultimately, a cloying sentimentality overwhelms the reader, much as in the manuscript version of *Journey for Margaret*, which Marion Ellet spotted when Bill asked her for advice. For example, the title, *The Little Toy Dog*, refers to a small plastic model of Snoopy, the dog in the "Peanuts" comic strip, given to the pilot, Maj. Willard Palm, by his eleven-year-old daughter. Torn from the pocket of his flight suit as he parachuted to his death, it rests in deep Arctic waters. In the preface Bill explains he insisted on that eccentric title, rather than the publisher's suggestion, "The RB-47 Story," because "it implores you not to forget that four brave and very nice young Americans died in the Barents Sea, leaving four little families who still grieve." More particularly, he maintains, it represents "the sob of a child for a lost father." To be successful, Bill's interview technique requires controlled, objective selectivity; he does not exercise that consistently enough in *The Little Toy Dog*.

For a while early that summer Bill promoted the book on the New York talk-show circuit. He appeared, for example, on the Arthur Godfrey show on CBS television. But in August, with sales faltering, he returned to Emporia and fell again into an emotional slump that lasted well into 1963. Though he wrote an occasional *Gazette* commentary that fall, he did not attempt any magazine projects. In December he returned five checks to the *Digest* covering July through November because, he wrote Wallace, "as I explained to you when we last met, I was unable to work."[54] But that winter he became interested in the four-month newspaper stoppage caused in New York City by a strike-lockout throughout the metropolitan area from December 8 to April 1. He covered that for the *Digest*, submitting an antiunion analytical article in the first part of May, after checking data with several of the publishers, whom he knew personally.[55] But "The Strike Nobody Won" did not appear until the September issue, which caused him some anxiety, since both his completed pieces and his story ideas seemed increasingly to get shunted aside.

Bureaucratic inertia contributed to Bill's failure to keep on track with the *Digest*. In the early 1960s Hobe Lewis had become nominal head of the firm, with Bill ostensibly reporting to him. But in reality Wallace was still very much in control, and Lewis deferred to him. Hobe was always most affable, as shown in his correspondence with Bill, but he was professionally adept at putting off a decision. With Bill he was especially indefinite because he regarded him as Wallace's responsibility.[56] That, for example, caused a major contretemps in 1964 when Bill refused on principle to sign off on a story about the anti-Communist revolution that year in Brazil, a story Wallace thought so important he ran it as a special tear-out booklet in the November issue and in all the international editions. Hobe Lewis handled the editing.

At their New York home on Easter Sunday 1964 the Whites had invited to dinner Bill's Harvard roommate Albert Byington, a prominent lawyer of São Paulo, Brazil. Phone calls to Byington from Brazil interrupted that meal because he had helped organize the "preventive revolution" that had ousted Brazilian leftist president Joãco Goulart just three days before. Bill immediately proposed to Lewis and Wallace that he fly down to cover the story. Both agreed, with Wallace insisting he not stay long but get back and write his account while it was timely, and not make it "too damned long." Bill spent sixteen days in Brazil, returned to New York, quickly wrote his story, submitted it, then at Hobe's suggestion rewrote and expanded it for August publication.[57] He then left for Turkey in late May to attend his first International Press Institute convention for another possible story. Before leaving, though, he gave Lewis his itinerary in case any questions came up about the final version.[58]

He returned to New York mid-July, but not until mid-August did Lewis send him in Emporia a copy of that edited article, which in the interim he had assigned to Gene Lyons to rewrite and expand even further with material from an earlier rejected story by roving editor Leland Stowe and new material from roving editor Clarence Hall, just back from Brazil. For by then Wallace had decided to run it as an extended special feature. After reading it, Bill found only sixteen of its forty-seven manuscript pages were his, though the article remained under his byline, and even those contained numerous, fundamental errors. He immediately wrote Lewis to explain that in his version, for example, he had written:

> "The women of Brazil . . . suddenly decided that politics had become far too important a matter to be entrusted to men.". . . These lines I wrote in New York, never having met Amelia Bastos [one of the revolutionary leaders]. The first sentence is, in fact, my modification of Georges Clemenceau's famous gag that "war is far too important a matter to be left to the generals," as you probably recognized. Turning now to the article you send, I find an interview with Amelia Bastos, who is quoted as saying, "I suddenly decided that politics had become too important to be left entirely to men.". . . Now I do not know how [that sentence], composed by me in America hopped out of my manuscript and landed back in Brazil between quotation marks as part of an interview with Amelia Bastos, presumably authorized by her. But this is why I never sign articles I have not written.[59]

That and other manufactured quotations plus what he thought were errors of emphasis stayed in, so Bill not only refused to put his name to it but sent back his payment for it, even though Wallace intervened to praise him for "this noteworthy scoop."[60] The booklet came out under Clarence Hall's byline, who then wrote Bill a letter of embarrassed apology.[61]

Through 1965 Bill sent Hobe a number of story ideas and a couple of manuscripts; he also attended several standard *Digest* luncheon conferences. During all of that "Hobe couldn't have been nicer," he wrote Wallace, in a detailed letter of protest early in 1966, but "I got no call."[62] That spring Wallace arranged a peace conference at Pleasantville between Hobe and Bill, which seemed to work out, for Bill wrote him: "Thanks, Boss, . . . no one but you could have done it. Hobe and I had a very pleasant lunch yesterday, and I think the show is back on the road."[63] But it really was not. In 1966 he placed an article about inflation in the magazine, and later a color story about the trees of Paris, used in 1972 as an international edition special, but that was it.[64] So he continued his practice of returning salary checks when unavailable for assignments. In 1969 he did stir Hobe into enthusiasm over a proposed annotated edition of President Nixon's speeches because, until Watergate, Lewis was a staunch Nixon backer. Hobe introduced him to James Keogh, a former senior editor at *Time*, who was in charge of the president's research and writing staff, and sent Bill a number of research tips. But because of illness he did not complete that project.[65]

With Wallace he maintained correspondence almost to the end of his life. After so many years "Wally" had become to Bill more than an editor or a boss. At the end of a long letter dated May 20, 1965, Bill wrote: "Excuse this out-pouring, but you have become a father-image. And I find that, even approaching age 65 . . . I am badly in need of one."[66] He was indeed in need of fatherly advice, then more than ever, because that winter he had alienated about half of Emporia.

The town Bill increasingly came home to in the late 1950s was changing, but his view of it had not kept pace. Because of conversion from steam to diesel and the many resulting changes in railroading in the early 1950s, the Santa Fe closed down its Emporia machine shops and large switching yard. By 1960 the town was but a nominal division point for Santa Fe train crews and section hands. The MKT railroad abandoned its line through Emporia late in 1957. Though the town's population had increased some— from 15,560 in 1950 to 18,190 in 1960—that was due mostly to increased enrollment at the Kansas State Teachers College, from 1,400 in 1950 to 3,400 in 1960. The College of Emporia was barely alive, with fewer than 300 students in the fall of 1960. In the late fifties the town did attract a few new small industries and became a busy intersection for Interstate 35, Highway 50, and the Kansas Turnpike in the early 1960s. But nothing truly offset the loss of its Santa Fe payroll.

In the fall of 1964, in order to attract significant new jobs, the city commission offered Interstate Bakeries, if that firm would build a plant in Emporia, a loan of $3.5 million through income tax-exempt industrial revenue bonds plus an abatement of local real estate taxes for ten years, a process approved by the Kansas legislature in 1961. Immediately, the county commission, worried about the potential tax loss, asked the Kansas attorney general if that were constitutional without a vote of the people. He replied yes, but the incentive plan caused a political cyclone in Emporia, especially after a local company, Didde-Glaser, a manufacturer of specialized printing equipment, also received city commission approval of industrial revenue bonds for plant expansion, with a ten-year tax exemption on both the expansion and its existing plant. Editorially, Bill joined local opposition to industrial revenue bonds for two reasons: first, as municipal bonds the interest was free from federal taxes, which he felt gave an unfair advantage to "unprincipled" firms; second, for ten years those firms also escaped the additional civic responsibility of property taxes, which in Kansas financed schools and local governmental services. Under the 1961 law, Bill explained, those exemptions could be "granted without an election," which is "in effect taxation without the consent of the governed." To him it was a matter of abstract principle, because earlier he had endorsed the establishment of an industrial park and continued to support other efforts to attract industry.[67]

Perhaps those industrial bonds became such a tempestuous local issue because, to their opponents, they raised a fundamental question about demographics. Was Emporia to continue a quiet, rural-market, two-college town ("the Athens of Kansas") or become a small-industry hub scrambling for low-wage payrolls at the expense of its schools and municipal services? But posed in that way the question was simplistic and illusory. The town had historically supported a sizable lunch-bucket side, because of the railroads, which were unionized and paid well. In the relatively near future the tiny College of Emporia would close, just as the 80- and 160-acre family farms lying along the river bottoms were disappearing.[68] Paradoxically, though, on this issue perception was to become reality, because later, in 1968, Iowa Beef Packers secured an industrial bond issue and used it to build a large Emporia slaughtering plant, which eventually employed over two thousand relatively unskilled, nonunionized workers, who did indeed change the demographics of the town.

The *Gazette* ran a postcard straw vote, with the returns coming in two-to-one against the city commission's bond and tax exemption offer. Unlike the earlier slot machine vote, though, this time the opposition was not a few shamefaced officers of fraternal clubs; it was the More and Better Jobs for Emporia Committee, made up of many of the town's retailers and chaired by a former mayor. The group conducted its own poll, which indicated by an even wider margin that the townspeople in fact supported the city commission. But Bill continued his strident opposition in editorials, through an expanded Wailing Place, through interviews and commentary on the *Gazette* Catfish channel, and by backing two antibond candidates for city commission elections in April.[69] As he later confided to DeWitt Wallace, "What followed was the dirtiest little political fight I had ever been through." His retail advertisers threatened to start an opposition daily and moved their business over to the local radio station, now called KVOE (Kansas Voice of Emporia). The city commission cited a clause in Bill's TV franchise agreement, in which he agreed to charge "reasonable rates," and ordered an investigation into the finances of his cable service.[70]

Emotions spiraled high as the town fragmented over the issue. Bill and his best friend Harold Trusler got into such a heated argument about *Gazette* coverage that Trusler publicly broke with him. Years of pent-up citizen resentment about Young Bill's paternalism surfaced in a verbal hate campaign that characterized him as an eccentric suitcase editor who used Emporia for an occasional rest cure and the *Gazette* as a source of easy money. Resentment had boiled over in the past, as in 1957 when a reader wrote in to protest his "obstructive" editorials about tapping into the Cottonwood River during the drought: "As a thoughtless boy with a toy, you dangle Emporia on a string—amused for a while, then dropping it to return to New York." Or as in 1962 when some College of Emporia students hanged him in effigy in front of the *Gazette* building because of his paper's frank coverage of high-handed dismissals at the college. (Typically, but unknown to them, Bill had left for New York at least three weeks before that hanging.)[71] This time, however, it seemed to him that much of the town was voicing aspersions.

In the April 1965 elections nearly 5,400 citizens voted, defeating Bill's candidates for city commission by a three-to-two margin, and the argument was over. But resentments and effects lingered on. An openly hostile city commission continued its probe of his Catfish rate structure. So Bill decided to sell the franchise rather than face a vindictive fight that he was sure to lose.[72] And his attitude toward his hometown changed, at least for a while. As he reported to Wallace, "it is as though somebody near and close to me had died. What has died, of course, was my illusion [of] the old Emporia I knew as a boy—[of a] solid, self-respecting little town, proud that it was a high-grade college town, too proud to bribe new people to come in by subsidizing factories. Some are left of course—the 40% who are pathetically grateful to me for having made the fight, even though we lost. The rest of the town I know is out in Maplewood Cemetery."[73]

But Bill rallied. In the summer of 1966 he joined a local fight against two city commission applications for federally funded urban renewal projects, one downtown and one residential. A zoning change request sparked the downtown project. In May out-of-town developers asked the advisory Metropolitan Planning Commission to change a parcel west of town from residential to commercial for construction of a shopping mall. Though that board turned down the request, city officials knew it would be approved on appeal to the county commission, or to the courts. Downtown merchants, threatened by potential mall competition, thought they could counter that threat with new or renovated buildings paid for with federal dollars. And prior to that zoning request, John King, president of the teachers college, had seen in urban renewal monies an expedient way to bulldoze a residential area near campus for future expansion.[74] Late in May townspeople formed an ad hoc advisory committee to work with the city commission and a hastily hired consulting firm to prepare two formal applications for federal funds.

Returning from a winter in New York early in June, Bill viewed both applications as tax swindles and boondoggles. So he mounted a four-month campaign of "informational" stories in the *Gazette*, starting July 14. Using maps and photos of the two proposed areas, the series featured nearly daily interviews of affected residents and merchants. He solicited letters to the Wailing Place and editorialized about how other communities addressed the same problems without federal help. Arguments over this issue polarized the town, much like the earlier debate over industrial bonds. But this time Bill was on the winning side, for by petition the residential project was placed on the November ballot and defeated by a three-to-two margin.[75] The city commission then dropped both it and the one for downtown.

In his opposition he was consistent. Since the courthouse fight he had advocated urban renewal through the renovation of existing structures, not through their destruction and replacement with parking lots and modernistic boxes paid for with federal dollars. He believed historical restoration created an aesthetic heritage and, frankly, was cheaper. With that in mind he and Kathrine in 1967, after their return from Asia, extensively renovated the *Gazette* building to expand the newspaper into the basement and first floor front of the building just north, built as an architecturally matched rental by his father. Bill restored the outside of the two structures to reflect their original architectural intent and preserved many of the old interior features. Now he could use the expanded and renovated *Gazette* building to prove his point about downtown renewal and to demonstrate his commitment to the town.[76]

Sometime in the late 1950s Kansas publisher Jack Harris involved Bill in the American Society of Newspaper Editors, an organization in which he became increasingly involved during the 1960s. From that association he went on to join the International Press Institute (IPI) and attend six of its annual conferences. Those meetings gave him and Kathrine, both at retirement age, a purpose for foreign travel, a chance to see fellow journalists, some of whom were old friends, and an opportunity, he hoped, for a *Digest* story. After each conference they then toured for varying periods. During each of those trips he wrote a series of travel letters for the *Gazette*, a narrative genre he obviously enjoyed because it allowed him to comment and reminisce at will.[77]

The most extensive of those trips was to New Delhi in 1966, after which he and Kathrine roamed the Far East for about seven months. He wanted to gather background on United States–Asian relations and firsthand information about escalating American military involvement in Vietnam, which greatly concerned him. During the tour he used both *Reader's Digest* and Associated Press staffs for research help and local contacts, plus friends he had run into, such as John Steinbeck, the author. He wrote both Lewis and Wallace progress reports and started in October what was to become a nearly yearlong series of travel commentaries in the *Gazette*. He also wrote to others about his impressions of the war in Vietnam, one being Ambassador-at-Large Henry Cabot Lodge, Jr., also of the Harvard class of 1924, who relayed Bill's views to President Lyndon Johnson.[78]

Though the *Gazette* series continued through September 1967, after his return early that April he bundled up the first group under the title "The Rim of Asia" and sent them to Hobe, who decided none was suitable for *Digest* condensation. Bill then turned the collection over to his agent, Elsie Stern, to peddle as a book, but the publishers she approached thought they lacked continuity and audience appeal.[79] That winter Bill reworked this collection to provide a better introductory narrative frame, to update and add more commentary, and to develop overall coherence. Eugene Reynal, another Harvard classmate of Bill's and his former editor at Harcourt, Brace, then offered to publish it through his own firm under the title *Report on the Asians*, but he died in March, just as it was going to press. The Reynal Company then arranged for printing and distribution through the William Morrow Company under the Reynal colophon. After some delay, Morrow issued it January 16, 1969, with minimal promotion, as booklists bulged with competitive titles about Southeast Asia.

Report on the Asians was not a success, securing but several trade reviews, all of which were mixed. For example, *Booklist*, a bulletin of the American Library Association, described it as a lively, provocative, but "largely superficial" travel volume.[80] As in his previous two "report" books, Bill interlards his narrative with social and political commentary, but this time he also includes long, simplistic historical essays. The overall focus is on Vietnam, with the centerpiece chapter his trip through Mekong Delta villages with Danh Thuh, a Buddhist member of South Vietnam's

Constituent Assembly. Though he is frank about widespread corruption first under United States–backed President Ngo Dinh Diem and family, and then under Gen. Nguyen Van Thieu and Air Marshal Nguyen Cao Ky, Bill nevertheless maintains that the government of South Vietnam has "a far more valid claim to represent a free people" than the "monolithic regime in the North."[81] While his comments are sometimes perceptive and his style is always colorful, his basic assumptions are those of the right-wing China Lobby.

As a result the book is but a period piece—of interest, perhaps, for its representative hawkish arguments for continued American involvement in South Vietnam and elsewhere in Asia to counter the enigmatic menace of Communist China. He offers no new insights. While the book was in press, he talked about America's role in Vietnam with newly elected President Richard Nixon, then sent him a marked advance copy, along with a four-page memorandum in which he assumed a negotiated peace could be achieved only through increased military pressure. He also argued that the peasantry could easily be won over by clearing up corruption, insisting on new elections, and distributing cheap chemical fertilizer to friendly villages. Only the fertilizer suggestion could be construed as new. There is no record of Nixon's response.[82]

Politically in the 1960s Bill stood firm as a pragmatic cold war GOP conservative, unmellowed by age. For example, in July of 1964 after the IPI convention in Istanbul, he flew back from Paris straight through to San Francisco to cover the Republican national convention, which nominated Barry Goldwater for president. In August he likewise reported in the *Gazette* the Democratic convention at Atlantic City, New Jersey, which nominated Lyndon Johnson. Bill had known both men on a first-name basis for years. Just after those conventions he wrote his old state-level political ally Kansas Supreme Court Justice William Smith that it will "be a joy to fight for Barry Goldwater and furthermore a joy uncontaminated by any hope of winning, for I do not see how he can be elected. Furthermore I think that Lyndon Johnson is the most corrupt man to come before the American voters in my lifetime. . . . I see no hope for beating him but it will be a pleasure to do what I can."[83]

That September and October he wrote a series of *Gazette* editorials supporting Goldwater and savaging Johnson, though he knew they would be no more heeded than "a belch in a whirlwind."[84] Yet within a year he was to write a memorable editorial staunchly supporting Johnson for his stand in Vietnam. Widely copied, that editorial, "The Long, Hard Road," elicited a personal letter of thanks from the beleaguered president. Directly, simply, it sums up Bill's belief, which he had held consistently since his 1944 trip to Russia, that the United States as leader of the world's democracies had a fundamental duty to oppose totalitarian international Communism. From Bill's point of view, by upholding that moral imperative, Johnson rose well above personal and financial peccadilloes to merit unflinching bipartisan support. The editorial explains why later, as increasing American involvement in the Vietnam War elicited widespread turbulent public protests, Bill splenetically attacked those in opposition as bearded "peaceniks" armed with guitars, who ignorantly advocated violent protests and provoked riots.

In 1968 he again attended both national conventions. At the Democratic one that August in Chicago he, like many others, experienced a profound visceral reaction to what he saw as an apocalyptic anarchy in the streets around the convention hall. Just before the election in a letter to Dan Longwell, the retired editor of *Life* magazine, he indicated a deepening sense of Armageddon and predicted that "whoever takes over in 1968 will have in his hands the terror of a sinking ship and within six months his popularity in the polls will drop to about the level Lyndon Johnson reached when he decided to bow out."[85] To him it seemed that America's ship of state was close to foundering on uncharted, treacherous rocks of protest. When riots erupted on the University of Kansas campus in the spring of 1970, after President Nixon flamboyantly ordered military incursions into Cambodia, Bill lamented to John Dos Passos "that today I have never seen our country more split up."[86] That is why, for example, when a student at the university, a fellow Phi Delt, wrote the *Gazette* to protest its editorial coverage of that campus protest and to present a substantive counter viewpoint, Bill printed the letter in the Wailing Place, then answered sarcastically but typically:

Brother: Before you get too deep into solving the problems of
over-population, pollution, dandruff, poverty and racism, I hope
you and your friends can find out and let us concerned alumni
know just who it was who burned down the Student Union,
just what social goal they think they have achieved by doing
it, and just who they think is going to pony up the money to
build a new one when the dedicated and socially involved Little
Darlings who burned down the first one are still running around
loose and out of jail.[87]

During those times, when an aging and crusty Bill White allowed
emotion to cloud his sense of editorial fair play, *Gazette* subscribers
could only sputter or shake their heads.

In the 1960s the *Gazette* automatically backed the Republican
state slate, with Bill or his staff commenting on the primaries only
when a candidate interested him personally. He kept up in general
with Kansas politics through a network of correspondents, but
he did not often bother to intervene editorially, except in the
politics of Lyon County. Whenever Bill was in Emporia, of course,
Republican officeholders or aspirants stopping through made sure
to look him up, because the *Gazette* and the White name still
carried political weight. In 1968, for example, Bill backed Robert
Dole in his successful first run for the United States Senate.
According to Ray Call, *Gazette* city editor, "W. L. put on a big
dinner at the Broadview Hotel and brought in most of the
Republican leaders from eastern Kansas to build support. The
dinner was pivotal to Dole's success."[88]

Early in 1972 Bill broke that pattern of Republican regularity
to come out editorially for Democratic governor Robert Docking,
running for an unprecedented fourth term, and to organize a group
called Republicans for Docking. A Democrat and a liberal on social
issues, Governor Docking was nevertheless a staunch fiscal
conservative, like his father before him, two-term Democratic
governor George Docking. Fiscal policy had been one of Bill's
chief concerns in the 1960s, inflation being the topic of his last
regular *Digest* piece. Thus he uncharacteristically backed Robert
Docking because he believed him best qualified in 1972 to fight

uncontrolled wartime inflation at the state level, an issue more important to Bill than party loyalty.[89]

During the last decade of his life, in fact, many of his *Gazette* commentaries had little to do with politics per se but were long, reflective color pieces or reminiscent essays. Some he published under standing heads—about life in New York City, about his annual fall auto tour of Emporia neighborhoods, about departed friends and nearly forgotten days; others were one of a kind—a commencement address at the College of Emporia, a speech at the opening of Wichita's new civic auditorium, a talk partly in French at a meeting of the American Society of Newspaper Editors in Montreal, Canada.[90] *Digest* editors returned the several such pieces he sent them because, as he groused to the elderly Sir Arthur Willert, a formerly prominent British journalist, those submissions "contained too many references with which the present generation was not familiar."[91] Yet he continued forwarding the occasional piece on to DeWitt Wallace almost out of habit. One of those, the 1960 editorial "Chicago," presents well the mellowed, sagacious tone the older W. L. W. sometimes adopted:

> As this is being read by whatever fond readers this journal may chance to have, this Editor will be in Chicago to attend the 1960 Republican convention, but he wishes now to describe the first national convention he ever attended, which again was in Chicago, but in 1916.
>
> What can a boy of 16, more than 40 years later, remember of a national convention? Well, first he remembers . . . what he wore, which was a blue jacket and a solitary pair of handsome white serge trousers. It was, in fact, the only outfit he had, and the theory was that this splendor would last for five days in the unairconditioned heat of old Convention Hall in Chicago. Those white serge trousers were first smeared with soot coming in through the little copper screens of the Santa Fe train going up to Chicago. This was many decades before trains were air-conditioned, and when all Pullman windows had to be kept open in the summer, since a little soot from the coal of the engine ahead was better than suffocation.

On their first day in Chicago the white serge trousers were slightly spotted, but passably decent. On the second day they were so smeared with soot, sweat and huge grease spots, that their wearer, left to his own ingenuity, got himself at a drug store a bottle of miracle spot-remover. It removed the spots from that scratchy white serge, all right, but transformed each spot into a light brownish ring. At the end of the third day he was, from the coat down, a mass of interlocking brown rings against this white serge background.

He remembers vividly the Congress Hotel, then Chicago's best. All of its mezzanine rooms were taken over by headquarters for long-forgotten candidates for Vice President—Weeks of Massachusetts, Sherman of Ohio—many more. He remembers his first smoke-filled room—a large one in which the Platform Committee of the Progressive Party (his father represented Kansas on it) was deliberating. In these days before air conditioning its windows were flung wide open, but still the blue cigar smoke stung his eyes. It was this boy's job, one afternoon, to stand guard at the door, while various Progressives in their shirt-sleeves debated the platform, with stern instructions to admit no reporters to watch the secret wrangling.

He remembers, down in the lobby of the Congress, its artistic piece de resistance—a life-sized white marble statue of a white marble lady, reclining in a white marble hammock. This languid lady in the hammock wore a conservative Grecian hair-do, but was otherwise jaybird-naked, and the boy remembers walking past her not just once, but on as many occasions as he could figure out a pretext; each time glancing at her, never directly, but always out of the corner of an eye. For there was nothing like this white marble lady in Emporia, either then or since. He was, remember, 16, and this is a wonderful age—many things still to learn, and you have all of life before you, during which not all the ladies will necessarily be of marble.

On this hideously hot July week both the Progressives and the Republicans were convening in Chicago; the Progressives to re-nominate their idol, Theodore Roosevelt who in 1912 had led them in a bolt from the Republican Party; the Republicans to nominate—well, the Progressives hoped Theodore Roosevelt.

It would be a gesture which would paste together the two severed wings of the old Republican party, so that they could flap gloriously to victory over Woodrow Wilson for his second term.

The Republicans, however, had other ideas. As the sweating hours passed, it became increasingly clear that they would nominate Charles Evans Hughes, whom the Progressives had sworn they would never accept. Instead these now planned defiantly to re-nominate Theodore Roosevelt, and to make a final lunge to victory against both Woodrow Wilson and Hughes.

Came, however, the horrible hour when, by telephone and from his summer home at Oyster Bay, Theodore Roosevelt's squeaky voice told his Chicago Progressive worshipers that he would not accept their nomination, and urged them to unite with the Republicans in endorsing Hughes!

Here was treason most foul—and most bewildering: the colorful hero who had founded the Progressive Party now pushing it headlong into its grave. It broke my father's heart, for he had dearly loved Theodore Roosevelt. I can remember him, after this day of agony and disappointment—one of the most terrible of his life—standing in the telephone booth from which he was calling my mother long distance in Emporia— trying to tell her of the terrible betrayal, but choking with sobs so that he could not go on, and finally crying like a baby with grief over his disappointment in Theodore Roosevelt—an unsettling thing for a 16-year-old son to watch.

And it made on me, perhaps, an even deeper impression than the white marble lady in the Congress lobby. Because, while in future decades I was to fall in love several times, luckily for me it has never been with a politician. I have admired them often, occasionally even liked them, but there it has always stopped. For which I am deeply grateful. . . .

And the 1916 issues? In that hour they mattered enormously, tremendously, poignantly. I can now only vaguely remember what they were, and to repeat them now would almost make a mockery of the earnestness with which they were then held. Yet the Convention itself—a living, breathing human organism— come together to make a mass judgment and pick a leader—this has changed not at all, and I have the greatest respect for it; and for the wise judgments that so often come out of the needed compromises any convention must make.

For it is gathered there to transact the solemn business of making those compromises. The callow may sneer at them, but they are the very stuff of democracy: without this give-and-take, free government could not exist. For what is any free government but the art and science of compromise; many divergent viewpoints, each yielding a little so that all may at last come together in that majority through which finally we rule ourselves? How could it be otherwise?—W. L. W.[92]

Such an attitude of nostalgia was not his forte, though, in the summer of 1970 when he and Dos Passos led a successful drive against organized opposition to get William F. Buckley, Jr., the conservative columnist and millionaire publisher, into the Century Club. Nor was that his attitude when in Emporia that year he opposed a new municipal golf course as too costly for too few. Nor when he offered the city $10,000 that same summer to help it buy and repair the town's old outdoor swimming pool, built privately in 1928 next to Peter Pan Park and leased to the city. He feared the pool would be sold and reopened as a commercial club with restricted membership. The city accepted his challenge, bought the pool, and rebuilt it for about $50,000—far less than the cost of a comparable new one.

The first several months of 1970 Bill was ill in New York City with a chronic lung infection that led to a persistent cough. He had been a heavy smoker much of his life, and though he showed no signs of lung cancer or emphysema at that time, his doctors ordered him off cigarettes entirely and suggested he lose twenty to thirty pounds. He immediately quit smoking and went on a diet but did not lose an ounce until he gave up his pre-dinner martinis. In a letter to John Roberts, a former *Gazette* reporter, Bill lamented: "As of this June I have lost twenty pounds, have not smoked a cigarette since Washington's birthday, nor had a drink since Easter. I feel twenty years younger, but to what point? Because all incentives to go on living have been removed."[93] Though he claimed to feel better and continued busy, traveling the next year to Finland and Russia, his health remained questionable. On May 23, 1972, after another bout with a persistent cough and a low-grade fever, he underwent surgery at Lennox Hill Hospital in New York City for removal of what proved to be a malignant tumor from his left rib cage. The diagnosis was widespread lung cancer, the prognosis death within a year. In a later memorial tribute, Ray Call, who had become the *Gazette*'s managing editor, reported:

> I saw the boss flinch only once during the ordeal. That was
> the first day he came down to the office after his return from
> New York where he had undergone surgery. He called Kenneth
> Williams [*Gazette* business manager] and me into the office in
> July of 1972 to say that he was dying of cancer . . . and for
> a moment tears came into his eyes. It was the only emotion
> of that sort I ever saw him show. He quickly composed himself
> and went ahead with other business.[94]

Part of that business was to provide for an orderly transition at the *Gazette*. With her father terminally ill, Barbara and her husband, David Walker, decided to move to Emporia with their four children so that he could become assistant publisher of the paper. After serving a tour with the air force, David had received his master of arts degree from Harvard Business School, worked toward a doctorate in education at Columbia University and at that time was a mid-level administrator at Colby College in Waterville, Maine. Bill welcomed the move and thought his son-in-law would provide much-needed help with the business end of the *Gazette*.[95]

Though weak and in pain Editor White insisted on attending the Republican national convention in Miami, Florida, that August to see President Nixon renominated but was too ill to withstand the hullabaloo at the convention hall. Ray Call, who accompanied the Whites to Miami, reported that Bill instead "visited with politicians and newsmen at the hotel where the Kansas delegation was staying, . . . [and] went to a few dinners with correspondents and to William Buckley's yacht to watch the convention on television."[96] That was his last hurrah. In November the Emporia City Commission, forgetting its recent history of

antagonism, renamed the auditorium in the civic building the
W. L. White Auditorium, the one Bill had filled past capacity just
after its dedication the spring of 1940 when he gave his personal
report on the start of war in Europe. He was too ill to attend the
naming ceremony, but he was not too ill to run the *Gazette* from
his bedside at 927 Exchange or to keep his sense of humor. On
May 24, 1973, he wrote his last *Gazette* commentary: a wry,
reminiscent postscript to a staff editorial reviewing the end that
spring of the town's public bus service, run for years at a loss by
Kansas Power and Light as a franchise requirement. He died at
Newman Memorial Hospital in Emporia on July 26, 1973.[97]

All of the many obituary tributes to Bill reprinted in the *Gazette*
just after his death referred in some way to his being the son of
the famous William Allen White of Emporia. Bill's dear friend
the columnist Irene Corbally Kuhn wrote simply: "It is seldom
that a great man has the good fortune to have a great son. All
too often something is filtered out of the second generation. This
was not so of Bill White who so ably filled his father's place on
the Emporia Gazette in Kansas, and went on to make his own
name and reputation in the world. He added lustre to the family
name, the family newspaper and to journalism." Marion Ellet of
the *Concordia Blade–Empire* observed shrewdly: "His style has been
compared to his father's. But there were sharp differences. Both
men had a puckish humor, but under 'Young Bill's' humor there
was a sharp and sometimes hard intellectual drive. And he had
a capacity for organizing his material which may have been a
reflection of Sallie White's pragmatism." Whitley Austin of the
Salina [Kansas] *Journal* noted more personally:

> He didn't particularly like to be called 'Young Bill,' preferring
> to be known for his own substantial accomplishments rather
> than reflect the fame of William Allen White, his father. But
> the adjective fitted him.
>
> He had the hankering for adventure, the itch for the humor-
> ous, the desire for full, joyful living that one somehow associates
> with the young, particularly the Irish young. Whatever his years,
> he always enjoyed a youthful bravura which he expressed in
> his person or on his typewriter.[98]

An Associated Press color story about Bill, issued the day of his death, began: "William Lindsay White was more than 40 years old before he could hear 'chip off the old block' and not wince. But there came a day when . . . the W. L. White byline proliferated around the world on war stories and broadcasts, travel reports and a dozen books. The William Allen White byline faded with a disappearing generation."[99] Maybe for the writer of that release, but not for the citizens of Emporia, Kansas. There the W. A. W. byline remained a vivid memory. In spite of Bill's becoming a nationally known author and journalist in his own right, in spite of his living and moving among the prominent on the East Coast, in spite of being a better stylist than his father, both with words and newspaper makeup, to most fellow townspeople he was but Young Bill White to the day of his death. At home, at least, his father's figure still cast its shadow.

Epilogue
Byline W. L. W.

"Hello, America, this is W. L. White talking to you tonight from somewhere in the Finnish war zone." During January 1940 that greeting reached millions of Americans as they listened anxiously to "Today in Europe," a CBS radio program broadcasting the developing story of World War II. For over a month, Bill White had brought listeners tightly written on-the-spot commentaries about the beseiged Finns, and his audience had grown nightly. To most his was a fresh voice, known to them only as W. L. White, a son of the American Midwest; few in that radio audience knew him as the son of Editor William Allen White, Sage of Emporia. This breakthrough for Young Bill occurred at age forty. At last he had stepped away from his father's shadow to emerge as a separate personality. To his radio audience he also brought a new perspective, for his was an unpretentious focus on human interest that personalized mechanized warfare as he retold in modern terms the ageless story of David and Goliath.

Late Christmas day, for example, he reported watching with other newsmen aerial dogfights above a small Finnish town near the front. His method was simple; first he reported the air battle in disinterested, almost ingenuous terms:

> Just as a spectacle, it was a magnificent sight. The planes would come over in squadrons of from four to seven, and in this zero weather, flying well over a mile in that cold air, a plane leaves behind it a cloud of frozen exhaust vapour which stays in the blue sky for at least a quarter and sometimes half an hour—a white brush stroke of mist which slowly fades out. We could not tell at that height which were Finns and which Russians, except that when little black powder puffs of smoke from anti-aircraft shrapnel appeared around a squadron, we could be sure it was Russian.

Next he brought the battle down to earth, to the human level:

> The Russians dropped one load of pamphlets—we could see them twinkling as they turned over and over in the clear sunlight high above, floating downward. Then a puff of smoke and a tongue of flame appeared in the sky four or five blocks away and we knew they had dropped at least one incendiary bomb. When we got there, the dog fights still going on above us, we found it had fired a house in the modest section of town where working people lived—struck the home of a soldier who had come back from the front with just four hours leave on Christmas day—he was sitting at table with his wife and his mother, aged 70, when the bomb struck another room, and a piece of it blew off his mother's arm. They had taken her to the hospital when we got there and we saw the poor soldier and his wife trying to save from the flames their little store of furniture, carrying out a Singer sewing machine with a family album on top of it.

Then after developing his report further he ended with a "kicker," a comment that turned the story back onto his audience. In fact, most of his commentary throughout his life ended with an ironic twist:

The bombing has been fairly steady—they landed a loud one near the studio as I spoke to you this afternoon—and it has continued off and on ever since. If you are bored by all these bombs, I admit that they also bore me and will be glad to be back in Helsinki tomorrow night so I can give you a more general and less personal picture of this war. Merry Christmas to America, and returning you now to Columbia in New York.[1]

Bill sensed that this time Goliath would slay David. And in his broadcasts he suggested the fate of the Finns would most likely be that of the other little European democracies soon to confront a combined Russia and Germany. That kind of anecdotal human interest reporting, with a serious subtext, established "W. L. White" as a widely recognized, independent byline throughout the war and afterward.

In his most successful war stories he developed a dramatic narrative technique subsumed under the interview mode but lacking its apparent methodology. His real-life personae seemed to tell their stories on their own, without prompting or direction, with enhanced emotional effect. It was a self-effacing technique that required empathy and discipline and art. Bill would amass hundreds of notecards during interview sessions, then selectively cut his tale to its essentials to put his narrative voices in the most minimal of frames. He once advised a would-be author that "you should labor to polish and condense your factual material, selecting the very best anecdotes to prove your point and cutting them down to the bone."[2] But for Bill himself that was not easy. DeWitt Wallace often cautioned him that his stories were too long for easy *Digest* editing. And he always faced an initial struggle to get into the flow of story and character. Interviewed himself on CBS television, he admitted that "with any book or any article I have a terrible time getting started. . . . [But] once you make up your mind that you're not writing for the ages and lose your self-consciousness, you—as a character in *Alice in Wonderland* says— begin at the beginning, go on till you get to the end and then stop. When you get in that frame of mind the rest is simple."[3] His phrase "lose your self consciousness" is key to his technique. Kathrine once, in recalling the effect of Bill's stories, commented

that his "identification with others was almost an illness."[4] In
his narratives he had the rare ability to sublimate his own ego,
to project himself into another's shoes, not the shoes of an
imagined character but those of another living being. That
empathy created the narrative immediacy of his most successful
war stories—*They Were Expendable, Queens Die Proudly, Land of
Milk and Honey*, and *Back Down the Ridge*.

The pages of the *Reader's Digest* contain William L. White the
popular reporter, one who wrote with color and verve. He also
wrote to the *Digest's* standards of brevity, optimistic simplicity,
and middle-class conservatism, or had his submissions edited to
fit those standards. But sometimes he wrote pieces too complex
or too controversial for *Digest* vetting, and sometimes a submission
got stuck in the editorial pipeline of the magazine until it lost
its timeliness. Or, much more often, his story suggestions just did
not fire Wallace's imagination during the obligatory *Digest* editorial
luncheons. By contrast, in the pages of the *Gazette*, from 1944
to 1973, William L. White became "W. L. W.," the small-town
publisher-editor who could comment about what and whom he
wanted, when and however he wanted. He could write long
commentaries for the *Gazette* with fanciful figures of speech, fully
developed anecdotes, and unabashed personal allusions. Still, his
commentaries seldom escaped one check, comparison by *Gazette*
subscribers to those by W. A. W.

As a practitioner of the journalist's art of putting the right words
one after another, Bill in that comparison surpassed his father,
who was his teacher. At the *Gazette* his father taught him, so he
once said, to drop the "ponderously Latinate vocabulary" learned
at Harvard and to use instead strong, short words. Bill admired
the writing of Ernest Hemingway and took him as a model for
concise narrative style. He also became interested in etymology
and delighted in crossword puzzles. His early sensitivity to terse
narration and to semantics paid off. He became an adept stylist.
Charles Cowan, for example, a frequent Emporia contributor to
the *Gazette's* Wailing Place, when asked to compare the two
Whites, said: "I always thought W. L. was a lot better writer than
his father. He could write so much more in a few pages than the
old man could write in a whole chapter, although it wasn't any

more interesting, but I mean he'd get to the point so much quicker.
. . . He had such a perfect command of the English language; he
knew every word and just where to put it."[5]

From his father, Bill also seems to have picked up his capacity
for compassion and his sense of irony. Both could write a poignant
obituary editorial, stock-in-trade for a small-town editor, and both
could invoke sympathy for the underdog or the wretched. Both
could also tweek the self-important with a combination of sly
understatement and deadpan exaggeration. But in his editorials
Young Bill usually conveyed a more outrageously humorous
attitude than his father, one that especially delighted in deflating
provincial pomposity, either in an event or a person. Considering
Bill's editorial career, Walter Butcher, a longtime political science
professor at Kansas State Teachers College (now Emporia State
University), remarked: "I've read every editorial that Young Bill
wrote, and I enjoyed his more than I did his father's. . . . You
could see at times that he was writing with his tongue in his cheek,
trying to stir people up and trying to make them mad. He would
make me mad once in a while—oh, mad as hops—but I would
read him anyway."[6] When Bill was in Emporia, the town's pace
quickened. At the editor's desk he often assumed the unpopular
but useful role of iconoclast, bringing to local affairs a wider
perspective, acting as an outside catalyst for civic improvement.
Of course, some townsfolk thought he acted more like the devil's
advocate.

In all his writings, whether for his syndicate, CBS, the *Reader's
Digest*, or the *Gazette*, Bill White had the uncomfortable integrity
to say what he believed and not to say what he did not believe.
He continued to attack the Nazis on the air, even though CBS
asked him to temper his remarks; he maintained that the Soviets
were an untrustworthy totalitarian regime, in spite of a slanderous,
Soviet-backed campaign against him; though a loyal employee of
the *Reader's Digest*, he refused Wallace's request to ghostwrite
articles and to sign an ersatz "special" about Brazil. In the *Gazette*,
where he was his own boss after his father's death, he could be
forthright and stalwart in his opinions, whether distrusting of
Alf Landon or Alger Hiss or municipal industrial bonds, or
supportive of FDR or Barry Goldwater or a renovated county

court house. Fred Markowitz, a former *Gazette* reporter and later dean of education at the teachers college, considered Bill White "one of the very important individuals in my life—not only from the point of view of what I learned from him about journalism and writing but what I learned about what men can be and what they should be. I'm speaking here of his sense of truth, his sense of honesty, his sense of justice, his sense of integrity, all of those things. You know, you don't really appreciate these qualities of Bill until you get to know him and until you've read quite a bit of what he writes."[7] No one in Emporia doubted that Bill White stood foursquare by his convictions.

Yet most had learned to expect from him the unexpected. In 1969, during a time of civil protest and campus riots, Bill gave the May commencement speech at the College of Emporia. His subject was cultural shock in a changing world, and he tailored it to a restive student body the college had recruited from the East Coast. He followed the traditional commencement speech formula of nostalgia, exhortation, and humor, but in his own peculiar way. For example, he commended that class, filled with New Yorkers, because

> in spite of this rinky-dink college in this two-bit midwestern town, half of you managed to survive and hang on, the boys, I understand, in the hope that the great Sexual Revolution, about which they had been reading so much in *Life* and *Look* and *Playboy*, soon would strike even Emporia and then they could get some action; . . . but almost seventy years of observation have demonstrated to me that while this great Revolution is both imminent and inevitable, it never is going on in any given place at the time you happen to be there. But you are young—so don't give up the faith. Of course it will reach Emporia—just after you leave.

He affirmed the true quality of their education and praised their ability to face cultural challenges. Then he moved to a singular peroration:

> So now you leave us, and I don't think you need be ashamed because you didn't try to close your college, or restructure it,

or even set fire to it. I don't know you but I do know well many members of your faculty who tell me that never in their memory has this college had a class as challenging, as lively, as likable and as smart as this class of 1969. Whatever you thought of us, we liked you. So now—

Pax Vobiscum!

Shalom Aleichem!

Go in Peace!

But be damn sure you return all the books to the library.[8]

In the *El Dorado Times*, editor Rolla Clymer, an alumnus of the College of Emporia, praised the unique appropriateness of that speech. In doing so he asserted what most fellow Kansans who knew Bill White could also assert, that he "is never banal. He does not follow set rules. He seldom conforms to the status quo. Above all, he is thoughtful—and entertaining."[9] And like his father before him, he was a brilliant small-town editor and nationally popular author, but by his own set of lights.

Notes

Acronymns Used Throughout the Notes

People

DW	DeWitt Wallace
HL	Hobart Lewis
KW	Kathrine White
LH	Lacy Haynes
SLW	Sallie Lindsay White
WAW	William Allen White
WLW	William Lindsay White

Sources

EG	*Emporia Gazette* (daily edition)
EGA	*Emporia Gazette* archives

ESU   William Allen White Memorial Library, Special Col-
           lections Division, Emporia State University
HHPL   Herbert Hoover Presidential Library, West Branch, Iowa
KSHS   Manuscript Division, Kansas State Historical Society,
           Topeka
KU   Spencer Research Library, Kansas Collection, University
           of Kansas, Lawrence
LC   Manuscripts Division, Library of Congress, Washington,
           D.C.
LCHM   Lyon County Historical Museum, Emporia
SHSW   State Historical Society of Wisconsin

Prologue: In the Shadow

1. WLW to Herbert Hoover III, August 25, 1969, KU.
2. For an excellent study of the early WAW see Sally Griffith, *Home Town News: William Allen White and the Emporia Gazette* (New York: Oxford University Press, 1989); for a brief general analysis see E. Jay Jernigan, *William Allen White* (Boston: Twayne, 1983).
3. WLW, "The Sage of Emporia," William Allen White Centennial Speech, February 12, 1968, William Allen White School of Journalism, University of Kansas, published in *Nieman Reports*, March 1969, 1–22. Quotation appears on pp. 15–16.
4. Whitley Austin to author, January 18, 1990.
5. Interview of Ed Shupe, March 19, 1974, in the Flint Hills Oral History Project, LCHM.

1. A Small-Town Kansas Childhood, with a Harvard Finish, 1900–1924

1. WAW to John Phillips, June 19, 1900, LC.
2. WAW to Maud Johnston, June 27, 1900, ESU.
3. WAW to John Phillips, July 14, 1990, LC; WAW to Auguste Jaccacci, July 14, 1900, LC.
4. Frank Clough, "Meet Bill White, A Small Edition of His Famed Dad," *Editor and Publisher*, November 18, 1940, 14.
5. Everett Rich, *William Allen White: The Man from Emporia* (New York: Farrar and Rinehart, 1941), 115.

6. *The Autobiography of William Allen White* (New York: Macmillan, 1946), 347.

7. WLW to Cecil ("Teet") Carle, [1938], KU.

8. In a letter to Edna Ferber, March 25, 1916, Will confided: "For twenty years [Sallie] has been more or less hampered by under-health. She could not do things that other women do, and she has been infinitely patient yet always more or less sad about it. Since we went to the hospital [the Mayo Clinic in 1914], she has had a strength that never came to her before. And she has felt joyous and exultant. When this thing [a gall bladder infection] hit her last month, she lost her nerve for the first time in all her life. She felt that it was a turn back to old conditions from which she had escaped." Ferber Papers, SHSW. And in a letter to Ferber dated May 24, 1920, he confessed: "I am having the dickens of a time. I broke down early in April and have been absolutely idle now for five or six weeks. The doctor has gone over me and says my heart, lungs, blood, blood pressure, kidneys and liver are all working beautifully, but when I try to use the typewriter or even dictate to my stenographer, anything that has any sort of literary form or even an editorial for the Gazette, I go all a-tremble and if I persist I break into a sweat and am completely exhausted within half an hour. . . . I can go my usual rounds of business, carry on conversation, and play around in politics, but just let me try to do anything that brings in any salary and I am a complete wreck without any salvage. I don't know how long the thing will last." Ferber papers, SHSW.

9. In a reminiscent speech commemorating his father's centennial Bill remarked about his mother: In a way she was less stable than my father; she had ups and downs. She would be sparkling and gay, and then could follow periods of depression. In another way she was more stable. She had hard common sense, and a deep sense of fairness. She also had, herself, some talent for writing, and shrewd literary judgment. These things he needed and depended on. He never wrote a piece of any importance without their going over it together. Usually, she read it aloud to him. Her pencil marks are all over his manuscripts; any top editor would agree that her suggestions for cuts or revision were highly professional. WLW, "Sage of Emporia," 9.

10. Aunt Kate was Mrs. William H. White (sometimes spelled Wight and a family not related to Dr. Allen White, Will's father), the only sister of Mary Ann (Hatton) White, WAW's mother. Her daughter, Catherine, Will's first cousin, was the mother of Gwen (Behr) and Roland Boynton, both of whom were to be regarded as close family by Bill, though they were but cousins twice removed.

11. Rich, *William Allen White*, 114.

12. WAW, *Autobiography*, 372.

13. See "Us Colored," EG, September 19, 1966.

14. WAW, *Autobiography*, 408.

15. Audiotape interview of WLW by Loren Pennington, January 30, 1973, EGA.

16. Teet Carle, "Mary" (unpublished book-length memoir), 29, ESU.

17. WAW to Eugene ("Gene") Howe, October 13, 1910, LC.

18. Ironically, several years after Will's congratulatory letter, Gene Howe, tired of conflict with his father and of being known only as "Ed Howe's son," left Atchison to start his own chain of newspapers in Texas. Later in his statewide newspaper column he wrote a sketch of his father, which the *Saturday Evening Post* published under the title "My Father Was the Most Wretchedly Unhappy Man I Ever Knew." Gene himself committed suicide. *Saturday Evening Post*, October 25, 1939; see "Old Tack," *Time*, July 7, 1952, 50.

19. As he wrote Thomas Johnston of the *Kansas City Star*, "Mrs. White's health is very seriously bad and we are going to try what California will do to improve it. Incidentally I am taking my interminable book [*In the Heart of a Fool*] along and hope to get something done with it." WAW to T. W. Johnston, December 18, 1912, LC. On medical advice Will delayed leaving Emporia until January 2, 1913.

20. Later that cousin would remarry and run the sanitarium Rancho Yucca Loma near Victorville, California.

21. WLW to Robert Boone, October 12, 1948, KU; Frank Atchinson to WLW, August 10, 1945, KU.

22. Carle, "Mary" 178.

23. WLW to Melvin Johnson, November 24, 1969, KU.

24. WLW to Pearl Lindsay, January 12, 1966, courtesy Joseph M. Lindsay.

25. Ibid.

26. WAW, *The Martial Adventures of Henry and Me* (New York: Macmillan Co., 1918).
27. WLW to WAW, August 30, 1917, EGA.
28. Years later he wrote a reminiscent piece entitled "Was There a Curtain?" about that epidemic. He recalls lying in a temporary infirmary watching orderlies move several fellow victims into a curtained off area to die, scared he would be next; see EG, October 15, 1966.
29. WLW to WAW, November 1918, LC.
30. WAW to SLW, December 14, 1918, LC.
31. Norman Angell was the pen name of Ralph Norman Angell Lane, manager of the *London Daily Mail* (continental edition) from 1904 to 1921.
32. See WLW, *Report on the Germans* (New York: Harcourt, Brace, 1947), 207–12, 234–39, for references to his role as a press courier during some of the conference and his personal observation of the volatile, labor-led Parisian general strike of May 1, 1919.
33. "Sees French Battlefields," EG, March 31, 1919, 6.
34. WLW to parents, [ca. October 1919], LC.
35. Audiotaped interview of WLW by Loren Pennington, February 11, 1973, EGA.
36. Fred Markowitz, a former *Gazette* reporter and later a professor and administrator at Emporia State University, observed in an interview after Bill's death that "as a personality he was certainly not very approachable, . . . not the kind of individual that you would want to strike up a casual conversation with at all . . . excepting when he would throw a party for the *Gazette* employees. And then he was right in the middle of things." Flint Hills Oral History Project, March 19, 1974, LCHM.
37. WLW to Paul Savage, February 10, 1943, KU.
38. WLW to Herbert Hoover III, August 25, 1969, KU; WAW to WLW, November 26, 1920, LC.
39. WAW, *Autobiography*, 595.
40. Unaddressed and undated form letter [ca. 1968], EGA.
41. WLW to parents, March 6, 1922, EGA.
42. His father wrote Edna Ferber proudly on March 21, 1921: "I am sending you . . . a copy of Bill's piece in the Boston Transcript. Bill seems to be employed as a dramatic writer and is doing one

piece a week in addition to his regular freshman work. He is . . . tremendously enthusiastic about Harvard and the whole situation he finds there." SHSW.

43. WLW to C. T. Copeland, January 23, 1943, EGA; J. Donald Adams, *Copey of Harvard* (Boston: Houghton Mifflin, 1910), 182.

44. Roger Hewlett, "An Historical Sketch," in *An Illustrated History of the Hasty Pudding Club Theatricals* (Cambridge: Hasty Pudding Club, 1933), n.p.

45. Samuel Eliot Morison, *Three Centuries of Harvard* (Cambridge: Harvard University Press, 1936), 427.

46. "Art," EG, June 30, 1966.

47. "Murdock Pemberton Was First Art Critic for *The New Yorker*," *New York Times*, August 21, 1982, 28; Leslie Frewin, *The Late Mrs. Dorothy Parker* (New York: Macmillan, 1986), 36, 42.

48. WLW to parents, [March 1921], EGA.

49. WLW to parents, February 22, 1922, EGA.

50. Henry Allen to SLW, May 11, 1921, LC.

51. WLW to Mary White, April 2, 1921, EGA.

52. Carle, "Mary," 16.

53. WLW to SLW, May 7, 1921, EGA; in a letter to Edna Ferber, September 17, 1920, Will White wrote: "Mary seems to have come into a new era in her life. Last year and the year before she was mighty careless, as you know, but this year she is bucking into her studies, . . . has an ambition to make grades and is tremendously impressed with the idea of going to Wellesley." SHSW.

54. Carle, "Mary," 258.

55. WLW to parents, May 11, 1922, EGA.

56. WAW to WLW, April 30, 1923, LC.

57. Frank Beach, "The Dunsany Play," EG, August 16, 1921, 8.

58. "A High-Brow Thriller," EG, August 6, 1921, 1.

59. "Do You Know When to Laugh?" EG, August 30, 1921, 2.

60. "The Highbrow Thriller," EG, September 1, 1921, 5.

61. Carle, "Mary," 12.

62. WLW to WAW, February 22, 1922, EGA.

63. WAW to WLW, April 27, 1922, LC.

64. WAW to WLW, April 27, 1922, LC.

65. Audiotape interview of WLW by Loren Pennington, January 30, 1973, EGA.

66. "Take a Look," EG, June 26, 1939. When home Bill functioned as his parents' chauffeur until his marriage in 1931. For example, somewhat reluctantly he drove his parents and Edna Ferber for ten days around north-central Oklahoma, where Will introduced her to places and friends for background to her novel *Cimarron*; Edna Ferber to Fannie Fox, [June 1928], SHSW.
67. "If," EG, July 31, 1923.
68. WAW to WLW, October 25, 1921, LC.
69. WAW to WLW, April 30, 1923, LC.
70. WLW to WAW, November 16, 1922, EGA.
71. WAW to WLW, December 5, 1922, LC.
72. WLW to parents, November 16, 1922, EGA.
73. WAW to WLW, December 5, 1922, LC.
74. WAW to WLW, October 25, 1923, LC.
75. WLW to WAW, November 14, 1923, EGA; WAW to WLW, November 22, 1923, LC; WAW to WLW, October 30, 1923, LC.
76. WAW to Milt Lindsay, June 6, 1924, LC.
77. Harvard class of 1924, "First Report," issued in 1925, listed W. L. White simply as "newspaper reporter."

2. The Heir Apparent, 1924–1934

1. "Walter E. Hughes," EG, September 6, 1932, 1.
2. "Blurred Outlines," EG, May 1, 1928.
3. Will did, however, eventually acknowledge that an unsigned editorial of December 17, 1932—an irreverently humorous comment on the Democrat's Agricultural Adjustment Administration (AAA) proposal to control hog production—was by his son, but only after it had been widely quoted as his. The *Gazette* reprinted that piece on February 11, 1933, with this disclaimer: "Last December while W. A. White was in New York, William L. White wrote an editorial entitled 'Persuading the Hogs.' It was sent out as a circular by various Chambers of Commerce and farm organizations. Nothing that has appeared in the Gazette in years has been so widely quoted."
4. WLW, "Sage of Emporia," 15; see also Russell H. Fitzgibbon, ed., *Forty Years on Main Street*, (New York: Farrar and Rinehart, 1937).
5. WLW, "Sage of Emporia," 13–14.

6. Edward Whitney to WLW, January 27, 1925, EGA.

7. WAW to Elbert Severance, December 19, 1925, LC.

8. WAW to WLW, April 1, 1926.

9. "The Odyssey of Young Bill," EG, June 15, 1926.

10. "The Odyssey of Young Bill," EG, June 22, 1926.

11. "The Odyssey of Young Bill," EG, July 13, 1926.

12. Telephone interview of Mrs. Martin Herrick, May 23, 1991.

13. WAW to WLW, June 12, 1926, LC.

14. "Italy's Non-Drinkers," New York Evening Post, August 10, 1926, 7; "How Americans Visiting in Paris Strike an Interested Observer from the Middle West," in "Spirit of the Press" column, New York Evening Post, August 14, 1926, 11.

15. Telegrams, WLW to WAW, May 17, April 21, July 13, and July 28, 1927, LC.

16. WAW to Robert Kane, August 29, 1927, LC.

17. Frank Clough, William Allen White of Emporia (New York: McGraw-Hill, 1941), 225.

18. "Al Smith's Record," EG, July 7, 1928.

19. Untitled manuscript version of "The Last Two Decades," KU.

20. "Smith Defended Saloon and Vice, White Charges," Christian Science Monitor, July 30, 1928, 3.

21. "White Renews Attack on Smith's Record, but Drops Vice Charge," Christian Science Monitor, July 31, 1928, 1.

22. WLW to WAW, August 10, 1928, LC.

23. In that address Bill remembered those events thus: "During the 1928 campaign when Al Smith was running against Herbert Hoover, Father made a trip alone to New York where some strategist on the Republican National Committee passed to him . . . a record of the vote cast by Al Smith in the New York legislature, against a bill purporting to abolish prostitution. In that period, the Republican picture was that Al Smith represented the Tammany Halls of America, the corrupt political machines of the big cities in which vice and alcohol were entwined. Who better than a Midwestern prohibitionist to throw down the gauntlet to this menace? But as the whole story presently came out, it became clear that the bill in question was a silly one. . . . I am happy to say that most of his biographers have either ignored or sloughed over this brief and unimportant episode. However much it deserves to be

forgotten, I revive it now because it completes the picture of my mother, who in this painful crisis told me that, had she gone with father on that New York trip, she would never have let him do it." WLW, "Sage of Emporia," 10–11.

24. "The Odyssey of Young Bill," EG, May 20, 1929.
25. "De Mortuis," *Chanute Tribune*, April 30, 1931, 2.
26. WAW to WLW, June 7, 1929, LC.
27. "Why?" *Chanute Tribune*, June 4, 1929, 2.
28. WAW to WLW, June 7, 1929, LC.
29. Telephone interview of Mrs. Russell Barnes, March 6, 1990.
30. "The Odyssey of Young Bill," EG, July 13, 1929.
31. WAW to Arthur Krock, August 24, 1929, LC.
32. See "Touring in a French Flivver Provides a Round of Thrills," *Kansas City Star*, September 6, 1929, 6.
33. "Facing American Charges in the German Trenches in the Argonne," *Kansas City Star*, September 15, 1929, C1, C7.
34. "In Kansas a Leader's Logic Wins: Success of Kansas Session Partly Due to W. L. White," *Kansas City Star*, March 25, 1933, 1.
35. "Finis," EG, June 18, 1930, 4.
36. Lee Rich in *Junction City Union*; reprinted under "Editorial Tributes," EG, August 10, 1973, 6.
37. Telegram, John Wheeler to WAW, March 31, 1931, LC.
38. John Wheeler to WAW, April 2, 1931, LC.
39. John Wheeler to WAW, April 8, 1931, LC.
40. "How a Viking Died," EG, April 1, 1931, 4.
41. EG, April 23 and 28, 1931.
42. WAW to John Wheeler, April 17, 1931, LC.
43. Barbara Walker, "Mother," EG, August 19, 1988.
44. *The Jayhawker* (University of Kansas yearbook), 1923 and 1926; John Nugent, University of Kansas Archives, to author, December 13, 1989; Dorothy Weidner, University of Wisconsin Office of Registrar, to author, July 25, 1991.
45. Telephone interview of Baronesa Ostman van der Leye, née Sally Ingalls, February 18, 1990.
46. Harry Ferguson, "The Memory Machine," *Atlantic Monthly*, March 1976, 72–73.
47. Telephone interview of Baronesa Ostman van der Leye, February 18, 1990.

48. Walker, "Mother."

49. *Emporia Weekly Gazette*, May 21, 1931; *Kansas City Star*, April 29, 1931, 2; KW to in-laws, September 14, 1943, EGA. This suitor may have been Phil Phillips, an Oklahoma oilman who attended the University of Kansas with Kathrine and remained a close friend.

50. WLW to parents, May 1, 1931, EGA.

51. "W. L. White Is Married," EG, April 29, 1931, 1; WLW to parents, May 1, 1931, EGA.

52. Interview of Barbara Walker, February 27, 1992; KW to John Dos Passos, [May–June 1966], EGA.

53. "Young Bill's Romance," EG, May 1, 1931, 1. An article, unsigned (per *Fortune*'s format), appeared on pp. 60–63 in the December 1930 issue entitled "Ale, Beer, Stout." Anticipating the end of Prohibition in the United States, the article—which was undoubtedly Kathrine's work—was a well-researched survey of prominent British brewers and their industry. An undated clipping from the *Kansas City Star* preserved in her passport issued August 4, 1930, reads: "Three years ago a talented girl went to New York to make her mark in the literary world, says the Ottawa Herald. . . . This summer, however, she found herself growing stale in New York so she sought the more stimulating atmosphere of Europe. There she found success. In a fall number of one of the swankiest magazines published in this country is to appear an article by this young woman. It is to be titled 'The Breweries of England, Ireland, Scotland and Wales'" According to customs entry stamps in Kathrine's passport, on that trip, which was her first abroad, she toured parts of England, Holland, and France. EGA.

54. "Editorial Correspondence," EG, April 23, 1931.

55. WLW to parents, May 1, 1931, EGA.

56. "5200 in Schools," EG September 15, 1931, 1.

57. Telegram, WLW to WAW, April 26, 1931, EGA.

58. WLW, *What People Said* (New York: Viking Press, 1938), 191. However, two years after that introduction, when the bank-bond scandal broke, Kathrine came to respect Mabel Finney's stalwart inner strength.

59. Ibid., 193–95.

60. For a while Belle was Mrs. Cavendish-Bentinck; see Maureen Montgomery, *Guilded Prostitution: Status, Money and Transatlantic Marriages, 1870–1914* (London: Routledge, 1989).

61. "Belle Livingston Returns to See Old Home Town," EG, July 6, 1931, 1, 2; see also Livingston's autobiography, *Belle Out of Order* (New York: Henry Holt, 1959).

62. "A Gazette Reminiscence: VI," in *The Emporia Gazette's Album of Memories*, n.d., n.p., EGA.

63. WAW to Henry Haskell, August 24, 1931, LC.

64. KW notes to Barbara Matthiessen manuscript, EGA.

65. Ibid.

66. Cited from an *El Dorado Times* clipping, n.d., n.p., EGA.

67. "A German Soviet?" EG, July 15, 1931; "A Rural Idyll," EG, July 16, 1931; "Wanted: 1,000 Jobs," EG, July 22, 1931; "Kansas Is Watching Young Mr. M'Gugin," *New York Times*, September 13, 1931, sec. 3, p. 8; "Rate Reductions Sought in Kansas," *New York Times*, October 25, 1931, sec. 3, p. 5; "85-Cent Oil Makes Mid-Continent Glad," *New York Times*, November 22, 1931, sec. 3, p. 5; "Tariff May Be Hit by Wheat Farmers," *New York Times*, November 29, 1931, sec. 3, p. 5; WLW to Arthur Krock, August 20, 1966, KU.

68. WAW to Robert Kane, January 5, 1932, LC.

69. "A Mexico Bullfight as It Looks to a Newspaperman from Kansas," *Kansas City Star*, April 28, 1932, 7.

70. Telegram, WLW to WAW, April 8, 1932, LC.

71. "Harmony," EG, December 21, 1932; "Peace in Kansas," *New York Times*, December 26, 1932, 22; "Is Our Face Red," EG, December 31, 1932.

72. "Stay West," EG, January 17, 1933.

73. Roscoe Le Gresley to WLW, March 11, 1972, KU; see also letter to the Wailing Place by Le Gresley, EG, August 11, 1973.

74. See "Challenge," EG, May 16, 1933; and "Innocent Bystanders," EG, June 17, 1933.

75. Twelve years later, when Bill was attacked viciously for besmirching his father's name by publishing an "unpatriotically critical" *Report on the Russians*, then wartime allies, Bill's defenders pointed to these pieces by Will as riposte.

76. Robert Bader, *The Great Kansas Bond Scandal* (Lawrence: University Press of Kansas, 1982), 14.

77. Lawrence: University Press of Kansas, 1982.

78. "Proud of Him," EG, August 12, 1933.

79. "Scandal and Politics," EG, August 17, 1933.

80. "A Friendship," EG, August 25, 1933.

81. "Too Soon," EG, September 6, 1933.

82. See "Following a Trail," EG, September 9, 1933.

83. "Dave Hinshaw," EG, August 29, 1933.

84. Whitley Austin to author, January 18, 1990.

85. Interview of Kenneth Scott, September 28, 1989.

86. See Jernigan, *William Allen White,* 17.

87. WAW to Erwin Canham, October 27, 1933, LC.

88. WLW to Lacy Haynes, August 29, 1933, KSHS.

89. In the *Gazette,* September 11, 1933, for example, Bill reprinted a *Kansas City Journal-Post* editorial that started out like this: "William Allen White is due home from Europe shortly. What a different Kansas he will find! What a different Emporia! . . . When the house of cards began to fall, Young Bill did his best, but it wasn't enough. He tried to keep Ronald Finney out of jail by going on his bond, but the bond was rejected. He tried by the use of his pen to justify his interest in the Finneys, but Emporia started buying out-of-town papers to get the facts about the Finney case.

"In justice, it must be said that Old Bill probably wouldn't have been able to do any better. The situation was too big even for a sage. . . . But we'll know more about this when Old Bill gets home. Kansas—and the nation—will watch with interest to see whether he joins in the crusade to clean up the state, let the chips fall where they may, or whether the self-righteousness which he has capitalized in the past becomes a pose when those involved belong to his own crowd."

Young Bill replied: "For years the Cities Service group, through the subsidized *Journal-Post,* has been hurling buffalo chips and juicy garbage at the office of the governor, the bank commissioner, the attorney general, and all others who have aided and abetted these in the fight for lower [gas] rates. . . . After years of hurling harmless garbage, at last several erring brethren present apparently defenseless and unprotected posteriors to the shillelagh of Cities

Service. . . . What a pleasant novelty it must be to the *Journal–Post* staff to be able to print an occasional truth, and still follow the instructions of their employer. "The Old 'Croc,'" EG, September 11, 1933.

90. WAW to Erwin Canham, October 27, 1933, LC.

91. The *Gazette* covered the trial as news so well that its back files were used by defense attorneys during the following appeals; their marginalia are now part of the microfilmed files.

92. WAW to Gwen Behr, November 9, 1933, LC. Boynton indeed seemed overwhelmed by the situation; Whitley Austin reported that Ronald Finney once said in private that "if he asked Boynton to jump off the Jayhawk Hotel roof, Boynton would jump." Whitley Austin to author, February 8, 1990.

93. Roland Boynton to WLW, October 29, 1933, LC.

94. After long, hard-fought legal delays, the court decided for the prosecution and on June 6, 1935, ordered Warren Finney's bond revoked. That afternoon, with his wife's knowledge, Warren Finney drove to their summer farm cottage and shot himself. The next day Bill wrote a poignant, initialed editorial description of the suicide, headed "A Hill with a View," which testified to his profound sympathy for that old family friend; EG, June 8, 1935; see Bader, *Great Kansas Bond Scandal*, 307, for a reprint, and 310–11 for Will's longer but equally poignant obituary.

3. Back East in Search of an Identity, 1934–1940

1. Telegram, WAW to Jessie Kane, March 20, 1934, LC.

2. WAW to WLW, April 3, 1934, LC.

3. KW to in-laws, April 24, 1934, EGA.

4. WLW to parents, April 28, 1934, EGA.

5. Telegram, WLW to parents, May 14, 1934, LC.

6. Telegram, WLW to parents, May 20, 1934, LC.

7. Telegram, WAW to WLW, June 1, 1934, LC.

8. WAW to Edna Ferber, June 26, 1934, LC.

9. WLW, "What Manner of Man?" EG, August 15, 1934; "Down with Speculators," EG, August 24, 1934; "Socialism of Else," EG, September 10, 1934; "New Theories for Old," EG, October 9,

1934; "Two Systems," EG, October 19, 1934; "Over the Top!" EG, December 10, 1934; telegram, WLW to WAW, September 12, 1934, EGA.

10. KW to in-laws, 1934, LC; correspondence over two decades between KW and Dr. Maurice Fremont-Smith exists but is unavailable to this author.

11. WAW to Mrs. Louise Quackenboss, November 9, 1934, LC.

12. Telegram, Whites to KW, November 8, 1934, LC.

13. In commenting about the White legacy in the centennial edition of the *Gazette*, Barbara Walker wrote, "Mental illness was never talked about in those days, and even in my father's lifetime my mother carefully covered up his illness, and my father referred to 'his sick old mud turtle days.'" EG, June 1, 1995, 4A.

14. Telegram, WAW to WLW, January 23, 1935, LC.

15. Telegram, WAW to WLW, February 11, 1935, LC.

16. WAW to Robert Kane, March 15, 1935, LC.

17. WAW to WLW, May 21, 1935, LC.

18. Telegram, WAW to WLW, May 29, 1935, LC.

19. KW notes to Matthiessen manuscript, EGA.

20. WLW, "Sage of Emporia," 15–16.

21. Telegram, WAW to WLW, May 21, 1935, LC.

22. Telegram, WLW to WAW, July 10, 1935, LC.

23. "W. L. White to Washington," EG, August 1, 1935, 1.

24. WAW to WLW, August 13, 1935, LC.

25. WAW to Mrs. Ella Peterson, October 10, 1935, LC.

26. WLW to parents, [September 1935], EGA.

27. "Backstage," *Esquire*, September 1937, 30.

28. "The Story Behind *They Were Expendable*," *New York Times Book Review*, November 1, 1942, sec. 7, p. 30.

29. WAW to Jessie Kane, February 24, 1936, LC.

30. Telegram, WLW to parents, March 25, 1936, LC.

31. WLW to parents, March 9, 1938, LC.

32. WLW to SLW, April 27, 1937, EGA.

33. WLW to parents, May 6, 1936, EGA.

34. From April 6 through June 13, 1936, Bill published forty-two initialed columns in the *Gazette*.

35. WLW to parents, July 4, 1936, EGA.

36. Telegram, WAW to WLW, September 2, 1936, LC.

37. WLW to parents, [September 1936], EGA.

38. WLW to parents, October 2, 1936, EGA.

39. WLW to C. T. Luddington, Jr., December 30, 1970, KU.

40. Taped interview of John Dos Passos by WLW, November 9, 1964, on Emporia's CATV, EGA.

41. WLW to parents, June 21, 1937, EGA.

42. WAW to Alf Landon as cited in Walter Johnson, ed., *Selected Letters of William Allen White* (New York: Henry Holt, 1947), 363.

43. That young instructor was Samuel Halper, for whom Will asked his son to help find a research job in New York City. WAW to WLW, May 24, 1938, LC.

44. Western Union day letter, WAW to WLW, March 29, 1937, LC.

45. WLW to parents, June 21, 1937, EGA.

46. WLW to parents, June 21, 1937, EGA.

47. KW to in-laws, [September] 1937, EGA.

48. WLW to parents, August 3, 1937, EGA.

49. WLW to WAW, November 5, 1937, EGA; "Café Society: The Yankee Doodle Saloon," *Fortune*, December 1937, 123-29, 180, 183-84, 186.

50. "The Birth Control Business: The Accident of Birth," *Fortune*, February 1938, 83-86.

51. WLW to parents, April 6, 1938, EGA.

52. Harold Strauss, "The People of a Country Town," *New York Times Book Review*, April 10, 1938, sec. 7, p. 2.

53. WLW to Truman Capote, October 25, 1965, EGA.

54. KW to in-laws, March 1, 1938, EGA; WLW to parents, March 9, 1938, EGA.

55. "Prairie America," *Christian Century*, May 11, 1938, 593.

56. *Springfield Republican*, April 17, 1938, 7.

57. Strauss, "People of a Country Town," 2.

58. WLW to WAW, April 6, 1938, EGA.

59. WLW to parents, May 28, 1938, EGA; WLW to parents, August 31, 1938, EGA.

60. Michael Emery and Edwin Emery, *The Press and America: An Interpretive History of the Mass Media*, 6th ed. (Englewood Cliffs, N.J.: Prentice-Hall, 1992), 536.

61. KW to in-laws, December 16, 1938, EGA.

62. WLW to parents, November 28, 1938, EGA.

63. WLW to parents, May 31, 1939, EGA.

64. WLW to parents, June 5, 1939, EGA.

65. WLW to SLW, July 22, 1939, EGA.

66. "Personals," *Editor and Publisher*, August 19, 1939, 13.

67. *New York Post*, September 1, 1939, sec. B, p. 7.

68. "Emporian Was on Ship Sunk as the War Began," EG, September 5, 1989, 1.

69. "New Style War Correspondent Will Tell What Europe's Humblest Are Thinking," *Richmond News Leader*, November 9, 1939, 7; "William L. White Writes a Brand New Idea in Columns," *Editor and Publisher*, January 20, 1940, 13.

70. WAW to John Wheeler, September 28, 1939, LC; John Wheeler to WAW, October 11, 1939, LC; promotion poster, [October 1939], EGA; WAW to John Wheeler, October 16, 1939, LC.

71. WAW to Cordell Hull, October 3, 1939, LC.

72. WAW to Sir Frederic Whyte, October 18, 1939, LC.

73. KW to WAW, [December 1939], EGA.

74. "Going," EG, October 27, 1939.

75. See *New York Post*, September 3, 1940, 16; September 4, 1940, 7; September 12, 1940, 7; September 16, 1940, 6.

76. See reference in WLW editorial "Debates on Battles," EG, September 11, 1951.

77. Quoted in "Take a Look," December 15.

78. "Take a Look," EG, December 18, 1939.

79. "Take a Look," EG, January 11, 1940.

80. Telegram, William L. Shirer to WLW, December 6, 1939, EGA; William L. Shirer, *Twentieth Century Journey: A Memoir of a Life and the Times*, vol. 2, *The Nightmare Years, 1930–40* (Boston: Little, Brown, 1984), 469.

81. Robert Sherwood to WAW, December 29, 1939, LC.

82. Transcript, December 13, 1939, EGA.

83. *Cue, the Weekly Magazine of New York Life*, January 6, 1940, 14.

84. KW to WAW, [December 1939], EGA.

85. Walter Schneider, "Newsmen Report Finnish War at 25 to 43 Below Zero," *Editor and Publisher*, January 13, 1940, 3.

86. Backed by fifteen Emporia businessmen, including Bill's friend Harold Trusler, the radio station took its call letters KTSW from the initials

of its two principal organizers, Kenneth Trimble and Sellek Warren; see "To Take the Air January 25," EG, January 12, 1939, 1.

87. KW to WAW, undated [January 1940], EGA.

88. Telegram, Paul White to WLW, January 19, 1940, EGA.

89. "Take a Look," EG, February 24, 1940.

90. "Take a Look," EG, February 25, 1940.

91. "CBS Broadcast," typescript, February 5, 1940, EGA.

92. "Bill White," *Book-of-the-Month Club News*, special supplement, September 1942, 2.

93. KW notes to Matthiessen manuscript, EGA.

94. Telegram, Paul White to WLW, February 13, 1940, EGA.

95. Telegram, WAW to WLW, February 24, 1940, LC.

96. See Bill's scathing analysis of upper-class British complacency at the time in his article "The Old School Tie," *Town and Country*, February 1942, 38, 74–76, 83–84.

97. Telegram, WAW to WLW, March 21, 1940, LC.

98. Advertisement headed "William L. White Writes a Brand New Idea in Columns," *Editor and Publisher*, January 20, 1940, 13.

99. Paul Fisher, "Young Bill White Carries on a Great Newspaper Tradition," *Kansas City Star*, June 17, 1940, 16.

100. Quoted in letter, WLW to parents, March 29, 1940, EGA.

101. Copy of cablegram, WLW to Ted Thackrey, [March 1940], EGA.

102. Telegram, WAW to WLW, March 28, 1940, LC.

103. Telegram, WAW to WLW, March 30, 1940, LC.

104. KW to WAW, [April 1940], EGA.

105. KW notes to Matthiessen manuscript, EGA.

106. WLW to parents, March 29, 1940, EGA.

107. In a letter of February 20, 1971, to Vermont Royster, Bill remembered Romania in 1940 as "the most delightfully crooked place I have ever seen." On his first day there he called on the minister of information, "a quadrilingual charmer" who confidentially offered him a better black market currency exchange rate than he could get elsewhere." KU.

108. "Take a Look," EG, April 29, 1940.

109. KW to in-laws, May 14, 1940, EGA.

110. KW to WAW, May 10, 1940, EGA.

111. KW to in-laws, May 21, 1940, EGA.

112. *Yale Review*, Autumn 1940, 92–108; *Cosmopolitan*, November 1940, 17, 75–76; WLW, "I Saw It Happen," in Stephen Vincent Benét et al., *Zero Hour: A Summons to the Free* (New York: Farrar and Rinehart, 1940), 117–75.
113. KW to in-laws, [October 1940], EGA.
114. "Personals," *Editor and Publisher*, October 12, 1940, 55.
115. John Wheeler to WAW, September 30, 1940, LC; WAW to John Wheeler, October 3, 1940, LC; WAW to John Wheeler, October 26, 1940, LC.

4. The *Reader's Digest*, the War, and the Passing of a Sage, 1940–1945

1. "Emporian Finds Few Scars of Nazi Bombings in England Today," EG, October 12, 1940, 1.
2. WLW to parents, [November 1940], LC.
3. Another original, "Death in the Dark," appeared in the *Reader's Digest*, July 1941, 64–70; the *Digest* planted the other two without reprinting them: "Invasion of England," *Atlantic Monthly*, May 1941, 542–47; and "Fighter Type," *McClean's*, September 15, 1941, 9–10, 49–54.
4. "Mounting Shipping Losses May Cause a New Crisis in Britain," EG, November 7, 1940, 1.
5. WLW to WAW, [November 1940], LC.
6. Richard Busvine, "Young White Finds Dad's Views Weak; Backs 'All-out' Aid," *Chicago Daily Times*, December 30, 1940, 5.
7. WLW to WAW, [January 1941], EGA.
8. WLW to parents, [November 1940], LC.
9. James Reston, "Lisbon's Refugees Now Put at 8,000," *New York Times*, December 15, 1940, 31; Reston implies the figure is closer to 10,000 and details conditions; KW to Mary Jo Wallace, January 13, 1941, EGA; "W. L. White Back from Europe with 3-Year-Old Adopted Girl," EG, February 10, 1941, 1.
10. The boy, named David, was later adopted by a British farm family.
11. WLW to WAW, April 3, 1941, EGA.
12. "Personals," *Editor and Publisher*, February 15, 1941, 37.
13. WLW to parents, June 26, 1941, EGA.

14. Christopher Morley, "Journey for Margaret," *Book-of-the-Month Club News*, December 1941, 12.

15. Telephone interview of Lambert Davis, March 13, 1990.

16. WLW to parents, June 26, 1941, EGA.

17. "His Majesty's Opposition," *Town and Country*, November 1941, 62–63, 100–02; "The Dying and the Buying," *Saturday Evening Post*, October 18, 1941, 9–11; "Out of the Doghouse," *Saturday Evening Post*, November 15, 1941, pp. 14–15, 123–27; "The Norse Travel Again," *Saturday Evening Post*, December 13, 1941, 14–15, 79–86.

18. WAW to Frank Motz, December 13, 1941, ESU.

19. Cited by KW in notes to Matthiessen manuscript, EGA.

20. Theodore Peterson, *Magazines in the Twentieth Century* (Urbana: University of Illinois Press, 1964), 232.

21. Lambert Davis as interviewed by Edison McIntyre, April 20, 1991.

22. James Wood, *Of Lasting Interest: The Story of the Reader's Digest* (New York: Doubleday, 1967), 92.

23. WLW to SLW, April 1, 1941, EGA.

24. WLW to parents, November 30, 1941, EGA.

25. "Books of the Times," November 13, 1941, 31.

26. Lacy Haynes to WLW, January 6, 1942, KSHS.

27. WLW to parents, February 9, 1942; WLW to WAW, February, 1942; WLW to WAW, February 15, 1942; WLW to WAW, February 22, 1942; WLW to WAW, March 13, 1942; WLW to WAW, April 14, 1942; WLW to WAW, April 17, 1942; WLW to Bill Stroock, April 22, 1942; WLW to WAW, May 11, 1942; WLW to SLW, August 1, 1942, EGA; WAW's and SLW's letters to Bill and to Kathrine during this period are not extant; their responses can only be inferred.

28. WAW to Frank Buxton, March 19, 1942, EGA.

29. Manuscript, KU.

30. Special supplement, September 1942, 6; Stephen Vincent Benét," History in a PT Boat," *Saturday Review of Literature*, September 12, 1942, 5.

31. Frank S. Adams, "Their Shields Were Plywood," *New York Times Book Review*, September 13, 1942, sec. 7, p. 1.

32. Telephone interview, March 13, 1990.

33. In 1956 at the Commencement Exercises of Harvard College, Senator John F. Kennedy told Bill he had gotten "into a hell of a lot of trouble" because he had read it, then "went right out and enlisted in motor torpedo boats." WLW, "Brief Encounter," EG, November 10, 1960.

34. See deposition of Robert B. Kelly by Edward F. McClennen, November 2, 1946, at 74–75, *Robert B. Kelly v. Loew's Inc.*, No. 5071 (Mass. Dist. Ct., March 4, 1948).

35. DW to Lt. James Van Alen, August 3, 1944, KU; Edison McIntyre to author, April 8, 1992.

36. WLW to DW, May 17, 1942, EGA.

37. Robert van Gelder, "The Story Behind 'They Were Expendable,'" *New York Times Book Review*, November 1, 1942, Sec. 7, pp. 2, 30.

38. WAW to Edna Ferber, July 21, 1942, ESU.

39. Telegram, KW to in-laws, October 20, 1942, LC.

40. KW to in-laws, November 15, 1942, EGA.

41. Manuscript copy, telegram, WLW to WAW, December 15, 1942, KU.

42. "War Romance May Stop Filming W. L. W.'s 'Expendable,'" EG, December 12, 1942, 1.

43. *Book-of-the-Month Club News*, special supplement, September 1942, 6.

44. Beulah Greenwalt Walcher to Edison McIntyre, July 9, 1991. In her deposition for the trial, in answer to the question "Looks like Mr. Kelly and Mr. White were pretty good reporters?" she replied, "Yes, they got the story told pretty much as it happened." Deposition of Beulah Greenwalt Walcher by Richard D. Shewmaker, April 15, 1948, at 115, *Beulah Greenwalt Walcher v. Loew's Inc.*, No. 5385, (Mo. Dist. Ct., May 29, 1950).

45. Robert Kelly, who became a navy career officer, sued MGM for libel over his portrayal in the screenplay as the character Rusty Ryan, played by John Wayne, even though Kelly had signed releases with both Bill for the book and MGM for the movie. Most of the suit was dismissed, but Kelly did win a small settlement from MGM. *Robert B. Kelly v. Loew's Inc.*, No. 5071 (Mass. Dist. Ct., March 4, 1948). The transcript of the lengthy testimony in the trial supports the honesty and verisimilitude of Bill's account.

46. WLW to DW, November 4, 1942, KU.

47. WLW to Paul Palmer, December 11, 1942, EGA.

48. Memorandum by Col. F. V. Fitzgerald, February 18, 1943; WLW to Herbert B. Swope, March 3, 1943; WLW to Herbert B. Swope, March 9, 1943; Col. John T. Winterich to WLW, March 15, 1943; WLW to Col. John T. Winterich, March 16, 1943, EGA.

49. Later the NANA through its Bell Syndicate offered it as a newspaper serial, just as it had *They Were Expendable*.

50. WLW to Lyndon Johnson, February 3, 1943; Lyndon Johnson to WLW, February 8, 1943, KU; see also Robert Caro, *The Years of Lyndon Johnson: Means of Ascent* (New York: Vintage, 1991), 44.

51. WLW to DW, May 10, 1943, EGA.

52. WLW to WAW, May 13, 1943, EGA.

53. WLW to WAW, June 14, 1943, EGA.

54. A. M. Stroock to Carol Hill, July 8, 1943; WLW to Brandt and Brandt, July 22, 1943; WLW to DW, July 27, 1943, EGA.

55. Eleanor Roosevelt, "My Day," *Detroit Free Press*, June 14, 1943, 5.

56. WLW to Mrs. Franklin D. Roosevelt, August 20, 1943, EGA.

57. Joseph Lash, *A World of Love* (New York: McGraw-Hill, 1984), 117.

58. WLW to SLW, April 5, 1944; WLW to SLW, April 25, 1944; WLW to Eleanor Roosevelt, August 8, 1944, EGA.

59. "W. A. White Goes to Mayo's," *New York Times*, October 13, 1943, 21.

60. KW to SLW, October 1943, EGA.

61. WLW to Lacy Haynes, October 23, 1943, KSHS.

62. For a report of one of those visits see "Take a Look," EG, August 5, 1940.

63. "Datebook 1943" EGA.

64. As cited in Bader, *Great Kansas Bond Scandal*, 333–34.

65. Ibid., 334.

66. WLW to Alf Landon, January 22, 1944, EGA.

67. WLW to DW, December 20, 1943, KU.

68. WLW, "Sage of Emporia," 21–22.

69. WLW to DW, February 29, 1944, KU.

70. Ibid.

71. WLW to Sallie Cabot Sedgwick, June 16, 1943, KU.

72. Wheeler gave Bill the same assignment at the same rate of pay—one thousand dollars plus expenses—to cover both conventions; John Wheeler to WLW, April 5, 1944, KU.

73. WLW to DW, March 22, 1944, KU.

74. Eric Johnston, "Your Stake in Capitalism," February 1943, 1-6; "Three Kinds of Capitalism," September 1943, 124-28; "A Talk to Britain," October 1943, 1-7; praising the Soviet war efforts were Maurice Hindus, "The Price that Russia Is Paying," April 1943, 47-50; and Paul Thompson, "The Nazis' Own Appraisal of the Russian Soldier," June 1943, 15-18; the critical leaders were Wendell Willkie, "Life on the Russian Frontier," March 1943, 1-7; and Max Eastman, "We Must Face Facts About Russia," July 1943, 1-14; Maurice Hindus, "The Russian Slogan: 'Work, Study, and Learn,'" February 1944, 59-60.

75. WLW to DW, April 5, 1944, KU.

76. John Wheeler to WLW, May 4, 1944, KU.

77. WLW to DW, April 5, 1944, KU.

78. WLW to KW, May 26, 1944, EGA; John Chamberlain, "Eric Johnston," *Life*, June 19, 1944, 96-108.

79. In his account of the trip, "Russian Visit," *Life*, September 11, 1944, 115, Johnston claimed, "I had purposely delayed making an appointment with the Marshal until I had inspected factories, seen the Red Army in action on the Finnish front and absorbed a little of the atmosphere of Russian daily life." But in *A Journey for Our Times* (New York: Harper and Row, 1983), 274, Harrison Salisbury wrote that it was really Johnston who was forced to wait.

80. WLW, *Report on the Russians* (New York: Harcourt, Brace, 1945), 34.

81. Bill was able to file only three stories to the NANA, one through Dick Lauterbach of Time-Life, two through James Aldridge, also accredited by the NANA; only Lauterbach's reached New York; John Wheeler to KW, June 21, 1944, EGA.

82. Eddy Gilmore recounts his and Bill's mutual experience of that raid in *Me and My Russian Wife* (New York: Doubleday, 1954), 208-19; Fletcher Pratt in "How the Censors Rigged the News," *Harper's*, February 1946, 98, asserts that White was the first journalist to publish the story. In a letter to a Dr. James T. Rountree, February 5, 1945, WLW responded to an inquiry about how much the *Reader's Digest* excerpts had been censored by replying that nothing was censored by anyone except for an unused chapter "which dealt with a visit I made to one of our shuttle bombing bases in Russia. Since I was a war correspondent and since this was an American military establishment, I followed the proper procedure of sub-

mitting this particular chapter to our War Department for censorship on my return to America. They took out very little and the changes they made were purely from the standpoint of military security and in no way did they alter or attempt to alter what might be call the political purport of my article." EGA.

83. Harrison Salisbury, *A Journey for Our Times*, 274–75; Richard Lauterbach, *These Are the Russians* (New York: Harper and Bros., 1945), 209–10.

84. WLW to Wilbur Forrest of the *New York Herald Tribune*, June 26, 1945, KU: "After we arrived in Russia, for the purpose of visiting the American Air Base at Poltava, I thought it appropriate to wear this uniform and present the American credentials to the Americans down there. When I took this matter up with our Russian hosts they said, in effect, 'Sure, why not?' I also wore the uniform on our trip out of the country because, by then, all of my civilian clothes were soiled. None of this at the time attracted any comment."

85. WLW, "Reds Lack Bombers to Raid German Cities," *Detroit News*, July 23, 1944, sec. 1, p. 6; Eric Johnston to WLW, August 10, 1944, KU; "Johnston Says Soviet Lacks Civil Liberties," *New York Times*, August 24, 1944, 19; "Johnston Defends Reds: W. L. White's Book 'Overemphasizes' the Bad, He Says," *New York Times*, March 15, 1945, sec. 1, p. 21.

86. Eric Johnston, "My Talk with Joseph Stalin," *Reader's Digest*, October 1944, 1-10; "Russian Visit," *Life*, September 11, 1944, 100–16; letter WLW to mother, July 22, 1944, EGA: "Ever since I got back from Russia, I have been working . . . on an interview between Eric Johnston and Stalin, which Eric wanted me to put into shape." Though DeWitt Wallace paid Bill for a manuscript version of that interview, Wallace wrote Bill, September 6, 1944, KU: "Alas! Eric wanted to write his own version of the Stalin interview. It is not as lively as yours."

87. KW to SLW, June 29, 1944, EGA: "I think maybe I've bought a house but I'm not too sure. I just bought it a little bit and today I had an offer to sell it for 5000 more. . . . I didn't want to sign the final papers until Bill got back."

88. "Little Joe's Star," *McCall's*, December 1944, 16–17, 61, 64, 66; letter WLW to DW, October 3, 1944, EG: "I took a day off last week to do a piece which McCall's magazine had been badgering me

for, for their Christmas issue, about the family of a boy who has been killed overseas."

89. Barmine was a *Reader's Digest* contributor who himself wrote two books about the Soviet Union: the first in 1938, *Memoirs of a Soviet Diplomat: Twenty Years in the Service of the U.S.S.R.* (London: Lovat Dickson, Ltd., 1938); the other was his popular exposé, *One Who Survived: The Life Story of a Russian Under the Soviets* (New York: G. P. Putnam's Sons, 1945); see his "The New Communist Conspiracy," *Reader's Digest* October 1944, 27–33. The FBI questioned Barmine closely a number of times from 1945 on about Soviet agents in the United States and he gave a series of inconsistent and conflicting responses. He was the source for Bill's erroneous "inside information" that Owen Lattimore, a specialist in Asian studies at Johns Hopkins University, was a longtime Soviet spy, which contributed to Bill's later support of the ultraconservative China Lobby. See Robert P. Newman, *Owen Lattimore and the "Loss" of China* (Berkeley and Los Angeles: University of California Press, 1992), 185–89.

90. On November 17, 1944, Bill signed a contract with Kathrine assigning her the movie, radio, and newspaper syndication rights to the book in acknowledgment of her "research, editing and revision"; copy EGA. Associated Newspapers syndicated the book to seventeen subscribers; memo Harry Gilbert to WLW, June 7, 1945, KU; also see advertisement, *Editor and Publisher*, April 21, 1945, 81. Lambert Davis to WLW, November 3, 1944, KU; KW to WLW, November 10, 1944, KU; KW to WLW, [November 1944], KU; KW to WLW, November 29, 1944, KU.

91. "A Scratched Ticket," EG, November 2, 1944; FDR to WLW, November 27, 1944, EGA.

92. For example, W. H. Lawrence, "Pravda Charges White Lied in Book," *New York Times*, December 10, 1944, sec. 1, p. 35.

93. DW to WLW, December 11, 1944, KU.

94. Bennett Cert, "Tradewinds," *Saturday Review of Literature*, December 30, 1944, 17.

95. Cerf's rather personal attack caused the *Kansas City Star*, for example, to comment editorially: "This appraisal of the White report strikes us as unfair. We see no evidence in the articles of anti-Russian bias. They seem on the contrary the attempt of a competent

American reporter to tell the truth about things as he saw them." January 14, 1945, p. 10D. A letter from Burton Rascoe, a prominent New York City book editor, newspaper columnist, and literary critic, to WLW, January 22, 1947, KU, indicates how much some in the trade resented Cerf's assumptions: "I remember [Harcourt, Brace assistant editor] Spencer Scott's telling me that day at the Dutch Treat Club when [I] told him what a snide, unethical thing Cerf had done, that Cerf could not have read the book because no review copies had gone out, and, moreover, his office had not yet received copies from the binder. . . . It is not an extenuation of Cerf's ethical culpability in this matter to say that he had read the RD condensation of it. In my books, it would have been just as unethical of Cerf to make that remark, if he had a review copy and had *not been a publisher* (though that fact compounds the offense). No ethical book reviewer would, at the beginning of the year, single out one unpublished book and predict that it would be the *worst* of the year."

96. WLW to Leigh White, November 6, 1946, KU; KW to Bill Stroock, January 24, 1949, KU. In May 1945 Lauterbach published his own signally uncritical *These Are the Russians* (New York: Harper and Bros.). Advertised as an "answer" to W. L. White, it was a credulous, statistics-packed account of Soviet war efforts, containing Finnish atrocity stories, the full Soviet version of the Katyn Forest massacre, and fulsome praise of Stalin as a benevolent lover of peace who had no intentions of expanding into Central or Western Europe. See Francis Hackett's review comparing the two books in the *New York Times*, May 31, 1945, sec. 1, p. 13.

97. In 1983 Kathrine wrote the following in response to Harrison Salisbury's attack on Bill's integrity in *A Journey for Our Times*, 287–88: "Ugly, anonymous mail was coming from Boston addressed to me at our hide-out office in New York. This mail began shortly after Bill got home from Russia. The gist of its message was that Bill was to be ruined as a reporter when it was discovered that his account of slave labor in Russia and his story about panic in Moscow were false. For some mysterious reason, the nameless writer blamed me for a 'change' in Bill which was to be his downfall. Bill paid little attention to this mail but it troubled me." "Salisbury reply," 2, KU. Significantly,

the *Reader's Digest* version did not include the Moscow pannic account.

98. Letters of January 12, 1945, as cited by Jean Folkerts in "An Analysis of the Controversy Surrounding William Lindsay White's 1945 Account of Russia," an unpublished paper delivered at the July 1982 convention of the Association for Education in Journalism at Athens, Ohio. I have not found those letters in the several accessible White collections; they may have been destroyed, along with other manuscript materials of this period, when 927 Exchange was vandalized in 1980.

99. Transcript of personal interview of Lambert Davis by Edison McIntyre, July 20, 1991.

100. Telephone interview of Lambert Davis by author, March 13, 1990; ironically Davis also edited Corliss Lamont's *The Peoples of the Soviet Union*, an uncritical, highly sympathetic account issued by Harcourt, Brace in the spring of 1946.

101. Corliss Lamont to WLW, May 17, 1945, KU; they continued to be political adversaries after Roger Baldwin in 1948 secured Bill's election as a moderate to the executive board of the American Civil Liberties Union (ACLU), on which Lamont led the left-wing faction until his ouster in 1953. Unfortunately, Lamont's outspoken but polite disagreements with Bill over ACLU policy, as demonstrated by their several extant letters from the late 1940s and early 1950s, turned into cranky disdain in old age. In a November 8, 1989, note to the author, responding to a request for an interview, Lamont wrote, "I do not recall anything about Bill White at Harvard and little else afterward. I just remember that he turned into a fanatical reactionary and menace to human decency. I do not think he deserves a biography."

102. WLW to Sen. Arthur Capper, one of the sponsors of the council, May 30, 1945, KU; WLW to Edmund Wilson, November 27, 1945, KU.

103. As cited in *The Truth About the Book the Nazis Like* (New York: National Council of American-Soviet Friendship, 1945), 3, KU.

104. George Moorad to WLW, March 8, 1945, KU. See Moorad's *Behind the Iron Curtain* (New York: Fireside Press, 1947), 84–87, for a full account of the reception of that petition in Moscow.

105. KW wrote Bill Stroock, January 24, 1949, that "our farm house was

broken into and all papers searched, many removed, while stealable things were overlooked," KU; WLW to Sen. Arthur Capper, May 30, 1945, KU. For WLW's own published account of who was behind the council's campaign, see his letter, "Anti-White Organization," in the *Saturday Review of Literature*, December 28, 1946, 21-22. Monya Gordon in the *Saturday Review of Literature* column "Strictly Personal," May 19, 1945, 22, asserted that "the real purpose of the organized campaign [against White] is apparently not to interrupt or to kill the circulation of 'Report on the Russians.' Indeed, the actual objective seems more remote but is infinitely more serious. It is an effort to prevent any book that is not one hundred percent pro-Soviet or an Intourist handout from being published." For two later accounts of the campaign against Bill, see Irene Corbally Kuhn, "Why You Buy Books that Sell Communism," *American Legion Magazine*, January 1951, 55, 58-59; and William L. O'Neill, *A Better World* (New York: Simon and Schuster, 1982), 90-92. O'Neill, an academic, concluded that "White's real sin was prematurity. His book was remarkably accurate, considering his short visit and lack of special knowledge. But White's truths were something that few liberals and fewer progressives wanted to hear. They suggested what was actually the case, that Stalin's Russia would not be easy to get along with after the war."

106. EG, August 24, 1939.

107. WLW, *Report on the Russians*, 19.

108. Ibid., 26.

109. Ibid., 61.

110. The Moscow panic story was told to him, he claimed, by a correspondent whose name he "hesitated" to disclose "for fear what he told me might be embarrassing professionally"; ibid., 165. No foreign correspondent was in Moscow at the time; in a letter to Bill Stroock, January 24, 1949, KU, KW identified Bill's source as "a high official in the Embassy." Much later, in an obituary editorial Bill identified that official as Llewellyn ("Tommy") Thompson, who in 1944 was second secretary at the American Embassy in Moscow and who was the "custodial officer" there during October 1941; "Tommy," EG, February 10, 1972.

111. WLW, *Report on the Russians*, 211.

112. Harrison Salisbury's delayed reaction in his memoir presents an

interesting case: "Bill told a number of stories and reported on various seamy matters, described concentration camps and political repressions which he said he learned about in the course of the trip. That stuck in my craw because these things had not happened. . . . Apparently what Bill had done was to use the Johnston trip as a clothesline on which to hang various yarns, some of which may have been true, which he had picked up even before he left New York. It was a shoddy business." *A Journey for Our Times*, 287–88. Sometime in November 1944 Dick Lauterbach had asked Bill if he would help out Salisbury by writing him into a particular scene in the book. Salisbury had a Russian girlfriend and his being placed there in print would somehow alleviate marital difficulties. Amused, Bill obliged, writing him that "everything is fixed and to make doubly sure, I inserted your name in a couple of other places so that there could be no possibility of misunderstanding." WLW to Harrison Salisbury, January 25, 1945, KU. After Salisbury's attack in 1983 on Bill's journalistic integrity, Kathrine wrote him a long letter refuting his assertions point by point and reminding him of that favor. KW to Harrison Salisbury, October 19, 1983, KU. Salisbury replied: "Bill was a wonderful, wacky and lovable companion on that famous trip—a delight and a comfort, the slow grin, the twinkle in his eye, the drawling wisecrack. . . . What drew me into the wrangle was plain factual reporting. . . . Bill said he got his scoop by talking to some engineers in Omsk. That was a kick in my pants. I was with Bill every minute in Omsk. If he could get a scoop like that what about me, Joe Reporter on the beat? It made me look, you should pardon the expression, like a horse's ass. When Bill said he used 'Omsk' to protect his sources that didn't help an iota. I *knew* the only American engineers in Russia. Hell, I played poker with those guys in the Metropole long before Bill hit town. I knew their yarns. So far as I was concerned that was what the shooting match was about—Bill claiming to scoop me on my own watch!" Harrison Salisbury to KW, December 21, 1983, KU. Curiously, nearly forty years after the event, and ten years after Bill's death, Salisbury's still-remembered resentment of him as a visiting fireman erupted into that disingenuous published attack on his honesty. For Bill's own account of his source for the Omsk engineers, see his letter to the editor in *Saturday Review of Literature*, November 16, 1946, 19–20.

113. WLW, *Report on the Russians*, 223; Lauterbach reported the same episode in *These Are the Russians*, 196–200, but his version of that conversation is not so pointed: "'This is certainly different from Moscow,' I said to Bill, indicating the NKVD Captain," 200.

114. WLW, *Report on the Russians*, 309.

115. While in Emporia Bill wrote thirty-three initialed editorials for the *Gazette*, most a full column or longer, on both local and national affairs, from November 2, 1944, through March 5, 1945; when in town he usually focused on his newspaper.

116. Lambert Davis to WLW, March 16, 1945, KU.

117. Dwight Bentel, "White's Book Creates Reviewer Furor," *Editor and Publisher*, March 31, 1945, 60.

118. "William Allen White Wouldn't Have Done It? But He Did," *Editor and Publisher*, March 31, 1945, 60.

119. Roscoe Ellard, "Report on White's Report," *Editor and Publisher*, March 31, 1945, 64; "W. L. White's Book," *Editor and Publisher*, March 31, 1945, 38.

120. "W. L. White on the Russians," *Saturday Review of Literature*, April 14, 1945, 20–23, 66. To his unqualified support, for instance, came John Chamberlain in "The Gang-Up on Bill White," *New Leader*, April 14, 1945, 5, and William H. Chamberlin in "W. L. White and His Critics," *American Mercury*, May 1945, 625–31.

121. See WLW to James Powell, October 21, 1946, about the continued refusal of the Wichita, Kansas, Public Library and others to purchase *Report on the Russians*, KU.

122. WLW to Lambert Davis, February 4, 1969, KU; see also interview transcript of WLW by Raymond Henle, March 1, 1968, 9, HHPL: "I discovered I lost all my old friends, here in New York particularly, and was making some new ones . . . and this was the beginning . . . of a quite long friendship [with Herbert Hoover] which lasted until his death."

123. Of the reviews of *Report on the Russians* listed in the *Book Review Digest* for 1945 most were mixed, only three were wholly positive, several were almost as negative as those of Zaslavsky and Davies. The *Reader's Digest* came to his defense in its July issue by reprinting on both sides of its back cover a staunchly supportive

review by J. Donald Adams in the *New York Times Book Review*, April 29, 1945, sec. 7, p. 2, which the *Digest* headed "The Un-American Effort to Suppress White's 'Report on the Russians.'" The White archives at KU contain over three hundred letters sent that summer to WLW about *Report on the Russians*.

124. Stella Gonser to WLW, June 24, 1945, KU.

125. Capt. Wilbur Van Horn, Jr., to WLW, March 30, 1945, KU.

126. "A Letter to William L. White," *Soviet Russia Today*, March 1945, 11.

127. WLW to Watson Kirkconnell, April 13, 1944; Watson Kirkconnell to WLW, April 23, 1944, KU.

128. WLW, "Report on the Critics," *Saturday Review of Literature*, October 5, 1946, 38.

129. E. T. Lowther as business manager then executive editor and Ted McDaniel as city editor, with the help eventually of Everette Barr as business manager, ran the *Gazette* in Bill's virtual absence for nearly a decade, with Lowther writing many of the editorials.

Eugene T. Lowther, son of Lloyd Lowther, longtime superintendent of Emporia public schools, started on the *Gazette* in 1915 as a summer reporter. After graduating from the University of Kansas, serving in World War I, and spending nearly a year at the Sorbonne in Paris, he returned to the *Gazette* in 1919, where he served forty straight years until 1959, when he retired as "co-editor and publisher."

Ted McDaniel started on the *Gazette* in 1924 as a proofreader. He retired as managing editor in 1970, though he did leave Emporia twice, once for a year to attend Marquette University in Milwaukee, Wisconsin, and once for three years to serve with the United States Navy in World War II.

Everette Barr started with the *Gazette* in 1948 when he leased its job-printing shop. In 1952 he became business manager, leaving that position to become assistant publisher in 1968, then retiring in 1970.

130. Interview of Ed Shupe, March 19, 1974, Flint Hills Oral History Project, LCHM.

131. WLW to Ted McDaniel, July 23, 1949, KU.

132. WLW, "Destiny," EG, April 13, 1945.

5. A Search for Peace and a Story, 1945–1951

1. John Dos Passos to WLW, April 26, 1945; WLW to John Dos Passos,

May 2, 1945, KU. See Townsend Ludington, *John Dos Passos* (New
York: Dutton, 1980), 398; Virginia Carr, *Dos Passos* (New York:
Doubleday, 1984), 395–98; and invitations from Herbert Hoover
to WLW, March 19, April 9, and April 14, 1945, HHPL.

2. KW to SLW, June 14, 1945, EGA; Clare Boothe Luce to WLW, July
25, 1945, KU; WLW to Herbert Hoover, August 2, 1945, HHPL.

3. WLW to Burt MacBride, October 11, 1945, KU; Capt. Jack Adams
to WLW, July 27, 1945, KU.

4. WLW to DW, September 20, 1945, KU.

5. Howard Chappell to WLW, January 1, 1946, KU; WLW to Howard
Chappell, January 8, 1946, KU.

6. WLW to DW, November 16, 1945; WLW to Howard Chappell, November 29, 1961; WLW to Mrs. L. F. Marriott, January 18, 1951, KU.

7. Telephone interview with Lambert Davis, March 13, 1990; interview
with Barbara Walker, September 29, 1989.

8. After returning to Emporia from a long absence, Bill would often write
a number of initialed *Gazette* editorials, almost as if to prove to
himself he could still do so; this time he wrote thirteen, from
October 4 through October 18.

9. WLW to Dorothy Canfield Fisher, December 5, 1945, EGA.

10. WLW to Mary Heaton Vorse, March 1, 1955, KU.

11. WLW to SLW, September 13, 1945, EGA.

12. WLW to W. G. Clugston, January 7, 1946, KU.

13. WLW to John Wheeler, March 1, 1946, KU.

14. WLW to James Byrnes, March 9, 1946, KU; see also WLW to Herbert
Hoover, March 9, 1946, requesting help, HHPL.

15. Interview with Barbara Walker, July 8, 1994.

16. "Freedom Exists in Red-Dominated Poland, W. L. White Discovers,"
datelined "Warsaw, May 3—(By Wireless)—(Delayed)," EG, May
9, 1946, 1, 6; and "Issue of Communism Adds to the Polish Food
Problem, Says WLW," datelined "Warsaw, May 4—(By Wireless)—
(Delayed)," EG, May 10, 1946, 1, 3.

17. KW to Morris Ernst, April 26, 1946, KU.

18. WLW to Jack Harris, August 24, 1946, KSHS.

19. WLW to LH, September 12, 1946, KSHS.

20. In a letter to DW Bill explained why he was unable that spring to
give his full attention to a *Digest* assignment: "As soon as I was
able to leave [Kathrine, who had undergone surgery], I started

West to look into a 4-H Club story suggested by Burt MacBride and also to see about the paper here which I hadn't been able to give attention to for more than a year. I had not expected to be in Emporia long but while I was here a very important and complicated matter came up concerning a local radio station, which is largely responsible for the fact that I have been tied up here for more than six weeks." WLW to DW, May 23, 1947, EGA.

21. WLW to LH, May 8, 1947, KSHS.

22. WLW to DW, October 7, 1946, KU.

23. WLW to Lambert Davis, October 17, 1946, KU.

24. See W. G. Calhoun, owner of Newman's Department Store, to WLW, December 1, 1947, EGA; WLW to LH, October 22, 1947, KU.

25. WLW to Lambert Davis, December 5, 1946, EGA.

26. Lambert Davis to WLW, December 10, 1946, EGA.

27. WLW to Herbert Hoover, December 17, 1946, HHPL; WLW to DW, May 23, 1947, EGA.

28. WLW to Kenneth Payne, March 12, 1947, EGA.

29. Interview with Barbara Walker, February 22, 1993.

30. WLW to Oscar Stauffer, May 8, 1947, EGA; WLW to Ronald Finney, May 23, 1947, EGA.

31. WLW to Jack Harris, January 25, 1947, KU; WLW to Drew Pearson, February 15, 1947, EGA; WLW to Herbert Hoover, February 25 and March 4, 1947, HHPL; Anne McCormick to WLW, March 1, 1947, EGA.

32. "Germany Since World War II," *Chicago Sun Book Week*, July 20, 1947, 10.

33. Bill presented his position more directly in a *Gazette* editorial of October 7, 1947, headed "Another View," in which he supported George Kennan's advocacy of "containment" of a truculent Soviet Union through strengthening the free nations on its borders, including Western-held Germany. Bill ended that endorsement with the apocalyptic pronouncement that "we must continue to fight for 'One World' or we won't have any world at all." In this public policy debate Bill thus supported the view of Dorothy Thompson, a columnist and an old friend of Bill's, who resigned as president of the international organization Freedom House, of which he was a board member, in opposition to the majority on its board, led by Rex Stout, the detective novelist, who advocated

some version of the Morgenthau plan. See Marion K. Sanders, *Dorothy Thompson: A Legend in Her Time* (Boston: Houghton Mifflin, 1973), 314–17, and Peter Kurth, *American Cassandra: The Life of Dorothy Thompson* (Boston: Little, Brown, 1990), 330, 370.

34. He also joined the board of directors of a similar organization, the Citizens Conference on International Economic Union, for whose January 1946 newsletter he wrote a brief article about trade with the Soviet Union, which he thought well enough of to send on for consideration by the *Digest*. WLW to Kenneth Payne, January 14, 1946, KU.

35. William Jackson, "Apologia for Auschwitz," *Saturday Review of Literature*, August 9, 1947, 18.

36. In a 1954 letter to Hal Lehrman, a friend and regular contributor to *Commentary*, a magazine of American Jewish opinion, Bill wrote: "Looking back on it all, I like to speculate what would have happened had we remained technically neutral until about 1944 or 45. By committing ourselves too early, we lost all bargaining power either with our enemies or our allies.

"For instance, if we stayed neutral, American public opinion would still have been a factor in Germany in 1943, and about 3½ million Polish Jews would be alive today. Also, had we measured out our lend lease aid to Moscow with an eye-dropper, instead of pushing it onto them with a bulldozer, we could have given them just enough to clear their own soil of German troops, but not enough to flood out into Europe. And we could have dictated a peace. Or so I think." WLW to Hal [Harold A.] Lehrman, September 29, 1954, KU.

37. In 1949 Bill put the Colorado compound in the hands of a rental agency, then eventually deeded it to the National Park Service.

38. WLW to LH, October 22, 1947, KU: "I have been busy here putting the finishing touches on a new story and settling the details of the sale of the movie rights of a book that I finished last summer in Colorado." The new story was "How It Feels to Starve," which appeared in *Woman's Home Companion*, January 1948, 40–41.

39. Lambert Davis left Harcourt, Brace to become executive editor of the North Carolina University Press; telephone interview, March 13, 1990.

40. "Across the Line," April 5, 1948, 18.

41. As quoted by Larry Ceplair and Steven Englund, *The Inquisition in Hollywood: Politics in the Film Community, 1930–1960* (New York: Anchor, 1980), 340.

42. Though based on Bill's book the screenplay itself was the work of others. See "Hoeing His Own Row: A Case History of Louis de Rochemont and His New Film 'Lost Boundaries,'" *New York Times*, June 26, 1949, sec. 2, p. 3, which describes *Lost Boundaries* as the first of a de Rochemont series of "real life" films from *Reader's Digest* stories. For a time de Rochemont considered filming Bill's next book, *Land of Milk and Honey*; see Eugene Lyons, "Louis de Rochemont: Maverick of the Movies," *Reader's Digest*, July 1949, 23–27. Bosley Crowther in the *New York Times* commentary "Issues of the Day," July 3, 1949, sec. 2, p. 1, compared the film *Lost Boundaries* to Republic Picture's *The Red Menace*, one of many anti-Communist films Hollywood studios began hastily turning out in response to pressure from HUAC. *Lost Boundaries*, he wrote, "visualizes most powerfully a significant drama of race and thereby contributes immensely to the airing of a problem of great size"; whereas *The Red Menace* "garbles in cheap and lurid terms the ever-pressing realities of Communist infiltration in this land." See also Margaret Lillord, "Family, Cast to Reunite for 'Lost Boundaries,'" *Keene* [New Hampshire] *Sentinel*, July 22, 1989, 19; and "'Lost Boundaries' Exciting New Book Tells Case History of a Family that Passed for 20 Years," *Ebony*, May 1948, 45–49.

43. WLW to DW, December 1, 1946, KU.

44. The three articles ran in the January 17, 24, and 31, 1948, issues.

45. WLW to Leon Volkov, [ca. July 1949], KU.

46. WLW to DW, February 24, 1948, KU.

47. WLW to DW, December 1, 1946, KU.

48. See *New York Times Book Review*, January 9, 1949, sec. 7, p. 7.

49. Philip Mosely, "Inside Soviet Russia," *Yale Review*, Summer 1949, 755.

50. WLW to George Moorad, January 12, 1949, KU.

51. WLW to Robert Littell, September 24, 1948, KU.

52. Memo from Roy C. Abbott to DW re William L. White, December 1, 1947, KU.

53. WLW to LH, October 22, 1947, KSHS.

54. WLW to George Moorad, January 12, 1949, KU.

55. The Century, founded by William Cullen Bryant, had been "long considered the City's most cultural club." Harmon Goldstone and Martha Dalrymple, *History Preserved: A Guide to New York City* (New York: Simon and Schuster, 1974), 210; Herbert Hoover to Mark Sullivan, March 18, 1948, HHPL.

56. WLW to "Dear Son," February 26, 1955, KU.

57. WLW to Freda Kirchwey, August 5, 1948, KU; see also later letter to Archibald MacLeish expressing outrage over that continued school board ban, July 14, 1949, KU.

58. WLW to Corliss Lamont, November 6, 1948, KU.

59. "That Common Man," EG, March 22, 1948; "The State of the Nation," EG, June 3, 1948; "Some Peerless Leaders," EG, June 4, 1948; "Thomas E. Dewey," EG, June 5, 1948; "Harold Stassen," EG, June 7, 1948; "Robert Taft," EG, June 8, 1948; "Our Choice," EG, June 9, 1948.

60. See Donald McCoy, *Landon of Kansas* (Lincoln: University of Nebraska Press, 1966), 534–38.

61. WLW to William Smith, November 26, 1947, KU.

62. "Kansas Grouches," EG, April 29, 1948.

63. WLW to DW, June 11, 1948, KU.

64. Willard Greene to WLW, May 11, 1948, KU.

65. WLW to Willard Greene, May 17, 1948, KU; in contrast, in reply to a Mrs. G. P. Kelly, who in a protest letter to the *Gazette* defending Senator Capper accused Young Bill of being an upstart, he wrote, "I want to thank you from the bottom of my heart for calling me an upstart. It happens that I am bald with three teeth missing and full crowns on most of the others, so under these circumstances being called an upstart is the most pleasant thing that has happened to me for months. It is like a breath of spring again." Mrs. G. P. Kelly to WLW, May 1, 1948; WLW to Mrs. G. P. Kelly, May 5, 1948, KU.

66. *Gazette* staff memo, June 30, 1949, KU; E. T. Lowther to Chase County treasurer, December 11, 1947, EGA.

67. WLW to Ronald Finney, August 4, 1948, EGA.

68. Mrs. Kathy ("Chuck") Southard to author, March 3, 1990.

69. WLW, "Palestine—I," EG, May 31, 1948; "Palestine—II," EG, June 1, 1948.

70. WLW to Paul Palmer, January 24, 1949, KU.

71. Telegram, [Paul] Thompson to Paul Palmer, January 26, 1949, EGA.

72. Mrs. Kathy ("Chuck") Southard to author, February 3, 1990.

73. WLW to Hans Alexander Lehmann, June 16, 1949, EGA.

74. WLW to Paul Palmer, May 26, 1949, KU.

75. Later, in 1951, along with the journalists Dorothy Thompson, Lowell Thomas, and Vincent Sheean, among others, Bill became a sponsor of the pro-Arab organization American Friends of the Middle East (AFME) and continued to play an active role in that organization until the early 1960s; see letter, WLW to Roy Durham, May 2, 1953, EGA. Major support for the AFME came from foundations that were CIA conduits. As in his sponsorship of Radio Liberty, Bill, with his close ties to Allen Dulles and to officials in the State Department, was undoubtedly aware of that connection. See Sanders, *Dorothy Thompson*, 337–38, and Kurth, *American Cassandra*, 536–37, n. 1.

76. WLW to Paul Palmer, May 26, 1949, KU.

77. WLW to Harold Ickes, July 14, 1949, KU.

78. WLW to DW, August 29, 1949, EGA; Paul Palmer to WLW, September 7, 1949, KU.

79. LH to WLW, October 14, 1949, _SHS; see also WLW to LH, November 1, 1949, KSHS.

80. WLW to Gen. Omar Bradley, October 7, 1949, KU; Lt. Col. C. V. ("Ted") Clifton to WLW, October 17, 1949, KU.

81. WLW to DW, November 18, 1949, KU.

82. In a letter to Keith Kane, a fellow Harvard Overseer, May 1953, KU, Bill wrote that "during the Conspirital Thirties I lived in Washington and knew, rather more than casually, both Whittaker Chambers and Alger Hiss. The second trial (I attended as a reporter) was an Old Home Week for me. I had at least a nodding acquaintance with a fair share of the witnesses on both sides."

83. "Hiss Loses Poise," *Kansas City Star*, December 4, 1949, 1A, 2A; "Spin Out Hiss Drama," *Kansas City Times*, December 12, 1949, 1, 2; "Fate of Alger Hiss Could Be Decided on a Word or Phrase," *Kansas City Times*, December 26, 1949, 2; "Vast Spy Impact," *Kansas City Times*, January 23, 1950, 1, 2.

84. WLW to John Wheeler, December 7, 1949, KU; apparently Wheeler felt that story packed too much dynamite, for he sent it back; John Wheeler to WLW, December 20, 1949, KU.

85. Whittaker Chambers to WLW, January 19, 1950, KU; WLW to Henry Luce, January 31, 1950, KU.

86. WLW to Allen Dulles, March 10, 1950, KU; WLW to Whittaker Chambers, April 27, 1950, KU.

87. *Reader's Digest*, May 1950, 145–80.

88. WLW to Bernard Baruch, January 16, 1950, KU.

89. WLW to DW, April 12, 1950, KU.

90. October 7, 1950, 133.

91. WLW to DW, April 4, 1950, KU.

92. WLW to DW, November 13, 1950, KU.

93. "Emporia or Tia Juana?" EG, October 3, 1949.

94. Harold Trusler to WLW, November 25, 1949, KU.

95. "A New Courthouse," EG, December 28, 1949.

96. WLW to Calvin Lambert, December 12, 1949, KU.

97. "A Plea to Topeka," EG, March 1, 1951.

98. "How Stupid Are We?" EG, April 3, 1951; "A Courthouse Vote," EG, June 16, 1952; for results of the straw vote see EG, June 19, 20, and 23, 1952; "Legal and Wasteful," EG, December 30, 1952.

99. "Farewell to Rink," EG, December 30, 1948; "Ruth Pemberton," EG, February 25, 1948.

100. Barbara Walker to author, September 21, 1993.

101. The White Memorial Foundation continues as a local nonprofit charitable organization sometimes confused with the White Corporation, the privately held family business entity.

102. "Herbert Hoover—II," EG, October 24, 1964; Roger Morris, *Richard Milhous Nixon: The Rise of an American Politician* (New York: Henry Holt, 1990), 577; transcript of interview of WLW by Raymond Henle, March 1, 1968, 22, HHPL; Gen. Leslie Groves, of the Atomic Energy Commission, and Bill shared a cabin together.

103. WLW to Joseph Alsop, May 29, 1952, KU; Joseph Alsop to WLW, June 2, 1952, KU.

104. WLW to Ralph Lowell, February 5, 1954, KU; WLW to Roy Larsen, February 8, 1954, KU; WLW to Robert Bradford, February 16, 1954, KU; WLW to Keith Kane, [March 1954], KU; and WLW to Paul Palmer, [1954], KU; see also "Harvard Teacher Is Indicted by U.S.," *New York Times*, December 18, 1954, 7.

105. WLW to Andrew Schoeppel, "Memorandum on the McCarthy Uproar," April 1950, KU; WLW to Andrew Schoeppel, April 11,

1950, KU; see also WLW to Herbert Hoover, April 11, 1950: "Anybody who makes his charges first and then goes running around frantically trying to collect evidence to back them up (as McCarthy did) is obviously an idiot." HHPL.

106. WLW to Roger William Riis, December 3, 1952, KU.

107. WLW to Dwight Eisenhower, January 8, 1953, KU; see Sig Mickelson, *America's Other Voice: The Story of Radio Free Europe and Radio Liberty* (New York: Praeger, 1983), 61–62.

108. WLW to Ernest Lindley, May 6, 1954, KU; "Thinks Oppenheimer Is Loyal," *New York Journal American*, April 17, 1954, clipping, EGA; WLW to Robert Oppenheimer, April 20, 1954, KU; "A Conversation with Dr. J. Robert Oppenheimer," on "See It Now," January 4, 1955.

109. WLW to J. Edgar Hoover, November 15, 1951, KU; WLW to Robert Lovett, November 15, 1951, KU; "Robert Lovett," EG, September 13, 1951.

110. "Russia Can't Lose," EG, July 1, 1950.

111. "A Note on Wars," EG, December 4, 1950.

112. See also "Cinderella in Mink," EG, March 5, 1951; "Wanted: Some Plans," EG, March 12, 1951; "More Trouble Ahead," EG, March 13, 1951; "The Chess Game," EG, July 3, 1951.

113. See, for example, William Manchester, *The Glory and the Dream* (Boston: Little, Brown, 1974), 10–19.

114. "Story of a Smear," *Freeman*, October 22, 1959, 51–53; *Reader's Digest*, December 1951, 49–53.

115. "A Voice from the Past," EG, September 29, 1951; see EG September 29, October 1, 2, 3, 4, 5, 6, and 8, 1951.

6. A Cold War Conservative Libertarian and an Award-Winning Small-Town Editor, 1951–1973

1. WLW to DW, November 4, 1951, KU; telegram, WLW to Gen. Dwight Eisenhower, November 5, 1951, KU; Jean Bright to WLW, November 5, 1951, KU; Arthur Krock to WLW, November 6, 1951, KU. According to the *New York Times*, when Eisenhower deplaned Sunday, November 4, he brushed aside all questions about politics and even refused to "indicate his own personal political affiliation." By Monday, November 5, he had softened that stance to say "that

he was not ready to talk politics with anyone 'just now.'" Then at a news conference on Tuesday morning, November 6, before enplaning for Paris, he enunciated "an 'open door' policy toward efforts to draft him for the President." Monday evening he had talked in private with Sen. James Duff of Pennsylvania, one of his principal backers for the Republican presidential nomination. Arthur Krock's observation about the effect of Bill's telegraph seems moot. W. H. Lawrence, "Military Leaders Meet Eisenhower," *New York Times*, November 5, 1951, 22; W. H. Lawrence, "Eisenhower Sees President, Bars Any Politics 'Just Now'," *New York Times*, November 6, 1951, 1; W. H. Lawrence, "Eisenhower Gives Backers New Hope of Draft for 1952," *New York Times*, November 7, 1951, 1.

2. Dwight Eisenhower to WLW, November 28, 1951, KU. Eisenhower sent this letter a little more than a month after he had privately committed himself in a letter to Sen. James Duff; see William Ewald, Jr., "Ike's First Move," *New York Times Magazine*, November 14, 1993, 57.

3. WLW to Dwight Eisenhower, July 14, 1952, KU.

4. Bruce Bliven, "War Is Still Hell," April 6, 1953, 28.

5. John Dos Passos to WLW, February 18, 1953, KU.

6. WLW to Louis de Rochemont, January 5, 1953, KU.

7. Gene Reynolds to WLW (posthumous), March 12, 1976, KU.

8. DW to WLW, August 12, 1953, KU.

9. For local color in Bill's unique narrative style see, for example, his three-column endorsement of Lyon County Sheriff Al Locke, EG, November 1, 1952.

10. WLW to Samuel Miller, July 22, 1960, EGA.

11. Alfred Dashiell to WLW, July 21, 1954, KU.

12. James Spadea to author, January 17, 1990; James Spadea to author, February 6, 1990; manuscript chapter of unpublished memoir by James Spadea.

13. "'No' Says Col. Robert R. McCormick,"; "'Yes' Says William L. White," *Freedom and Union*, November 1952, 8–11; "Thunder from Olympus," EG, January 17, 1953.

14. WLW to Dwight Eisenhower, March 10, 1953, KU; "No Answers Yet," EG, March 10, 1953; WLW to Herbert Hoover, March 11, 1953, HHPL; WLW to Wes Roberts, March 16, 1953, KU; "The

Roberts Case," EG, March 23, 1953; WLW, "There's Trouble in Kansas," Spadea Syndicate release, March 30, 1953, KU.

15. "Tandy Is Released at Emporia State," EG, January 20, 1953, 1; "McCarthyism?" EG, May 25, 1953; WLW to Walter Fees, February 10, 1953, KU; "Education vs. Concrete," EG, May 14, 1953.

16. Paul Palmer to WLW, May 15, 1953, EGA; Bill also submitted the manuscript to the Curtis Brown Agency, but they had no luck placing it; Mrs. Sewell Haggard to WLW, July 21, 1954, KU.

17. WLW to Paul Palmer, April 21, 1954, KU.

18. "Manly and Purposeful Ax Handle," Reader's Digest, October 1954, 42–45.

19. "Europe and Emporia—I," EG, October 16, 1953.

20. "Could We Give You Black Headlines?" EG, November 9, 1954; "Old Stones Provide Our News Headlines," EG, November 10, 1954.

21. "The Comics," EG, December 15, 1954; "That Dang Tabloid," EG, December 16, 1954.

22. Interview with Ernie Williams, September 24, 1994.

23. See long, detailed memorandum, WLW to Everette Barr, April 27, 1957, KU, analyzing the Ayer critique.

24. "Ridiculous Waste in the Armed Services," Reader's Digest, April 1955, 39–44; "W. L. White Story in Reader's Digest Subject of Inquiry," EG, April 8, 1955, 1; WLW to DW, April 25, 1955, KU. The other four Digest articles were: "The Personal Injury Racket," January 1955, 105–108; "Should Unions Have Monopoly Powers?" August 1955, 33–42; "The New Look in Defense Spending," November 1955, 97–100; "400,000 Boys Are Members of the Club," February 1956, 71–77.

25. WLW to Herbert Hoover, May 15, 1955, HHPL.

26. Maurice Ragsdale to WLW, May 18, 1956, KU; Maurice Ragsdale to WLW, August 31, 1956, KU.

27. WLW to Herbert Hoover, Jr., November 1956, KU; Hansen's book was published in 1957 by Van Nostrand as Heroes Behind Barbed Wire.

28. WLW to Col. William Robinette, July 30, 1957, EGA: "Since in the reviews very few have criticized my handling of the subject, and most people have praised it highly, I can only ascribe the low sale to the low public interest in the Korean War at this point."

29. "Soldiers Under Stress," New York Times Book Review, May 19, 1957, Sec. 7, p. 7.

30. See "New Journey for Margaret: A Best-Seller Subject Grows Up and Is Married," *Life*, August 19, 1957, 49–50; compare to "Journey for Margaret: A War Refugee Comes to U.S." *Life*, December 8, 1941, 83–86.

31. "Feasts for Kings," EG, June 16, 1957; see interview with Ed Shupe, March 19, 1974, Flint Hills Oral History Project, 41–42, LCHM.

32. DW to WLW, September 6, 1955, EGA.

33. DW to WLW, December 12, 1955, EGA.

34. WLW to DW, December 1955; DW to WLW, January 1956, EGA.

35. DW to WLW, February 7, 1957, KU.

36. Gene Lyons to WLW, December 18, 1957, KU.

37. DW to WLW, December 16, 1957, EGA.

38. Samuel Schreiner, Jr., *The Condensed World of the Reader's Digest* (New York: Stein and Day, 1977), 54–55; John Heidenry, *Theirs Was the Kingdom: Lila and DeWitt Wallace and the Story of the Reader's Digest* (New York: Norton, 1993), 111–13, 418–21.

39. "The Right to Work: Our Hottest Labor Issue," August 1958, 32–37; "India Sees Main Street," October 1958, 111–13; "Why Should Labor Leaders Play Politics with the Workers' Money?" October 1958, 157–64; "Why Can't We Have Pay TV?" November 1958, 57–61; "Words—Our Most Ancient Legacy," November 1958, 130–34.

40. WLW to Congressman John Rhodes, October 25, 1957, EGA.

41. WLW to DW, September 20, 1958, KU.

42. HL to Cuyler MacRae, June 19, 1959; WLW to HL, July 1959, KU; WLW to HL, September 14, 1959, EGA.

43. WLW to DW, December 1959, KU.

44. "Truth's Torch," EG, August 15, 1958; "We Can't Win," EG, September 3, 1958; "Prince Hal," EG, October 23, 1959; "Cyclones vs. Trees," EG, June 25, 1958; "Lost Editorial," EG, August 27, 1958.

45. "Ayer Cup for Typographical Excellence Won by Gazette," EG, April 21, 1960, 1.

46. "Earning a Living," EG, December 7, 1963.

47. "Gazette Again Wins Award in Typographical Contest," EG, April 22, 1966, 1; Whitley Austin to author, January 18, 1990; in 1969 Bill was asked to explain his award-winning typographical formula for *Seminar: A Quarterly Review for Newspapermen by Copley*

Newspapers; see his "Redesigning for Readability," September 1969, 27–29; as a testimony to his increased interest in format and typography rather than in social commentary, Bill finally killed the *Emporia Weekly Gazette* in 1964. His father had used that weekly from 1895 on as a convenient vehicle for editorial "exchanges." See "Today We Die!" EG, October 7, 1964.

48. See WLW to D. A. Peterson, June 20, 1960, EGA, asking about community television masts in Dallas, Texas.

49. See KW's lament to Bill Stroock, January 9, 1964, KU: "I must get in shape to know where we are [re Catfish capitalization] and I don't, I don't, I don't."

50. Taped interview, WLW of John Dos Passos, November 9, 1964, EGA; see Charles O'Rear, "CATV Subscribers Get Local News Instantly," *Editor and Publisher*, August 7, 1964, 15; "One CATV in the News Act," *Television Magazine*, February 1965, 62–63.

51. "Purely Personal," EG, June 28 and 30, 1962; WLW to DW, April 6, 1961, KU.

52. WLW to Vermont Royster, November 13, 1961, EGA.

53. E. P. Dutton firm to John McKone, October 12, 1965, KU; John McKone to author, February 7, 1992.

54. WLW to DW, December 18, 1962, KU.

55. WLW to John Whitney, April 23, 1963, KU.

56. According to former *Digest* editor Samuel Schreiner, "Lewis had a habit of shelving letters, memos, verbal propositions. Perhaps it was the cautious reaction of a man with a long shadow over his shoulder, or perhaps it was a personal characteristic." *The Condensed World of the Reader's Digest*, 218. HL to author, November 13, 1989.

57. See Kathrine's reminiscent note, February 5, 1980, KU; WLW to HL, August 24, 1964, KU. Bill reported that trip in fifteen travel letters to the *Gazette* under the heading "Brazil's Revolution," EG, May 28–June 23, 1964.

58. See his forty-three travel letters to the *Gazette* about that Turkish International Press Institute convention under the heading "Turkey," EG, June 24–August 26, 1964.

59. WLW to HL, [August 1964], KU; ten years earlier Bill had refused several requests from Wallace to ghostwrite articles, a standard

Digest practice; see WLW to DW, April 18, 1955, KU, and Heidenry *Theirs Was the Kingdom*, 351–52.

60. DW to WLW, August 24, 1964, KU.

61. Clarence Hall to WLW, September 22, 1964, EGA.

62. WLW to DW, February 15, 1965, KU.

63. WLW to DW, April 8, 1966, KU.

64. In the *Gazette*, October 12, 1966, 6, under the heading "Reprints," Bill announced uncharacteristically that the *Digest* had reported that "more than 88,000 reprints of his article on inflation have been sold, and that orders continue to come in."

65. HL to WLW, June 2, 1969; WLW to HL, June 1969; WLW to James Keogh, June 25, 1969; Pat Buchanan to WLW, June 26, 1969, KU.

66. WLW to DW, May 20, 1965, KU.

67. See "Emporia's Salute to Industry," EG, April 21, 1966, special section, B1–B16.

68. After years of administrative turmoil and financial crises, the College of Emporia permanently shut its doors in December 1973.

69. "New Industries," EG, January 13, 1965; "A Short History of Tax Dodging," EG, January 18, 1965; "Your Hoarse Watch Dog," EG, February 1, 1965, 1; "Farmers Join Poll on Tax Exemptions," EG, February 12, 1965, 1; "Tax Exemptions Rejected by Voters in Post Card Count," EG, February 15, 1965, 1; "Fair to All," EG, February 19, 1965; "Back on the Rails," EG, February 22, 1965; "A Perversion," EG, February 26, 1965; "Tax Exemptions," EG, March 18, 1965; "What Happened to Our Main Street?" EG, March 29, 1965.

70. "Catfish TV Rates Will Be Studied," EG, March 4, 1965, 1, 8; "City Probe of Catfish Is Started," EG, March 5, 1965, 1, 6.

71. Mary Penny, "Loathes Us," Wailing Place, EG, July 17, 1957; "Publisher of Gazette Is Hanged in Effigy," EG, January 17, 1962, 1.

72. After negotiations with several out-of-town firms, the Whites sold Catfish in the summer of 1966 to Oregon CATV, headquartered in Denver, Colorado. "Sale of Catfish Cable TV System Here Is Announced," EG, August 16, 1966, 1. The new company immediately changed its Emporia name to Cable Vision, dropped the local programming, added different commercial channels, and increased rates.

73. WLW to DW, May 20, 1965, KU.

74. John King's acceptance of the University of Wyoming presidency in June diminished the push behind the campus expansion project; see WLW to Clarence Beck, July 13, 1967, KU.

75. See that series of fifty-eight features in the *Gazette* from July 14, "Urban Renewal and Emporia I," pp. 1 and 8, through November 5, 1966, "Emporians Find Ballot on Renewal Plan Puzzling," pp. 1 and 10, plus the sundry editorial commentaries and special letters to the editor during that period; see also "Renewal Ordinance Wins Nearly 2–1—Voters Take Pro–Shopping Center Stand," EG, November 9, 1966, 1.

76. See "No, Not Remodeling," EG, December 18, 1967; later, in 1974, Kathrine moved the pressroom from its former basement location to a below-street site in the next building north and included a window view of it as an addition to the remodeled façade. In the late 1980s Kansas Power and Light gave to the city the corner building north of that to be demolished for a street-corner park commemorating the editors White. Paid for mostly by private donations, that razed and reconstructed area was dedicated October 28, 1988, as White Memorial Park. It features a life-sized bronze bust of WLW and excerpts in tile from several of WAW's and WLW's best-known commentaries.

77. See "Turkey," 43 letters, EG, June 24–August 26, 1964; "Atlantica," 31 letters, EG, July 22–August 30, 1965; "The Big Blow [the Far East]," 78 letters, EG, October 20, 1966–September 20, 1967; "Africa," 17 letters, EG, June 27–July 25, 1968; and "Finland," 7 letters, EG, June 11–August 9, 1971.

78. See "The Office," EG, October 28, 1966, and "Hotels," EG, October 29, 1966, for a detailed account of how important *Digest* referrals and introductions were to a roving editor; Lyndon Johnson to WLW, March 18, 1967; WLW to Lyndon Johnson, April 14, 1967, KU.

79. Eleanor Rawson to Elsie Stern, July 20, 1967, KU.

80. *Booklist* 65(1969): 1110.

81. WLW, *Report on the Asians*, 207.

82. WLW to Richard Nixon, January 4, 1969, KU.

83. WLW to William Smith, August 17, 1964, EGA.

84. See "Brave and Wise," EG, October 13, 1964; "The Johnson Victory Hymn," EG, October 19, 1964.

85. WLW to Dan Longwell, October 12, 1968, KU.

86. WLW to John Dos Passos, July 20, 1970, KU.

87. "Student Is Concerned," EG, May 26, 1970.

88. "The Second Generation," EG, June 1, 1995, 3A.

89. "Robert Docking," EG, April 4, 1972.

90. See "Report on New York," EG, September 20, 1965; "Our Town," EG, November 6, 1968; "Mike and Jack," EG, April 14, 1969; "To C. of E.'s Class of 1969," EG, June 25, 1969; "The Wahoo Bird," EG, February 23, 1968; "A Canadian Fuss," EG, June 13, 1966.

91. WLW to Sir Arthur Willert, January 20, 1972, KU.

92. "Chicago," EG, July 25, 1960, 4.

93. WLW to John Roberts, June 22, 1970, KU.

94. "Remembering the Boss," EG, December 21, 1973.

95. "The Walkers," EG, August 5, 1972.

96. "Remembering the Boss," EG, December 21, 1973.

97. Kathrine took over as editor of the Gazette and president of the family corporation until her own death in Emporia, also from cancer, August 17, 1988.

98. "Tributes to William Lindsay White," EG, July 30, 1973, and August 10, 1973.

99. "Mr. White Soon Overcame 'Chip-Off-the-Old-Block' Tag," EG, July 26, 1973.

Epilogue: Byline W. L. W.

1. Transcript, December 25, 1939, EGA.

2. WLW to Ronald T. Vinnard, June 12, 1955, KU.

3. WLW on "The Arthur Godfrey Show," CBS television, August 15, 1962, transcript, EGA.

4. KW notes to Mathiessen manuscript, EGA.

5. Interview, Charles Cowan, December 6, 1973, Flint Hills Oral History Project, LCHM.

6. Interview, Walter W. Butcher, April 25, 1974, Flint Hills Oral History Project, LCHM.

7. Interview, Fred Markowitz, March 19, 1974, Flint Hills Oral History Project, LCHM.

8. "To C. of E.'s Class of 1969," EG, June 25, 1969.

9. "White's Commencement Speech," clipping from *El Dorado Times*, EGA.

Bibliography

William Lindsay White

Kathrine White gave about half of her husband's papers to the University of Kansas, Lawrence; they are housed uncatalogued in the Kansas Collection of the Spencer Research Library. Some of his early letters are at the Library of Congress, in Washington, D.C., catalogued among the William Allen White Papers in the Manuscript Division. A few are catalogued in the Special Collections Division of the William Allen White Memorial Library at Emporia State University; in the Manuscript Division of the Kansas State Historical Society, Topeka; and in the Herbert Hoover Presidential Library, West Branch, Iowa. The rest of his papers are presently held uncatalogued in the *Emporia Gazette* archives by his daughter, Barbara Walker.

W. L. White published well over one thousand initialed editorials in the *Gazette*, plus hundreds of travel letters. For sixteen months he also wrote the column "Take a Look," distributed at its peak to about fifty daily newspapers by the *Des Moines Register-Tribune* Syndicate. And he wrote occasional commentaries or reports variously distributed by the North American Newspaper Alliance (NANA) and the Spadea Syndicate. Almost all of those syndicated materials appeared under his byline in the *Gazette*. But fewer than a dozen libraries hold complete files of the *Gazette* (daily edition) on microfilm; among them are the William Allen White Memorial Library at Emporia State University and the Spencer Research Library at the University of Kansas. More widely accessible are Bill's books and magazine articles; for that reason the following primary bibliography is limited to them.

Books

What People Said. New York: Viking Press, 1938.
Journey for Margaret. New York: Harcourt, Brace, 1941.
They Were Expendable. New York: Harcourt, Brace, 1942.
Queens Die Proudly. New York: Harcourt, Brace, 1943.
Report on the Russians. New York: Harcourt, Brace, 1945.
Report on the Germans. New York: Harcourt, Brace, 1947.
Lost Boundaries. New York: Harcourt, Brace, 1948.
Land of Milk and Honey. New York: Harcourt, Brace, 1949.
Bernard Baruch: Portrait of a Citizen. New York: Harcourt, Brace, 1950.
Back Down the Ridge. New York: Harcourt, Brace, 1953.
The Captives of Korea: An Unofficial White Paper on the Treatment of War Prisoners. New York: Charles Scribner's Sons, 1957.
The Little Toy Dog: The Story of the Two RB-47 Flyers, Captain John R. McKone and Captain Freeman B. Olmstead. New York: E. P. Dutton, 1962.
Report on the Asians. New York: Reynal, 1969.

Articles

"Making a Note of It." *Esquire*, September 1937, 73, 110.
"Trouble in the UAW." *New Republic*, August 10, 1938, 6–10.
"Joseph V. Connolly." *Scribner's Magazine*, November 1938, 9–13, 64–65.
"Pare Lorentz." *Scribner's Magazine*, January 1939, 7–11, 42.
"A Voice from Main Street, U.S.A." *Survey Graphic*, February 1939, 133–35.
"The Middle West Drifts to the Right." *Nation*, June 3, 1939, 635–38.

"As I Saw It." *Yale Review*, Autumn 1940, 92–108.

"Coming Home." *Cosmopolitan*. November 1940, 17, 75–76.

"Atlantic Crossing on U.S. Detroyer." *Life*, December 2, 1940, 39–46.

"Aboard a U.S. Destroyer, Bound for Britain." *Reader's Digest*, January 1941, 70–73 (from *Life*, December 2, 1940).

"A Day of Sweeping Mines off Dover." *Reader's Digest*, March 1941, 95–99.

"London Fire, 1940." *Reader's Digest*, March 1941, 6–14.

"Invasion of England." *Atlantic Monthly*, May 1941, 542–47.

"Death in the Dark." *Reader's Digest*, July 1941, 64–70.

"Fighter Type." *Maclean's*, September 15, 1941, 9–10, 49–54.

"The Dying and the Buying." *Saturday Evening Post*, October 18, 1941, 9–11.

"His Majesty's Opposition: Loyal and Disloyal." *Town and Country*, November 1941, 62–63, 100–102.

"Journey for Margaret." *Reader's Digest*, November 1941, 34–38.

"Out of the Doghouse." *Saturday Evening Post*, November 15, 1941, 14–15, 123–27.

"The Norse Travel Again." *Saturday Evening Post*, December 13, 1941, 14–15, 79–86.

"Nuns Wearing Field Boots." *New Republic*, January 19, 1942, 76–78.

"The Old School Tie." *Town and Country*, February 1942, 38, 74–76, 83–84.

"Negro Officers: 1917 and Now." *Survey Graphic*, April 1942, 192–94.

"The Negro in the Army." *Reader's Digest*, April 1942, 51–54 (from *Survey Graphic*, April 1942).

"The Boys Who Fight the Subs." *New Republic*, April 20, 1942, 536–38.

"The Boys Who Keep 'Em Down." *Reader's Digest*, May 1942, 1–5 (from *New Republic*, April 20, 1942).

"Four New Falcons." *Atlantic Monthly*, May 1942, 620–26.

"To the Four Far Corners." *Atlantic Monthly*, July 1942, 58–61.

"Out to the Four Far Corners." *Reader's Digest*, July 1942, 9–13 (from *Atlantic Monthly*, July 1942).

"Up and out, in a Hurry!" *American Legion Magazine*, July 1942, 14–15, 38.

"Escape Test." *Reader's Digest*, July 1942, 74–77 (from *American Legion Magazine*, July 1942).

"They Were Expendable." *Reader's Digest*, September 1942, 5–9, 147–76.

"Eastern Sea Frontier." *Reader's Digest*, October 1942, 102–107.

"They Were Expendable." *Life*, October 26, 1942, 114–16, 118–24.

"It's the Pig Boats that Dish It Out." *Look*, December 15, 1942, 34–39.

"Mexico at War." *Town and Country*, March 1943, 49, 72, 88–89.

"Queens Die Proudly." *Reader's Digest*, April 1943, 11–15, 113–44; May 1943, 111–44.

"Queens Die Proudly." *Magazine of Sigma Chi*, July–August 1943, 65–104 (from *Reader's Digest*, April and May 1943).

"Dream Jobs." *Redbook*, November 1943, 24–25, 61–62.

"They Fight with Cameras." *American Mercury*, November 1943, 537–42.

"Fliers Who Fight Without Guns." *Reader's Digest*, November 1943, 91–94 (from *American Mercury*, November 1943).

"Flat Top—Where Courage Is Routine." *Reader's Digest*, December 1943, 109–16.

"This Is Jungle Fighting." *Reader's Digest*, March 1944, 35–45.

"AMG Takes Over." *American Legion Magazine*, July 1944, 9, 31–32.

"How You Go in." *Reader's Digest*, July 1944, 97–100 (from *American Legion Magazine*, July 1944).

"We Govern a Sawdust Empire." *Saturday Evening Post*, August 12, 1944, 6.

"Little Joe's Star." *McCall's*, December 1944, 16–17, 61–66.

"Report on the Russians." *Reader's Digest*, December 1944, 101–22; January 1945, 106–28.

"Some Affairs of Honor." *Reader's Digest*, December 1945, 136–53.

"Report on the Critics." *Saturday Review of Literature*, October 5, 1946, 15–17, 38.

"Report on the Poles." *Reader's Digest*, January 1947, 149–70.

"Killer of Women." *Ladies' Home Journal*, November 1947, 51, 108–10.

"Lost Boundaries." *Reader's Digest*, December 1947, 135–54.

"How It Feels to Starve." *Woman's Home Companion*, January 1948, 40–41.

"Spot Check for Cancer." *Reader's Digest*, June 1948, 56–58 (from *Ladies' Home Journal*, November 1947).

"Vasili's First Days in America." *Reader's Digest*, January 1949, 1–8.

"Land of Milk and Honey." *Reader's Digest*, May 1949, 135–56.

"Sergeant Culin Licks the Hedgerows." *Reader's Digest*, February 1950, 81–84.

"Bernard Baruch, Portrait of a Citizen." *Reader's Digest*, October 1950, 167–80.

"The Isle of Detention." *American Mercury*, May 1951, 556–63.

"Foreign Students: An Opportunity." *Reader's Digest*, September 1951, 113–16.

"The Story of a Smear." *Freeman*, October 22, 1951, 51–53.

"Home Was Never Like This!" *United Nations World*, December 1951, 48–50.

"The Story of a Smear." *Reader's Digest*, December 1951, 49–53 (from *Freeman*, October 22, 1951).

"The Way We Look to Them." *Reader's Digest*, January 1952, 16–19 (from *United Nations World*, December 1951).

"'On the County'—Then and Now." *Reader's Digest*, March 1952, 110–13.

"Should the NATO Nations Form an Atlantic Federal Union? 'Yes.'" *Freedom and Union*, November 1952, 9–10.

"Back Down the Ridge." *Reader's Digest*, February 1953, 149–68.

"What's Happened to Independence Day?" *Better Homes and Gardens*, July 1954, 43, 142.

"Manly and Purposeful Ax Handle." *Reader's Digest*, October 1954, 42–45.

"The Personal-Injury Racket." *Reader's Digest*, January 1955, 105–108.

"Ridiculous Waste in the Armed Services." *Reader's Digest*, April 1955, 39–44.

"Should Unions Have Monopoly Powers?" *Reader's Digest*, August 1955, 33–42.

"The New Look in Defense Spending." *Reader's Digest*, November 1955, 97–100.

"400,000 Boys Are Members of the Club." *Reader's Digest*, February 1956, 71–77.

"Strike Without End—The Kohler Story." *Reader's Digest*, October 1957, 91–98.

"The Right to Work: Our Hottest Labor Issue." *Reader's Digest*, August 1958, 32–37.

"India Sees Main Street." *Reader's Digest*, October 1958, 111–13.

"Why Should Labor Leaders Play Politics with the Workers' Money?" *Reader's Digest*, October 1958, 157–64.

"Your Oldest Heirlooms." *Saturday Review of Literature*, October 4, 1958, 12–13.

"Why Can't We Have Pay TV?" *Reader's Digest*, November 1958, 57–61.

"Words—Our Most Ancient Legacy." *Reader's Digest*, November 1958, 130–34 (from *Saturday Review of Literature*, October 4, 1958).

"The Liquidation of Herbert Hoover." *Reader's Digest*, May 1960, 215–26.

"The Disappearance of Earl Ellis." *Reader's Digest*, September 1960, 177–80.

"How Russia Treats the Jews." *Reader's Digest*, June 1961, 92–94.

"The Little Toy Dog: The Story of an Air Force Mission." *Reader's Digest*, July 1962, 106–11, 217–40.

"Brave Yanks in a Moscow Jail." *True, the Men's Magazine*, August 1962, 107–21.

"The Strike Nobody Won." *Reader's Digest*, September 1963, 155–62.

"The Rising Risk of Runaway Inflation." *Reader's Digest*, August 1966, 128–32.

"Who Needs Newspapers?" *Bulletin of the American Society of Newspaper Editors*, December 1968, 1–2, 6.

"Redesigning for Readability." *Seminar Quarterly*, September 1969, 27–29.

"Under the Trees of Paris." *Reader's Digest* (British edition), April 1972, 133–39.

Index